SAN JUAN ISLANDS
A Boater's Guidebook

By
Shawn Breeding and Heather Bansmer

San Juan Islands: A Boater's Guidebook
First Edition

Shawn Breeding and Heather Bansmer

Published by Blue Latitude Press LLC
P.O. Box 2773
Kirkland, WA 98083-2773
(360) 421-1934
www.bluelatitudepress.com

ISBN: 978-0-9800901-3-0

Library of Congress Control Number: 2013931319

Printing History
1st edition - 2013

Printed in South Korea

While the Authors and Blue Latitude Press LLC have made every effort to ensure that the data and information within this guide is accurate and error-free, errors may occur. We ask that you notify us immediately of any errors that you may discover. The authors and publisher do not assume and hereby disclaim any liability to any party for any loss or damage caused by errors or omissions, whether such errors or omissions result from negligence, accident or any other cause.

Blue Latitude Press LLC and the Authors make no claims, promises or guarantees about the accuracy, completeness, or adequacy of the contents of this guide and expressly disclaim liability for errors and omissions in the contents of this guide. No warranty of any kind, implied, expressed or statutory, including but not limited to the warranties of non-infringement of third party rights, title, merchantability, fitness for a particular purpose, is given with respect to the contents of this guide. Reference in this guide to any specific commercial products, processes, or services, or the use of any trade, firm or corporation name is for the information and convenience of the public, and does not constitute endorsement, recommendation, or favoring by Blue Latitude Press LLC and the Authors.

This guide does not replace prudent seamanship. It is intended as a reference and planning aid and not for navigation. The skipper of the vessel is solely responsible for the safe operation and navigation of his/her vessel and the safety of the crew and/or passengers.

Table of Contents

 24
 48
 61
 75
 89

Table of Contents

123

139

184

224

240

About the Authors

Long before Shawn and Heather first met, their adventurous spirits were guiding them on travels around the world. Catching glimpses of different cultures and meeting many fantastic friends along the way fueled their desire to pursue more adventures.

Born in Youngstown, Ohio and later moving to Bowling Green, Kentucky, Shawn, along with his partner in crime and identical twin brother, took up scuba diving and boating among the many lakes surrounding Kentucky and the warm waters off Florida. In his mid-twenties, Shawn had the unique opportunity to crew on two sailboats through the South Pacific and New Zealand where he quickly fell in love with sailing and the cruising lifestyle. Shortly after returning to Kentucky, Shawn packed his belongings and moved to the coastal town of Bellingham, Washington to pursue his dream of buying a sailboat and preparing himself and the boat for future adventures at sea.

Heather, who was born and raised in the sagebrush hills of Yakima in eastern Washington, pursued a far different passion from the typical aspiring sailor, that of a cowgirl. She grew up riding through miles of apple orchards and along the irrigation canals found on the outskirts of her home town. After moving to Bellingham, Washington to attend college and unable to pack her horse in her suitcase, she traded in horseback riding for sea kayaking and white water rafting.

Working next door to each other in Bellingham, Shawn and Heather became quick friends and shared their tales of past adventures and dreams of new adventures. Armed with his new purchase of a stoutly built Westsail 32 named *Om Shanti*, Shawn wooed Heather with sunset sails on Bellingham Bay and taught her the finer points of sailing. Excited about dreams of living a cruising lifestyle and traveling to new destinations by boat, they concentrated their efforts to making the dream come true.

On June 1, 2003, *Om Shanti* left the dock in Bellingham Bay to take her crew on a magical ride, sailing to unbelievably wonderful adventures. From Bellingham they headed north, sailing with orcas and feasting on salmon while exploring the vast array of islands along British Columbia's southwestern coast. After circumnavigating Vancouver Island, they began the voyage south, down the west coast of the United States and Baja California. By early December, *Om Shanti* arrived in Cabo San Lucas and began a new, beautiful adventure in sunny Mexico.

For seven years, Heather, Shawn and *Om Shanti* explored the west coast of Mexico, relishing the beauty of this foreign land so close to home. Their love of boating and cruising in the coastal waters of Mexico lead to the development of their first cruising guides, in hopes of sharing the unique beauty and richness of life Mexico has to offer.

In 2007, Heather and Shawn launched their publishing company, Blue Latitude Press LLC, and shortly there after, released their first book, *Sea of Cortez: A Cruiser's Guidebook*. By October of 2009, a second edition of this widely popular guide was released. The following October, Heather and Shawn released a second guide, *Pacific Mexico: A Cruiser's Guidebook*, detailing the cruising destinations of mainland Mexico from Mazatlan south.

Yearning for home, a tough decision was made to move *Om Shanti* back to her home waters in Puget Sound in the spring of 2010. While the winter months in Washington are far different than those in Mexico, summer cruising in the Pacific Northwest can't be beat. With their trusty boat back in Bellingham, the couple looked to share the beauty of their home waters with fellow boaters, and developed their newest guide, *San Juan Islands: A Boater's Guidebook*.

Shawn, who is a licensed boat captain, has used his 20 years of experience as a graphic designer and cartographer to create the GPS-accurate charts, while Heather has pursued her passion of writing and graphic design to compose an informative and easy to follow guide. With their combined efforts, they have created one-of-a-kind guidebooks, filled with beautiful photography, accurate charts and descriptive text to help inspire and guide fellow boaters.

Boat Notes

Om Shanti is a cutter-rigged, Westsail 32, based on a Colin Archer design, and was built in 1976, in Costa Mesa, California. She is a 32-foot (40-foot LOA), fiberglass, full keel, double-ender, weighing 20,000 pounds (25,000 pounds fully loaded). She has a 5-foot draft and an 11.5 foot beam.

Om Shanti has been outfitted with a 27-horsepower Yanmar 3GM30F engine. A Monitor windvane acts as a third crew member to help steer when the boat is sailing, and a Simrad TP32 tiller-attached autopilot helps to steer when the boat is motoring in calm conditions.

Om Shanti carries a variety of cruising sails to take her through various wind conditions. The main sail, made by Kern Sails, has full battens and two reef points. The hank-on staysail is made by Taylor and has one reef point. The roller furling jib, also made by Kern, is a 100% super yankee. A light weight nylon drifter, made by Kern, is stored in a spinnaker sock for easy deployment and dousing. *Om Shanti* also carries a set of storm sails: a storm trisail that attaches to a dedicated track on the mast, and a storm jib that hanks on to the inner forestay.

Her battery bank is 440 amp hours with charging from the engine's high output alternator or the 75-watt solar panel. She carries 75 gallons of diesel in her fuel tanks. A Pur Power Survivor 35 water maker keeps the two 35-gallon water tanks topped up.

In the galley, Adler-Barbour Super ColdMachine keeps the beer cold. She has a two-burner propane stove with oven, and carries two 6-pound aluminum propane tanks.

Her ground tackle consists of a primary 44-pound Bruce anchor with 275 feet of 5/16" HT chain, and a 35-pound secondary CQR with 30 feet of 5/16" HT chain joined with 300 feet of 5/8" nylon rode. A 21-pound Fortress anchor is carried for backup and occasional use as a stern anchor. A Simpson-Lawrence 555 "Sea Tiger" manual windlass is used to raise and lower the anchors.

Om Shanti carries a Metzeler, 9-foot long rigid bottom inflatable with Hypalon tubes. A 9.8 horsepower Nissan outboard is able to plane the dinghy with two passengers, and was essential in the research of this guide. *Om Shanti* also carries an Eddyline "Merlin LT" plastic kayak on her top deck.

For short distance communication, the boat carries a Standard Horizon VHF radio and an Icom M72 handheld. For long distance communication, an Icom 718 ham radio transmits and receives SSB and ham frequencies, as well as sending email via an SCS Pactor modem.

Depth information is gathered by two boat mounted depth sounders: a Raymarine depth sounder and a Hummingbird fish finder. Navigation equipment includes a couple of Garmin GPS, Coastal Explorer and iNavx navigation software, and a Furuno radar.

Salty Dog

Salty is the newest addition to *Om Shanti*. After years of waiting for the "right" time, the plunge was taken and a new puppy was welcomed onto the boat. Part golden retriever and part border collie, Salty has been raised solely on the boat, making him a true and wonderful salty dog.

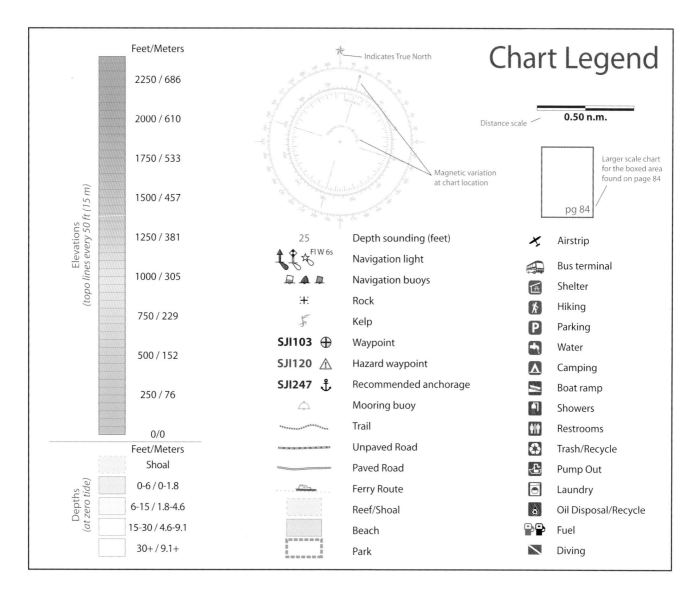

Chart Legend

Feet/Meters

Elevations (topo lines every 50 ft (15 m))	
2250 / 686	
2000 / 610	
1750 / 533	
1500 / 457	
1250 / 381	
1000 / 305	
750 / 229	
500 / 152	
250 / 76	
0/0	

Feet/Meters

Depths (at zero tide)

Shoal	
0-6 / 0-1.8	
6-15 / 1.8-4.6	
15-30 / 4.6-9.1	
30+ / 9.1+	

Indicates True North

Magnetic variation at chart location

Distance scale — **0.50 n.m.**

pg 84 — Larger scale chart for the boxed area found on page 84

25	Depth sounding (feet)
Fl W 6s	Navigation light
	Navigation buoys
	Rock
	Kelp
SJI103 ⊕	Waypoint
SJI120 ⚠	Hazard waypoint
SJI247 ⚓	Recommended anchorage
	Mooring buoy
	Trail
	Unpaved Road
	Paved Road
	Ferry Route
	Reef/Shoal
	Beach
	Park

	Airstrip
	Bus terminal
	Shelter
	Hiking
	Parking
	Water
	Camping
	Boat ramp
	Showers
	Restrooms
	Trash/Recycle
	Pump Out
	Laundry
	Oil Disposal/Recycle
	Fuel
	Diving

How to Use the Book

This book has been created to provide boaters exploring the San Juan Islands with the most up-to-date and complete information currently available. Whether your boat is power or sail, large or small, this guide is designed to help provide mariners with the information needed to confidently and comfortably cruise the islands. Because boating does not end once the boat stops moving, this guide, in addition to the maritime information, will also inform you of things to do once you are swinging on the hook or tied up at a marina. Places to get fuel, water, and provisions are included, as well as our favorite spots to stretch your legs, tour a museum, eateries to escape the galley for a meal out, or local haunts to get a cold beverage. The information used to create this guide has been gathered by us during many years of traveling and exploring the San Juan Islands.

Every effort has been made to include all of the popular (and not so popular) anchorages that a boater may travel to while exploring the San Juan Islands. With 172 islands within San Juan County, the San Juan Islands offer many more undiscovered gems outside the scope of this book for those adventurers wishing to get off the beaten path and blaze their own trail. This guide focuses on the well-traveled routes to and from the major islands of the San Juans, as well as the cities of Bellingham and Anacortes.

The charts used throughout the book have been created from scratch by combining on-site surveys, satellite and aerial photography, US digital elevation models, radar topography/bathymetric data, NOAA's ENC chart data, topographic maps and anything else we could get our hands on. The charts use WGS 84 datum, and all of the GPS waypoints used throughout this guide (unless otherwise noted) are our own personally gathered waypoints.

Shorelines for the charts used in this guide have been taken from and referenced to NOAA's electronic navigation charts (ENC) and the USGS National Elevation Dataset for unparalleled detail.

Depths found on the following charts are a combination of NOAA chart data as well as our own personal surveys. All depths included are given at zero tide. Depth contours indicated on the charts by varying shades of white to blue are included to give boaters a general idea of the bottom contours of a given area.

Waypoints are also included on each chart as a reference to help aid boaters in locating certain anchorages or hazards. Waypoints are included only as a reference tool and are not meant to be used for navigation or entering into autopilots. Approach waypoints included for a few of the anchorages are strictly meant for the use in locating specific bays. Because we cannot determine from which direction boats will be arriving and what kind of land or rock features may be in between, approach waypoints or any other waypoints should not replace prudent, hands on navigation.

Mileage table example:

Friday Harbor to:		
	Anacortes	19 nm
	Bellingham	26 nm
	Blaine	31 nm
	Blind Bay (Shaw Island)	7 nm
	Echo Bay (Sucia Island)	17 nm
	Fisherman Bay (Lopez Island)	5 nm
	Roche Harbor (San Juan Island)	11 nm
	Rosario (Orcas Island)	10 nm
	Sidney (Canada)	19 nm
	Spencer Spit (Lopez Island)	8 nm
	Victoria (Canada)	27 nm

Mileage tables are provided as a quick reference for distances to possible "next stops" from the anchorage being discussed. With so many "next stop" possibilities, locations used in the tables try to reference a major destination within a general cruising area. For instance, Friday Harbor to Echo Bay on Sucia Island will give you an exact mile count between the two locations, but will also give you an approximate idea on mileage to nearby islands of Patos and Matia, as well as other anchorages found on Sucia Island. A more inclusive mileage table can be found on the inside back cover, detailing mileage for each destination listed in the guide.

Throughout this book, the mileages used for distances over water are given in nautical miles, distances over land are given in statute miles. These distances are not straight-line "as the crow flies," but calculated to reflect the distance one would logically travel under actual circumstances.

For some of the larger islands and towns, a brief history and few of the sights to see are listed. Supplies and services including marine chandleries, grocery stores, and restaurants are also included. Please keep in mind though, that these lists are not exhaustive and more stores or services may be found in that particular town. Our lists are based on ease of access, personal experience, referrals and research. As much as we would like to include all the businesses available throughout the San Juan Islands, unfortunately, our guide just is not big enough! We welcome all of you to share any of your experiences and recommendations with us for inclusion in future editions.

As new information becomes available, including updates, changes or errors, we will post the information on our web site at **www.bluelatitudepress.com/bl_updates.html.** We want everyone to have the most accurate and up-to-date information available and welcome any comments or suggestions.

Using this guide, you will be equipped with the latest, most up-to-date cruising information available, but nothing will substitute for having a safe and sound vessel, always keeping a good watch, carrying an up-to-date set of nautical charts for the area, and operating your vessel with the utmost respect of the environs you are exploring. This guide does not replace prudent seamanship. It is intended as a reference and planning aid and not for navigation. The skipper of the vessel is solely responsible for the safe operation and navigation of his/her vessel and the safety of the crew and/or passengers.

Keep in mind when using this book that while every attempt has been made to ensure this information is as accurate as possible, things change and mistakes are possible. We welcome any corrections, updates or any other information you would like to share with your fellow cruiser. You can contact us at:

Blue Latitude Press, LLC
Shawn Breeding and Heather Bansmer

PO Box 2773
Kirkland, WA 98083
(360) 421-1934
(801) 454-1934 fax
www.bluelatitudepress.com
info@bluelatitudepress.com

Islands Information

The following list of topics provides information to help facilitate a cruise through the San Juan Islands, from government charts to information on local weather.

Charts

Charts are one of the single most important items to have on a boat to help you navigate the intricate waterways found within the San Juan Islands, as well as to help you avoid reefs and shallow water dangers. The National Oceanic and Atmospheric Administration, or NOAA, produces and maintains a suite of nautical charts that cover the coastal waters of the United States including the San Juan Islands. NOAA's charts are available in a variety of formats, including traditional paper charts, print-on-demand charts which are up-to-date paper charts with current Notice to Mariners corrections, Raster Navigational Charts (NOAA RNC®) which are bitmap electronic images of paper charts, and Electronic Navigational Charts (NOAA ENC®) which are vector charts that conform to international standards. For further information or to view these charts online, visit NOAA's website at: **www.nauticalcharts.noaa.gov.**

NOAA Region 2: Pacific Coast, Coastal & Harbor Charts

Chart #	Chart Name
18400	Strait of Georgia and Strait of Juan de Fuca
18421	Strait of Juan de Fuca to Strait of Georgia
18423	Bellingham to Everett including San Juan Islands
18424	Bellingham Bay
18427	Anacortes to Skagit Bay
18428	Oak and Crescent Harbors
18429	Rosario Strait-southern part
18430	Rosario Strait-northern part
18431	Rosario Strait to Cherry Point
18432	Boundary Pass
18433	Haro Strait-Middle Bank to Stuart Island
18434	San Juan Channel

Chart kits and books are also available from various publishers which include regional reproductions of NOAA charts in more convenient nav table sizes. These include Maptech's *San Juan Islands* chartbooks, Evergreen Pacific's *San Juan Islands Cruising Atlas*, and the Yachtsman's *Northwest Chart Book*.

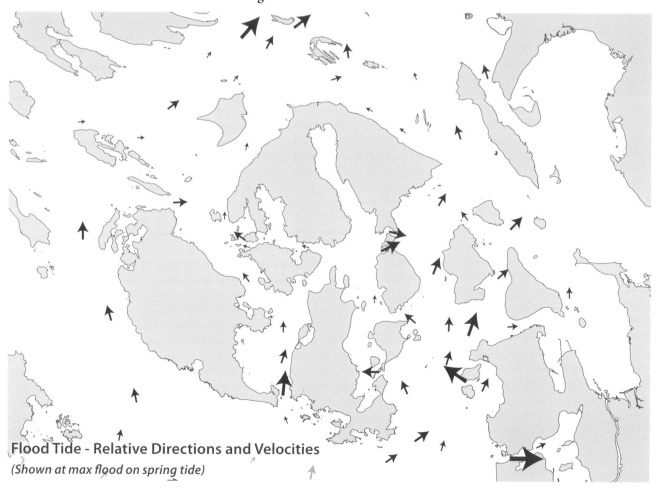

Flood Tide - Relative Directions and Velocities
(Shown at max flood on spring tide)

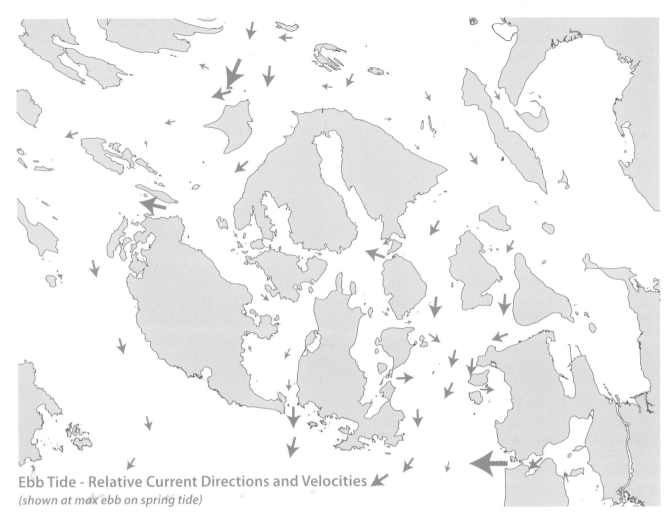

Ebb Tide - Relative Current Directions and Velocities ◢
(shown at max ebb on spring tide)

Currents and Tides

The maze of islands and reefs along with the variable bathymetry of the ocean floor, results in a complex flow of currents ebbing and flooding around the San Juan Islands. Tides dictate the times and intensities of these currents with two high tides and two low tides occurring each day. Tidal differences average around 7 to 9 feet, although they can reach up to 12 feet on extreme tides. In areas where land restricts the flow of water, currents can be forceful, for example at Deception Pass, between Whidbey and Fidalgo Islands, peak currents regularly flow 6 to 7 knots.

Along with charts, tide tables and a current atlas are essential resources to have on board your boat to help you navigate through the islands. Knowing when slack and peak current times are throughout the day will help you plan your route and your departure time. Knowing what level the tide is at and what the future level will be, can also help you determine a safe location and depth to anchor. A number of publications are available for tides and currents in the San Juan Islands including NOAA's online website: **tidesandcurrents.noaa.gov**. Others include the Canadian Hydrographic Service Publication, *Current Atlas for Juan de Fuca Strait to the Strait of Georgia* (for use with the yearly *Washburne's Tables* updates), the annual *Ports and Passes* tide and current tables book, and the annual *Capt'n. Jack's Tide and Current Atlas.*

Emergency Contacts
EMERGENCIES
Dial 9-1-1 or (360) 378-4141

Hospitals and Medical Centers
Inter Island Medical Center
550 Spring Street, Friday Harbor, WA 98250
(360) 378-2141

Island Hospital
1211 24th Street, Anacortes, WA 98221
(360) 299-1300

PeaceHealth St. Joseph Medical Center
2901 Squalicum Parkway, Bellingham, WA 98225-1898
(360) 734-5400

Sheriff's Offices

San Juan County Sheriff's Office (non-emergency)
96 Second Street, Friday Harbor, WA 98250
(360) 378-4151

Skagit County Sheriff's Office (non-emergencies)
600 South Third Street, Mount Vernon WA 98273
(360) 428-3211

Whatcom County Sheriff's Office (non-emergency)
311 Grand Avenue, Bellingham, Washington 98225
(360) 676-6650

Wildlife

Report illegal poaching in progress or dangerous wildlife complaints (all reports are anonymous):
EMERGENCY: Dial 9-1-1
NON-emergency: 1-877-933-9847

Ferries

Washington State operates passenger and vehicle ferries through the San Juan Islands. The ferries operate daily with ferry terminals at Anacortes, Lopez Island, Shaw Island, Orcas Island, San Juan Island and Sidney, British Columbia. The ferries make for convenient and inexpensive trips into the islands. During the summer months, reservations are highly recommended for vehicle traffic.

On the water, the ferries have regular scheduled routes through the islands. These ferries move quickly and have limited maneuverability. When sharing the waters with these large ships, it is best to stay out of the ferry's path especially around the ferry terminals. Five short blasts of the ferry's horn means the captain is signaling for a boat to move out of the way of the ferry's path. With the law of mass on their side, it is best to alter course and let ferries pass before continuing on your route.

For current ferry sailing schedules or for additional information on Washington State Ferries, visit their website at: **www.wsdot.wa.gov/ferries/** or by phone: 1-888-808-7977.

Fishing Licenses

The Washington Department of Fish and Wildlife requires a fishing license for all individuals 15 years of age and over. Licenses are broken down into resident or non-resident status with time frames from annual to multi day licenses. Different licenses are available for the specific type of fishing you plan on doing including freshwater, saltwater, shellfish/seaweed, and razor clams. Catch record cards are issued for sturgeon, steelhead, salmon, halibut and Dungeness crab in order to monitor and better manage the recreational harvest of these fish and shellfish. The department is now requiring the return of these catch records (including records for children under the age of 15) each season. Failure to return the cards will result in a small fine the next time you go to purchase a fishing license.

For further information regarding licenses, a list of local license vendors, or to purchase your license online, contact:

Washington Department of Fish and Wildlife
Licensing Division
600 Capitol Way North
Olympia, WA 98501-1091
(360) 902-2464
licensing@dfw.wa.gov
fishhunt.dfw.wa.gov

Fuel

Fuel docks are widely available throughout the San Juans, catering to the large numbers of summer pleasure boat travelers and charterers throughout the islands. The following is a list of fuel docks available:

Anacortes

Fido's Fuel
Located within Cap Sante Boat Haven (page 52) near the entrance. Offering both gasoline and diesel fuels. A small store sells bait, ice, pop and ice cream. Open everyday with seasonal daytime hours.
Phone: (360) 293-0694 or VHF channel 66A

Marine Servicenter Fuel
Located within Anacortes Marina near the south entrance (page 58). Offering gasoline and diesel fuels. Open everyday with seasonal daytime hours. Phone: (360) 293-8200

Skyline Marina Fuel
Located within Skyline Marina near the entrance (page 54). Offering gasoline and diesel fuels. Open everyday with seasonal daytime hours. Phone: (360) 293-5134

Bellingham

Harbor Marine Fuel
Located within Squalicum Harbor Marina (page 29) next to Bellingham Cold Storage. Offering both gasoline and diesel fuels. Open everyday with seasonal daytime hours. Phone: (360) 734-1710

Hilton Harbor Fuel
Located near the east entrance to Squalicum Harbor Marina (page 34), next to the U.S. Coast Guard Station. Offering gasoline fuel only. Phone: (360) 733-1110

San Juan Island

Island Petroleum Services
Located within the Port of Friday Harbor Marina (page 192) near Breakwater D and the Spring Street Landing. Of-

Fuel Stops Map

fering both gasoline and diesel fuels. Open everyday with seasonal daytime hours. Phone: (360) 378-3114

Roche Harbor Fuel
Located within Roche Harbor Marina near the dinghy dock and the grocery store (page 203). Offering gasoline and diesel fuels. Open everyday with seasonal daytime hours. Phone: (360) 378-2155

Orcas Island

Deer Harbor Marina Fuel
Located within Deer Harbor Marina (page 145) near the visitor dock on the south side. Offering both gasoline and diesel fuels. Open every day with seasonal daytime hours. Phone: (360) 376-3037 or VHF channel 78A

Rosario Resort Fuel
Located at Rosario Resort (page 170) near the entrance to the marina. Offering both gasoline and diesel fuels. Phone: (360) 376-2152 or VHF channel 78A

West Sound Marina Fuel
Located within West Sound Marina (page 156) near the visitor dock on the south side. Phone: (360) 376-2314

Lopez Island

Lopez Islander Marina Fuel
Located within the Lopez Islander Marina (page 97) near the seaplane dock on the north side of the marina. Offering both gasoline and diesel fuels. A small convenience store is also found at the top of the ramp. Phone: 800.736.3434

Blakely Island

Blakely Island Marina Fuel
Located outside the entrance to the Blakely Island Marina (page 79). Offering both gasoline and diesel fuels. Phone: (360) 375-6121

Parks and Camping

Washington State, San Juan County, the city of Anacortes and the Washington Department of Natural Resources (DNR) have set aside a number of sites, as well as entire islands, for the public to enjoy throughout the San Juan Islands. Many of the state marine parks offer docks, mooring buoys, floats or linear mooring options for boaters visiting these islands. Daily use fees are charged by the parks year-round for these options. If you plan to visit and use these moorage options frequently throughout the year, purchasing an annual state park moorage permit may save you money. Annual permit fees are currently

Cascadia Marine Trail

The Cascadia Marine Trail is a salt water trail that stretches over 140 miles from the Canadian border to south Puget Sound. This trail was developed exclusively for non-motorized boats. Currently there are over 50 campsites along the trail, included within the San Juans:

Blind Island State Park	Point Doughty
Griffin Bay	Posey Island State Park
James Island State Park	San Juan County Park
Jones Island State Park	Shaw County Park
Obstruction Pass	Spencer Spit State Park
Odlin County Park	Stuart Island State Park

Specially designated CMT campsites are set aside for those arriving by wind or human powered boats. For further information on the trail, visit the Washington Water Trails Association's website at: www.wwta.org.

based on boat length, and can be a very economical way to enjoy the state marine park moorage options. The money from these annual permits and daily use fees goes directly into the maintenance of the park as well as the mooring buoys and docks. Without revenue, these mooring options will lack the proper maintenance and upkeep they need in order to safely secure your boat. When the wind picks up in the middle of the night and the boat starts bobbing, you will sleep a little easier knowing your money and your neighbor's money has been well spent on new fittings and dive inspections on your mooring buoy or dock!

For those looking to camp for the night, keep in mind that summer is the busiest time for these parks. It is a good idea to reserve your campsite ahead of time as many of the parks, especially on the weekends, will be full.

For further information on Washington State Parks or to purchase your annual permit online, visit their website at: **www.parks.wa.gov/boating/moorage/**, or phone: (360) 902-8844. For information on San Juan County parks, visit their website at: **www.co.san-juan.wa.us/parks/**, or phone: (360) 378-8420. For information on Anacortes City parks (Washington Park) visit their website at: **www.cityofanacortes.org**, or phone: (360) 293-1918. For information on DNR sites, visit their website at: **www.dnr.wa.gov**, or phone: (360) 856-3500.

US Customs

When entering the United States by boat from Canada, even if you are a U.S. citizen, all boats along with their crew MUST clear in with United States Customs and

Washington Marine Parks Map

Border Protection. Upon arrival at the customs dock, only the boat's captain may disembark the boat, all crew must stay on board. The captain must present the custom's officer with passports for everyone on board, along with boat registration or documentation papers. U.S. Customs designated ports of inspection are located at:

Friday Harbor
271 Front Street
Friday Harbor, WA 98250
(360) 378-2080

Roche Harbor
195 Reuben Memorial Drive
Roche Harbor, WA 98250
(360) 378-2080

Point Roberts
50 Tyee Drive
Point Roberts, WA 98230
(360) 945-2314 or (360) 945-5211

Anacortes
1019 Q Avenue
Suite F
Anacortes, WA 98221
(360) 293-2331

Port Angeles
138 West First Street
Suite 204
Port Angeles, WA 98362
(360) 457-4311

U.S. Customs also offers the Small Vessel Reporting System (SVRS). The SVRS enables boaters to report quickly and easily to CBP their arrival from foreign waters. It is a free, easy-to-use, voluntary program that you enroll for online. SVRS is available to all U.S. citizens, nationals and lawful permanent residents; Canadian citizens and permanent residents of Canada who are nationals of a Visa Waiver Program country. The enrollment system is Web-based (**svrs.cbp.dhs.gov**). New applicants register online and self-schedule an interview with a CBP officer at an authorized reporting location of their choice. Participants receive a welcoming email with their Boater Registration (BR) number and password for SVRS.

For frequent boating travelers between the United States and Canada, there are alternative inspection programs including the Canadian Border Boat Landing Permit Program (I-68) and the NEXUS Program. The Canadian Border Boat Landing Permits are inspected and issued an I-68 permit for the entire boating season. The I-68 permit allows boaters to enter the United States from

Tips on Entering the U.S.

The following are a few tips on restricted items you can and cannot bring into the U.S. (regardless of your citizenship). This list can change due to disease outbreaks and other factors. For up-to-date information, check the U.S. Customs' website at: **www.cbp.gov** and the USDA's website at: **www.aphis.usda.gov**.

Fruits and vegetables grown in Canada are generally admissible, if they have labels identifying them as products of Canada. Fruits and vegetables merely purchased in Canada are not necessarily admissible, i.e. citrus or tropical fruits, which were not grown in Canada due to climate limitations.

Food products from Canada, including pet food and fresh (frozen or chilled), cooked, canned or otherwise processed products containing beef, veal, bison, and cervid (e.g. deer, elk, moose, caribou etc.) are now permitted from Canada. Products containing sheep, lamb, or goat will not be allowed entry. Proof of origin of beef, pork, poultry, cervid meat, and pet food must be provided in order to bring them into the United States. Examples of proof of origin include the grocery store receipt where the product was purchased or the label on the product indicating the province in which it was packaged.

The Centers for Disease Control and Prevention (CDC) requires that dogs be vaccinated against rabies at least 30 days prior to entry, except for puppies younger than 3 months and dogs originating or located for 6 months in areas considered to be free of rabies. A dog with an unexpired health certificate meets these requirements.

Generally, one liter of alcohol per person may be entered into the U.S. duty-free by travelers who are 21 years or older.

Prescription medications should be in their original containers, and it is advised that you travel with no more than personal use quantities. A rule of thumb is no more than a 90 day supply. If your medications or devices are not in their original containers, you should have a copy of your prescription with you or a letter from your doctor.

Canada for recreational purposes by reporting to CBP by telephone upon their arrival. The NEXUS Marine program is a joint Canada-U.S. initiative that offers facilitated customs and immigration clearance for recreational low-risk boaters entering either country through registration into the program. NEXUS is valid for 5 years and satisfies the boat operator's legal requirement to report to a port-of-entry for face-to-face inspection, but boaters must still phone in their arrival.

Participants in these programs may report their arrival to U.S. Customs and Border Protection (CBP) by calling **1-800-562-5943**. Unless directed by a CBP officer, participants in these programs do not have to report for an in-person inspection. All boat captains must phone in their arrival and have the following information available:

- Name, date of birth and citizenship of all persons on board (including passport numbers)
- Name of the boat and/or boat registration number
- CBP user fee decal number (if 30 feet or longer)
- Homeport and current location
- Return contact number
- Trusted Traveler document info readily available (i.e. I-68, Nexus, "BR#)

Whales

Sightings of orca, or killer, whales are one of the true highlights during a visit to the San Juan Islands. A community of orcas return each year to the inland waters of Washington and British Columbia, known as the Southern Resident population. These local residents are made up of three matriarchal family pods - the J, K and L pods. These whales spend the summer months in the Pacific Northwest feeding on fish, including salmon, herring and cod.

The residents are generally found swimming the inland waters from June through September. While the J pod has been observed in Washington and British Columbia year-round, the movement of K and L pods during the winter and spring months is mostly unknown. Tracking studies on the K and L pods have shown the whales offshore of Vancouver Island and Monterrey, California.

Aside from resident whales, transient orca whales are also spotted occasionally in the inland waters of Washington and British Columbia. These whales travel in small family groups of three to four, feeding on marine mammals including seals, sea lions, porpoise, dolphins and whales. Residents and transients differ in their diet, the shapes of their dorsal fins, vocalizations, and travel patterns.

Orcas are the largest mammal of the dolphin family, characterized by their black and white markings. Males weigh up to approximately 12,000 pounds and measure between 24 to 31 feet in length. Females generally weigh up to 8,000 pounds and measure up to 26 feet in length. One of the easiest ways to distinguish between mature males and females is by their dorsal fins. Females have small curved fins (whale in the above photo on the left) and males have a long straight fin up to six feet in length (whale on the right).

In the dark waters of the Pacific Northwest, orcas are able to locate food sources by using sonar, or echolocation.

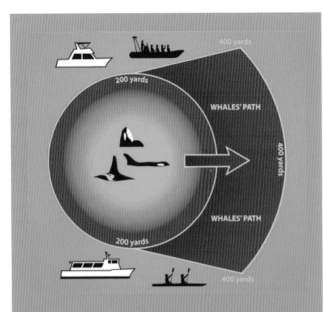

Be Whale Wise

BE CAUTIOUS & COURTEOUS: approach areas of known or suspected marine wildlife activity with extreme caution. Look in all directions before planning your approach or departure.

SLOW DOWN: reduce speed to less than 7 knots when within 400 metres/yards of the nearest whale. Avoid abrupt course changes.

KEEP CLEAR of the whales' path. If whales are approaching you, cautiously move out of the way.

DO NOT APPROACH whales from the front or from behind. Always approach and depart whales from the side, moving in a direction parallel to the direction of the whales.

DO NOT APPROACH or position your vessel closer than 200 metres/yards to any whale.

If your vessel is not in compliance with the 200 metres/yards approach guideline, place engine in neutral and allow whales to pass.

STAY on the **OFFSHORE** side of the whales when they are traveling close to shore.

LIMIT your viewing time to a recommended maximum of 30 minutes. This will minimize the cumulative impact of many vessels and give consideration to other viewers.

DO NOT swim with, touch or feed marine wildlife.

DO NOT drive through groups of porpoises or dolphins to encourage bow or stern-riding.

Should dolphins or porpoises choose to ride the bow wave of your vessel, avoid sudden course changes. Hold course and speed or reduce speed gradually.

Whales can produce a rapid clicking sound which travels through the water in the form of sound waves. These waves bounce off anything in the whale's path and return to sensors within the whale.

According to the Center for Whale Research in Friday Harbor, approximately 85 whales made up the southern resident community as of 2012. For further information on whales visit the Center for Whale Research website at: **www.whaleresearch.com**, or get a hands on approach at the Whale Museum (see page 195) in Friday Harbor.

Weather

Nestled within the lee of mountain ranges found on both the Olympic Peninsula and Vancouver Island, the San Juan Islands are uniquely protected from the direct force of weather that arrives along the Pacific coast of Washington and British Columbia. These mountain ranges also help to create a rain shadow effect over the islands, resulting in a much drier climate than the majority of western Washington and western Vancouver Island which can average approximately 120 to 160 inches of rain a year. Average annual rainfall within the islands ranges from 20 inches in the south to 30 inches in the northern islands, with the majority of rain falling in the winter months.

The San Juans are also affected by seasonal conditions. The summer months from June through September are characterized by warmer, drier and calmer conditions with average temperatures ranging in the 50's to 70's F. The winter months of November through February are more typically cold, wet and windy, with average temperatures ranging in the 30's to 40's F. During the winter months, storms hitting the Pacific coast create wetter and windier conditions than during the more benign summer months.

While the surrounding mountain ranges help to shield the islands from large weather systems, the intricate maze of islands and surrounding waterways can create localized weather conditions within the San Juans. Predominate winds are typically from the southerly quadrant, from southeast to southwest, however north and west winds are not uncommon. Hills, points and the islands themselves can change the wind direction and velocity as it funnels or bends around land masses. A popular example is the effect of north winds flowing through East Sound, known as gap winds. Due to the high restricting hills on either side, wind is funneled down the sound with increasing velocity. Boats approaching East Sound from the calm, protected waters of Obstruction Pass or Harney Channel are many times taken by surprise with the sudden, brisk wind as they round into the sound.

Waves generated by wind and/or by current is also something to take into account when boating in the San Juans. Large, open stretches of water have a greater distance (fetch) for wind driven waves to build. Open waterways like Bellingham Bay, Haro Strait and San Juan Channel are examples of areas that are unobstructed, where wind and waves can build. Combining these conditions with an opposing current will create waves with increased height and shortened wave length.

During the spring, summer and autumn months, fog can also affect the area, blanketing the islands and greatly reducing visibility. As moist ocean air condenses, it creates a morning fog layer, and as the day heats up, the fog generally burns off quickly.

The National Oceanic and Atmospheric Administration's (NOAA) National Weather Service provides valuable marine weather forecasts, updated four times daily. Marine weather reports for the northern inland waters including the San Juan Islands are available via VHF weather channels or online at:
www.ndbc.noaa.gov/data/Forecasts/FZUS56.KSEW.html
www.atmos.washington.edu/data/marine_report.html

Canadian weather forecasts including the Gulf Islands and the Strait of Georgia are also available via VHF weather channels and online at:
www.weatheroffice.gc.ca/marine/index_e.html

VHF Automated Radio Checks

In order to address increasing traffic on VHF channel 16, which is used solely for calling ships and shore stations and as an international distress frequency, Sea Tow began setting up automated radio check stations on the East Coast of the United States in 2010 (it is illegal to use 16 for radio checks). The radio checks use the old radio telephone channels (24, 26, 27 and 28) to record your transmission, then transmit an announcement and play back the brief recording of your call.

Learning of this new system and desiring to have something similar within his home waters, current Friday Harbor resident, Steve Roberts, has implemented a VHF automated radio check on channel 28. Based in Friday Harbor on San Juan Island, Roberts' automated system allows boaters to call on VHF channel 28, and if the transmission is picked up by Roberts' station, it will record and play it back to you after a brief announcement. This allows boaters to know exactly how far away their transmission is getting out, how clear their signal is, and most importantly, keeps illegal radio check traffic off channel 16. For further information or to contact Roberts, visit his website at: nomadness.com.

Yacht Clubs

There are a number of yacht clubs within the San Juans including Anacortes and Bellingham. The following is a list of local yacht clubs and their contact information:

Anacortes Yacht Club
504 Seventh
Anacortes, WA 98221
Website: www.anacortesyachtclub.org

Bellingham Yacht Club
2625 Harbor Loop
Bellingham, WA 98225
Website: www.byc.org

Corinthian Yacht Club of Bellingham
PO Box 101
Bellingham, WA 98227
Website: www.cycbellingham.org

Flounder Bay Yacht Club
2400 Skyline Way
Anacortes, WA 98221
Website: fbyc.com

Friday Harbor Sailing Club
PO Box 62
Friday Harbor, WA 98250
Website: fridayharborsailing.com

Lopez Island Yacht Club
PO Box 22
Lopez Island, WA 98261
Website: lopezislandyachtclub.com

Orcas Island Yacht Club
PO Box 686
Eastsound, WA 98245
Website: www.oiyc.org

Roche Harbor Yacht Club
PO Box 94426
Seattle, WA 98124
Website: www.rhyc.org

San Juan Island Yacht Club
PO Box 67
Friday Harbor, WA 98250
Website: www.sjiyc.com

Seattle Yacht Club
(Outstations at Friday Harbor and Henry Island)
1807 East Hamlin Street
Seattle, WA 98112
Website: www.seattleyachtclub.org

Squalicum Yacht Club
PO Box 735
Bellingham, WA 98227
Website: www.squalicumyc.org

Sample Itineraries

The following itineraries are a sample of cruises designed to fit a variety of schedules and interests. These itineraries are easily adjusted for adding or removing various ports of call. Depending on weather, some locations may not be suitable for anchoring, and may end up changing the itinerary.

Islands Marina Tour

For those dreaming of peaceful nights securely tied to the dock or sunset cocktail hours spent socializing with new neighbors, pack your dock chairs and get your fenders ready to sample the Islands Marina Tour. Marina hopping is a perfect way to experience the island way of life - eat at local restaurants, partake in seasonal island festivities, and meet fellow boaters living the dream.

Total Mileage: 73 nautical miles	
Anacortes to Rosario Resort (Orcas Island):	16 miles
Bellingham to Rosario Resort (Orcas Island):	*21 miles*
Rosario Resort to Fisherman Bay (Lopez Island):	9 miles
Fisherman Bay to Friday Harbor (San Juan Island):	5 miles
Friday Harbor to Roche Harbor (San Juan Island):	11 miles
Roche Harbor to Deer Harbor (Orcas Island):	8 miles
Deer Harbor to West Sound (Orcas Island):	4 miles
West Sound to Blakely Island Marina (Blakely Island):	8 miles
Blakely Island Marina to Anacortes:	12 miles
Blakely Island Marina to Bellingham:	*18 miles*

The Perfect Charter

Many get the chance to first experience the beauty of the San Juan Islands by charter boat, and there are numerous companies in the area to assist in outfitting you with the ideal boat for your travels. The Perfect Charter itinerary is designed specifically to help those on a limited time schedule get a real flavor for the islands and to visit a few not-to-be-missed gems. Whether traveling with a family or on a solo adventure, these six-night, seven-day itineraries take you past lush green islands, amazing wildlife, tours of local towns, and ample shoreside activities.

Total Mileage: 78 nautical miles	
Anacortes to Echo Bay (Sucia Island):	21 miles
Bellingham to Echo Bay (Sucia Island):	*19 miles*
Echo Bay to Prevost Harbor (Stuart Island):	15 miles
Prevost Harbor to Jones Island:	8 miles
Jones Island to Friday Harbor (San Juan Island):	6 miles
Friday Harbor to Indian Cove (Shaw Island - lunch):	4 miles
Indian Cove to Fisherman Bay (Lopez Island):	3 miles
Fisherman Bay to Pelican Beach (Cypress Island):	12 miles
Pelican Beach to Anacortes:	9 miles
Pelican Beach to Bellingham:	*13 miles*

Total Mileage: 77 nautical miles	
Anacortes to Fossil Bay (Sucia Island):	21 miles
Bellingham to Fossil Bay (Sucia Island):	*19 miles*
Fossil Bay to Reid Harbor (Stuart Island):	14 miles
Reid Harbor to Garrison Bay (San Juan Island - lunch):	6 miles
Garrison Bay to Roche Harbor (San Juan Island):	2 miles
Roche Harbor to Blind Bay (Shaw Island):	11 miles
Blind Bay to Spencer Spit (Lopez Island):	5 miles
Spencer Spit to Eagle Harbor (Cypress Island):	10 miles
Eagle Harbor to Anacortes:	8 miles
Eagle Harbor to Bellingham:	*13 miles*

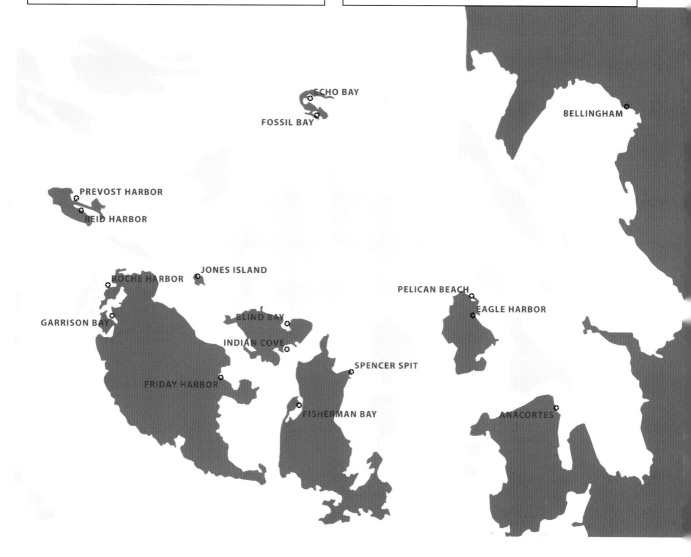

Hiker's Bounty

For the intrepid outdoorsman who wants to combine two great passions for land and sea into one fantastic adventure, is the Hiker's Bounty itinerary. Strap on your boots, grab your PB&J and get ready to conquer the lush trails of the San Juan Islands. From summiting the 2,409 foot peak on Mt. Constitution (Orcas Island), to trekking the nearly ten miles of waterfront trails at Sucia Island, you will enjoy the best of the islands' trail systems. Check with the respective anchorage descriptions to see if digital versions of trail maps are available for download to your computer or smart phone.

Total Mileage: 110 nautical miles

Anacortes to Eagle Harbor (Cypress Island):	8 miles
Bellingham to Eagle Harbor (Cypress Island):	*13 miles*
Eagle Harbor to Matia Island:	12 miles
Matia Island to Echo Bay (Sucia Island):	3 miles
Echo Bay to Patos Island:	6 miles
Patos Island to Prevost Harbor (Stuart Island):	12 miles
Prevost Harbor to Garrison Bay (San Juan Island):	9 miles
Garrison Bay to Jones Island:	8 miles
Jones Island to Griffin Bay (San Juan Island):	11 miles
Griffin Bay to Watmough Bay (Lopez Island):	10 miles
Watmough Bay to James Island (lunch stop):	5 miles
James Island to Rosario Resort (Orcas Island):	10 miles
Rosario Resort to Anacortes:	16 miles
Rosario Resort to Bellingham:	*21 miles*

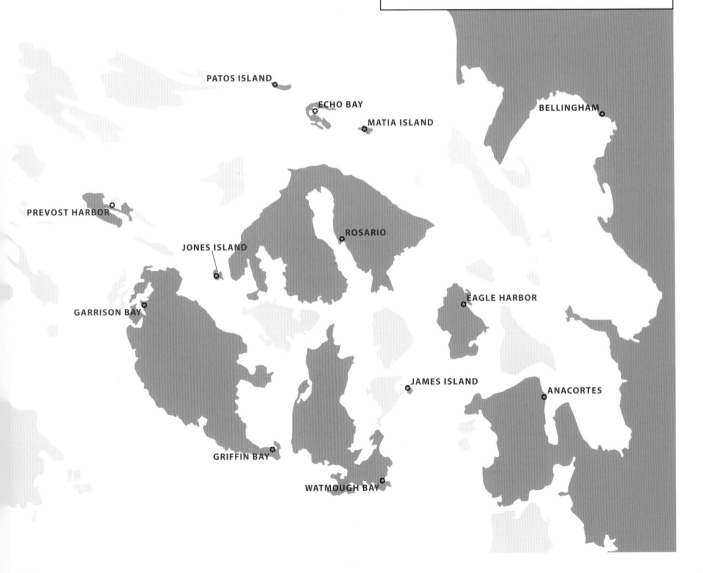

Weekend Warrior (Anacortes)

As the ever-watched clock on Friday afternoon strikes 5pm, reward yourself for a job well done and hit the water running. The Weekend Warrior itinerary is designed to recharge, reinvigorate and revive your spirit after a lengthy week of work. Cut the docklines and knock that shaggy green mane from the bottom of your boat by taking advantage of the summer season's long daylight hours. Grab a crab pot, a pack of sausages and a few cold ones for the cooler to enjoy a weekend out at anchor. Catch an amazing sunset, get the heart pumping with an exhilarating hike and find out why siestas should be mandatory in day to day life.

Total Mileage: 30 nautical miles

Anacortes to Eagle Harbor (Cypress Island):	8 miles
Eagle Harbor to Spencer Spit (Lopez Island):	10 miles
Spencer Spit to Anacortes:	12 miles

Total Mileage: 26 nautical miles

Anacortes to James Island:	9 miles
James Island to Watmough Bay (Lopez Island):	5 miles
Watmough Bay to Anacortes:	12 miles

Total Mileage: 48 nautical miles

Anacortes to Fisherman Bay (Lopez Island):	18 miles
Fisherman Bay to Jones Island:	9 miles
Jones Island to Anacortes:	21 miles

Total Mileage: 42 nautical miles

Anacortes to Pelican Beach (Cypress Island):	9 miles
Pelican Beach to Fossil Bay (Sucia Island):	12 miles
Fossil Bay to Anacortes:	21 miles

FOSSIL BAY

JONES ISLAND

PELICAN BEACH

EAGLE HARBOR

SPENCER SPIT

JAMES ISLAND

ANACORTES

WATMOUGH BAY

Weekend Warrior (Bellingham)

Total Mileage: 35 nautical miles

Bellingham to Pelican Beach (Cypress Island):	13 miles
Pelican Beach to Clark Island:	6 miles
Clark Island to Bellingham:	16 miles

Total Mileage: 40 nautical miles

Bellingham to Inati Bay (Lummi Island):	7 miles
Inati Bay to Echo Bay (Sucia Island):	14 miles
Echo Bay to Bellingham:	19 miles

Total Mileage: 49 nautical miles

Bellingham to Rosario Resort (Orcas Island):	21 miles
Rosario Resort to Spencer Spit (Lopez Island):	7 miles
Spencer Spit to Bellingham:	21 miles

Total Mileage: 28 nautical miles

Bellingham to Chuckanut Bay:	5 miles
Chuckanut Bay to Eagle Harbor (Cypress Island):	10 miles
Eagle Harbor to Bellingham:	13 miles

Dog Days of Summer

The Dog Days of Summer itinerary is designed for boaters who are looking to share the beauty of the islands with their furry best friend at their side. While not all destinations in the San Juans appreciate your pup as much as you, the following list of locales will help to insure that you and your buddy have a wonderful time romping on the beaches and enjoying a good game of fetch without treading on private property. For the courtesy of others and to protect the fragile island eco-system, please be sure to pick up after your pet and to have them leashed at all times.

Total Mileage: 77 nautical miles

Anacortes to Spencer Spit (Lopez Island):	12 miles
Bellingham to Spencer Spit (Lopez Island):	*21 miles*
Spencer Spit to Friday Harbor (San Juan Island):	8 miles
Friday Harbor to Jones Island:	6 miles
Jones Island to Garrison Bay (San Juan Island):	8 miles
Garrison Bay to Reid Harbor (Stuart Island):	6 miles
Reid Harbor to Fossil Bay (Sucia Island):	14 miles
Fossil Bay to Clark Island (lunch stop):	7 miles
Clark Island to Eagle Harbor (Cypress Island):	8 miles
Eagle Harbor to Anacortes:	8 miles
Eagle Harbor to Bellingham:	*13 miles*

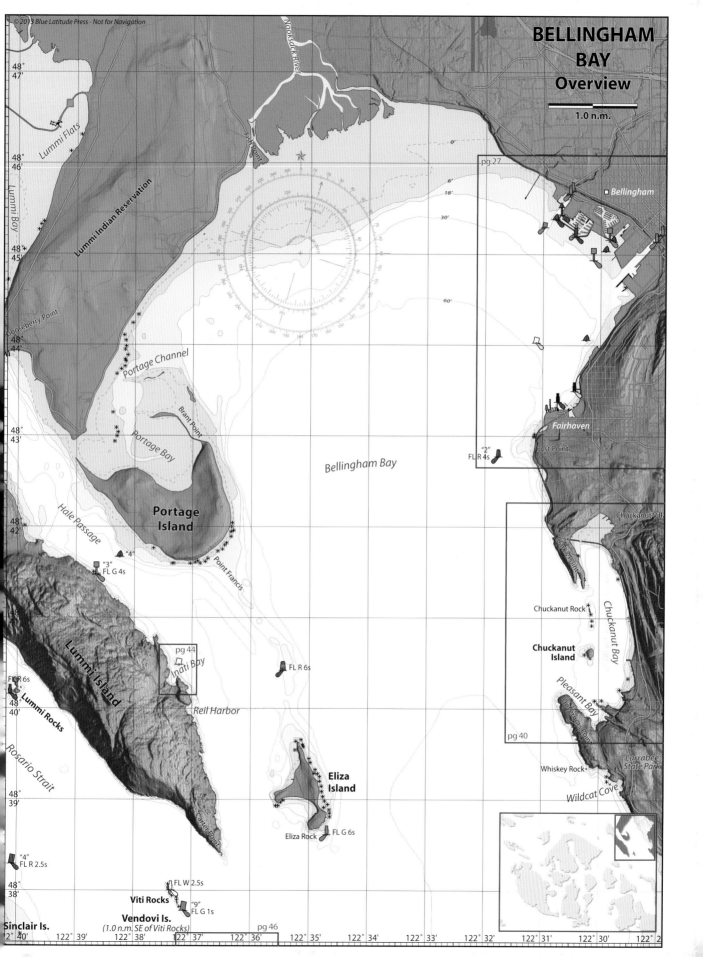

© 2013 Blue Latitude Press - Not for Navigation

BELLINGHAM BAY
Overview

1.0 n.m.

Lummi Flats

Lummi Bay

Nooksack River

Lummi Indian Reservation

Fish Point

pg 27

Bellingham

0

6'

18'

30'

60'

Gooseberry Point

Portage Channel

Brant Point

Portage Bay

Fairhaven

Post Point

"2"
FL R 4s

Bellingham Bay

Chuckanut Vill.

Clark's Point

Portage Island

Hale Passage

"3"
FL G 4s

"4"

Point Francis

Chuckanut Rock

Chuckanut Bay

Chuckanut Island

Lummi Island

pg 44

Inati Bay

FL R 6s

Pleasant Bay

Governor's Point

pg 40

FL R 6s

Lummi Rocks

Reil Harbor

Whiskey Rock

Larrabee State Park

Rosario Strait

Wildcat Cove

Eliza Island

Carter Point

Eliza Rock

FL G 6s

"4"
FL R 2.5s

FL W 2.5s

Viti Rocks

Vendovi Is.
(1.0 n.m. SE of Viti Rocks)

"9"
FL G 1s

Sinclair Is.

pg 46

48° 47'
48° 46'
48° 45'
48° 44'
48° 43'
48° 42'
48° 40'
48° 39'
48° 38'

122° 40'   122° 39'   122° 38'   122° 37'   122° 36'   122° 35'   122° 34'   122° 33'   122° 32'   122° 31'   122° 30'   122° 2

Michael Bertrand www.michaelbertrandphotography.com

Bellingham

Flanked by snow capped mountains to the east and the island studded waters of the Salish Sea to the west, Bellingham is a city like no other. It is a place where locals are proud to call home. This picturesque city provides nearly instant access to the area's best sailing, hiking, mountain biking, golfing, skiing, snowboarding and even kite boarding. Aside from its beauty and laid back atmosphere, Bellingham also offers the services, facilities and shopping centers found in most large marine based towns.

Bellingham is a city of approximately 80,000 people and lies nearly midway between the urban centers of Seattle and Vancouver, Canada. The city has one main marina operated by the Port of Bellingham with roughly 1,400 slips, as well as anchoring options near Fairhaven. A number of charter boat companies, both sail and power, bare boat or skippered, operate out of the marina as well. Access to Bellingham is made convenient with direct flights from a number of west coast cities including Seattle, Los Angeles, San Diego, Oakland, Las Vegas, Phoenix, Denver and even Honolulu.

Bellingham is located in the far northeastern corner of Bellingham Bay, approximately 16 nautical miles north of Anacortes. Due to the drainage of the Nooksack River, as well as Whatcom Creek and Squalicum Creek, much of the head of Bellingham Bay remains relatively shallow.

Approaches to Bellingham Bay can be taken from the south near Vendovi Island, or from the southwest via Hale Passage between Lummi Island and the mainland. Approaching the bay from the south is relatively straight forward with open stretches of water. If approaching from Hale Passage, be sure to check your charts as shallow areas can be found

Bellingham to:		
	Anacortes	16 nm
	Blaine	29 nm
	Blind Bay *(Shaw Island)*	23 nm
	Deer Harbor *(Orcas Island)*	26 nm
	Eagle Harbor *(Cypress Island)*	13 nm
	Echo Bay *(Sucia Island)*	19 nm
	Fisherman Bay *(Lopez Island)*	25 nm
	Friday Harbor *(San Juan Island)*	26 nm
	Prevost Harbor *(Stuart Island)*	32 nm
	Roche Harbor *(San Juan Island)*	34 nm
	Rosario *(Orcas Island)*	21 nm
	Sidney *(Canada)*	42 nm
	Spencer Spit *(Lopez Island)*	21 nm

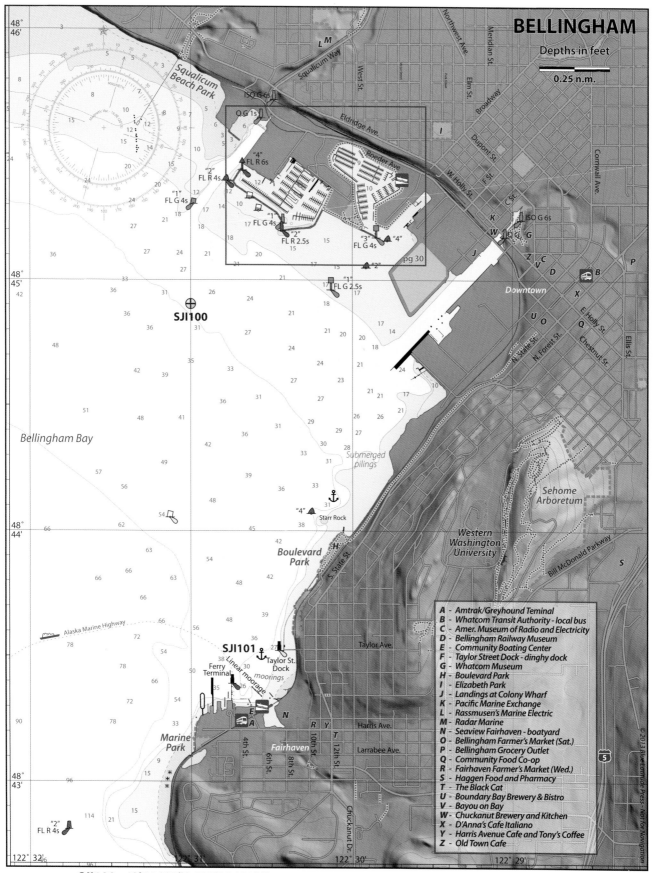

BELLINGHAM

Depths in feet

0.25 n.m.

Squalicum
Beach Park

MAGNETIC

ISO G 6s

Q G 1s

"4"
FL R 6s

"2"
FL R 4s

"1"
FL G 4s

"1"
FL G 4s

"2"
FL R 2.5s

"3"
FL G 4s

"4"

"2"

"1"
FL G 2.5s

Roeder Ave.

Eldridge Ave.

Squalicum Way

West St.

Northwest Ave.

Meridian St.

Elm St.

Broadway

Dupont St.

W. Holly St.

C St.

ISO G 6s

Cornwall Ave.

Downtown

pg 30

SJI100

Bellingham Bay

Submerged
pilings

"4"
Starr Rock

Sehome
Arboretum

Western
Washington
University

Boulevard
Park

S. State St.

N. State St.

N. Forest St.

Chestnut St.

E. Holly St.

Ellis St.

Bill McDonald Parkway

Alaska Marine Highway

SJI101

Taylor St.
Dock

Linear moorage
moorings

Taylor Ave.

Ferry
Terminal

Marine
Park

4th St.

6th St.

8th St.

10th St.

12th St.

Fairhaven

Harris Ave.

Larrabee Ave.

Chuckanut Dr.

5

A - Amtrak/Greyhound Teminal
B - Whatcom Transit Authority - local bus
C - Amer. Museum of Radio and Electricity
D - Bellingham Railway Museum
E - Community Boating Center
F - Taylor Street Dock - dinghy dock
G - Whatcom Museum
H - Boulevard Park
I - Elizabeth Park
J - Landings at Colony Wharf
K - Pacific Marine Exchange
L - Rassmusen's Marine Electric
M - Radar Marine
N - Seaview Fairhaven - boatyard
O - Bellingham Farmer's Market (Sat.)
P - Bellingham Grocery Outlet
Q - Community Food Co-op
R - Fairhaven Farmer's Market (Wed.)
S - Haggen Food and Pharmacy
T - The Black Cat
U - Boundary Bay Brewery & Bistro
V - Bayou on Bay
W - Chuckanut Brewery and Kitchen
X - D'Anna's Cafe Italiano
Y - Harris Avenue Cafe and Tony's Coffee
Z - Old Town Cafe

"2"
FL R 4s

© 2013 Blue Latitude Press - Not for Navigation

SJI100 - 48°44.900'N 122°31.000'W   **SJI101** - 48°43.490'N 122°30.550'W

Mt Baker and the Bellingham waterfront

Taylor Street dock near Fairhaven

Bellingham offers anchorage, mooring buoys and marina options for visiting boats. Boats looking to anchor can find protection from prevailing southerly winds near the aptly named historical district of Fairhaven, just north of Post Point. Additional anchorage is also available north of Fairhaven near Boulevard Park.

The Bellingham Bay Community Boating Center (see page 34) also operates mooring buoys and a linear side-tie mooring system within Fairhaven. Both mooring options are available for seasonal use May through October. Mooring buoys are available for boats up to 35 feet in length, and the linear moorage is available to visiting boats for up to three days.

To dinghy ashore in Fairhaven, the best location is at the Taylor Street Dock. The dock connects to the boardwalk trail system near Fairhaven, and is available for dinghies to tie up for short term visits to shore. To dinghy ashore near Boulevard Park, there are a handful of small sand beaches for landing around the park, with the most popular being at the very north end. These locations are not necessarily secure so be sure to take precautions if leaving your dinghy on shore.

For boats heading into Squalicum Marina (see page 29), there are three entrances: West, South and East. The west entrance includes access to the fuel dock, pumpout dock, Seaview North shipyard, and gate 3 west. The south entrance includes access to the gate 3 visitor dock, boathouses, and gates 3 east and 5. The east entrance has access to the gate 9 and 12 visitor docks, the launch ramp, and gates 6 through 12.

in this area. This is especially true around Portage Island and the water between Portage and Eliza Island. Be sure to pass outside of red buoy #4, and do not cut between the buoy and Portage Island due to shoal areas. The red and green lighted buoy lying between Portage and Eliza Islands marks a small, shallow reef just north of the buoy.

Bellingham Bay is roughly 10 nautical miles from north to south resulting in a large, open area of water. For this reason, Bellingham Bay is a favorite place for sailboats to hoist their sails and enjoy a pleasant day on the bay. During the winter months, when strong south to southeast winds are more likely, it is possible for chop to build in the bay due to this fetch. Depending on your direction of travel, this can make for a slow up wind slog, or a fast ride to Bellingham.

U.S. Department of Agriculture, Farm Service Agency

Squalicum Harbor Marina

The Port of Bellingham operates the enormous 1,400 slip marina at Squalicum Harbor. The two basin marina can accommodate boats up to 110 feet in length (depending on draft), along with 1,100 feet of side-tie guest moorage space. Each slip has access to power (30 amp and possible 50 amp) and water hook ups, with trash and recycling located at the top of each ramp. Services include a fuel dock, showers, laundry facilities, a four lane boat launch ramp, Fairhaven boat launch ramp, parking, two 4,000 pound cranes, pumpout facilities (including mobile pumpout carts), propane tank fills, and a used oil dump. Visiting boats have the option of tying up to one of the three visitor docks located at gates 3, 9 and 12, which are available on a first come basis (up to three days moorage). Visitors also have the option of contacting the marina for a loan-a-slip (up to 14 days) or a sublet (monthly stays). Staff at the marina office also operate a shuttle van for provisioning trips into town for visiting boaters.

Squalicum Harbor includes marine industry businesses, haul out yards, a commercial fishing fleet, restaurants, hotels and various shops can be found throughout Squalicum Harbor. A 2.5 mile trail also loops around the harbor, taking visitors on a scenic tour of the marina and its beauti-fully landscaped surroundings. Zuanich Point Park, which lies between the two marina basins, is a popular locale for its sweeping views of Bellingham Bay, along with the perfect breeze for kite flying. Squalicum Harbor lies only one mile from downtown Bellingham, making it an easy jaunt to explore more of this wonderfully eclectic city on the bay.

Squalicum Harbor Marina
Monitors VHF channel 16
722 Coho Way
Bellingham, WA 98225
(360) 676-2542
squalicum@portofbellingham.com
www.portofbellingham.com

Harbor Marine Fuel

Offering diesel and gasoline. Open everyday. Enter Squalicum Harbor via the west entrance. Located next to Bellingham Cold Storage (look for the large neon "ICE" sign). Phone: (360) 734-1710

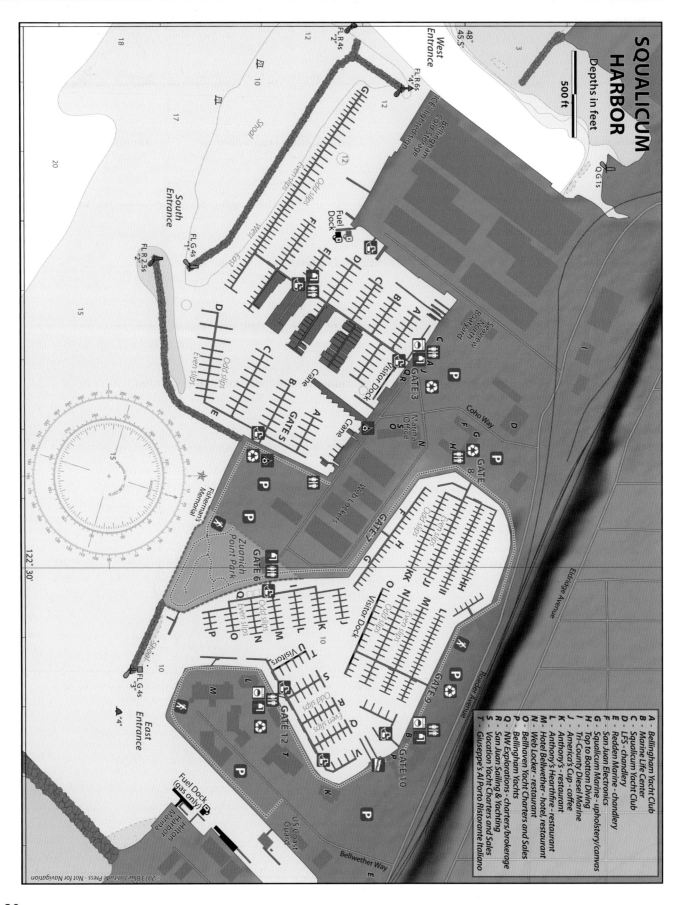

SQUALICUM
HARBOR

Depths in feet

500 ft

A - Bellingham Yacht Club
B - Marine Life Center
C - Squalicum Yacht Club
D - LFS - chandlery
E - Redden Marine - chandlery
F - San Juan Electronics
G - Squalicum Marine - upholstery/canvas
H - Top to Bottom Diving
J - Tri-County Diesel Marine
K - America's Cup - coffee
L - Anthony's Hearthfire - restaurant
M - Hotel Bellwether - hotel, restaurant
N - Web Locker - restaurant
O - Anthony's - restaurant
P - Bellingham Yachts
Q - Bellhaven Yacht Charters and Sales
R - NW Explorations - charters/brokerage
S - San Juan Sailing & Yachting
T - Vacation Yacht Charters and Sales
T - Giuseppe's Al Porto Ristorante Italiano

West
Entrance

South
Entrance

East
Entrance

Fisherman's
Memorial

Zuanich
Point Park

Fuel Dock

Marina
Office

Seaview
North
Boatyard

Web Lockers

Coho Way

Roeder Avenue

Eldridge Avenue

Bellwether Way

Hilton
Harbor
Marina

Fuel Dock
(gas only)

US Coast
Guard

© 2013 Blue Latitude Press - Not for Navigation

30

Bellingham waterfront with the Whatcom Museum and the old GP complex

History of Bellingham

The lands surrounding Bellingham Bay were first inhabited by the Coast Salish people including the Lummi, Nooksack, Samish and Semiahmoo. In the late 1700's, English and Spanish explorers began to arrive. During Captain George Vancouver's exploration of Puget Sound in 1792, Bellingham Bay was given its name in honor of Vancouver's colleague, Sir William Bellingham. Along the shores of Bellingham Bay, four small towns including Whatcom, Fairhaven, Bellingham and Sehome were established around the mid 1800's.

The site of first European settlement was established around 1852, along the mud flats where Whatcom Creek empties into the bay. With timber in high demand, a mill was built along the shores of the creek where lumber could then be transported by train and ship. This site, including the mud flats which are now covered, was the town of Whatcom.

When coal was discovered, the towns of Sehome (the current location of downtown Bellingham) and Bellingham (near present day Boulevard Park), sprang up to accommodate the company towns. The Sehome Dock was the only deepwater dock in Bellingham Bay for a number of years. The town of Fairhaven was established north of Post Point,

and had the conveniences of a deep water port with protection from the prevailing southeast winds.

In 1858, the Fraser River Gold Rush brought tens of thousands of people to the area as they traveled north with hopes of striking it rich. Unfortunately, the gold rush was short lived and many ended up returning to Whatcom county in search of jobs. With the industries of coal and sandstone mining, logging, rail lines, ship building and fishing, Bellingham Bay experienced tremendous growth over the next thirty years. On the front page of the holiday issue of the Fairhaven Herald, they posted the population change over 16 months from 180 in 1889 to 8,000 in 1890.

As the Depression of 1893 settled in across the nation, Whatcom county's boom era began to stall, eventually leading to a downturn in the local economy. In an effort to share municipal costs during this hard time, the two remaining towns of Whatcom and Fairhaven were consolidated and incorporated under the official city name of Bellingham in 1903.

As the national economy rebounded, Bellingham once again became a thriving town, relying on its abundant natural resources. Numerous wharves extended into the bay, all linked by rail cars aiding in the transport of lumber, shingles, coal and canned salmon to be shipped to distant des-

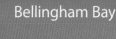

tinations. Before the construction of roads, ships played an important role in the area, transporting goods and people throughout Puget Sound and British Columbia.

Bellingham continued its growth with new hotels, shops, waterfront businesses, schools and government offices. In 1899, the New Whatcom Normal School opened with an initial enrollment of 88 students. Today, Western Washington University, as it is now known, has a current enrollment of 15,000 students.

While Bellingham continues to rely on its natural resources, tourism and the service industry have slowly begun to take more prominent positions in diversifying the city's economy. With an ever expanding population, now over 80,000 people, Bellingham continues to entice people to its shores where the mountains meet the sea.

Sights to See

For those staying at the marina, one of the first and most popular activities is to stretch your legs and take the scenic and beautiful walking tour of the harbor. A roughly 2.5 mile, paved loop trail circles the marina, taking visitors past the various areas of the marina, including Zuanich Point Park, marine chandleries and service centers, and tasty restaurants and cafes.

While enjoying your tour of the harbor, be sure to stop at the Marine Life Center to catch a glimpse of what lies beneath the water (**www.marinelifecenter.org**). The center showcases marine life and habitat in Bellingham Bay, Puget Sound and on the Washington Coast, with a number of aquariums and even a touch pool for an up close experience. The center is located in the building adjacent to the launch ramp at the marina.

If you happen to be in Bellingham on a Saturday, a trip to the Bellingham Farmer's Market is definitely a "not to miss" event. During the summer months the market is alive with activity including local farmers, bakers, cheesemongers, and artisans displaying their colorful wares, as well as delicious food vendors and live music. The market is open from 10am to

Walking trail at Squalicum Harbor and Zuanich Point Park

3pm, and is located downtown at the Depot Market Square at Railroad and Chestnut Streets (**www.bellinghamfarmers.org**).

From the market, the start of the popular greenway trail to Boulevard Park begins. This hard packed dirt and gravel trail follows the shoreline south to one of Bellingham's most treasured ocean front parks known as Boulevard Park. From the park, a paved boardwalk path leads over the water to the historic and quaint district of Fairhaven.

For those anchored or moored in Fairhaven, a walk through this historic and very picturesque district is well worth a visit. One of the original founding towns of the area, Fairhaven has retained its historical charm, as well as a number of the old brick buildings. Fairhaven boasts a number of excellent restaurants, shops, a grocery store, post office, banks and even a haul out yard. The Village Green is also home to the Fairhaven Farmer's Market on Wednesday afternoons in the summer months. Fairhaven is also a great place to pick up the 6.5 mile dirt and gravel Interurban Trail leading to Larrabee State Park.

For those looking to explore the history, art and culture of Bellingham and Whatcom county, there is no better place to visit than the Whatcom Museum. The museum occupies three buildings: the Syre Education Center which houses per-

manent historical exhibits and archive photos, the historical and very distinctive Old City Hall building which houses historical exhibits, and the modern new Lightcatcher building which houses a rotating schedule of art exhibitions as well as a Family Interactive Gallery. The Whatcom Museum is located downtown on the corner of Prospect and Flora Streets. Visit their website at: **www.whatcommuseum.org**.

Bellingham Trail Guide

With hundreds of miles of trails traversing the city and surrounding forest land, Bellingham is the perfect stop to get off the boat and stretch your legs with a nice stroll through the park, a hike through the Chuckanut mountains or a pleasant bike ride exploring the town. The city of Bellingham has put together a wonderful trail guide, including descriptions and maps, illustrating the various parks and trails the city is known for. For a complete listing and a downloadable version of the guide, visit the city's website at: **www.cob.org/services/recreation/parks-trails/**.

Two additional museums located in downtown are well worth a visit, including the American Museum of Radio and Electricity, and the Bellingham Railway Museum. Each museum provides a historical look through photographs and exhibits, and are well worth a stop. The radio and electricity museum is located at 1312 Bay Street (www.sparkmuseum.org), and the railway museum is located at 1320 Commercial Street (www.bellinghamrailwaymuseum.org).

One of the highlights during the summer season is the city of Bellingham's Concerts in the Park series. This free event takes place throughout the summer months at various parks and locales within the city. Locations are Boulevard Park (Saturdays at 7pm), Elizabeth Park (Thursdays at 6pm) and the Downtown Sounds (held at Holly and Bay Streets on Wednesdays at 5pm). For a current schedule, check the city's website at: www.cob.org/services/recreation/activities/concerts-in-the-park.aspx.

Marine Chandleries and Services

Bellingham Bay Community Boating Center
The CBC was founded in 2007 to fill the need for affordable and accessible boating for all in Bellingham. The CBC offers youth camps, adult classes, rentals and group events, and mooring buoy and linear moorage rentals in Fairhaven.
Phone: (360) 714-8891   Web: www.boatingcenter.org

Hardware Sales
A locally owned, family-run hardware store like no other that has been open since 1962. Well versed in the marine industry, Hardware Sales has a large supply of tools, fasteners, painting supplies, plumbing, electrical, and even a rigging shop.
Phone: (360) 734-6140   Web: www.hardwaresales.net

Hilton Harbor
Hilton Harbor offers land-based boat and trailer storage, as well as a haulout facility, a gasoline fuel dock, maintenance,

repairs and painting. Located across from the U.S. Coast Guard Station at the south end of Hilton Avenue.
Phone: (360) 733-1110   Web: www.hiltonharbor.com

Home Depot
Home Depot is a national chain home hardware warehouse complete with lumber, tools, plumbing and electrical supplies and much more. Located near the intersection of I-5 and Meridian at 420 Telegraph Road.
Phone: (360) 715-0090   Web: www.homedepot.com

Landings at Colony Wharf
Colony Wharf operates a crane lift with the ability to haul monohull and multihull boats up to 25 tons. This full service yard includes mast stepping, storage, painting, fabrication, sandblasting, repairs and much more. Located at 1001 C Street, on the Whatcom Creek waterway.
Phone: (360) 715-1000   Web: www.landingscolonywharf.com

Lowe's
Lowe's is a national chain hardware warehouse with tools, lumber, plumbing and electrical supplies and more. Located at 1050 East Sunset Drive, near I-5.
Phone: (360) 734-2659   Web: www.lowes.com

LFS - Lummi Fishery Supply
Originally opened in 1967 as a supplier to commercial fishermen, LFS has grown and diversified to include sport fishing supplies, pleasure boating supplies, kayaks and accessories, and outdoor clothing and shoes. Located at Squalicum Marina at 851 Coho Way, at the corner of Roeder and Coho.
Phone: (360) 734-3336   Web: www.lfsinc.com

Pacific Marine Exchange
Pacific Marine Exchange offers new, used and consignment marine equipment and supplies. The shop also offers a well stocked bookstore (new and used) as well as a marine art gallery. Located at 700 Holly Street.
Phone: (360) 738-8535   Web: www.pacificmarine.com

Radar Marine
Radar Marine specializes in marine electronics for commercial and recreational boaters. Services include sales, installations, repairs and training. Located at 909 Squalicum Way.
Phone: (360) 733-2012   Web: www.radarmarine.com

Rasmussen's Marine Electric
In operation since 1978, Rasmussen's offers sales, installation and repairs for marine electronics, as well as being a certified Suzuki outboard dealer. Located at 909 Squalicum Way.
Phone: (360) 671-2992   Web: www.rasmarineelectric.com

Redden Marine
Redden Marine opened in 1959 to supply the commercial fishing industry. Over the years, Redden has expanded to

supply a large selection of recreational boating supplies, clothing and fishing gear. Located at Squalicum Marina at 1411 Roeder Avenue, on the corner of Roeder and Bellwether Way.
Phone: (360) 733-0250   Web: www.reddenmarine.com

San Juan Electronics

San Juan Electronics has been in operation for 35 years, specializing in sales, installation, repairs and training of marine electronics for commercial and recreational boaters. Located at Squalicum Marina at 730 Coho Way.
Phone: (360) 733-6264   Web: www.sanjuanelectronics.com

Seaview North Boatyard

Seaview operates two yards, one conveniently located within Squalicum Marina and a second in Fairhaven. The yard operates a 165 ton travel lift for large vessels, as well as a 35 ton lift. Services at Seaview include mast restepping, painting, maintenance, repair and fabrication work. Seaview North is located at Gate 3 in Squalicum Marina. Seaview Fairhaven is located at 805 Harris Avenue, Buildings 4 and 5, in the Fairhaven Marine Industrial Park.
Phone: (360) 676-8282   Web: www.seaviewboatyard.com

ShipShape Your Yacht

ShipShape offers maintenance and repairs, along with scheduled checks, washing and waxing of your boat.
Phone: (360) 933-4656 Web: www.shipshapeyouryacht.com

Squalicum Marine

Squalicum Marine specializes in marine canvas and upholstery from repairs to custom projects, including sail repair. They are located within Squalicum Marina at 712 Coho Way.
Phone: (360) 733-4353   Web: www.squalicummarine.com

Top to Bottom Diving

Top To Bottom provides a variety of services ranging from light commercial diving work to yacht repair and maintenance. Top to Bottom provides general dive services as well as sunken boat recovery and 24 hour emergency response.
Phone: (360) 671-7022   Web: www.toptobottominc.com

Tri-County Diesel Marine

Tri-County Diesel provides authorized sales, service and parts for marine and industrial engines and generators from sailboats to large commercial vessels. Located near Squalicum Marina at 2696 Roeder Avenue.
Phone: (360) 733-8880 Web: www.tricountydieselmarine.com

West Marine

One of the nation's largest boating supply retailers, including marine parts, supplies, accessories, apparel, and electronics. Located at 3560 Meridian Street near Cornwall Park.
Phone: (360) 650-1100   Web: www.westmarine.com

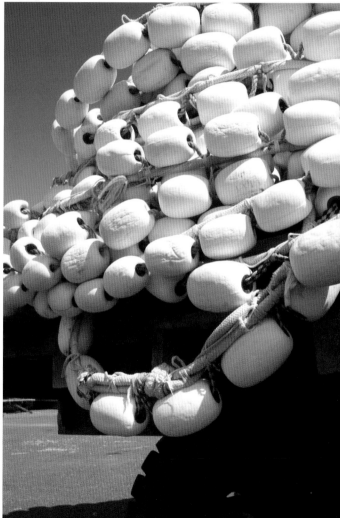

Sail and Power Boat Charter Companies
Bellhaven Yacht Charters and Sales

Bellhaven is brokerage and charter office offering a selection of power and sailboats for weekly charter. Located at Squalicum Marina at 714 Coho Way.
Phone: (360) 733-6636   Web: www.bellhaven.net

Bellingham Yachts

Bellingham Yachts is a brokerage company specializing in Sabre, Back Cove and Cutwater yachts. They offer weekly bareboat or crewed charters on a selection of power boats including Sabre and Back Cove yachts. Located at Squalicum Marina at 1801 Roeder Avenue, Suite 174.

Phone: (360) 671-0990   Web: www.bellinghamyachts.com

NW Explorations

NW Explorations specializes in Grand Banks yachts for both brokerage and charters. They offer weekly Grand Banks charters as well as guided flotillas to southeast Alaska and Desolation Sound. Located at Squalicum Marina near the entrance to Gate 3.

Phone: (360) 676-1248   Web: www.nwexplorations.com

San Juan Sailing & Yachting

San Juan Sailing offers one of the largest charter fleets in Bellingham. Their boats include power and sailboats, both monohulls and multihulls for weekly charters. Located at Squalicum Marina near the entrance to Gate 3.

Phone: (360) 671-4300   Web: www.sanjuansailing.com

Vacation Yacht Charters and Sales

Vacation Yacht Charters offers weekly bareboat and crewed charters, including both sail and power boats. Located at Squalicum Marina at 2620 Harbor Loop.

Phone: (360) 752-5754   Web: www.paryachtcharters.com

Provisioning and Other Services

Bellingham Farmer's Market

The Bellingham Farmer's Market is held in downtown Bellingham at the Depot Market each Saturday from April through December from 10am to 3pm. This festive outdoor market includes fresh local produce, bakery items, cheese, seafood, crafts and food vendors.

Phone: (360) 647-2060   Web: www.bellinghamfarmers.org

Community Food Co-op

With over 40 years of serving the community with natural foods, the Community Food Co-op is a great place to find fresh, local and organic foods. The grocery includes produce, dairy items, meats, seafoods, bakery items, staples, bulk foods, vitamins and even a deli and cafe. Located downtown on the corner of Holly and Forest Streets.

Phone: (360) 734-8158   Web: www.communityfood.coop

Costco

Costco is a warehouse style store that carries everything from groceries to home and office supplies. The warehouse requires a membership card to shop. Located at 4299 Guide Meridian Street.

Phone: (360) 671-6947   Web: www.costco.com

Fairhaven Farmer's Market

The Fairhaven Farmer's Market is held each Wednesday from noon to 5pm during the summer months at the Village Green in central Fairhaven. The Market is a wonderful place to spend the afternoon shopping for local produce and crafts.

Phone: (360) 647-2060   Web: www.bellinghamfarmers.org

Fred Meyer

Fred Meyer is a national chain super store including a grocery, pharmacy, clothes, electronics, household items, furniture, hardware items and a garden center. Two locations at 800 Lakeway Drive near downtown, and 1225 West Bakerview Road north of town.

Phone: (360) 676-1102   Web: www.fredmeyer.com

Haggen Food and Pharmacy

Haggen is a local area grocery store chain that opened back in 1933. The grocery carries fresh produce, dairy items, meats, seafood, bakery items, a pharmacy, and all the staples. A number of stores are found throughout the area including the closest to the water at 2814 Meridian and in Fairhaven at 1401 12th Street.

Phone: (360) 733-8720   Web: www.haggen.com

Trader Joes

Trader Joe's is a national grocery chain that has achieved quite a following for its name brand products, many of which are organic. Trader Joe's carries fresh produce, meats, dairy items and cheeses, a wine department and all the staples. Located at 2410 James Street.

Phone: (360) 734-5166   Web: www.traderjoes.com

Village Books

Village Books is a community-based, independent bookstore located in the historic Fairhaven district. This bookstore is like no other with three floors of new and used books, including weekly book readings. Located at 1200 11th Street.

Phone: (360) 671-2626   Web: www.villagebooks.com

Youngstock's Country Farms

Youngstock's is a local favorite produce and nursery stand. Fresh fruits and veggies available at very affordable prices. Located near Trader Joe's at 2237 James Street.

Phone: (360) 733-1866

Transportation
Airport

Bellingham International Airport (BLI) serves the commercial, general aviation, and corporate air transportation needs of the region. The Bellingham airport is located 90 miles north of Seattle, and 50 miles south of Vancouver. Airport services include car rentals, a foreign trade zone, customs brokerage, U.S. Customs international terminal, aircraft maintenance and air cargo services. Shuttle service is also available between Seattle's Sea-Tac International Airport and Vancouver's International Airport (see Buses below). Airlines servicing the airport include Alaska Airlines, Allegiant Air, Frontier Airlines, Island Air, Northwest Sky Ferry and San Juan Airlines.

Buses

Intracity buses are a convenient, easy, and inexpensive way to travel around the city of Bellingham. Bus service is available through the Whatcom Transit Authority. Schedules and fares are available at www.ridewta.com. Intercity bus travel is available through Greyhound Bus Lines for travel to or from Bellingham. The Greyhound terminal is located at the Fairhaven Transportation Center (schedules and fares can be found at www.greyhound.com). Shuttle services are also available for travel between Seattle and Vancouver's international airports. Schedules and fares are available at www.quickcoach.com, www.airporter.com and www.boltbus.com.

Cabs

Cab service is available throughout town, including transportation to and from the airport, bus terminal, train terminal and local area shopping. A number of services operate in town including Yellow Cab (Phone: (360) 733-TAXI, Web: www.yellowcabinc.com).

Trains

Scenic train transportation is available at the Bellingham terminal through Amtrak. The Bellingham train terminal is located at the Fairhaven Transportation Center. Schedules and fares can be found online at: www.amtrak.com.

Restaurants
America's Cup

Located at the top of the ramp at Gate 3 and next to the Bellingham Yacht Club, America's Cup offers piping hot coffee and delicious espresso drinks daily. The perfect spot to grab a cup and a pastry snack on your way down to the boat.

Anthony's at Squalicum Harbor

On of the most popular and beautiful settings on the waterfront at Squalicum Harbor. Serving fresh and delicious northwest fare including locally caught seafood. Happy hour daily from 3pm to 6:30pm. Located at 25 Bellwether Way.

Phone: (360) 647-5588   Web: www.anthonys.com

Anthony's Hearthfire

The Hearthfire is located just down the road from Anthony's original Bellingham restaurant. Overlooking the marina, the Hearthfire serves fresh northwest dishes including locally caught seafood. Happy hour daily from 3pm to 6:30pm. Located at 7 Bellwether Way.

Phone: (360) 527-3473   Web: www.anthonys.com

The Black Cat

The Black Cat is a classic in Fairhaven. With a french cabaret theme, the Black Cat is a popular stop for happy hour and dinner. Be sure to try their famous Caesar salad made fresh at your table.

Phone: (360) 733-6136 Web: www.blackcatbellingham.com

The Black Cat restaurant in Fairhaven

The Village Green in Fairhaven

A Lot of Flowers

Tony's Coffee and the Harris Avenue Cafe

Boundary Bay Brewery & Bistro

Bellingham's local and award winning brewery and bistro opened in 1995. A local favorite, Boundary serves excellent beer and northwest food with weekly live music lineups. Indoor and outdoor seating, located at 1107 Railroad Avenue.
Phone: (360) 647-5593   Web: www.bbaybrewery.com

Bayou on Bay

Bayou on Bay is a delicious and unique Cajun and Creole dining experience. Next door is their Oyster Bar, serving fresh local oysters along with a host of delectable cocktails. Located at 1300 Bay Street, on the corner of Bay and Holly.
Phone: (360) 75-BAYOU   Web: www.bayouonbay.com

Chuckanut Brewery and Kitchen

Located in Old Town, Chuckanut Brewery offers hand-crafted beers served with local, season dishes. Happy hour Sunday through Thursday. Located at 601 W Holly Street.
Phone: (360) 752-3377
Web: www.chuckanutbreweryandkitchen.com

Giuseppe's-Al-Porto

Located waterfront near the Bellwether Hotel, Giuseppe's is a fine dining Italian experience. Open for lunch and dinner with happy hour specials. Large outdoor seating is also available. Located at 21 Bellwether Way.
Phone: (360) 714-8412   Web: www.giuseppesitalian.com

Harris Avenue Cafe and Tony's Coffee

Harris Avenue Cafe and adjoining Tony's Coffee are located in the heart of Fairhaven in the historic Terminal Building. The cafe serves delicious, homemade breakfasts and lunches, while Tony's is your place for the perfect cup of coffee or espresso. Tony's Coffee is also available to purchase buy the pound at Tony's or at most Bellingham area grocery stores.
Phone: (360) 738-0802   Web: www.harrisavecafe.com
Phone: (360) 733-6319   Web: www.tonyscoffee.com

Old Town Cafe

Located in Bellingham's historic Old Town district, the Old Town Cafe is one of the most popular spots for breakfast and lunch. Serving fresh, local and organic entrees with a cozy down home atmosphere. Located at 316 West Holly Street.
Phone: (360) 671-4431   Web: www.theoldtowncafe.com

Web Locker Restaurant

Delicious food, coupled with a great location, the Web Locker is the central gathering place for breakfast and lunch at Squalicum Marina. From amazing omelettes to juicy burgers and fresh seafood, the Web Locker's casual indoor and outdoor atmosphere is sure to win you over. Located next to the Squalicum Marina office at 734 Coho Way.
Phone: (360) 676-0512

From Pleasant Bay looking north towards Chuckanut Bay

Chuckanut Bay

Beautiful Chuckanut Bay is situated alongside the thickly forested hillside of Chuckanut Mountain. The bay, which lies only five miles south from Bellingham, is a popular area for seakayaking and pleasure boating with its protected waters and scenic views. Like Sucia Island, the bay is lined with sandstone that has been worn away over the years by the lapping waters of Bellingham Bay, creating intricate lace-like formations. Near the middle of the bay lies Chuckanut Island, a Nature Conservancy preserve, which is open to the public and offers a walking trail around the island.

Chuckanut Bay is located along the eastern shore of Bellingham Bay, roughly three miles south of the historic area of Fairhaven and two miles north from the Larrabee State Park boat launch. The bay is formed by Clark's Point (locally named) to the north and Governors Point to the south. Near the southern portion of the bay, is a smaller cove with good southerly wind protection, named Pleasant Bay.

Entrance to Chuckanut Bay is guarded by Chuckanut Island, Chuckanut Rock and another unnamed reef lying between the two. Since these obstructions are extensive and unmarked, with many portions of the reefs covered at both high and low tides, consult your charts and navigate with caution.

Chuckanut Island is surrounded by an extending rocky shoreline, with larger reefs found off the western and southern portions of the island. Chuckanut Rock, with the center of the reef visible at high tide, is a long narrow reef, extending north to south. The nearby unnamed reef, which is an extension of Chuckanut Rock, is underwater at high tide and also extends from north to south. No passage is available between Chuckanut Rock and the unnamed reef.

Chuckanut Bay to:		
	Anacortes	11 nm
	Bellingham	5 nm
	Blaine	28 nm
	Blind Bay (Shaw Island)	19 nm
	Clark Island	14 nm
	Deer Harbor (Orcas Island)	23 nm
	Echo Bay (Sucia Island)	18 nm
	Eagle Harbor (Cypress Island)	10 nm
	Fisherman Bay (Lopez Island)	22 nm
	Friday Harbor (San Juan Island)	23 nm
	Inati Bay (Lummi Island)	5 nm
	Roche Harbor (San Juan Island)	30 nm
	Spencer Spit (Lopez Island)	18 nm

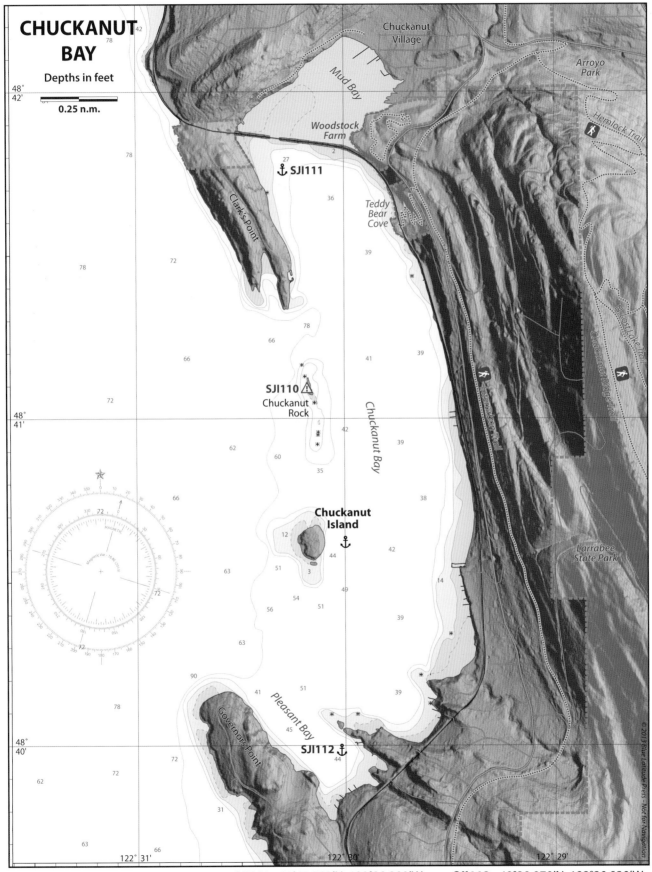

CHUCKANUT BAY

Depths in feet

0.25 n.m.

SJI111 ⚓

Clarks Point

Mud Bay

Chuckanut Village

Woodstock Farm

Teddy Bear Cove

Arroyo Park

Hemlock Trail

SJI110 ⚠
Chuckanut Rock

Chuckanut Bay

N Lost Lake Trail

Chuckanut Ridge Trail

Chuckanut Island ⚓

Interurban Trail

Larrabee State Park

Pleasant Bay

Governors Point

SJI112 ⚓

© 2013 Blue Latitude Press - Not for Navigation

SJI110 - 48°41.100'N 122°30.170'W   **SJI111** - 48°41.750'N 122°30.300'W   **SJI112** - 48°39.970'N 122°30.030'W

40

Anchored at Chuckanut Island

The largest and least obstructed entrance to the bay can be taken from the south between Governors Point and Chuckanut Island. Entrance from the north can be taken between Clark's Point and Chuckanut Rock, keeping in mind that reefs extend north off Chuckanut Rock. Passage can also be taken between Chuckanut Island and the unnamed reef, although rocks extend off both the island and the reef.

Once inside, the bay is relatively open to anchoring with the exception of a shallow, rocky area near the southeastern portion. Popular anchoring locations are found in the northern section of the bay near the railroad trestle, off the eastern side of Chuckanut Island, and also to the south in Pleasant Bay. Anchoring depths range from 5 to 8 fathoms over a mostly mud bottom.

Depending on weather conditions, anchorage can be taken in various portions of the bay for all around protection. In the northern portion, good protection from north, west and east winds are available, although it is open to the south. In Pleasant Bay, good protection from the area's predominate southerly winds is available as well as east and west wind protection, however the bay is open to the north.

While a large portion of the land surrounding Chuckanut Bay is privately owned, there are a number of activities including shoreside parks and preserves available to keep you well entertained. One of the favorite places to visit is the Nature Conservancy's, Cyrus Gates Memorial Preserve, on Chuckanut Island. Dinghy and kayak landings are available

on the northeast and west beaches. A walking trail meanders around the tree studded island, and the rocky shorelines are a perfect place to spot tidepools teaming with intertidal life. A bald eagle's nest is also found in one of the trees on the island with frequent sightings of these majestic birds.

Across the bay, on the northeastern shore, are two public parks: Teddy Bear Cove and Woodstock Farm. Teddy Bear Cove is best recognized by its sand and pebble beach, which also makes for a good dinghy or kayak landing location. A trail leads up from the beach to the road, Chuckanut Drive, as well as the gravel 6.5 mile Interurban Trail.

Nearby Woodstock Farm, named by civic leader Cyrus Gates, is a newly acquired 16 acre estate, which has been developed into a city park. Picturesque walking trails traverse the farm lands and barns with scenic views of Chuckanut Bay and nearby islands. Access to the park is available via the Teddy Bear Cove trail and the Interurban Trail.

Anchored at Pleasant Bay

One of the best highlights of Chuckanut Bay is taking a slow dinghy ride or kayak paddle along the diverse stretch of shoreline around the bay. Surrounded by limestone rocks and cliffs, intricately eroded lace-like formations are found throughout the area, lending to a unique and amazing shoreline. Clark's Point, Chuckanut Island and Pleasant Bay are all good locations to spot these complex stone creations.

For wildlife viewing, the peaceful waters of Chuckanut Bay support a wide variety of birds, mammals and fish. The isolated reef of Chuckanut Rock is a favorite haul out location for local harbor seals, as well as cormorants and sea gulls. Bald eagles and great blue herons are also frequently spotted in the area, especially in the spring months. Deer additionally frequent the area as they graze on the thick undergrowth found throughout the Chuckanut Mountain area.

Inati Bay (Lummi Island)

Inati Bay on Lummi Island is a favorite weekend getaway for many boaters coming from Bellingham. This remote little anchorage is the ideal spot to unwind from the hectic weekdays spent in the city, and allows boaters to get a jump start on weekend cruises out to the islands. Inati Bay lies only seven miles from Bellingham, making it an easy destination Friday evening during the summer's long daylight hours. Inati Bay is also an outstation for the Bellingham Yacht Club, whose members maintain the lawn, firepit and outhouses on shore. Because the yacht club leases the land surrounding the bay, onshore access is restricted to club members and guests only, although any boat is allowed to anchor within the protection of the bay.

Inati Bay is located on the southeastern shore of Lummi Island where Hale Passage meets Bellingham Bay. If approaching Inati Bay from Hale Passage, be sure to check your charts and note the shallow areas found within the pass. If approaching from Bellingham, note the red and green lighted buoy lying between Portage and Eliza Islands, which marks a small reef and should be avoided.

The entrance to Inati Bay is guarded by a small reef which is marked by a white buoy and kelp. This buoy is not lighted so care should be taken if approaching the anchorage at night. While passage into the bay can be taken either south or west of the reef, keep in mind that the reef extends north from the buoy and adequate room should be given to the reef on a northerly approach from Hale Passage.

Inati Bay to:		
	Anacortes	11 nm
	Bellingham	7 nm
	Blaine	23 nm
	Blind Bay (Shaw Island)	17 nm
	Echo Bay (Sucia Island)	14 nm
	Eagle Harbor (Cypress Island)	7 nm
	Fisherman Bay (Lopez Island)	19 nm
	Friday Harbor (San Juan Island)	20 nm
	Roche Harbor (San Juan Island)	27 nm
	Rosario (Orcas Island)	15 nm
	Sidney (Canada)	36 nm
	Spencer Spit (Lopez Island)	16 nm

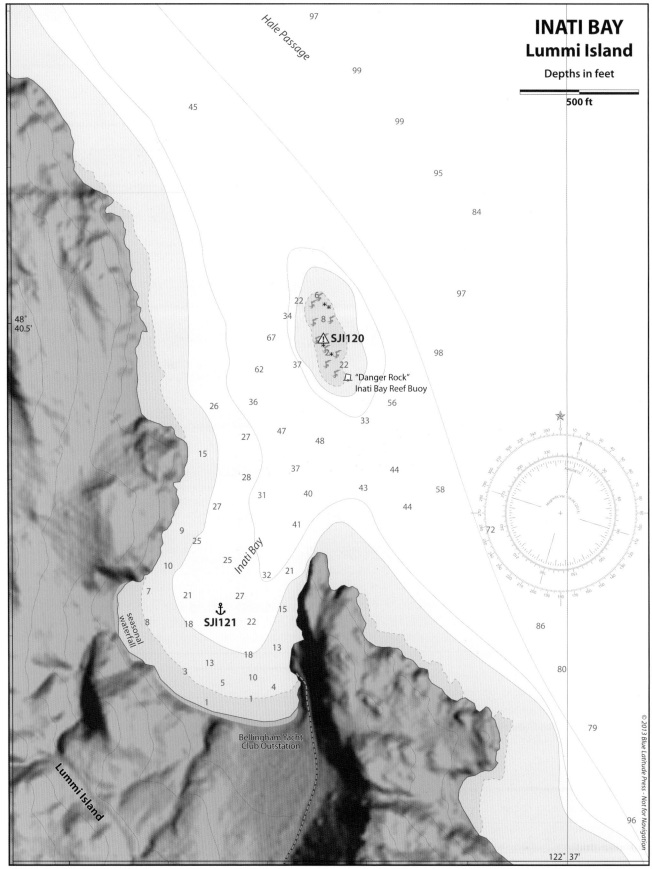

INATI BAY
Lummi Island
Depths in feet

500 ft

Hale Passage

97

99

45

99

95

84

97

22
34
8
67
⚠ SJI120
62
37
2
22
🔲 "Danger Rock"
Inati Bay Reef Buoy
56
26
36
33
47
48
27
15
37
44
28
43
58
31
40
44
27
41
9
25
58
10
25
32
21
Inati Bay
7
21
27
15
8
18
22
⚓ SJI121
13
18
3
13
10
4
5
1
1
seasonal waterfall

72

86

80

79

96

Bellingham Yacht
Club Outstation

Lummi Island

122° 37'

48°
40.5'

SJI120 - 48°40.490'N 122°37.240'W   **SJI121** - 48°40.320'N 122°37.340'W

Anchorage for a handful of boats can be taken within Inati Bay in 4 to 6 fathoms over a good holding, mostly mud bottom. In order to accommodate additional boats, many will stern tie to shore to prevent swinging into other anchored boats or the shoreside. The anchorage provides good protection from the area's predominately southerly winds, but is open to the north. For northerly winds, anchorage can be taken nearby off the south side of Eliza Island (see page 272) or within the northern portion of Chuckanut Bay.

For dinghy trips to shore for members of the Bellingham Yacht Club or reciprocals, Inati Bay has a large crescent shaped pebble beach for easy shoreside landings. The lush green lawn that is maintained by the Bellingham Yacht Club, tends to be a haven for spotting deer on Lummi Island. The yacht club also maintains two pit toilets, a beachside fire pit, and a picnic table for its members.

During the spring and winter months, a small waterfall can be found in the southwest corner of the beach, whose cascading water lends to the peaceful nature of the anchorage. For those looking to stretch their legs and take a walk, a logging road leads from the log skids found on the eastern side of the bay and meanders up the island. Evenings at Inati Bay are quiet times, where a beautiful backdrop of Bellingham's twinkling lights can be seen.

Inati Bay

White Buoy

Kelp

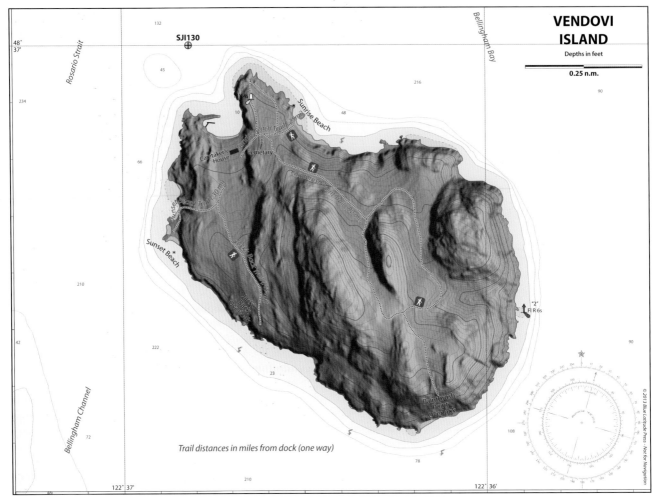

Trail distances in miles from dock (one way)

SJI130 - 48°37.000'N 122°36.820'W

Vendovi Island

Vendovi Island is one of the newest preserve acquisitions by the San Juan Preservation Trust (SJPT). The 217-acre island was purchased by the Trust in 2010 and is open to the public for day use during the summer months. Only two acres have been developed on the entire island, leaving the remaining island in pristine and native condition. Without the presence of deer on the island, a lush undergrowth has also lead to a vibrant flora, including an array of wildflowers, especially in the spring and summer months. The island's diversity includes beaches, forests, grasslands and wetlands. Midden (crushed shell) beaches found on the island are also telling that Vendovi was used for centuries by Coast Salish people as a seasonal camp.

Vendovi Island is located near the southeastern end of Bellingham Bay, 1.75 miles off the southern tip of Lummi Island. Vendovi's neighboring islands include Eliza, Sinclair, Guemes and Samish Islands. The only access to the island is found on the north side in a small cove protected by a rock breakwater. A nearly 80 foot dock with tie ups on either side

is found within the cove and is available for use by visitors to the island. No anchoring is allowed within the cove due to the preservation of sensitive eelgrass beds.

Vendovi Island is currently open to the public from 10am to 6pm, May through September, for day use only. An information kiosk as well as island caretakers provide helpful

Vendovi Island to:		
Anacortes		7 nm
Bellingham		9 nm
Blaine		27 nm
Blind Bay (Shaw Island)		14 nm
Echo Bay (Sucia Island)		15 nm
Eagle Harbor (Cypress Island)		4 nm
Fisherman Bay (Lopez Island)		16 nm
Friday Harbor (San Juan Island)		17 nm
Roche Harbor (San Juan Island)		24 nm
Rosario (Orcas Island)		12 nm
Spencer Spit (Lopez Island)		12 nm

island facts as well as maps to the island's trail system. Over two miles of trails cover the island including trails leading to midden and sand/pebble beaches.

Vendovi Island is a rare, relatively untouched gem within the San Juan Islands. Thanks to the foresight of the SJPT, the island will hopefully remain untouched for generations to come, however the Trust still has an outstanding loan to pay off before the island is permanently acquired. The purchase and maintenance of the island is funded entirely by donations. If you would like to help with the SJPT's campaign to "Save Vendovi Island," visit their website at **www.sjpt.org**, or take a trip to Vendovi Island to experience the rare beauty the island has to offer. Donations are encouraged and will help to further the ongoing efforts to protect Vendovi Island and other vitally sensitive areas within the San Juan Islands.

San Juan Preservation Trust

Founded in 1979, the San Juan Preservation Trust is a nationally accredited private, non-profit and membership-based land trust dedicated to helping people and communities conserve land in the San Juan Islands. The Preservation Trust has permanently protected more than 260 properties, 37 miles of shoreline and 15,000 acres on 20 islands, including land now managed as public parks, nature preserves, wildlife habitat, and working farms and forests. Some of their projects and easements include Watmough Bight Conservation Easement on Lopez Island, Turtleback Mountain Conservation Easement on Orcas Island, Kimball Preserve on Decatur Island, Mosquito Pass Preserve on Henry Island and their newest project, Vendovi Island Preserve. Without the foresight, dedication, and financial support of individuals and businesses, many of these protected areas would be part of future development sites and closed to the enjoyment of the public.

The San Juan Preservation Trust is not affiliated with any government agency with the majority of their funding coming from private donors. The Preservation Trust depends upon thousands of people to provide support in a number of ways to continue their efforts to protect and preserve lands throughout the San Juan Islands. The Preservation Trust relies on private financial and volunteer support from individuals, families, businesses, and foundations. If you would like to support the San Juan Preservation Trust or get further information about their organization, please contact the Trust at:

San Juan Preservation Trust
PO Box 327, Lopez, WA 98261
(360) 468-3202
info@sjpt.org
www.sjpt.org

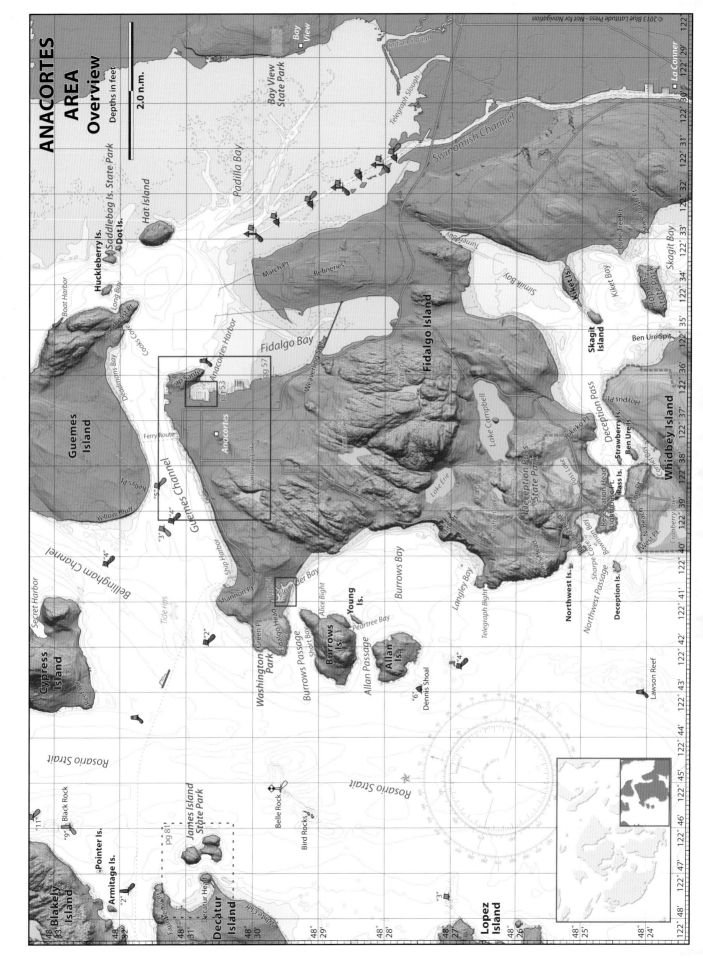

Depths in feet

2.0 n.m.

© 2013 Blue Latitude Press - Not for Navigation

La Conner

Bay View

Indian Slough

Bay View State Park

Telegraph Slough

Swinomish Channel

Padilla Bay

Hat Island

Saddlebag Is. State Park

Dot Is.

Huckleberry Is.

Boat Harbor

Southeast Pt.

Cooks Cove

Long Bay

March Pt.

Refineries

Turner Bay

Snee-oosh Pt.

Lone Tree Pt.

Skagit Bay

Deadmans Bay

Anacortes Harbor

Fidalgo Bay

Cap Sante

pg 57

pg 53

Fidalgo Island

Weaverling Spits

Lake Campbell

Whistle Lake

Similk Bay

Kiket Is.

Kiket Bay

HOPE Is. State Park

Skagit Island

Ben Ure Spit

Guemes Island

Ferry Route

Kellys Pt.

Yellow Bluff

"5"

"4"

"3"

Bellingham Channel

Anacortes

Cranberry Lake

Heart Lake

Pass Lake

Lake Erie

Stratton Lake

Trafton Lake

Deception Pass State Park

Yokeko Pt.

Deception Pass

Hoypus Pt.

Strawberry Is.

Reservation Head
Lighthouse Pt.

Ben Ure Is.

Bowman Bay

Sharpe Cove

Rosario Strait

"4"

Secret Harbor

Red Pass

Cypress Island

Ship Harbor

Shannon Pt.

Washington Park

Green Pt.

Fidalgo Head

Short Bay

Burrows Passage

pg 54

Flounder Bay

Alice Bight

Peartree Bay

Young Is.

Burrows Is.

Allan Passage

Allan Is.

Dennis Shoal

"6"

"4"

Burrows Bay

Langley Bay

Fish Pt.

Sares Head

Telegraph Bight

Northwest Is.

Northwest Passage

Deception Is.

Pearl Island Bay

Gun Pt.

Cornet Bay

N Beach

Cranberry Lake

Mac's Pt.

Whidbey Island

Tide rips

"2"

Lawson Reef

Rosario Strait

Belle Rock

Bird Rocks

James Island State Park

pg 81

Faunleroy Pt.

Decatur Head

White Cliff

Decatur Island

"2"

"11"

"9"

Black Rock

Pointer Is.

Armitage Is.

Blakely Island

Lopez Island

"3"

Michael Bertrand www.michaelbertrandphotography.com

Anacortes

Anacortes is situated on Fidalgo Island and is one of the most popular departure points for heading into the nearby San Juan Islands. With no shortage of marinas or anchoring locations, Anacortes caters to the boating crowd with numerous haulout yards, service centers and marine chandleries. The peaceful, small town charm of Anacortes quickly wins hearts over with its scenic vistas of nearby islands and mountain ranges, conveniently located shopping, and beautifully landscaped surroundings.

Anacortes has a modest population of roughly 16,000 people, spread across an island with only a handful of traffic lights. Although many people mistake Anacortes and Fidalgo Island as part of the mainland, it is in fact separated by the navigable Swinomish Channel. A number of marinas are scattered around the island with the majority found along the island's northeastern shore.

The town of Anacortes is located on the northern shores of Fidalgo Island and directly across from Guemes Island. Approaches to the town can be made from east or west via Guemes Channel, or from the north off the east side of Guemes Island. Due to traffic from the Washington State Ferries, the Skagit County Ferry and commercial tankers serving the oil refineries at March Point, Guemes Channel and the water east of Guemes Island are well marked with lighted navigation buoys. Be aware that current floods (east current) and ebbs (west current) through Guemes Channel, and can reach up to 5 knots at times. Tidal rips can be found off Southeast Point on Guemes Island during flooding and ebbing currents.

The majority of Anacortes and its marine facilities are centered around Fidalgo Bay which is located between

Anacortes to:		
	Bellingham	16 nm
	Blaine	34 nm
	Blind Bay (Shaw Island)	16 nm
	Deer Harbor (Orcas Island)	20 nm
	Eagle Harbor (Cypress Island)	8 nm
	Echo Bay (Sucia Island)	21 nm
	Fisherman Bay (Lopez Island)	18 nm
	Friday Harbor (San Juan Island)	19 nm
	Mackaye Harbor (Lopez Island)	18 nm
	Roche Harbor (San Juan Island)	28 nm
	Rosario (Orcas Island)	16 nm
	Sidney (Canada)	36 nm
	Spencer Spit (Lopez Island)	12 nm
	Victoria (Canada)	38 nm

Anacortes Marina

Fidalgo Bay
Anchorage

Seafarer's Park
Dinghy Dock

Fuel Dock

Entrance to Cap
Sante Marina

Green Beacon #5

Red Beacon #4

Green Beacon #3

March Point and Cap Sante. While Fidalgo Bay is shallow, it is well marked with navigation aids to lead boats safely into marinas and haul out facilities. The Cap Sante Waterway is a dredged channel (approximate 11 foot depth) marked with day beacons on the south side of Cap Sante. The waterway leads boats into the Port of Anacortes' Cap Sante Marina (see page 52) where transient moorage and a fuel dock are available. The entrance to the waterway begins with lighted red beacon #2 and green beacon #1. The waterway continues into the marina where lighted red beacon #6 and lighted green beacon #5 mark the entrance breakwaters. Be sure to stay within the channel markers upon approach to avoid shallow water and rocks.

A second dredged channel is found south Cap Sante (approximate depth of 13 feet). This channel leads further into Fidalgo Bay where a number of haulout yards and service centers are located as well as a few private marinas (see pages 57-60 for further information on these businesses). The channel is marked by lighted buoys beginning with lighted green and red buoy "A" and green buoy #3.

For boats looking to anchor out for the day or the night, ample shallow water anchoring room is available next to town within Fidalgo Bay. The majority of the northern portion of Fidalgo Bay is fairly uniform at 1 ½ fathoms with a mud bottom. Anchorage can be taken south of Cap Sante where dinghy dock access is available at Seafarer's Memorial Park or

From Cap Sante looking east at the oil refineries on March Point

within Cap Sante Marina on "Q" dock. Grocery stores, marine chandleries, restaurants and shops are located within a few block radius of Cap Sante Marina for easy walking access.

Additional anchorage is also available in Ship Harbor near the Washington State Ferry terminal. Ship Harbor is a large bay with ample anchoring room in 1 to 4 fathoms. The head of the harbor is shoal so be sure to check your depth sounder when exploring the anchorage. With the ferry terminal located on the northwestern edge of the harbor, ferry traffic and noise will be noticed here, although the ferries do shut down for the night making for a peaceful sleep. Keep in mind that Ship Harbor has been known to have poor holding and should not be used during strong winds.

Michael Bertrand www.michaelbertrandphotography.com

Note: This photo was taken prior to new construction on docks F, E and C, as well as the fuel dock in 2012.

Cap Sante Marina

Operated by the Port of Anacortes, Cap Sante Marina is located in the heart of downtown Anacortes, within easy walking distance of marine chandleries, shopping and restaurants. The 950-slip marina offers permanent and transient moorage, accommodating boats up to 120 feet in length. Each slip has access to water and power (20, 30 and 50 amp hookups), along with portable pumpout carts and a floating pumpout dock. Services include a fuel dock (Fido's Fuel page 11), small boat hoist, showers, laundry facilities, free wireless internet, boat trailer parking, and RV parking/camping. The marina also operates a monorail trailer boat launch which can lift boats up to 25,000 pounds and 37 feet in length. Cap Sante is an official Port of Entry with a conveniently located U.S. Customs office near the marina office.

Cap Sante is a favorite place for boaters, locals and tourists alike with its picturesque vistas and paved walking paths. During the summer months you can enjoy free concerts at the marina each Friday beginning at 7pm. And for your boat-bound furry best friend, a large, fenced dog park is located across from the marina for a lively game of fetch.

Cap Sante Boat Haven
Monitors VHF channel 66a
100 Commercial Ave
Anacortes, WA 98221
Phone: (360) 293-0694
Fax: (360) 299-0998
marina@portofanacortes.com
www.portofanacortes.com

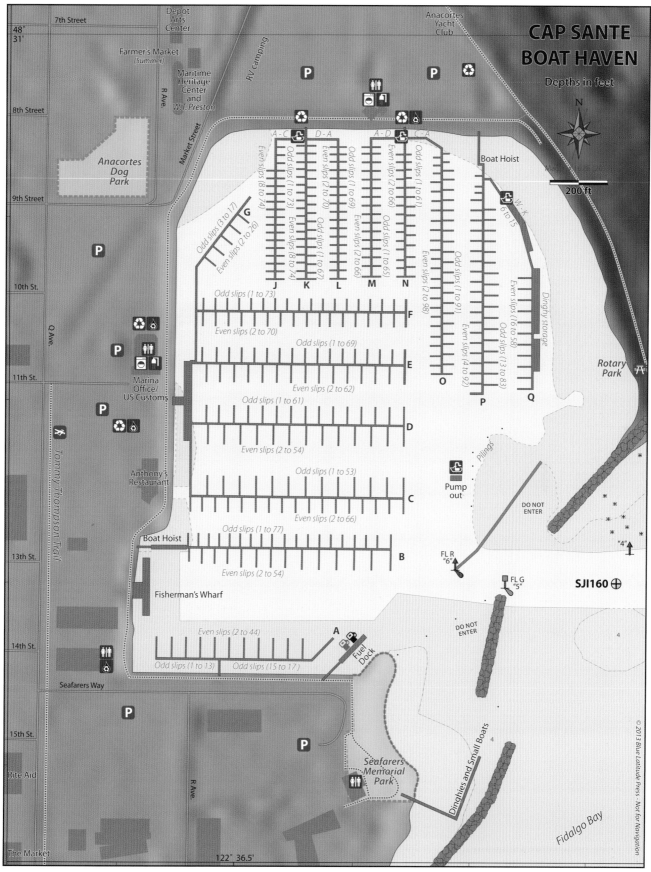

CAP SANTE BOAT HAVEN

Depths in feet

200 ft

7th Street
Depot Arts Center
Anacortes Yacht Club
Farmer's Market (Summer)
Maritime Heritage Center and W.T. Preston
RV camping
8th Street
Anacortes Dog Park
Market Street
R Ave.
9th Street
10th St.
Q Ave.
11th St.
Marina Office/ US Customs
Anthony's Restaurant
Boat Hoist
Tommy Thompson Trail
Fisherman's Wharf
13th St.
14th St.
Seafarers Way
15th St.
Rite Aid
R Ave.
The Market

Boat Hoist
W-K 6 to 15
Dinghy storage
Rotary Park
Pilings
DO NOT ENTER
Pump out
FL R "6"
FL G "5"
SJI160
DO NOT ENTER
"4"
4
Fuel Dock
Seafarers Memorial Park
Dinghies and Small Boats
Fidalgo Bay

Odd slips (3 to 17)
Even slips (2 to 26)
G
Odd slips (8 to 74)
Even slips (1 to 73)
Odd slips (1 to 73)
Even slips (8 to 74)
Odd slips (2 to 70)
Even slips (1 to 67)
Odd slips (1 to 69)
Even slips (2 to 66)
Odd slips (2 to 66)
Even slips (1 to 65)
Odd slips (1 to 61)
Even slips (2 to 98)
Odd slips (1 to 91)
Even slips (4 to 92)
Odd slips (13 to 83)
Even slips (16 to 58)
J K L M N
O P Q
A-C D-A A-D C-A

Odd slips (1 to 73)
F
Even slips (2 to 70)
Odd slips (1 to 69)
E
Even slips (2 to 62)
Odd slips (1 to 61)
D
Even slips (2 to 54)
Odd slips (1 to 53)
C
Even slips (2 to 66)
Odd slips (1 to 77)
B
Even slips (2 to 54)

Even slips (2 to 44)
A
Odd slips (1 to 13)   Odd slips (15 to 17)

SJI160 - 48°30.700'N 122°36.175'W

48° 31'
122° 36.5'

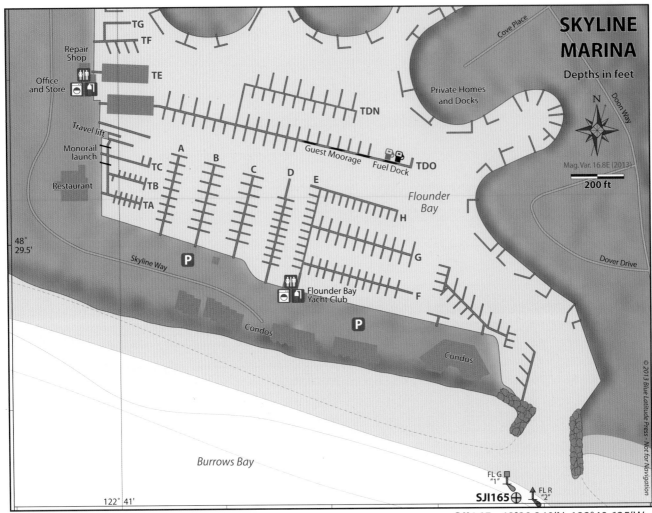

SKYLINE MARINA

Depths in feet

Mag. Var. 16.8E (2013)

200 ft

Cove Place

Doon Way

Private Homes and Docks

TG

TF

Repair Shop

Office and Store

TE

Travel lift

Monorail launch

Restaurant

TDN

Guest Moorage

Fuel Dock

TDO

Flounder Bay

A

B

C

D

E

H

G

F

TC

TB

TA

48° 29.5'

Skyline Way

P

Flounder Bay Yacht Club

Condos

P

Condos

Dover Drive

Burrows Bay

122° 41'

FL G "1"

SJI165

FL R "2"

© 2013 Blue Latitude Press – Not for Navigation

SJI165 - 48°29.340'N 122°40.625'W

Skyline Marina

Skyline Marina is located west of downtown Anacortes, on the north side of Burrows Bay. The marina offers 710 slips, a combination of private and condo style docks, along with transient slips, each with power and water hookups. Services include a fuel dock, showers, laundry facilities, pumpout services and a small grocery/deli nearby (see Old Salt's Deli on page 60). The marina includes a monorail lift for trailer boats, as well as a 50-ton travel lift and haulout yard for repairs and storage.

Skyline Marina
2011 Skyline Way
Anacortes, WA 98221
Phone: (360) 293-5134
Fax: (360) 293-7557
betty@skylinemarinecenter.com
www.skylinemarinecenter.com

History of Anacortes

The Coast Salish people, including the Swinomish, Skagit and Samish tribes, have a long history of living on Fidalgo Island, dating back thousands of years. In 1855, the tribes signed the Treaty of Point Elliott with the United States reserving the southeast peninsula of Fidalgo Island where the Swinomish Reservation stands today.

Early Spanish and English explorers began entering the Strait of Juan de Fuca and Puget Sound in the late 1700's. Finding the area rich and abundant with wildlife and natural resources, a number of the early western inhabitants of the area were trappers, fishermen and farmers.

One of the first areas to be settled by early pioneers on Fidalgo Island was the land around March Point (where today's Shell and Tesoro refineries are located). While much of the island was thickly forested, March Point was desirable for its open prairie land, leaving the area easier to clear for homestead sites and farming.

By the mid 1800's, settlers began trickling in to the region and developing small communities. Lumber mills, farms and fishing fleets supported the early economy of Fidalgo Island. In 1877, island visionaries Amos Bowman and his wife Anne Curtis established a wharf and store near Ship Harbor and opened the island's first post office and newspaper. They named the community at the northern end of the island Anacortes, a derivation of Anne's maiden name.

Furthering Anacortes' growth, the western terminus of the Northern Pacific railway was up for grabs in the late 1800's. Due to its proximity to the entrance to the Strait of Juan de Fuca, the large yet protected Ship Harbor, and the nearby access through the Cascade Mountain range to the east, made Anacortes a front runner. Early speculation sparked development throughout the community. Streets and buildings began springing up across town, with land prices skyrocketing in anticipation of the coming railroad. By 1891, the year the town was incorporated, it was clear that Anacortes would not be the western terminus for the railroad, thus ending the town's boom years. Development was further slowed across the region and the nation by the Depression of 1893.

Still rich with natural resources, Anacortes relied on the industries of fishing and timber to build its economy once again in the early 1900's. With up to eleven fish processing plants operating, Anacortes was one of the nation's leading

The W. T. Preston *snag boat*

Mt Baker from Seafarers Park

Statue at Seafarers Park

processors of salmon and cod. Although most of the fish processors had closed by the mid 1900's, Trident Seafoods, Sugiyo, and Seabear continue to operate today.

In 1922, one of the first passenger and car ferries left the dock at Q Avenue, starting the popular run between Sidney, British Columbia and Anacortes. The Puget Sound Navigation Company (Black Ball Line) was the original transport company offering ferry service throughout Puget Sound. The company opened in 1913 and continued operations until 1951, when Washington State took over the ferry line. In 1960, the Anacortes ferry terminal was moved to its present day location at Ship Harbor. Today Washington State Ferries operates five ferries traveling between Anacortes, the San Juan Islands, and Sidney, BC including the *Evergreen State* (built in 1954), *Hyak* (1967), *Elwha* (1967), *Yakima* (1967), and the *Chelan* (1981).

In 1953, Shell Oil announced plans to establish an oil refinery on March Point, with Texaco following shortly thereafter in 1958 with a second refinery. Today, Shell operates the Texaco refinery after a merger in 1998 with the company, and Tesoro operates the second refinery after purchasing it from Shell.

In 1977, Dakota Creek Industries relocated to Anacortes from Blaine, where they specialize in shipbuilding and repair. Able to handle vessels up to 400 feet in length, DCI has produced tug boats, offshore support vessels, research vessels, fireboats, ferries and fishing vessels.

Throughout the years, Anacortes has seen change, all the while retaining its coastal town charm with a wonderful mixture of a working waterfront and tourist attractions.

Sights to See

With its small town charm, Anacortes boasts a wealth of activities and festivals throughout the year to keep visitors busy for days. Much of the activities are centered around the downtown area allowing visitors on foot easy access to all the town has to offer. Anacortes also has a Visitor Information Center, located on the corner of 9th Street and Commercial Avenue, staffed with wonderful volunteers who can help answer questions on local sights to see.

One of the first activities that most visitors take advantage of is the walking trails throughout town. The Tommy Thompson Trail is a paved walking and biking trail over three miles in length following the Fidalgo Bay shoreline. Beginning at 11th and Q Street, the trail heads southwest across town and ends at March Point. Another scenic trail leads around the Cap Sante marina to Rotary Park. Be sure to walk up Cap Sante (access from 4th St.), the headland to the east of the marina where sweeping views of the city, marina, Mount Baker, Skagit Valley and islands can be found.

Scattered throughout town are a number of additional parks and walking trails, perfect for stretching your legs after a few days on the boat. Washington Park, on the northwestern side of Fidalgo Island, is a 220 acre park (campsites

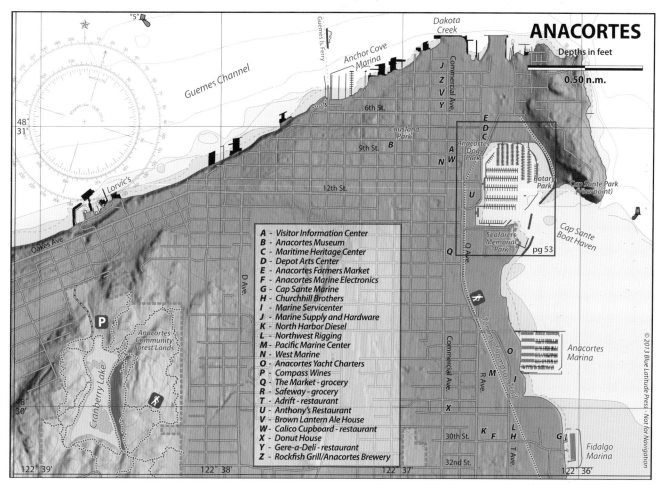

ANACORTES

Depths in feet

0.50 n.m.

A - Visitor Information Center
B - Anacortes Museum
C - Maritime Heritage Center
D - Depot Arts Center
E - Anacortes Farmers Market
F - Anacortes Marine Electronics
G - Cap Sante Marine
H - Churchhill Brothers
I - Marine Servicenter
J - Marine Supply and Hardware
K - North Harbor Diesel
L - Northwest Rigging
M - Pacific Marine Center
N - West Marine
O - Anacortes Yacht Charters
P - Compass Wines
Q - The Market - grocery
R - Safeway - grocery
T - Adrift - restaurant
U - Anthony's Restaurant
V - Brown Lantern Ale House
W - Calico Cupboard - restaurant
X - Donut House
Y - Gere-a-Deli - restaurant
Z - Rockfish Grill/Anacortes Brewery

© 2013 Blue Latitude Press - Not for Navigation

and a boat launch are available) with a 2.3 mile loop road available for cars, bikes and foot traffic. The park provides a perfect location for watching the sunset across the San Juan Islands. Other nearby parks with extensive trail systems include Cranberry Lake, Heart Lake, Whistle Lake, Mount Erie, Deception Pass and Rosario Beach. Park maps for the lakes are available at the Visitors Information Center or online at: **www.pnt.org/trail.html**.

For a look back in time and to get a real sense of the history of Anacortes, be sure to stop by the Anacortes Museum located at 1305 8th Street. The museum features exhibits on the history of the area including the fishing and logging industries, canneries and fish processing plants, Native American artifacts, and historical photographs. The museum also operates the Maritime Heritage Center located next to Cap Sante Marina. The center features one of the last remaining sternwheeled snag boats, the *W. T. Preston* which plied the waters of Puget Sound since 1929. For further information check their website at: **museum.cityofanacortes.org**.

Don't forget to take a stroll through historic Old Town Anacortes. There are a variety of restaurants, boutiques, antique stores, book stores, coffee shops, bakeries and art galleries. If you happen to be in town in the summer months on a Wednesday or Saturday, be sure to check out the Anacortes Farmers Market for fresh, local produce, as well as cheeses, meats, fresh baked goods, craft items and much more. The market is located in the plaza at 7th and R Streets, next to the Depot Arts Center and the Maritime Heritage Center. For more information including market hours see their website at: **www.anacortesfarmersmarket.org**.

Anacortes is also home to a number of festivals throughout the year. A few of these large festivals take over the downtown area, closing portions of Commercial Avenue for vendors and pedestrian traffic. Events include Trawler Fest, the Waterfront Festival, Shipwreck Festival, Anacortes Arts Festival, Oyster Run, and Oktoberfest. For further information including annual dates, see the Anacortes Chamber of Commerce site at: **www.anacortes.org**.

Marine Chandleries and Services
Ace Hardware
Ace Hardware is conveniently located near Cap Sante Marina with a wide range of hardware, plumbing, electrical, and painting supplies including housewares, outdoor and sporting gear. Located at 1720 Q Avenue.
Phone: (360) 293-3535 Web: www.acehardwareanacortes.com

Cap Sante Marina

facility. The yard operates a 55 ton travel lift, with services including top and bottomside painting, maintenance, repair, fabrication work and a boat watch program. The yard also operates a fuel and pumpout dock. Located at 2417 "T" Avenue.
Phone: (360) 293-8200   Web: www.marinesc.com

Marine Supply & Hardware Co.
Originally opened in 1910, Marine Supply & Hardware Co. has been serving the needs of Anacortes' marine market for decades. Selling a little bit of everything, from antiques to crab pots, Marine Supply is a shop not to miss. Located at 202 Commercial Ave.
Phone: (360) 293-3014
Web: www.marinesupplyandhardware.com

North Harbor Diesel
North Harbor Diesel is a full service haulout and dry storage yard. Services include yacht sales, mechanical repairs and maintenance, painting, varnishing, fiberglass and wood work, and more. Using a Sea-Lift hydraulic trailer with cushioned air bunks, North Harbor is able to haul most hull types with boats up to 65 feet in length and up to 45 tons. Located at 720 30th Street.
Phone: (360) 293-5551   Web: www.northharbordiesel.com

North Harbor Propeller
North Harbor Propeller specializes in new installs, repairs and maintenance of propellers, shafts, cutlass bearings, zincs (a large assortment of zincs in stock) and more. With computerized equipment, they are also able troubleshoot problems and balance propellers. Located at 401 34th Street.
Phone: (360) 299-8266
Web: www.northharborpropeller.com

North Island Boat Company
North Island Boat Company is a full service boat maintenance, repair and boat yard facility offering a wide range of services. North Island is located at Skyline Marina.
Phone: (360) 293-2565   Web: www.northislandboat.com

Northwest Rigging
Northwest Rigging is a family owned business specializing in marine rigging for sail and power boats, including standing rigging, furling systems, dinghy davits, line splicing, steering cables and lifelines. Located at 2901 T Avenue.
Phone: (360) 293-1154   Web: www.northwestrigginginc.com

Pacific Marine Center
Pacific Marine Center is situated on nearly 36 acres with a 34,000 square foot refit building and a 350 foot service dock. Pacific Marine operates a 30 ton and a 45 ton submersible trailer for boats up to 70 feet in length. Located next to Anacortes Marina at 2302 T Avenue.
Phone: (425) 418-7658   Web: www.pacmarinecenter.com

Anacortes Marine Electronics
Anacortes Marine Electronics specializes in installation and maintenance of navigation, communication, and safety systems, as well as systems integration. Located at 620 30th Street.
Phone: 360-293-6100   Web: www.anacortesmarine.com

Cap Sante Marine
Cap Sante Marine operates two offices in Anacortes, one at 2915 W Avenue, and their newest at Skyline Marina. The W Ave office operates two travel lifts can haul boats up to 50 tons, with services including painting, repairs, installation, maintenance and fabrication. The new office in Skyline offers dinghy and outboard sales as well as parts and servicing.
Phone: (360) 293-3145   Web: www.capsante.com

Churchhill Brothers
Churchhill Brothers specializes in marine canvas repair and custom projects including upholstery, covers, biminis and dodgers. Located at 2901 T Avenue. Phone: (360) 293-2700

Marine Servicenter
Marine Servicenter is conveniently located at Anacortes Marina, offering haulout services, yacht sales and dry storage

Sebo's Hardware & Equipment Rental
Sebo's is located downtown, within easy walking distance of Cap Sante Marina. Featuring a full selection of tools and hardwares including rentals. Located at 1102 Commercial.
Phone: (360) 293-4575   Web: www.sebos.com

West Marine
One of the nation's largest boating supply retailers, including marine parts, supplies, accessories, apparel, and electronics. Located at 918 Commercial Avenue in downtown Anacortes.
Phone: (360) 293-4262   Web: www.westmarine.com

Sail and Power Boat Charter Companies
Anacortes Yacht Charters
Anacortes Yacht Charters is the largest charter company in Anacortes, offering a wide selection of charter boats from power to sail, bare boat to crewed. AYC also offers boating and sailing courses, as well as a brokerage company.
Phone: 800-233-3004   Web: www.ayc.com

Ship Harbor Yacht Charter
Ship Harbor Yachts, located at Skyline Marina, offers both sail and power boat charters from bare boat to fully crewed. Sailing and boating courses are also offered.
Phone: 877-772-6582   Web: www.shipharboryachts.com

Provisioning and Other Services
Airport
The airport at Anacortes is operated by the Port of Anacortes where private, charter, scenic or scheduled flights, fuel, hangars, tie downs and aircraft service is available. San Juan Airlines operates several flights a day to various destinations in the San Juan Islands, Bellingham and other destinations. Transportation to and from the airport is available through taxis and rental car agencies (Alamo, Enterprise and Anacortes U-Save Rental). Located off Anacopper Road towards the ferry terminal.
Phone: (360) 299-1829   Web: www.portofanacortes.com

Compass Wines
Compass Wines carries an extensive collection of Washington wines, as well as California, Bordeaux, Burgundy, Italian and many more. This well stocked store also offers a tasting bar, climate controlled wine storage, gourmet foods, wine accessories, wine clubs and free delivery to any of the local marinas around Anacortes. Located on the corner of Commercial Avenue and 14th Street near Cap Sante Marina.
Phone: (360) 293-6500   Web: www.compasswines.com

The Market at Anacortes
The Market is a well stocked grocery store with everything including fresh produce, meats and seafood, dairy items, baked goods and all the staples. In store cafes include Da-

Washington Park boat launch

Anthony's restaurant at Cap Sante Marina

Vinci Classic Subs and Starbucks. A Bank of America branch is also found within the store. Located between Commercial and Q Avenue on 15th Street near Cap Sante Marina.
Phone: (360) 588-8181   Web: themarketswa.com

Old Salt's Deli & Market
Old Salt's Deli & Market is a fixture near the Skyline Marina area. Featuring a small grocery and deli items. Located at 1900 Skyline Way.
Phone: (360) 293-0618

Safeway
Safeway is a popular grocery store chain and is conveniently located next to Cap Sante Marina. The store carries fresh produce, dairy items, meats, seafood, fresh baked goods and all the staples. In store cafes include Starbucks Coffee and Jamba Juice. A Peoples Bank branch is also found in the store. Located across from Cap Sante Marina on the corner of Q Avenue and 11th Street.
Phone: (360) 293-5393   Web: www.safeway.com

Restaurants

Adrift
Fresh, local food is combined with an artistic love of cuisine to create the amazing menu found at Adrift. From delicious burgers to savory seafood dishes, Adrift will quickly win your heart and your stomach. Located downtown at 510 Commercial Avenue.
Phone: (360) 588-0653   Web: adriftrestaurant.com

Anthony's Restaurant
Opened the summer of 2011, Cap Sante Marina is the sight of one of the newest Anthony's restaurants. With beautiful architecture, Anthony's has a prime location overlooking the marina, serving delicious and fresh Northwest delicacies for lunch, and dinner, along with daily happy hour specials.
Phone: (360) 588-0333   Web: www.anthonys.com

Brown Lantern Ale House
The Brown Lantern is a local staple in the Anacortes scene, serving delicious pub style favorites including sandwiches, burgers, salads and seafood. Live music is offered on the weekends and game nights are featured throughout the week. Located in downtown Anacortes at 412 Commercial Avenue.
Phone: (360) 293-2544   Web: www.brownlantern.com

Calico Cupboard
The Calico Cupboard features delicious homemade breakfasts and lunches in an old fashioned country farmhouse setting. The cafe also has an assortment of fresh bakery items including pies, cookies, muffins, scones, cinnamon rolls, breads and more. Located across from Cap Sante Marina on the corner of Commercial and 9th.
Phone: (360) 293-7315   Web: www.calicocupboardcafe.com

Donut House
No trip to Anacortes is complete without a morning stop at the Donut House for a fresh, warm donut and a cup of Fidalgo Bay coffee. Whatever your favorite, the Donut House has it from raised donuts to cake to buttermilk, with vanilla creme, chocolate, mocha, Bavarian cream and jelly fillings. Located on the corner of 28th Street and Commercial Ave.
Phone: (360) 293-4053

Gere-a-Deli
An Anacortes lunchtime institution, Gere-a-Deli serves homemade traditional family recipes including sandwiches, soups, salads, desserts, breads and pastries all which are prepared from scratch daily. One look at the pastry counter and you'll be back to sample each and every delicacy. Located on the corner of 5th Street and Commercial Avenue.
Phone: (360) 293-7383   Web: www.gere-a-deli.com

Rockfish Grill
The Rockfish Grill serves fresh, Northwest cuisine including pizza from their wood-fired oven. The restaurant also features Anacortes Beer from their inhouse brewery, and live music featured throughout the week. Located downtown at 314 Commercial Avenue.
Phone: (360) 588-1720   Web: www.anacortesrockfish.com

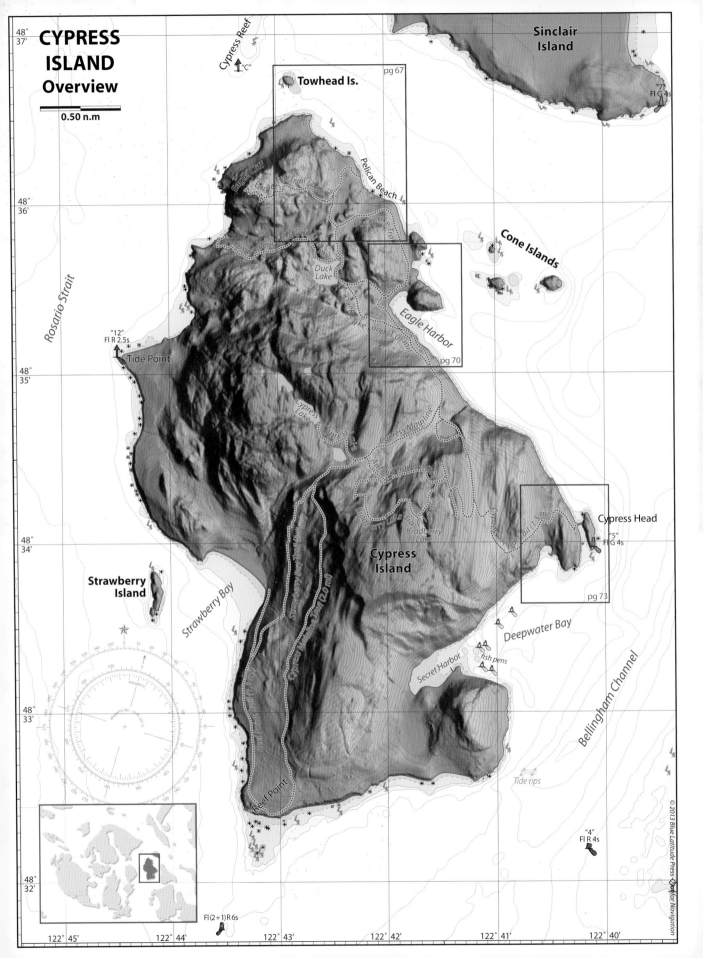

CYPRESS ISLAND
Overview

0.50 n.m

Sinclair Island

Cypress Reef
"C"

Towhead Is. — pg 67

Pelican Beach

Eagle Cliff
Eagle Cliff Trail (1.0 mi)
Duck Lake Trail
Smugglers Cove Trail (0.7 mi)

Duck Lake

Duck Lake Loop (1.0 mi)

Cone Islands

Eagle Harbor

pg 70

Rosario Strait

"12"
Fl R 2.5s
Tide Point

Cypress Lake

Cypress Lake

Cypress Mainline

Anchor Trail (0.1 mi)

Cypress Head Trail (1.5 mi)

Cypress Head
"5"
Fl G 4s

Bradberry Lake Trail (0.4 mi)

Bradberry Lake

Cypress Island

pg 73

Strawberry Island

Strawberry Bay

Smugglers Cove Trail (1.5 mi)

Cypress Mainline Trail (2.0 mi)

Reef Point Trail (1.1 mi)

Reef Point

Deepwater Bay

Secret Harbor   fish pens

Bellingham Channel

Tide rips

MAGNETIC
MAGNETIC Var:

"4"
Fl R 4s

48° 37'
48° 36'
48° 35'
48° 34'
48° 33'
48° 32'

Fl(2+1)R 6s

122° 45'   122° 44'   122° 43'   122° 42'   122° 41'   122° 40'

Anchored at Eagle Harbor with Mt Baker in the background

Cypress Island

Majestic Cypress Island is one of the largest islands within the San Juan archipelago that has remained mostly undeveloped. Due to its proximity to both Bellingham and Anacortes, Cypress Island is a favorite weekend getaway for those looking for a quick escape to these tranquil islands. With miles of trails crisscrossing the mostly undisturbed island, hiking and wildlife viewing are some of the most popular pastimes.

Cypress Island is comprised by a total of 5,500 acres of lush forest lands, wetlands, and grasslands. 4,800 of those acres are protected and managed by the Department of Natural Resources (DNR), with the majority of the island open to the public. Two seasonal campgrounds with mooring buoys are found on the island: Pelican Beach on the island's northern end, and Cypress Head, on the island's eastern shore. Both campgrounds, including the mooring buoys at Eagle Harbor, are managed and maintained by the DNR. All DNR sites on Cypress Island are open year round with the exception of the campgrounds, which are open only during the spring and summer months. For further information regarding DNR services, facilities or trail maps, visit their website at: **www.dnr.wa.gov**.

History of Cypress Island

Cypress Island is a rugged and mountainous island, home to diverse species of plant and animal wildlife. Like many of the surrounding islands, Cypress was once used for seasonal camps by the Coast Salish people who plied the waters of Puget Sound in search of natural resources to sustain their families. With lakes, marsh lands and fresh water streams, Cypress Island had a wealth of resources as well as a strategic location within the migration path of annual salmon runs.

In 1791, the first European explorers arrived in Puget Sound, lead by Spanish captain, Juan Francisco de Eliza, commander of the ship, *Santa Saturnina*. Jose Maria Narvaez originally named the island "Isla de San Vincente," although it is believed he never actually landed on shore. It was later changed to Cypress by English explorers who mistakenly labeled the island after what they thought were Cypress trees on shore. The following year Captain George

Pelican Beach

Duck Lake

Vancouver lead an expedition into Puget Sound, sending Lt. William Broughton into the San Juan Islands sailing on board the ship, *Chatham*. Broughton anchored for the night within Strawberry Bay on Cypress Island and named the bay after the wild berries found on shore.

Cypress Island remained largely forgotten by its European explorers for the next 60 to 70 years. It was not until the mid to late 1800's that Cypress Island began to see it's first European settlements at Strawberry Bay, Eagle Harbor and Secret Harbor. Early occupations on the island included farming, logging, fishing and boat building.

As the number of homesteaders increased on the island, the need for a public school and post office arose. In 1891, the Cypress School District was formed and in 1892, the first school, located near Reef Point, opened its doors to students. By 1907, due to a lack of students, the Cypress School District was absorbed by the nearby Sinclair Island School District. The post office on the island had a somewhat more spotty history with a series of openings and closings. The very first post office was operated out of Eagle Harbor by homesteaders living nearby.

Farming on the rugged island was not an easy venture, with most homesteaders only lasting a year or two before moving on. Fish traps were popular especially in Strawberry Bay before the government banned their use in 1935.

With its thick forest, Cypress was also a prime location for logging which resulted in the cutting of a number of dirt roads that are still in use today. The island also has a history of mining, with olivine being extracted (near Olivine Hill) as well as chromite (near Cypress Dome).

By the 1960's, Cypress Island still remained relatively undeveloped as compared to other surrounding islands. Scientists and locals began looking to Cypress as a possible

Cypress Island Trail Maintenance

With limited public funding, the expansive trail system on Cypress Island can quickly become engulfed by the local flora of the island. The Department of Natural Resources relies on volunteer efforts to help maintain the accessibility of Cypress Island's trails. If you would like to donate your time and help with volunteer efforts on the island, please contact:

Department of Natural Resources
Northwest Region, Cypress Island Steward
919 N Township Street
Sedro Woolley, WA 98284-9384
Phone: (360) 856-3500
northwest.region@dnr.wa.gov
www.dnr.wa.gov

Bald Eagles

The bald eagle is the only eagle unique to North America, with the majority of the population living near the coastal waters from the Pacific Northwest to Alaska. Eagles of the Pacific Northwest feed mainly on salmon and other fish, using their massive talons to capture fish as they swoop over the water. The birds are also well known as opportunistic feeders, scavenging the carcasses of dead fish and mammals, or stealing food from other predators. Mature female bald eagles tend to be larger than males, weighing 10 to 14 pounds, with an average wingspan of 6 to 7 feet. Males average 8 to 10 pounds and have a 6-foot wingspan. Eagles reach adulthood between four to five years of age, at which time juveniles loose their mottled brown and white plumage.

It is believed that eagles mate for life, building a large nest they return to year after year to raise their young. Mating season takes place between the late winter and spring months. During courtship, eagles can be seen in acrobatic aerial displays, locking talons and plummeting towards the ground before releasing to fly away. After laying one to three eggs, both parents take turns in the nest while the eggs incubate for over 35 days. Once the eggs are hatched, both parents continue to take care of and feed the chicks until they are ready to leave the nest.

nature preserve to protect the wild and natural beauty of the island. Washington's Department of Natural Resources (DNR) already had land holdings on the island and pushed for the purchase of additional land to add to the preserve.

During this time, a developer began purchasing large plots of land on the island in hopes of creating a prosperous new community. An airfield was built with plans to build a marina, golf course, condominiums, conference center and additional buildings. Although the developer's plans were approved, community opposition through the "Save Cypress Island Committee," led to the land eventually being sold to the state's DNR.

In 1987, 3,933 acres on Cypress Island were designated a Natural Resources Conservation Area (NRCA), one of the first four areas to be protected under the NRCA title in the entire state. In addition, 1,073 acres have been designated Natural Area Preserve lands for specific areas on the island with more fragile plant and animal communities. Natural Area Preserve lands are the highest level of preservation within the state, and are set aside for the conservation purposes of protecting ecological systems and providing low-impact use options to the public. Today, nearly the entire island of Cypress has been protected and preserved for the enjoyment of all as well as providing a unique and educational location for Pacific Northwest research and studies.

Sights to See

No voyage to Cypress Island would be complete without taking advantage of at least one of the many trails found meandering across the island. Cypress has nearly twenty miles of scenic trails traversing the island, keeping even the avid hiker busy for days. From hilltop bluffs to beachside walks, Cypress Island has a unique trail to suit everyone's desire for exploration. Trailheads, along with maps can be found at Eagle Harbor, Pelican Beach and Cypress Head.

One of the more popular trails crosses the island from Eagle Harbor or Pelican Beach, to the west side of Cypress Island at Smuggler's Cove. This trail takes hikers past an old log cabin, a relic from Cypress Island's homesteading days, and past the thickly vegetative, Duck Lake. Surrounding the lily pad-filled lake are numerous snags, or dead trees, which are favorite resting locations for the island's population of bald eagles. Once at Smuggler's Cove, a small picturesque stream, draining from Duck Lake, empties onto the pebble beach and into Rosario Strait.

Other popular hikes include a trek to the top of the 752 foot high Eagle Cliff. This trail affords amazing views of the surrounding islands and Rosario Strait, and is also a good vantage point for watching bald eagles soaring over the island. Because this is a favorite nesting site, the trail is closed to the public from February 1st to July 15th, to protect the nesting raptors and their young. Another good hike explores the east side of Cypress, and takes visitors up to the island's grass airstrip, nearly 1,000 feet high. From this open vantage point, sweeping views of the San Juans Islands, along with countless soaring bald eagles, can be found. Be sure to pack your camera, lunch and some water for this wonderful adventure!

Pelican Beach

Pelican Beach boasts one of the finest beaches along Cypress Island's shores, and has become a favorite overnight camp for kayakers paddling the protected waters of the San Juans. The anchorage affords scenic vistas of the surrounding islands, including a view of nearby Mt. Baker. Whether from the beach or your boat, Pelican Beach is also a prime location to sit back and watch recreational boats traveling through the islands, as well as watching commercial vessels transiting Rosario Strait. The park is run by the Department of Natural Resources (DNR), along with the help of various local volunteer clubs and organizations. Campsites, composting toilets, fire pits, and endless miles of trails traversing the island make this a popular spot for boaters and campers alike.

Pelican Beach is located on the far northeastern side of Cypress Island, gaining protection to the northeast from nearby Sinclair Island. For boats approaching Pelican Beach from the west, passage can be taken between the northern extreme of Cypress Island and Towhead Island, allowing boaters to avoid nearby Cypress Reef. Cypress Reef is located 0.25 miles west-northwest of Towhead Island, and whose southern most point is marked with a triangular day

beacon. Portions of the reef are covered by kelp, helping to reveal its location. This reef should be avoided and given a wide berth when passing.

For boats approaching from the north, be sure to navigate with caution and to locate the dangers of Boulder Reef off the northwestern side of Sinclair Island (the northern most point is marked by a lighted red buoy), Buckeye Shoal within Rosario Strait (marked by a lighted red buoy), and the previously mentioned Cypress Reef.

Pelican Beach to:		
Anacortes		9 nm
Bellingham		13 nm
Blaine		26 nm
Blind Bay (Shaw Island)		10 nm
Echo Bay (Sucia Island)		13 nm
Fisherman Bay (Lopez Island)		12 nm
Friday Harbor (San Juan Island)		14 nm
Roche Harbor (San Juan Island)		21 nm
Rosario (Orcas Island)		9 nm
Sidney (Canada)		29 nm
Spencer Spit (Lopez Island)		8 nm

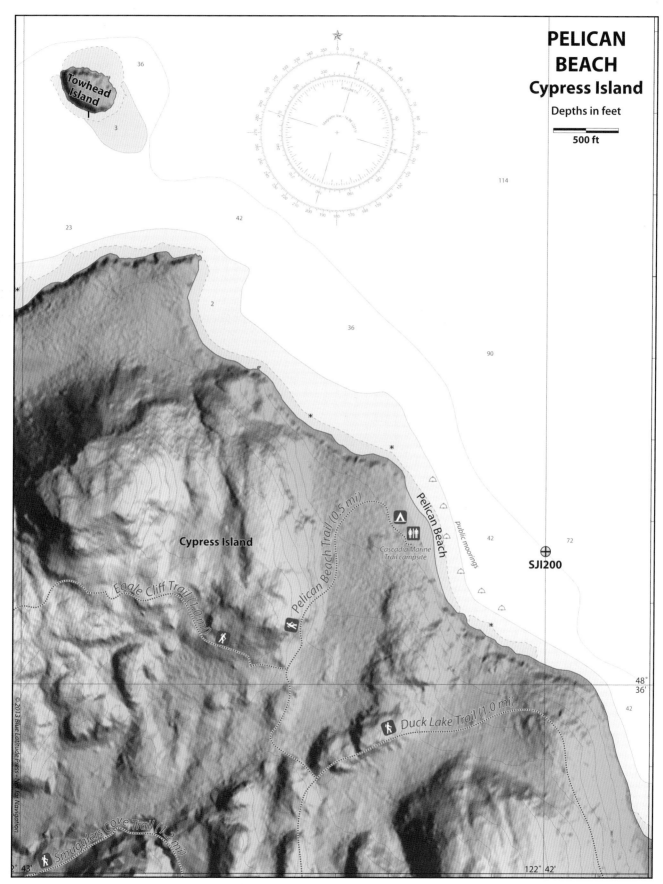

PELICAN BEACH
Cypress Island
Depths in feet

500 ft

Towhead Island

36

3

114

23

42

2

36

90

Cypress Island

Pelican Beach Trail (0.5 mi)

Pelican Beach

public moorings

42

72

Cascadia Marine Trail campsite

SJI200

Eagle Cliff Trail (1.0 mi)

48°
36'

42

Duck Lake Trail (1.0 mi)

© 2013 Blue Latitude Press - Not for Navigation

Smugglers Cove Trail (1.2 mi)

2° 43'

122° 42'

SJI200 - 48°36.170'N 122°42.000'W

Due to the steep gradient found off Pelican Beach, as well as current running between Cypress and Sinclair Islands, anchoring off Pelican Beach can be difficult. Luckily, DNR has made six park mooring buoys available for use and provides a good alternative to anchoring. Depending on the tidal conditions for the day, current through the anchorage can be swift. It is therefore a good idea to have a secondary mooring line as a backup should there be any chafe problems with your primary line. Pelican Beach provides protection from southwest and westerly winds, but is relatively exposed to winds from the north, east and southeast. The anchorage is best suited during periods of light or calm weather.

The one minor draw back to Pelican Beach is the occasional boat wake that can pass through the anchorage. Many boats travel through the pass between Cypress Island and Towhead Island, as well as commercial boat traffic through Rosario Strait. Depending on the size of the boat wake, waves can reach the anchorage and cause a slight roll, but it is short lived.

Dinghies and kayaks can be landed anywhere along the beach for trips to shore. The long sand and pebble beach is dotted with driftwood and the campsites are near the tree line. For those looking for the perfect bocce beach or rock skipping competition, look no further than Pelican Beach. The beach is littered with small, flat stones, perfect for a lively sunset skipping competition. For hikers, island information, including a map, as well as the trailhead are located at the top of the beach near the picnic shelter.

For boats approaching from the south, passage can be taken between the eastern shore of Cypress Island and the west side of the Cone Islands. Keep in mind that the northern most Cone Island has a shallow area extending off its northwestern shore which is generally marked by kelp.

Eagle Harbor

True to its name, Eagle Harbor is alive with bald eagles soaring overhead on the island's breezes during the spring and summer months. Their distinctive sharp cries alert you to their presence, and the striking white head is unmistakable against the lush forest backdrop. Eagle Harbor is a favorite stop on Cypress Island for its beautiful scenery, protected anchorage and access to the many miles of trails crisscrossing the island. It's close proximity to both Bellingham and Anacortes make it a great destination for weekend getaways to the islands.

Eagle Harbor is located on the northeastern shore of Cypress Island, just west of the Cone Island group. Approaches to Eagle Harbor from the south can be made via Bellingham Channel, or from the north via the passage between Sinclair Island and Cypress Island. When approaching from the northeast, be aware of tidal rips and current found off the eastern shore of Sinclair Island which can slow your travels and alter your course.

For boats arriving from the northern portion of Rosario Strait or for boats that are crossing the Strait from Peavine or Obstruction Passes, check your charts and be aware of a few hazards that are found in the area. These include Boulder Reef off the northwestern shore of Sinclair Island (marked

Eagle Harbor to:		
Anacortes	8 nm
Bellingham	13 nm
Blaine	27 nm
Blind Bay *(Shaw Island)*	11 nm
Echo Bay *(Sucia Island)*	14 nm
Fisherman Bay *(Lopez Island)*	14 nm
Friday Harbor *(San Juan Island)*	15 nm
Jones Island	16 nm
Roche Harbor *(San Juan Island)*	22 nm
Rosario *(Orcas Island)*	10 nm
Spencer Spit *(Lopez Island)*	10 nm
Victoria *(Canada)*	38 nm

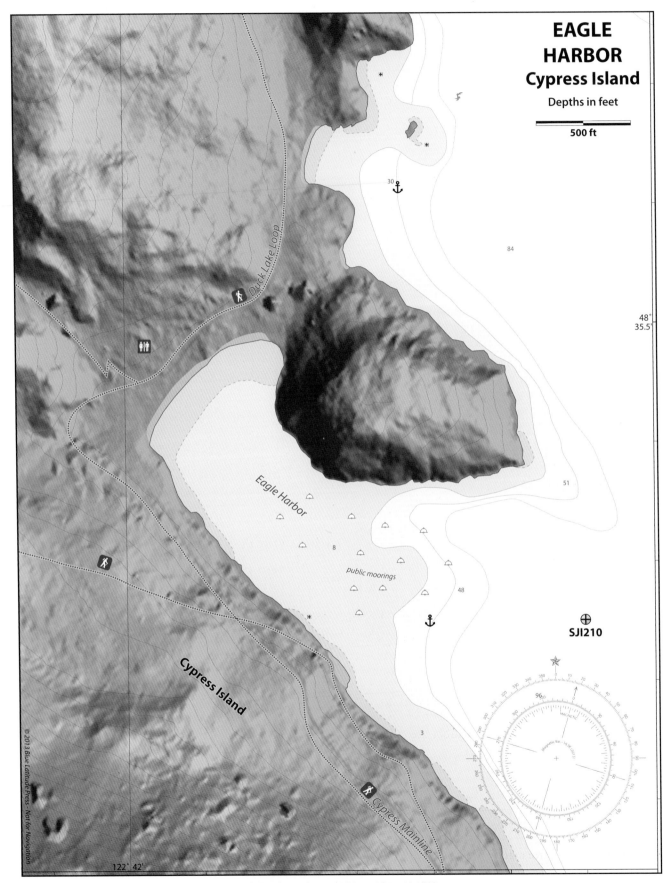

EAGLE HARBOR
Cypress Island
Depths in feet

500 ft

48°
35.5'

Duck Lake Loop

30

84

51

Eagle Harbor

8

public moorings

48

SJI210

96

3

Cypress Island

Cypress Mainline

122° 42'

SJI210 - 48°35.240'N 122°41.400'W

by a lighted red buoy), Buckeye Shoal near the eastern side of the traffic lane in Rosario Strait (marked by a lighted red buoy), Cypress Reef lying just north of Cypress Island (marked by a red and green beacon) and Lydia Shoal found east of Obstruction Pass (marked by a lighted green buoy).

For boats transiting Rosario Strait, keep in mind that this is a commercial shipping channel and to be on the lookout for large, fast moving ships as well as tugs towing barges. Rosario Strait is also affected by current so watch your compass and compensate for set and drift if crossing the strait. Once across the strait, clear passage can be taken between the northern extreme of Cypress Island and Towhead Island, allowing boaters to avoid nearby Cypress Reef and its kelp beds.

Lying just to the east of Eagle Harbor are the picturesque gumdrop islands known as the Cone Islands. These islands are undeveloped state park islands and are open to the public. Rocks and kelp surround some of these islands, including a detached shallow area off the northern most island, so be sure to navigate with caution here.

Once within Eagle Harbor, a number of public mooring buoys are available for free nightly use. In an attempt to protect the eelgrass and fragile marine environment from boat

anchors and dragging chain, the Department of Natural Resources (DNR) installed 13 mooring buoys within Eagle Harbor. Over the years, some of these moorings have lost their floats and due to lack of funding, they have not been replaced. Instead, a number of these missing floats have been replaced by crab pot floats to mark their location and hold up the mooring line/chain.

For trips to shore, a sand and pebble beach is located at the head of the harbor. A second landing option is also available at the south end of the harbor along a small cleared patch of shoreline. This option is sometimes preferred at low tide as the head of the harbor can become quite shallow.

On shore a number of trails lead off and around the island. Near the head of the harbor, along the main trail, is a map of the island which includes a trail guide as well as information about the island. Trails to the north lead to Pelican Beach, Eagle Cliff (closed February 1 to July 15 to protect nesting bald eagles), Duck Lake and Smuggler's Cove. Trails to the south lead to Cypress Lake, Reed Lake, the old airfield, Cypress Head, Bradberry Lake, Strawberry Bay and Reef Point.

Cypress Head

The anchorage at Cypress Head is a pleasant little cove located on the eastern shore of Cypress Island. A thin isthmus of land (tombolo) connects the headland to the main island of Cypress. A couple of public mooring buoys and campsites at Cypress Head make this a choice spot for boaters and paddlers alike. With views of nearby Guemes Island and Anacortes, Cypress Head is a wonderful spot to enjoy a beachside campfire while watching the twinkling lights of the distant towns. Cypress Head is also a great location to jump on one of the many miles of trails traversing this diverse island.

Cypress Head is located on the far eastern side of Cypress Island, lying only 0.75 miles west of Guemes Island. The long and narrow headland is attached to Cypress Island by a small stretch of sand (known as a tombolo) which forms a north cove and a south cove. For protection from the area's predominate southerly winds, the northern cove is the primary location for visiting boats and the location of the moorings.

Approaches to Cypress Head can be made via Bellingham Channel which lies between Guemes and Cypress

Islands. Depending on the tides, Bellingham Channel can have a strong current flowing north and south between the islands, especially near Cypress Head where the channel becomes restricted.

A few Department of Natural Resources' (DNR) mooring buoys are located in the north cove at Cypress Head for free use. Due to the deep and steep-to sides of the small cove, anchoring can be difficult here, making the moorings a nice

Cypress Head to:	
Anacortes	6 nm
Bellingham	16 nm
Blaine	34 nm
Blind Bay (Shaw Island)	16 nm
Echo Bay (Sucia Island)	21 nm
Fisherman Bay (Lopez Island)	18 nm
Friday Harbor (San Juan Island)	19 nm
Roche Harbor (San Juan Island)	28 nm
Rosario (Orcas Island)	16 nm
Sidney (Canada)	31 nm
Spencer Spit (Lopez Island)	12 nm

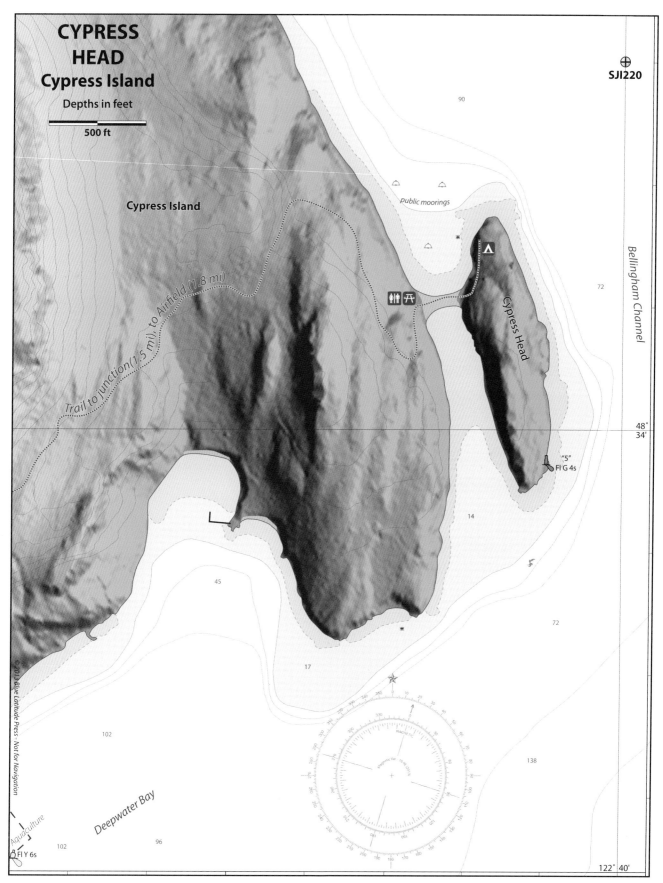

CYPRESS HEAD
Cypress Island
Depths in feet

500 ft

Cypress Island

90

Public moorings

Bellingham Channel

72

Cypress Head

Trail to junction (1.5 mi), to Airfield (1.8 mi)

48° 34'

"5"
Fl G 4s

14

72

45

17

© 2013 Blue Latitude Press - Not for Navigation

102

138

Deepwater Bay

Aquaculture

102

96

Fl Y 6s

122° 40'

option. No mooring buoys are found in the south cove and due to the predominate south winds, this cove is not used much by anchoring boats. This south cove is also shallow, preventing anchoring within the majority of the cove.

For trips to shore, a gradual sand and gravel beach is found at the head of the north cove. Picnic tables and firepits are found along the sandy isthmus, with campsites scattered in the trees on Cypress Head. Pit toilets are located near the isthmus on the Cypress Island side.

For hikers, Cypress Head offers access to the miles of trail systems found throughout the island. One main trail leads from Cypress Head up the hill for 1.5 miles before intersecting with two trails leading to Reed Lake, Bradberry Lake and the old airfield. Views from the airfield are fantastic and well worth the hike up the hill. The cleared airfield provides a vantage point to see many of the surrounding islands, as well a great location to spot many of the island's eagles soaring on thermal currents. From here, it is only a short walk to the Cypress Island Mainline trail, which bisects the island from north to south, and the trail to Cypress Lake. With so many trails, days can be spent hiking the island and enjoying the beautiful sites and wildlife found on Cypress.

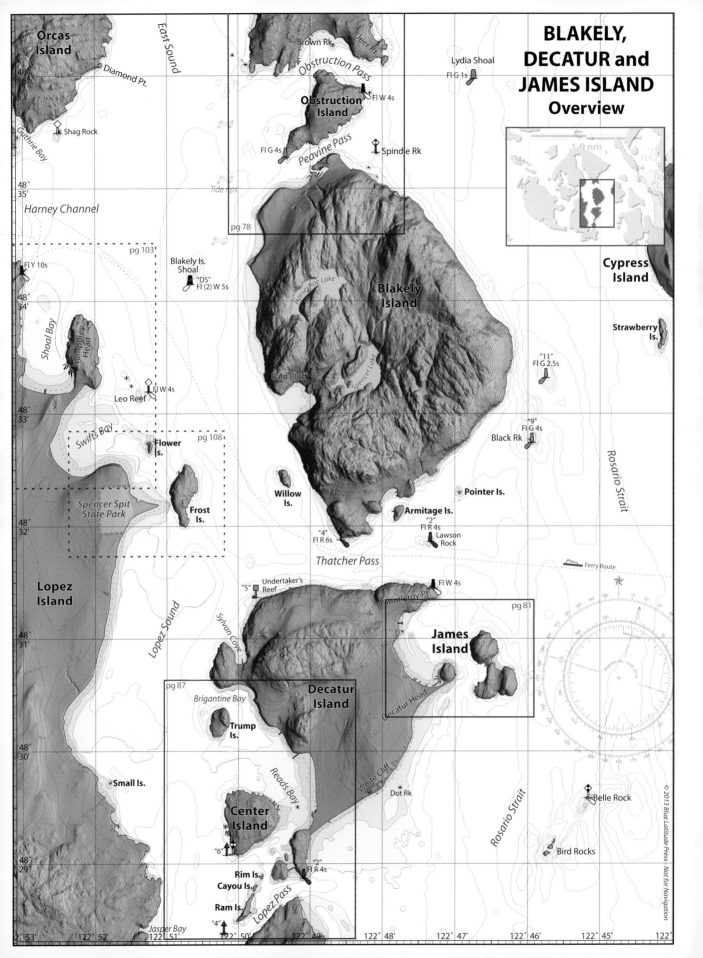

Orcas Island

East Sound

Diamond Pt.

48° 36'

Guthrie Bay

Shag Rock

Harney Channel

48° 35'

pg 103

Fl Y 10s

48° 34'

Blakely Is. Shoal

"DS"
Fl (2) W 5s

Shoal Bay

Humphrey Head

Leo Reef

Fl W 4s

48° 33'

Swifts Bay

Flower Is.

pg 108

Spencer Spit State Park

Frost Is.

48° 32'

Lopez Island

Lopez Sound

48° 31'

Sylvan Cove

pg 87

Brigantine Bay

Trump Is.

48° 30'

Small Is.

Reads Bay

Center Island

"6"

48° 29'

Rim Is.
Cayou Is.

"2"
Fl R 4s

Ram Is.

"4"

Lopez Pass

Jasper Bay

Brown Rk

Deer Pt.

Obstruction Pass

Obstruction Island

Fl W 4s

Peavine Pass

Fl G 4s

Spindle Rk

Tide rips

pg 78

Lydia Shoal

Fl G 1s

Blakely Island

Horseshoe Lake

Bald Bluff

Spencer Lake

Cypress Island

Strawberry Is.

"11"
Fl G 2.5s

"9"
Fl G 4s

Black Rk

Rosario Strait

Willow Is.

Pointer Is.

Armitage Is.
"2"
Fl R 4s
Lawson Rock

"4"
Fl R 6s

Thatcher Pass

Ferry Route

"5"
Undertaker's Reef

Fl W 4s

Fauntleroy Pt.

pg 81

James Island

Decatur Island

Decatur Head

White Cliff

Dot Rk

Belle Rock

Rosario Strait

Bird Rocks

© 2013 Blue Latitude Press - Not for Navigation

48° 2' 53' 122° 52' 122° 51' 122° 50' 122° 49' 122° 48' 122° 47' 122° 46' 122° 45' 122°

1.0 nm

Fl R 2

Tide Pt.

Blakely Island Marina

Blakely Island

Blakely Island is one of the largest private islands within the San Juan Island group. Though most of the island remains undeveloped, a small, private housing community centered around the marina and airstrip is located on the north side of the island. With its heavily forested 4,700 acres, Blakely Island had a long history in the logging industry in the late 1800's and early 1900's, with a large sawmill operation located in Thatcher Bay. Thanks to generous donations from island residents, Blakely Island is also home to Seattle Pacific University's, Blakely Island Field Station, where education and research in field-based environmental and physical sciences takes place.

Blakely Island is located south of Orcas Island and north of Decatur Island, with its eastern shore along Rosario Strait. The island lies between two of the most popular eastern entrances into the heart of the San Juan Islands, Peavine Pass and Thatcher Pass. If approaching from the south via Thatcher Pass, be aware of Lawson Rock which lies north of Fauntleroy Point on the eastern side of the pass. Lawson

Rock is marked by a lighted buoy. If approaching from the north or east via Peavine Pass, be aware of Spindle Rock lying on the eastern side of the pass. Spindle Rock is marked by a beacon. Due to the restricted widths of both these passes, current will be experienced on both the flood and ebb tides.

Blakely Island Marina to:		
Anacortes	12 nm
Bellingham	18 nm
Blaine	28 nm
Blind Bay *(Shaw Island)*	5 nm
Echo Bay *(Sucia Island)*	15 nm
Fisherman Bay *(Lopez Island)*	7 nm
Friday Harbor *(San Juan Island)*	9 nm
Hunter Bay *(Lopez Island)*	8 nm
Jones Island	10 nm
Roche Harbor *(San Juan Island)*	16 nm
Rosario *(Orcas Island)*	4 nm
Sidney *(Canada)*	25 nm
Spencer Spit *(Lopez Island)*	3 nm

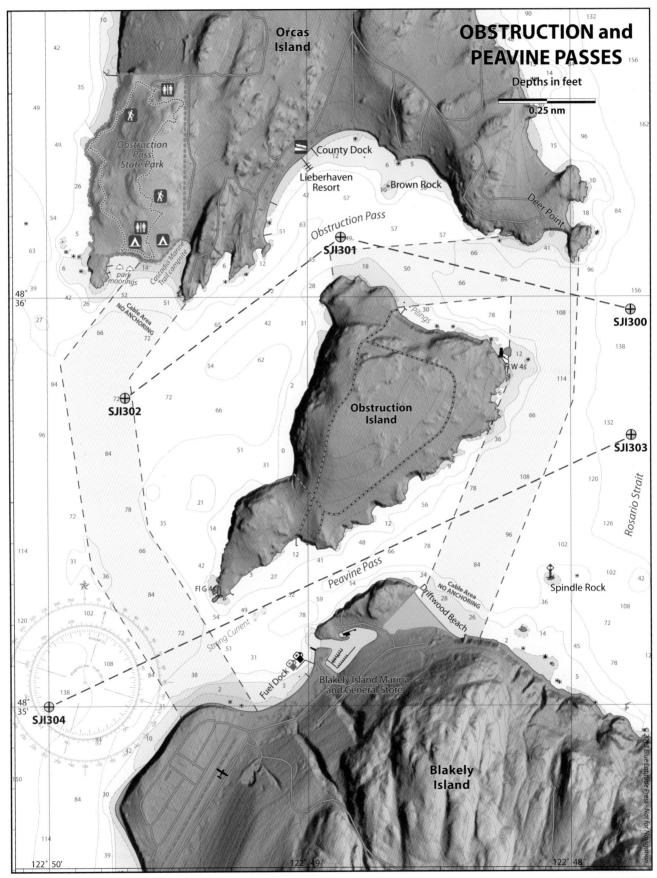

OBSTRUCTION and PEAVINE PASSES

Depths in feet

0.25 nm

Orcas Island

County Dock

Lieberhaven Resort

Brown Rock

Deer Point

Obstruction Pass

SJI301

SJI300

Obstruction Pass State Park

Cascadia Marine Trail campsite

park moorings

Cable Area NO ANCHORING

SJI302

Pilings

W 4s

Obstruction Island

SJI303

Rosario Strait

Spindle Rock

Peavine Pass

Cable Area NO ANCHORING

Driftwood Beach

Fl G 4s

Strong Current

Fuel Dock

Blakely Island Marina and General Store

SJI304

Blakely Island

SJI300 - 48°35.970'N 122°47.770'W   **SJI301** - 48°36.130'N 122°48.870'W   **SJI302** - 48°35.750'N 122°49.700'W

SJI303 - 48°35.660'N 122°47.760'W   **SJI304** - 48°35.000'N 122°50.000'W

Dock and fuel dock at Blakely Island Marina

Blakely Island Marina and General Store

Though Blakely is one of the larger islands, it's shoreline does not provide many places for pleasure boats to anchor. At the north end of the island is the Blakely Island Marina and fuel dock. The small, nearly landlocked marina offers transient slips for visiting boaters, with dock side power and water available. Marina amenities include restrooms, showers and laundry facilities, along with a diesel and gasoline fuel dock located at the entrance.

Next to the marina is the Blakely Island General Store. The store carries a number of grocery staples, including ice, fishing supplies, beverages, beer, ice cream and snacks. The store also offers espresso, donuts, hot dogs and wireless internet. A small picnic area next to the store provides a nice setting to enjoy the view of Peavine Pass and the San Juan Islands. The land and park area surrounding the marina are privately owned by the homeowners association and are not available for public use. The store and fuel dock are closed in the off season, and are open daily from Memorial Day weekend through Labor Day.

Blakely Island Marina and General Store
Monitors VHF channel 66A
1 Marina Drive
Blakely Island, WA 98222
(360) 375-6121

Blakely Island General Store

Thatcher Bay

Located on the southwest side of Blakely Island is Thatcher Bay. Thatcher Bay was once the site of a sawmill with a number of pilings still in place on the north side of the bay. The majority of the bay is shallow, with the head of the bay becoming shoal. Anchorage can be taken in 1 fathom over a mud bottom. With decades of use as a logging site, be cautious of submerged debris on the bottom. The surrounding land is privately owned so shore access is restricted.

James Island

Lying a mere six miles west of Fidalgo Island is the quiet, picture perfect state park of James Island. This small, 113 acre island offers an easily reached destination from Anacortes. It allows boaters and kayakers alike to enjoy the serenity of the islands for which the San Juans are known. The marine state park island offers a dock and moorings buoys, as well as campsites and hiking trails traversing the south side of the island. With sweeping views of nearby Mt. Baker and the surrounding Cascade mountain range, James Island is an ideal stop to soak in the enchanting beauty of the Pacific Northwest and the island studded waters of Puget Sound.

James Island lies directly east of Decatur Island along the western fringes of Rosario Strait. Approximately 400 yards separate James Island from nearby Decatur Head. Common approaches to the island are made via Thatcher Pass located between Blakely and Decatur Islands to the northwest, or via Rosario Strait. The majority of James Is-

land's shoreline is rocky and surrounded by kelp so use caution when transiting or fishing around the island.

Moorage options are available in both coves found on the east and west sides of the island. Three mooring buoys

James Island to:		
	Anacortes	9 nm
	Bellingham	19 nm
	Blaine	31 nm
	Blind Bay (Shaw Island)	8 nm
	Eagle Harbor (Cypress Island)	8 nm
	Echo Bay (Sucia Island)	18 nm
	Fisherman Bay (Lopez Island)	11 nm
	Friday Harbor (San Juan Island)	12 nm
	Roche Harbor (San Juan Island)	19 nm
	Rosario (Orcas Island)	10 nm
	Spencer Spit (Lopez Island)	4 nm
	Victoria (Canada)	31 nm

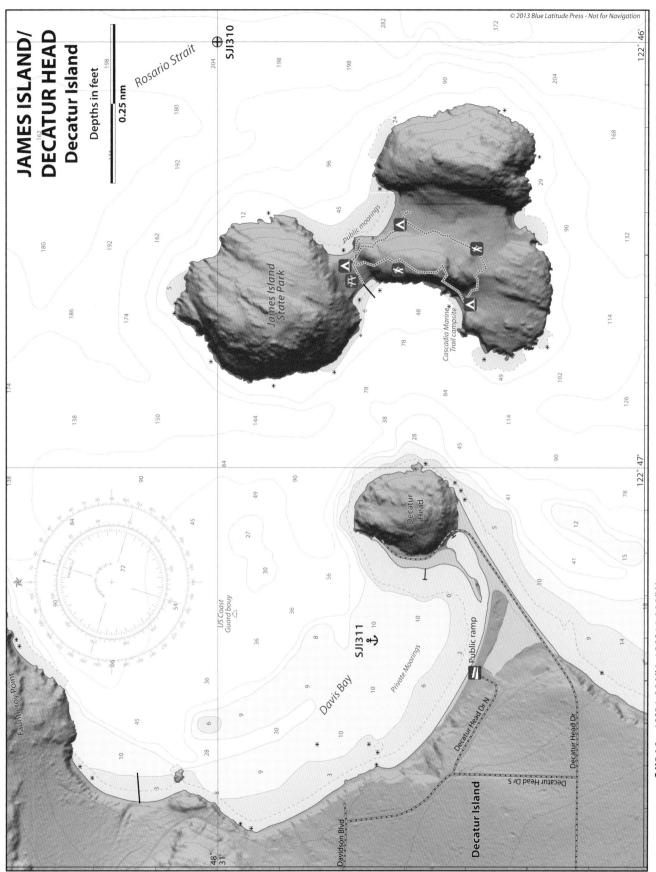

JAMES ISLAND/ DECATUR HEAD
Decatur Island

Depths in feet

0.25 nm

© 2013 Blue Latitude Press - Not for Navigation

Rosario Strait

SJI310

James Island State Park

public moorings

Cascadia Marine Trail campsite

Decatur Head

US Coast Guard bouy

SJI311

Davis Bay

Private Moorings

Public ramp

Decatur Head Dr N

Decatur Head Dr S

Decatur Head Dr

Davidson Blvd

Decatur Island

Fauntleroy Point

SJI311 - 48°30.750'N 122°47.400'W

SJI310 - 48°31.000'N 122°46.000'W

are located in the east cove, and a 44-foot dock is found in the west cove, which are operated by the state park. The dock is available for use during the summer months, and is removed for winter in October and replaced in April. When using the mooring buoys found in the east cove, keep in mind that wake from commercial traffic transiting Rosario Strait may cause an occasional roll in the anchorage. Due to the rocky and steep shoreline around much of the island, anchorage options are fairly limited making the use of mooring buoys and dock space a convenient option.

Dinghy trips to shore are easily made in both the east and west coves of the island where pebble beaches or the dock can be found. James Island is part of the Cascadia Marine Trail and offers 13 campsites scattered around the island

Wildflowers of the San Juan Islands

An explosion of color on the open grasslands and forests heralds the arrival of spring each year in the San Juan Islands. This is a favorite time of year for many to visit, viewing and photographing brightly colored fields of blues, purples, yellows, whites and pinks. Small-flowered Blue-eyed Mary, Common and Great Camas, Seashore Lupine, Nootka Rose, Taper-tip Onion, and Field Chickweed are just a few varieties of flowers that can be spotted. The best months for viewing the wildflowers of the islands are April through July.

Anchored on the east side of James Island along Rosario Strait

along with pit toilet facilities. No potable water is available at the island however. A park information bulletin board and pay station for use of the dock, buoys and campsites can be found up the hill from the dock in the low saddle area between the east and west coves.

Island activities include hiking trails, fishing and wildlife viewing. A 1.5 mile looping trail winds around the southwestern portion of the island, taking visitors through the forest and up to a bluff overlooking the clear blue waters of the western cove. The northern portion of the island has been preserved as a Natural Forest Area, and is not open to hikers. With its pristine beauty and superb location, James Island is a perfect spot to grab your camera and photograph some of the best island scenes in the San Juans. From the island, there are clear views of Rosario Strait with the towering backdrop of Mt. Baker and the Twin Sisters. This area is well traveled by boaters, pleasure and commercial, including the Washington State Ferries. From lush forests and colorful madrona trees, to crystal clear water alive with flowing kelp, James Island is a true picture perfect location.

Looking south at Decatur Head

Decatur Island

Decatur Island is a popular summer home location with roughly 400 part-time residents and 50 full time residents. Lying only nine miles west of Anacortes, Decatur is an easily reached destination with a quiet peacefulness only the islands can bestow. With a diverse shoreline, Decatur offers an array of anchorage options around the island. The island is also home to a small public school, part of the Lopez Island School District, for grades kindergarten through eight. The island recently had a small store and deli, however it is currently closed. Although the vast majority of the island is privately owned, a public boat ramp is located at Decatur Head, providing access to visitors looking to walk the quiet county roads. At the far south end of the island, Kimball Preserve, owned by the San Juan Preservation Trust, offers an additional option for the public to explore this beautiful island.

Decatur Head

Decatur Head lies on the island's northeastern shore, only a mere quarter of a mile from James Island State Park. The nearly spherical headland is connected to Decatur Island by a narrow and sandy isthmus (tombolo) at the southern end of the bay which doubles back to form a small lagoon. This low isthmus provides the perfect window for watching the occasional commercial ship transiting nearby Rosario Strait. The northeast portion of the bay opens towards the east entrance to Thatcher Pass, a popular route for boats entering the San Juan Islands, including the iconic Washington State Ferries.

The large crescent shaped anchorage is formed by Decatur Head to the south and Fauntleroy Point to the north (see page 81 for the chartlet to Decatur Head). Approaches to the bay can be made via Thatcher Pass to the west or Rosario Strait to north and south. For boats approaching from the south, passage can be taken between James Island and Decatur Head. When rounding the headland, be aware of shallow water and old pilings extending off the west shore of Decatur Head.

The bay forming the anchorage is mostly shallow with a steep gradient rising from 6 fathoms to 1 fathom in a very short distance. Near the southwestern side of the bay are a handful of charted rocks to be cautious of, with one rock lying roughly 160 yards off the beach. Anchorage can be taken within the bay in 1 to 7 fathoms over a mostly mud bottom. Be aware that a large number of private moorings are scattered throughout the southern portion of the bay. The anchorage at Decatur Head provides protection from most weather with the exception of northerly winds to which the bay is open. The low isthmus found at the head of the bay provides good wave protection from southeasterlies, but offers little in the way of wind abatement.

Decatur Head is one of two locations on the island where public shore access is available. A public boat ramp is found at the head of the bay where dinghies can be landed. Visitors can walk along the county roads, but keep in mind most of Decatur Island is privately owned, and visitors should respect the privacy of land owners here.

Sylvan Cove and the Decatur Northwest community

Sylvan Cove

Sylvan Cove lies on the northwestern shore of Decatur Island, overlooking the northern entrance to Lopez Sound. The land surrounding the cove, including the dock and mooring buoys within the cove are privately owned and are part of the Decatur Northwest housing community. This community operates a private water taxi that runs between Sylvan Cove and Skyline Marina in Anacortes.

Sylvan Cove can be approached via Thatcher Pass to the east, Lopez Sound to the south and the waters between Blakely and Lopez Islands to the north. If approaching via Thatcher Pass, be aware of the marked, Undertakers Reef, lying offshore and northeast of the entrance to Sylvan Cove. Anchorage can be taken within the cove in 3 to 4 fathoms. The dock and mooring buoys are reserved for the use of Decatur Northwest property owners and their guests. Sylvan Cove affords protection from east, south and west weather, but is open to the north. Better northerly protection can be found around the corner at Brigantine Bay or at Spencer Spit on Lopez Island.

Due to private property surrounding the cove, shore access is not available to the public at Sylvan Cove. For those looking to stretch their legs on the beach, a mile and a half to the northeast is Spencer Spit State Park which offers a lengthy stretch of sand beach for strolling and exploring.

Brigantine Bay

Brigantine Bay is found around the headland and to the south of Sylvan Cove on Decatur Island. Trump Island, which lies just southwest of the anchorage, provides a beautiful backdrop and adds to the labyrinth-like feel of the waters along the west and southwest portions of Decatur Island.

Brigantine Bay is located on the eastern side of Lopez Sound off Decatur Island. Approaches to the bay can be made from the north or south in Lopez Sound. Be aware that the shoreline around Trump Island is rocky, with shallow water found off its western side. Anchorage can be taken within the bay under the protection of the headland in 6 to 7 fathoms. Brigantine Bay affords north and east wind protection, but is open to the south and west.

The land surrounding Brigantine Bay, including Trump Island, is private with no public shore access. However, the protected waters of Lopez Sound and nearby Reads Bay provide an excellent location to drop the kayak in the water to explore the shorelines of the various islands and National Wildlife Refuges in the area.

Reads Bay and Decatur Island

Reads Bay

Reads Bay is located on the southwestern shore of Decatur Island, one mile southeast of Brigantine Bay. This large bay has become a popular mooring and anchorage site for private homeowners on the nearby islands.

Reads Bay is found between Center Island to the west and Decatur Island to the east. Approaches to the bay can be made from Lopez Sound, either from the north or south. If approaching from the north, be cautious of shallow water found off the west side of Trump Island. If approaching from the south, it is best to enter the bay by rounding the west and north side of Center Island. While some boats do transit between Center Island and Decatur Island, the passage contains shoal areas and rocks. This passage is best left to those with local knowledge and shallow draft boats. The western shore of Center Island is rocky with a few detached rocks in places so be sure to give this shoreline ample room when passing.

Anchorage can be taken throughout this large bay in 3 to 6 fathoms over a mostly mud bottom. The shoreline along Decatur Island becomes shoal at low tide with shallow water extending out into the bay, including the east side of Center Island. In the southern portion of the bay, a charted shallow rocky patch is found. Before dropping the anchor, be sure to note two cable crossing locations, one from Lopez to Decatur, and another from Decatur to Center Island. Be sure your anchor does not fall into one of these cable crossing zones.

Reads Bay offers protection from easterly and southerly weather, but is open to the west and northwest. Due to the low, narrow land found on the south end of Decatur Island, little wind abatement from southerlies will be found here, although it does provide good wave protection.

While there is not public beach access within Reads Bay or on Center Island, nearby Kimball Preserve (see page 88) offers visitors the chance to stretch their legs on shore. Reads Bay is a good location to drop the kayak or dinghy in the water to explore many of the surrounding smaller islands. If paddling towards Ram, Cayou or Rim Islands, be aware that current can be stronger in this area due to Lopez Pass. Be sure to check your current and tide tables.

Reads Bay to:		
	Anacortes	12 nm
	Bellingham	24 nm
	Blaine	35 nm
	Blind Bay (Shaw Island)	9 nm
	Fisherman Bay (Lopez Island)	11 nm
	Friday Harbor (San Juan Island)	12 nm
	Hunter Bay (Lopez Island)	3 nm
	James Island	5 nm
	Rosario (Orcas Island)	10 nm
	Shallow Bay (Sucia Island)	22 nm
	Spencer Spit (Lopez Island)	3 nm

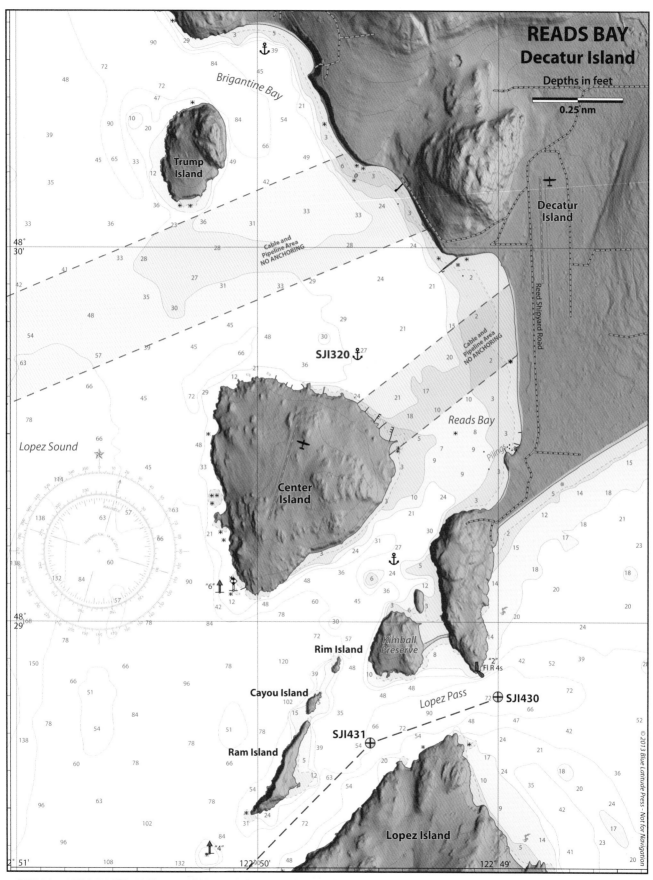

READS BAY
Decatur Island

Depths in feet

0.25 nm

Brigantine Bay

Trump Island

Decatur Island

Reed Shipyard Road

Cable and Pipeline Area NO ANCHORING

Cable and Pipeline Area NO ANCHORING

SJI320

Reads Bay

Pilings

Lopez Sound

Center Island

Kimball Preserve

Rim Island

"2" Fl R 4s

Cayou Island

"6"

SJI430

SJI431

Ram Island

"4"

Lopez Pass

Lopez Island

© 2013 Blue Latitude Press - Not for Navigation

SJI320 - 48°29.710'N 122°49.590'W   **SJI430** - 48°28.800'N 122°49.000'W   **SJI431** - 48°28.690'N 122°49.520'W

SJI432 - 48°28.200'N 122°50.240'W *(not shown, see pg 112)*

Looking south at Kimball Preserve

Kimball Preserve

Kimball Preserve is a unique little nook tucked into the far southern tip of Decatur Island. A tombolo, or deposited sand bar, stretches from Decatur to connect a small off lying island. This special piece of land was donated by outdoorsman and conservationist, Dr. Walter Kimball in the 1980's to the San Juan Preservation Trust (see page 47). Today, the 56 acre preserve is open to the public, only one of two locations on Decatur Island with public beach access.

Kimball Preserve is located on the very southern end of Decatur Island, under the protection of Center Island to the north. Approaches can be taken via Lopez Sound to the north and south, or via Lopez Pass to the east. If approaching via Lopez Sound to the north, be aware of day beacon "6," marking a reef lying off the southern end of Center Island.

If approaching from the south, be on the lookout for day beacon "4," marking a reef lying roughly 300 yards southwest of Ram Island. If approaching via Lopez Pass, keep in mind that current flows through the pass on the flood and ebb tides. Passage can be taken between Decatur Island and Rim Island, the northern most of the chain islands (Ram, Cayou and Rim) in an 8 fathom channel. If using this route, be aware of shallow water extending off the southern tip of Decatur Island. The passage from Reads Bay to Kimball Preserve off the east side of Center Island contains shoal areas and rocks. Although a few boats use this passage, it is best left to those with local knowledge and shallow draft boats.

Anchorage can be taken between Decatur and the southeast shore of Center Island. The small cove north of the tombolo is mostly shallow, with shoal water at the head of the cove. The small island found within the cove has shoal water on the south side. An isolated 1 fathom patch, along with shallow water extending west from Decatur Island lie within the anchorage. Consult your charts prior to entering this area and make sure to set your anchor in a location that gives you ample room to swing without hitting the bottom at low tide.

For trips to shore, dinghies can be landed on the beach at the head of the cove. As this is a nature preserve, be sure to "leave no trace" when visiting this area.

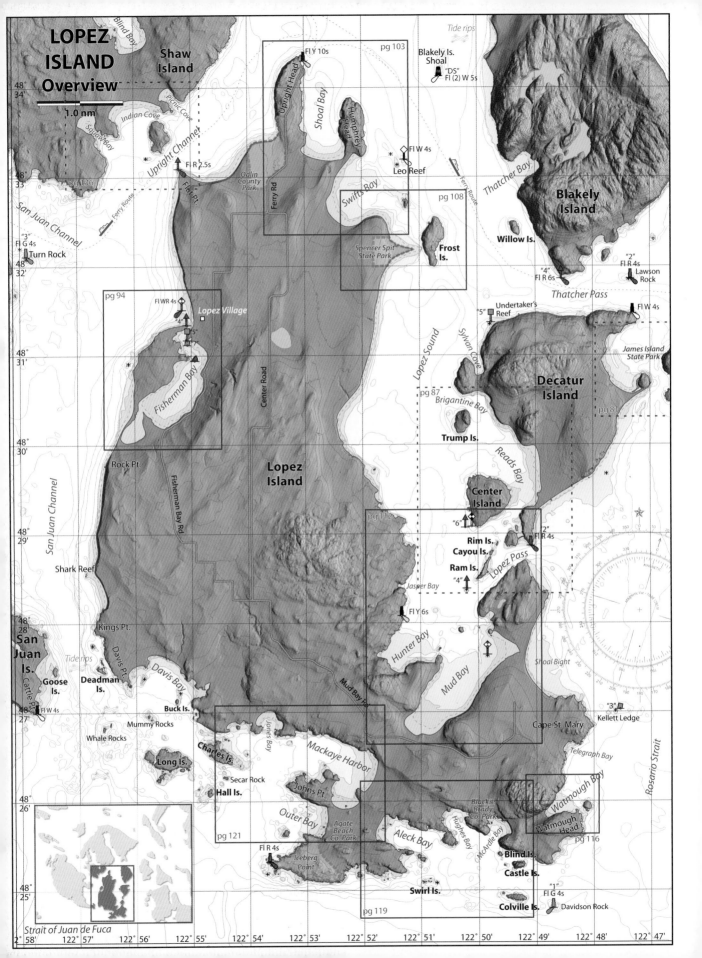

LOPEZ ISLAND
Overview

1.0 nm

48° 34'

48° 33'

48° 32'

48° 31'

48° 30'

48° 29'

48° 28'

48° 27'

48° 26'

48° 25'

Shaw Island

Blind Bay

Squaw Bay

Indian Cove

Picnic Cove

Upright Channel

Flat Pt.

Fl R 2.5s

pg 136

San Juan Channel

"3"
Fl G 4s
Turn Rock

pg 94

Fl WR 4s

"4"
"5"

Lopez Village

"3"

Fisherman Bay

Rock Pt.

Fisherman Bay Rd

Center Road

Lopez Island

San Juan Is.

Kings Pt.

Davis Pt.

Goose Is.

Deadman Is.

Davis Bay

Buck Is.

Cattle Pt.

Fl W 4s

Mummy Rocks

Whale Rocks

Long Is.

Charles Is.

Hall Is.

Secar Rock

Jones Bay

Mackaye Harbor

Johns Pt.

Outer Bay

Agate Beach Co. Park

pg 121

Fl R 4s

Iceberg Point

Swirl Is.

Colville Is.

pg 119

Shark Reef

Upright Head

Shoal Bay

Fl Y 10s

pg 103

Odlin County Park

Ferry Rd

Humphrey Head

Fl W 4s
Leo Reef

Swifts Bay

Ferry Route

pg 108

Spencer Spit State Park

Frost Is.

Lopez Sound

Sylvan Cove

Undertaker's Reef
"5"

pg 87

Brigantine Bay

Trump Is.

Reads Bay

Center Island

"6"

Rim Is.
Cayou Is.
Ram Is.

"2"
Fl R 4s

Lopez Pass

"4"

Jasper Bay

Fl Y 6s

Hunter Bay

Mud Bay Rd

Mud Bay

Shoal Bight

Cape St. Mary

pg 112

Blakely Is. Shoal
"DS"
Fl (2) W 5s

Tide rips

Thatcher Bay

Blakely Island

Willow Is.

"4"
Fl R 6s

"2"
Fl R 4s
Lawson Rock

Thatcher Pass

Fl W 4s

James Island State Park

Decatur Island

pg 81

Rosario Strait

"3"
Kellett Ledge

Telegraph Bay

Watmough Bay

Watmough Head

pg 116

Blackie Brady Co. Park

Hughes Bay

McArdle Bay

Blind Is.

Castle Is.

"1"
Fl G 4s
Davidson Rock

Aleck Bay

Strait of Juan de Fuca

122° 58' 122° 57' 122° 56' 122° 55' 122° 54' 122° 53' 122° 52' 122° 51' 122° 50' 122° 49' 122° 48' 122° 47'

Lopez Island

Third largest of the San Juan Islands, Lopez Island is well known for its rural farmlands, artistic flare and genuine island hospitality that keeps visitors coming back year after year. "Island time" is the norm here, where locals are at the ready with a friendly wave to all.

The island has a population of approximately 2,400 residents, with multiple daily ferry sailings to and from the island. Lopez has one main commercial shopping area known as Lopez Village, situated around Fisherman Bay. Lopez Village has a good selection of restaurants, gift shops, and grocery stores. Landlocked Fisherman Bay is the hub of boating activity for the island with two marinas, a fuel dock, a haul out yard and easy access to the village.

With an amazingly diverse shoreline, Lopez Island features an eclectic array of protected bays and anchorages, perfect for gunkholing and exploring by boat. From remote sand covered beaches and rocky islets to public state parks, Lopez Island has endless opportunities for adventure.

History of Lopez Island

With its numerous protected bays adjacent to some of the area's best fishing locations, Lopez Island has a long history of settlers coming to the island. The earliest visitors to Lopez Island were the Coast Salish people, including the Lummi and Samish tribes, who frequented the island for its bountiful resources of fish, shellfish, deer, lumber and vegetation.

By the late 1700's, Spanish and English explorers began entering the Puget Sound area. It was from one of these early exploration trips that Lopez Island derived its name from Spanish pilot, Gonzalo Lopez de Haro. Although exploration of the Washington and British Columbia coasts was well under way, it took many decades before settlers began trickling into the San Juan Islands.

One of the first European settlers to the island is believed to have been Hiram E. Hutchinson in 1850. Hutchinson arrived at Fisherman Bay and established a trading post and later a post office near present day Lopez Village. Over the next twenty years, more settlers arrived. The 1870 Census reported nearly 90 people living on the island, though some are thought to have lived on neighboring islands. Islanders made their living by fishing, farming, hunting and logging.

Lopez Island began to develop and thrive with towns rising up around Lopez Village to the west, Richardson to the south and Port Stanley to the north. With its roots as a trading center already established, Lopez Village, which is located near the protected waters of Fisherman Bay, offered wharves and warehouses for goods coming to and leaving

the island. Richardson, with direct access to the bountiful salmon fishing grounds, became the center for fishing operations. Piers and canneries sprang up to accommodate the growing fleet, including reefnetters and fish traps. The Richardson canneries employed more than 400 workers during their peak. To the north, Port Stanley, with its open pasture lands and farms, became the center for farmers raising livestock and planting crops of fruits, vegetables and grains.

In the early 1900's, as irrigation efforts began to increase throughout eastern Washington, larger farms producing more crops were beginning to spring up east of the mountains. This resulted in a declining demand for Lopez Island produce and meat. With the Great Depression of the 1930's, economic growth on the island further diminished.

In 1926, the Puget Sound Navigation Company, also known as the Black Ball line, added ferry service to Lopez Island. By the 1940's, increasing operating costs led the Puget Sound Navigation Company to sell its ferry fleet and terminals. In 1951 the state of Washington purchased the majority of the company and holdings, with the exception of the Port Angeles to Victoria route which is still in operation today by the Black Ball Ferry Line.

Ferry service began to carry tourists from the mainland cities to the islands. This new tourism, along with its solid roots in farming, invigorated Lopez's economy after the end of World War II. With its gentle topography and beautiful scenery, Lopez Island has become a favored destination within the archipelago. Today, Lopez is one of the top island destinations for cyclists who relish the quiet country roads and lack of mountainous terrain. The annual "Tour de Lopez," a noncompetitive bike ride around the island, brings 900 cyclists to the island each spring.

Michael Bertrand www.michaelbertrandphotography.com

Fisherman Bay

Fisherman Bay, a nearly landlocked gem, is situated near the village hub of Lopez Island. With a narrow, winding entrance, the bay opens into a wonderful expanse of protected water, perfect for anchoring or taking a slip at one of the two marinas. Savor the thrill of seaplanes taking off and landing in your "backyard" while relaxing on deck, surrounded by the island's beauty. A short walk or dinghy ride to town takes visitors into the heart of Lopez Village where travelers can enjoy the local restaurants, art galleries and shops that give Lopez Island its delightful charm.

Fisherman Bay is located on the western shores of Lopez Island, across from San Juan and Shaw Islands. Approaches to the bay can be taken via Upright Channel to the north, or San Juan Channel to the west and south. Due to the narrow confines of these channels, particularly between Canoe Island and Flat Point as well as Cattle Point and Davis Point, current on the flood and ebb tides will be experienced in these areas. The entrance to Fisherman Bay is marked by a lighted beacon north-northwest of the entrance.

The entrance to Fisherman Bay is narrow, winding and shallow, requiring careful attention to the tides and navigational charts. With a narrow entrance and a large bay

within, current flows through the channel with the tides. When planning your trip into Fisherman Bay, be sure to time it appropriately with the tides and the draft of your boat. For example, at zero tide, there are certain areas where the depth is about 5 feet, so plan according to the draft of your boat and the tide level to allow for sufficient maneuvering room. For newcomers to the bay, the entrance may seem a little daunting for the first time, but keep in mind

Fisherman Bay to:		
	Anacortes	18 nm
	Bellingham	25 nm
	Blaine	35 nm
	Blind Bay *(Shaw Island)*	6 nm
	Eagle Harbor *(Cypress Island)*	14 nm
	Echo Bay *(Sucia Island)*	22 nm
	Friday Harbor *(San Juan Island)*	5 nm
	Mackaye Harbor *(Lopez Island)*	9 nm
	Reid Harbor *(Stuart Island)*	15 nm
	Roche Harbor *(San Juan Island)*	14 nm
	Rosario *(Orcas Island)*	9 nm
	Spencer Spit *(Lopez Island)*	7 nm
	Victoria *(Canada)*	25 nm

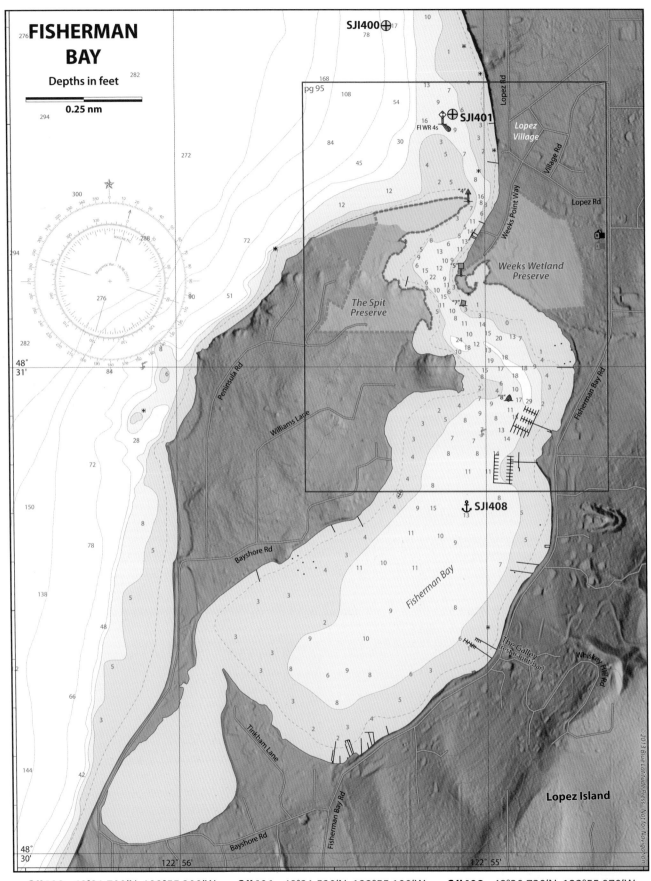

FISHERMAN BAY

Depths in feet

0.25 nm

SJI400

SJI401

Lopez Village

Lopez Rd

Fl WR 4s

Weeks Wetland Preserve

The Spit Preserve

Weeks Point Way

Village Rd

Peninsula Rd

Williams Lane

Fisherman Bay Rd

Bayshore Rd

SJI408

Fisherman Bay

The Galley (restaurant/bar)

Whiskey Hill Rd

Tinkham Lane

Bayshore Rd

Fisherman Bay Rd

Lopez Island

pg 95

© 2013 Blue Latitude Press. Not for Navigation.

48° 31'

48° 30'

122° 56'

122° 55'

94

SJI400 - 48°31.700'N 122°55.300'W   **SJI401** - 48°31.520'N 122°55.100'W   **SJI408** - 48°30.720'N 122°55.070'W

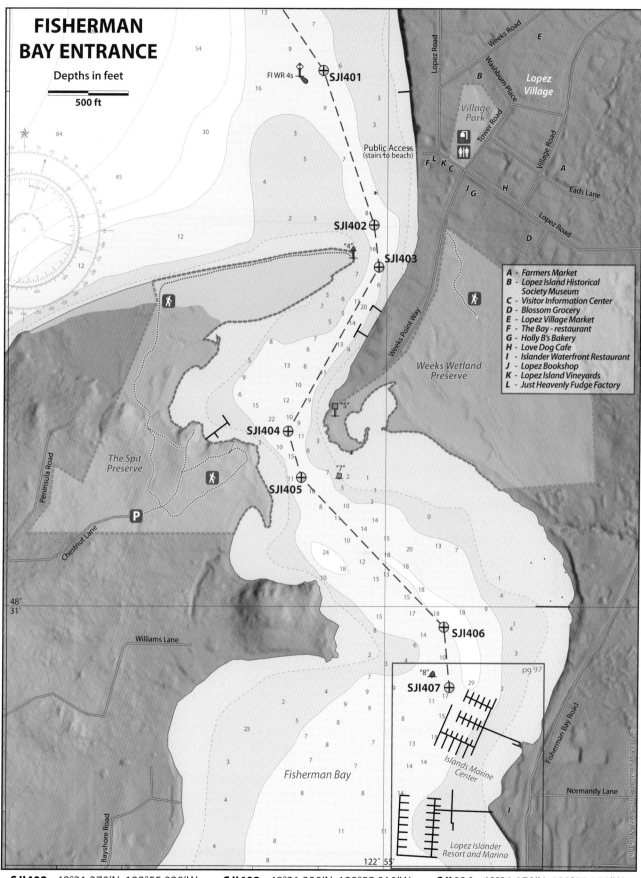

FISHERMAN BAY ENTRANCE

Depths in feet

500 ft

Fl WR 4s   SJI401

Public Access
(stairs to beach)

SJI402

"A"   SJI403

Weeks Point Way

Weeks Wetland
Preserve

"5"

SJI404

The Spit
Preserve

P

Chestnut Lane

"7"

SJI405

A - Farmers Market
B - Lopez Island Historical
       Society Museum
C - Visitor Information Center
D - Blossom Grocery
E - Lopez Village Market
F - The Bay - restaurant
G - Holly B's Bakery
H - Love Dog Cafe
I - Islander Waterfront Restaurant
J - Lopez Bookshop
K - Lopez Island Vineyards
L - Just Heavenly Fudge Factory

Peninsula Road

Williams Lane

Bayshore Road

Fisherman Bay

48°
31'

SJI406

"8"   pg 97

SJI407

Islands Marine
Center

Lopez Islander
Resort and Marina

Fisherman Bay Road

Normandy Lane

122° 55'

Lopez Road
Weeks Road
Washburn Place
Lopez Village
Village Park
Tower Road
Village Road
Eads Lane
Lopez Road

© 2013 Blue Latitude Press Not for Navigation

SJI402 - 48°31.370'N 122°55.020'W   **SJI403** - 48°31.330'N 122°55.010'W   **SJI404** - 48°31.170'N 122°55.150'W
SJI405 - 48°31.125'N 122°55.130'W   **SJI406** - 48°30.980'N 122°54.910'W   **SJI407** - 48°30.920'N 122°54.900'W   95

Red buoy #8

Green buoy #7

Green Beacon #5

Red Beacon #4

Lighted Beacon north
Fisherman Bay entranc

Michael Bertrand www.michaelbertrandphotography.com

that numerous boats enter and leave this well marked bay every day. The key to a successful entry and exit is allowing for ample water during the tidal cycle and paying attention to the channel markers. Prudent mariners, enter on a rising tide in the event that a grounding should occur. On a rising tide, you will only have to wait a short duration for the tide to rise and float your boat, rather than many hours for low tide to complete its cycle and begin rising once again.

Upon approaching the entrance to the bay, be aware that the shoreline of Lopez Island near this area is shallow, and that it is best to stand off when approaching. A lighted beacon stands north of the entrance to Fisherman Bay. Due to shallow water south of this beacon, pass to the north and east of the beacon - do not cut between the beacon and red beacon #4. Red beacon #4 lies on the peninsula of land forming the western entrance point. At low tide this beacon appears to be on the beach and at high tide is surrounded by water. Keep in mind the water just south and west of beacon #4 becomes shallow, but the main channel has deeper water. This is also an area where current can be experienced depending on the tide. US Chart #18434 also depicts a rock off the east side of the entrance and northeast of red beacon #4, so be sure to navigate with care in this area.

The next channel marker is green beacon #5, located at the tip of land where the channel turns towards the south east. Near this beacon the water is shallow, but deeper water is found in the main channel just to the west. Nearby and to the south is green buoy #7. Green buoy #7 marks the shoal water found to the northeast, east and southeast of the buoy. Further down the channel is the final navigation aid to the channel, red buoy #8. This buoy marks shallow water found to the west side of the buoy. While it is tempting to cut the corner before red buoy #8, be sure to stay within the channel and round the buoy to the north and east.

After passing the final marker, Fisherman Bay opens ahead with ample shallow water anchoring room and two marinas nearby. Good anchorage can be taken within the bay in 1 to 2 fathoms over a mud bottom. A number of moorings are found throughout the bay, however these are private moorings and not available for public use. For boats looking for a slip at the marina, two options are available at the Lopez Islander Resort and the Islands Marine Center (see pages 97 for further information).

For trips to shore and Lopez Village, dinghy and kayak landing is available on the small public beach next to The Bay restaurant along the entrance channel to Fisherman Bay. Dinghy wheels are especially helpful landing and launching on this rock and sand beach if you happen to have a heavy dinghy. Dinghy docks are also available at both Lopez Islander Resort and Islands Marine Center.

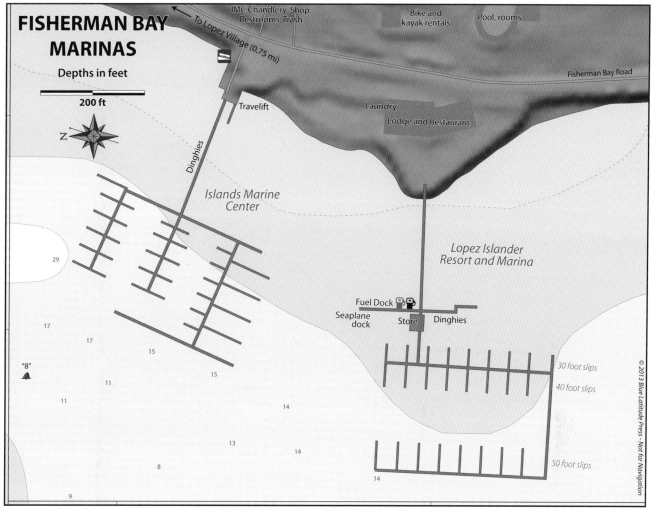

FISHERMAN BAY MARINAS

Depths in feet

200 ft

IMC Chandlery, Shop, Restrooms, Trash

To Lopez Village (0.75 mi)

Bike and kayak rentals

Pool, rooms

Fisherman Bay Road

Travelift

Laundry

Lodge and Restaurant

Dinghies

Islands Marine Center

Lopez Islander Resort and Marina

Fuel Dock

Seaplane dock

Store

Dinghies

30 foot slips

40 foot slips

50 foot slips

29

17

17

15

15

"8"

11

11

14

14

13

14

8

9

© 2013 Blue Latitude Press - Not for Navigation

Islands Marine Center (IMC)

Islands Marine Center or IMC, is a 100 slip marina, offering transient and permanent moorage, including a 250 foot side tie dock, all within the protection of Fisherman Bay. IMC also operates a 25 ton marine travel lift, haulout yard, storage facility and a well stocked marine chandlery and parts department. The marina offers restroom and shower facilities, a pumpout system and a boat launch.

Islands Marine Center
Monitors VHF channel 16
2793 Fisherman Bay Road
Lopez Island, WA 98261
(360) 468-3377
www.islandsmarinecenter.com

Lopez Islander Resort

Next door to IMC is the Lopez Islander Resort, offering transient and permanent moorage within its 60-slip marina. A 340 foot side tie dock is able to accommodate boats of varying lengths. The marina offers a fuel dock, seaplane dock, small convenience store, restaurant, camping facilities and lodging. Guests at the marina have use of the resort's showers, swimming pool and jacuzzi. A coin operated laundromat is also located at the resort, next to the restaurant.

Lopez Islander Resort
Monitors VHF channel 16
2864 Fisherman Bay Road
Lopez Island, WA 98261
(360) 468-2233
desk@lopezfun.com
www.lopezfun.com

Sights to See

One of the highlights of visiting Fisherman Bay is a walk through Lopez Village, the main town on Lopez Island. The village offers a number of shops and delectable restaurants to tour. The village is also a great place to sample some of the island's local creations from Lopez Island Vineyards and Lopez Island Creamery. The winery has a tasting room located across from Village Park, featuring its estate grown organic wines as well as its Yakima Valley wines. Nearby at Just Heavenly Fudge, grab a cone of locally produced ice cream from Lopez Island Creamery and head to the public beach to enjoy the waterfront island vista. Lopez is also an island known for its talented artistic residents, with the village featuring a number of galleries showcasing their works of art.

While in town, be sure to visit the Lopez Island Historical Society Museum. The museum holds a wealth of information about the island's past, with rotating exhibits on display. These include digital recordings of stories from longtime island residents, large photo collections, an outdoor maritime exhibit, natural history and first islanders exhibits. For a current schedule of events and hours, check their website at: **www.lopezmuseum.org** or call (360) 468-2049. The museum is located on the corner of Weeks Road and Washburn Place, near the Village Park.

If you happen to be lucky enough to time your visit to the island on a Saturday, be sure to stop by the Lopez Island Farmer's Market (10 am to 2 pm during the summer months). The farmer's market is spread throughout a park located on Village Road. Local farmer's and crafts people display colorful booths filled with fruits, vegetables, bakery items, artwork and more.

For those looking to stretch their legs and enjoy the nearby nature of the island, follow the trails through the Weeks Wetland Preserve and the Fisherman Bay Spit Preserve. From town, follow Weeks Point Way south to the trailhead for the wetland preserve. The short trail leads to a viewing platform where visitors can take in the 24 acre wetland preserve, viewing migratory birds and other wetland wildlife. The Spit Preserve is located on the peninsula of land at the entrance to the bay and can be reached by car, dinghy or kayak. The preserve includes 29 acres of coastal sand dunes and wetlands area. Trails lead through an old orchard and former homestead site. On the spit are old reef net fishing boats, a reminder of Lopez Island's historic fishing fleet.

Marine Chandleries and Services

Islands Marine Center (IMC)

IMC includes a marina, chandlery, haul out yard, and a service and sales center. The well stocked chandlery carries a wide selection of marine parts, as well as charts, fishing supplies and nautical gifts. For further information on IMC see page 97.

Provisioning and Other Services

Blossom Grocery

Blossom Grocery, located on Lopez Road, just southeast of the Lopez Plaza building, carries a large selection of local and organic products. The grocery carries fresh produce, local meats and seafood, regional cheeses, beer and wine, bulk foods, supplements, coffee, and even fine chocolates.
Phone: (360) 468-2204   Website: www.blossomgrocery.com

Lopez Bookshop

Lopez Bookshop has a nice selection of fiction, nonfiction and children's books, specializing in regional Pacific Northwest books and mysteries. Located next to Holly B's Bakery in the Lopez Plaza Building on Lopez Road.
Phone: (360) 468-2132   Website: www.lopezbookshop.com

Kenmore Air

Kenmore Air provides daily, year-round flights between Seattle and seven locations in the San Juan Islands, including Fisherman Bay.
Phone: (425) 486-1257   Web: www.kenmoreair.com

Lopez Village Market

Lopez Village Market is the main grocery store on Lopez Island, featuring a wide selection of fresh produce, meats, seafood, wines, and dairy items. The market also carries a nice variety of locally made products including farm fresh produce, dairy items, meats and wines. Located near the museum on Weeks Road.
Phone: (360) 468-2266   Website: www.lopezvillagemarket.com

United States Postal Service

The Lopez Village post office is open Monday through Friday from 8am to 3pm. The office is located at 209 Weeks Road, just up the road from Lopez Village Market.
Phone: (360) 468-2282   Web: www.usps.com

Visitor Information Center

Operated by the Lopez Island Chamber of Commerce, the Lopez visitor center is a wealth of information, including maps, directions, sights to see and other helpful island information. Located on Lopez Road, next to the Bay Cafe and the public beach access area.
Phone: (360) 468-4664   Website: www.lopezisland.com

Restaurants

The Bay

Enjoy a fine dining experience overlooking San Juan Channel from the cozy setting of The Bay. Specializing in farm fresh, local ingredients, The Bay is the perfect place to watch the sun setting over the San Juan Islands with a delicious meal.
Phone: (360) 468-3700   Website: www.bay-cafe.com

The Galley Restaurant

Overlooking Fisherman Bay, The Galley Restaurant has a wide selection of homemade meals including fresh seafood, burgers, pizza and Mexican entrees. The restaurant is open for breakfast, lunch and dinner, and also has a dinghy dock and mooring buoys available for visitors arriving by boat. The restaurant is located on the southeast side of the bay with a large dock in front.
Phone: (360) 468-2713   Website: www.galleylopez.com

Holly B's Bakery

Judging by the crowd lingering out front, it's no secret that Holly B's is one of the finest bakeries in the islands. The bakery specializes in fresh baked breads, pizzas, cinnamon rolls, cookies, scones, muffins and more. Be sure to try the delectable cheesy ham biscuits! Located in the Lopez Village Plaza, next to the Lopez Bookshop.
Phone: (360) 468-2133   Website: www.hollybsbakery.com

Islander Waterfront Restaurant

The Islander Waterfront Restaurant is located at the Lopez Islander Resort. Indoor and outdoor seating overlooking Fisherman Bay is perfect for catching sunsets or soaking up the summer sun. Serving northwest favorites for breakfast, lunch and dinner.
Phone: (360) 468-2233   Website: www.lopezfun.com

Love Dog Cafe

The Love Dog Cafe features fresh and local northwest cuisine in a beautiful setting. Serving breakfast, lunch and dinner, including vegetarian and vegan meals. Located across from the Lopez Village Plaza on Lopez Road.
Phone: (360) 468-2150   Website: www.lovedogcafe.com

Odlin County Park

Odlin County Park is situated on the northeastern shore of Lopez Island along Upright Channel. The county park offers a beautiful, sandy beach setting along with mooring buoys and campsites. The 80-acre park is part of the Cascadia Marine Trail system and is a popular site for kayakers paddling the waters of the San Juan Islands. Located in the heart of the islands, Odlin is a wonderful stop to relax on the beach or launch the kayak for a paddle in protected waters.

Odlin County Park is located west of Shoal Bay on Lopez Island, across the narrow stretch of land forming Upright Head. Approaches to the park can taken from Upright Channel which separates Shaw and Lopez Islands. This channel experiences current on the flood and ebb tides due to the constriction of the channel between the islands, particularly near Flat Point and Canoe Island. Upright Channel is also used by the Washington State Ferries so be on the lookout for ferry traffic.

The park offers five mooring buoys off the beach for a nightly fee. Due to the steep gradient of the shoreline and current in this area, anchoring can be difficult, making the moorings a nice option.

For trips to shore, a beautiful sand beach is available to land dinghies and kayaks. A small park dinghy dock is also available east of the anchorage for day use. The park offers 30 campsites, restrooms, water, firepits, a beach boat launch and even a baseball field. Walking trails traverse the park, leading visitors past old growth trees and up along the cliffside for views of Shaw and Canoe Islands.

Odlin Park to:		
	Anacortes	15 nm
	Bellingham	22 nm
	Blaine	33 nm
	Blind Bay *(Shaw Island)*	3 nm
	Deer Harbor *(Orcas Island)*	6 nm
	Fossil Bay *(Sucia Island)*	18 nm
	Friday Harbor *(San Juan Island)*	5 nm
	Pelican Beach *(Cypress Island)*	9 nm
	Reid Harbor *(Stuart Island)*	15 nm
	Roche Harbor *(San Juan Island)*	14 nm
	Spencer Spit (Lopez Island)	4 nm
	Victoria *(Canada)*	28 nm

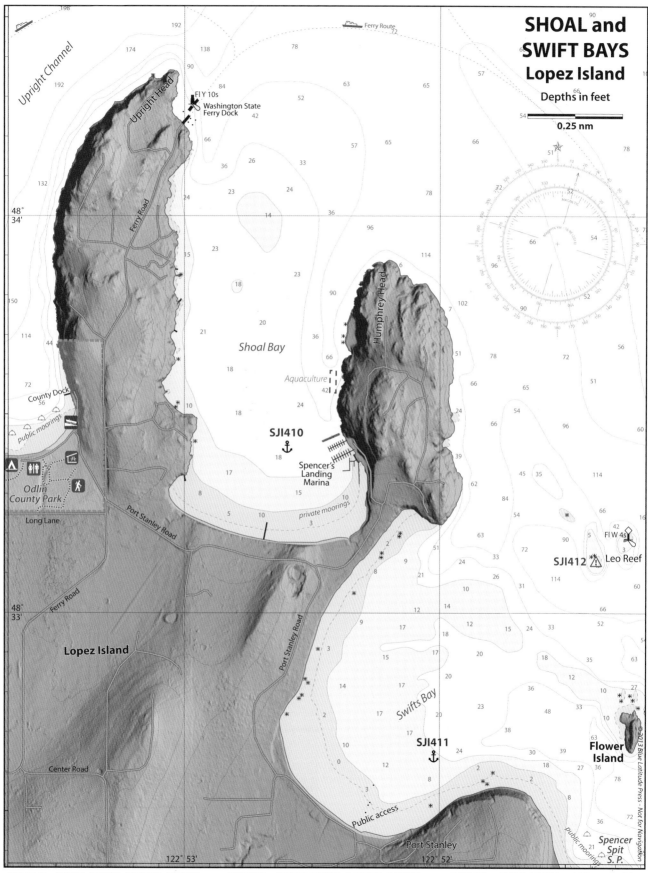

SHOAL and SWIFT BAYS
Lopez Island
Depths in feet

0.25 nm

Upright Channel

Ferry Route

Upright Head

Fl Y 10s
Washington State
Ferry Dock

Ferry Road

48° 34'

MAGNETIC

Shoal Bay

Humphrey Head

Aquaculture

SJI410
⚓

Spencer's
Landing
Marina

County Dock

public moorings

Odlin
County Park

Long Lane

Port Stanley Road

private moorings

Leo Reef
SJI412 ⚠

Fl W 4s

48° 33'

Ferry Road

Lopez Island

Port Stanley Road

Swifts Bay

SJI411
⚓

Flower
Island

©2013 Blue Latitude Press - Not for Navigation

Center Road

Public access

Spencer
Spit
S. P.

public moorings

Port Stanley

122° 53'   122° 52'

SJI410 - 48°33.410'N 122°52.600'W   **SJI411** - 48°32.620'N 122°52.060'W   **SJI412** - 48°33.130'N 122°51.380'W

Shoal Bay

The long stretching arms of Humphrey Head and Upright Head provide a perfectly shaped bay on the northern tip of Lopez Island known as Shoal Bay. While this anchorage is occasionally outshined by its nearby neighbors of Spencer Spit or Blind Bay on Shaw Island, Shoal Bay offers nearly all round protection in a peaceful and tranquil setting. The Lopez Island ferry terminal is located at the head of the bay, providing a distinctive San Juan Islands scene as you watch the stately ferries glide by with the dramatic backdrop of Orcas Island's towering Mt. Constitution.

Shoal Bay is located on the far northern end of Lopez Island, protected by the peninsulas of Humphrey Head and Upright Head. Approaches to the centrally located Shoal Bay can be taken from a variety of channels and passes, depending on your direction of travel. These approaches include Upright Channel, Harney Channel, Eastsound, Obstruction and Peavine Pass, Thatcher Pass and Lopez Sound. When approaching from the east, be sure to locate Blakely Island Shoal off the western side of Blakely Island and Leo Reef off the southeastern side of Humphrey Head, both of which have lighted navigation aids.

As the name suggests, Shoal Bay is relatively shallow, and therefore provides good anchoring depth throughout the bay. A number of private mooring buoys are located near the head of the bay, along with a private marina. Anchorage can be taken inside the bay in 2 to 4 fathoms over a solid holding mud bottom.

Spencer's Landing Marina, in the southeast portion of the bay is private with no transient slips available. Services

Shoal Bay to:		
Anacortes		12 nm
Bellingham		21 nm
Blaine		31 nm
Blind Bay *(Shaw Island)*		4 nm
Deer Harbor *(Orcas Island)*		7 nm
Eagle Harbor *(Cypress Island)*		10 nm
Fisherman Bay *(Lopez Island)*		6 nm
Fossil Bay *(Sucia Island)*		17 nm
Friday Harbor *(San Juan Island)*		7 nm
Jones Island		11 nm
Roche Harbor *(San Juan Island)*		14 nm
Sidney *(Canada)*		23 nm

Humphrey Head, the eastern shore of Shoal Bay

at the marina include Tanbark Marine, a full yacht management service. Tanbark Marine specializes in mechanical, electrical, and desalination systems installation and service. Contact Tanbark at: (360) 468-4390 or by email: tanbark@rockisland.com.

Shoal Bay provides protection from nearly all directions, with the exception of northerly weather. During periods of strong southeast winds, the anchorage will provide protection from waves, however due to the low narrow isthmus of land found in the southeast corner, little wind abatement will be found here.

Unfortunately, there is no public beach access at Shoal Bay. A number of homes line the low bank waterfront and beach access is reserved to the property owners. For those looking to get off the boat and stretch their legs, public beaches are available at nearby Spencer Spit State Park and Odlin County Park.

Swifts Bay

Swifts Bay is the quiet, unassuming neighbor to the often visited and nearby Spencer Spit State Park. This large and shallow bay is narrowly separated from Shoal Bay by Humphrey Head. With its easy access to the State Park, Swifts Bay can be a quiet alternate anchorage if Spencer Spit happens to be full, or if you prefer an anchorage mostly to yourself. The historical hamlet of Port Stanley is found at the head of Swifts Bay, where the renovated Port Stanley schoolhouse, built in 1917, can still be seen today. With public beach access, Swifts Bay is a great place to land your bicycles and go for a ride on the peaceful country roads.

Swifts Bay is located on the northern end of Lopez Island, lying between Shoal Bay to the northwest and Spencer Spit to the southeast. When approaching Swifts Bay, be aware of the rocky Flower Island and Leo Reef near the entrance to the bay. Flower Island is located east of the bay and is protected as a National Wildlife Refuge, and therefore closed to the public to protect marine wildlife. The island's

Frost Island

Lopez Sound

Spencer Spit

Flower Island

Lopez Island

Leo Reef

Detached rocks
west of Leo Reef

Orcas Island

Leo Reef

Once inside the bay, anchorage can be taken in 2 to 4 fathoms over a good holding mud bottom. A number of moorings are found in this bay, however they are private and not available for use by the public. The bay provides good protection from most winds with the exception of north and east winds.

For dinghy trips to shore, a small 45 foot stretch of beach is available for public access near the far southern end of the bay. This access is connected to Port Stanley Road and is typically marked by signs. Immediately around the corner from Swifts Bay is the 138 acre state park at Spencer Spit. This park is a great place to get off the boat and stretch your legs on a sandy beach (see page 107 for Spencer Spit information).

north end has a number of detached rocks and should be given a wide berth if traveling between Leo Reef and Flower Island. Leo Reef lies north of Flower Island and northeast of the entrance to Swifts Bay. The eastern edge of the reef is marked by a lighted beacon. A detached portion of the main reef lies west of Leo Reef, and should be given adequate room when passing. Passage can be taken between Leo Reef and Humphrey Head on Lopez Island, between Flower Island and Leo Reef, or between Flower Island and Lopez Island. Keep in mind that the shoreline along Lopez Island is shallow in this area. Rocks are found off the northern end of Flower Island and around Leo Reef, so be sure to allow for ample room when transiting in this area.

Looking north from Spencer Spit at Flower Island

U.S. Department of Agriculture, Farm Service Agency

Spencer Spit

Lying within the heart of the San Juan Islands, the magical 138 acre state park at Spencer Spit is a must stop on any cruising boat's itinerary. The unique sand spit stretching from the northeastern shore of Lopez Island invites countless visitors for a pleasant stroll or a relaxing nap on the soft sand and pebble beach. A large lagoon near the beach also provides the perfect habitat for spotting a variety of the many shore birds found within the islands. With plenty of anchoring room and state park mooring buoys found on either side of the sand spit, boats of all shapes and sizes can easily enjoy the beauty of Spencer Spit State Park.

The triangular shaped point of Spencer Spit is located around the corner from Swifts Bay on the northeastern side of Lopez Island. With the low lying land of Spencer Spit, the high cliffsides of nearby Frost Island help to provide a good visual aid for locating the anchorage. With its central location, Spencer Spit can be approached from a number of directions including Lopez Sound to the south, Thatcher Pass to the east, Harney or Upright Channels to the northwest, or Peavine or Obstruction Passes to the northeast.

Anchoring and mooring options are available on both the north and south side of the spit. Depending on the approach and which side of the spit to anchor, two options are available for boats to travel to the north or south side of the spit. The first option and most obvious is transiting off the east side of Frost Island. This option has deep water and plenty of maneuvering room. The second option is to use the narrow waterway between the west side of Frost Island

Spencer Spit to:	Anacortes	12 nm
	Bellingham	21 nm
	Blaine	31 nm
	Blind Bay *(Shaw Island)*	5 nm
	Fisherman Bay *(Lopez Island)*	7 nm
	Fossil Bay *(Sucia Island)*	17 nm
	Friday Harbor *(San Juan Island)*	8 nm
	James Island	4 nm
	Pelican Beach *(Cypress Island)*	8 nm
	Roche Harbor *(San Juan Island)*	16 nm
	Watmough Bay *(Lopez Island)*	9 nm
	Victoria *(Canada)*	31 nm

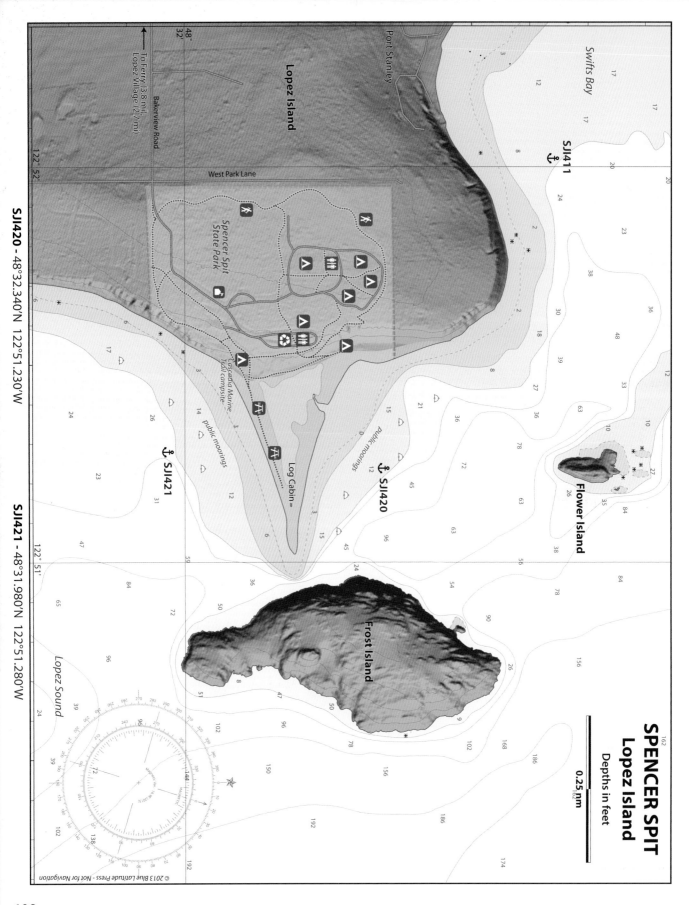

Lopez Island

Port Stanley

Swifts Bay

SJI411

SPENCER SPIT
Lopez Island
Depths in feet

0.25 nm

West Park Lane

Spencer Spit
State Park

Bakerview Road

To Ferry (3.8 mi)
Lopez Village (2.7 mi)

SJI420 - 48°32.340'N 122°51.230'W

Cascadia Marine
Trail campsite

public moorings

public moorings

Log Cabin

SJI421

SJI420

Flower Island

Frost Island

SJI421 - 48°31.980'N 122°51.280'W

Lopez Sound

The passage between the tip of Spencer Spit and Frost Island

and the tip of Spencer Spit. Depending on the tide level, this passage is roughly 250 feet in width at its narrowest. Deeper water is found closer to Frost Island, with shallow water found off the tip of the spit. Staying in the deeper water channel closer to Frost Island and away from the tip of the spit, the shallowest depths range from 25 feet to 30 feet just south of the narrowest section of the passage.

For boats approaching from the north, be aware of the rock dangers at Leo Reef and Flower Island (see page 106 for pictures of the reef and island). Leo Reef, which lies north of Flower Island, is marked by a lighted beacon. Detached rocks lie off the western side of the marked reef so be sure to give this area ample room when passing. Flower Island, which lies north of Spencer Spit, has rocks that lie off the northern end of the island. Flower Island is also a National Wildlife Refuge for nesting seabirds and other marine animals, and therefore closed to the public.

Anchorage options as well as state park mooring buoys are available on both the north and south side of Spencer Spit. Both sides have good access to dinghy landings on shore and the park amenities. The south side of the spit offers northerly and west wind protection. The northern side of the spit offers south, east and west wind protection. While the low land of the spit will do little for wind abatement, the spit and Frost Island provide good wave protection.

Looking south at Spencer Spit and Decatur Island

If anchoring or picking up a mooring on the north side of the spit, be aware that shallow water surrounds the drainage area from the lagoon near the western side of the spit. Anchorage can be taken on the north side of the spit in 2 to 7 fathoms over good holding sand and mud. Anchorage can be taken on the south side of the spit in 2 to 6 fathoms also over good holding sand and mud.

Spencer Spit is a popular destination in the islands, especially during the peak summer months. Park moorings fill up quick, but there are plenty of anchoring options available, including those at nearby Swifts Bay (see page 105). Keep in mind that there is a fee for using the state park mooring

buoys. Payment envelopes and drop boxes are available on shore or at the ranger station.

For trips to shore, the low sandy spit provides good landing locations on either side. A small log cabin lies near the tip of the spit with interpretive signs and history of the

area. Picnic tables line the shoreline and are popular gathering places for lunches or sunset cocktails. The beach is a great location for rousing games of bocce, fort building with the abundant supply of driftwood, or a lively game of fetch with your furry friend.

The park offers 37 campsites and is also part of the Cascadia Marine Trail system. Two miles of hiking trails cover the park property, and kayak rentals and tours are available on the beach during the summer months. The park also offers the educational, Junior Ranger program from June through August for children looking to learn more about the history and wildlife that surround the park.

Hunter Bay

Nestled around the bend from Mud Bay lies the large, peaceful waters of Hunter Bay. Surrounded by thick forests of evergreens on the nearby hillsides, Hunter Bay is an ideal spot to relax and enjoy a sunset barbecue on the boat. Nearby Crab Island provides good entertainment and the perfect location to watch curious harbor seals bobbing about and sunning themselves on the island. With room for dozens of boats, a county dock and boat launch ramp, Hunter Bay can accommodate everyone's boating needs.

Hunter Bay is located on the southeastern side of Lopez Island, just northwest of Mud Bay, within the protected waters of Lopez Sound. Approaches to the bay can be made from the north via Lopez Sound and from the east via Lopez Pass. If approaching via Lopez Pass, the eastern entrance point is marked by a lighted red buoy off the southern most point of Decatur Island. Once through the pass be aware of a reef found southwest of Ram Island which is marked by a red day beacon. Current also flows through Lopez Pass on the flood and ebb tides.

Anchorage can be taken within Hunter Bay over a fairly uniform 2 to 3 fathom mud bottom. The bay offers good holding with protection from nearly all winds except from the north. Due to the lower saddle of land found at the head

of the bay, strong winds blowing through the Strait of Juan de Fuca can occasionally spill over into Hunter Bay. If the weather forecast for the east Strait is for strong winds, there is a chance that some of that wind will flow over the south end of Lopez and through the saddle into the bay. If so, good protection can be taken in the southern portion of the bay near the head.

For trips to shore, a county dock is located near the eastern entrance point to the bay. A boat launch ramp and parking is also available here. To stretch your legs and pick

Hunter Bay to:		
	Anacortes	12 nm
	Bellingham	26 nm
	Blaine	36 nm
	Blind Bay (Shaw Island)	10 nm
	Eagle Harbor (Cypress Island)	12 nm
	Fisherman Bay (Lopez Island)	12 nm
	Fossil Bay (Sucia Island)	22 nm
	Friday Harbor (San Juan Island)	13 nm
	Roche Harbor (San Juan Island)	20 nm
	Rosario (Orcas Island)	11 nm
	Spencer Spit (Lopez Island)	5 nm
	Victoria (Canada)	32 nm

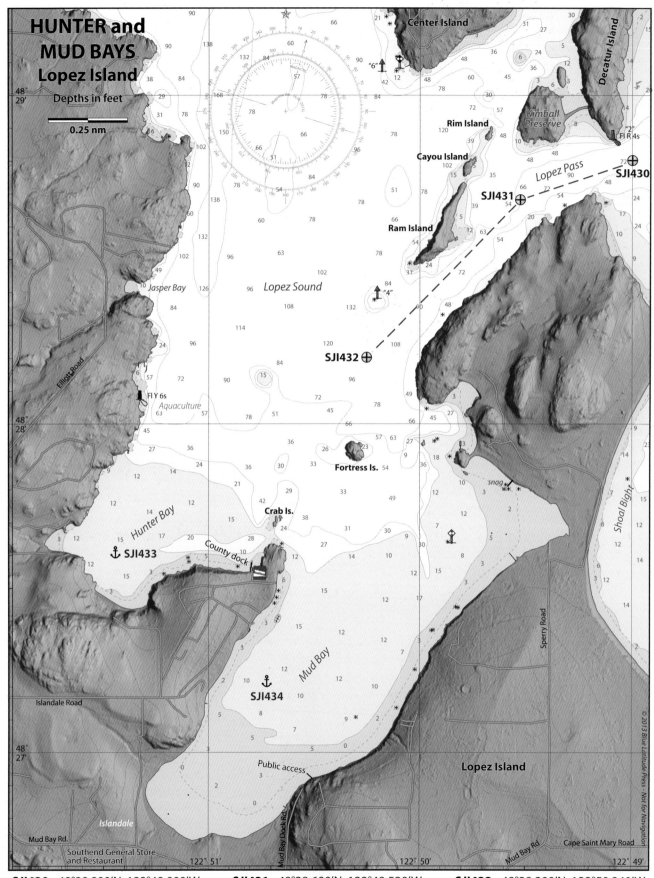

HUNTER and MUD BAYS
Lopez Island

Depths in feet

0.25 nm

Center Island

Decatur Island

Kimball Preserve

"2" Fl R 4s

Rim Island

Cayou Island

Lopez Pass

SJI430

SJI431

Ram Island

Lopez Sound

Jasper Bay

"4"

SJI432

Fl Y 6s

Aquaculture

Fortress Is.

Shoal Bight

Hunter Bay

Crab Is.

County dock

SJI433

Mud Bay

SJI434

Islandale Road

Lopez Island

Public access

Sperry Road

Elliott Road

Islandale

Mud Bay Rd.

Southend General Store
and Restaurant

Mud Bay Dock Rd.

Mud Bay Rd

Cape Saint Mary Road

© 2013 Blue Latitude Press - Not for Navigation

122° 51'

122° 50'

122° 49'

SJI430 - 48°28.800'N 122°49.000'W   **SJI431** - 48°28.690'N 122°49.520'W   **SJI432** - 48°28.200'N 122°50.240'W
SJI433 - 48°27.560'N 122°51.450'W   **SJI434** - 48°27.210'N 122°50.710'W

Harbor seals on Crab Island

up a treat, visit the South End General Store where you can find most of your grocery needs, including island raised meats, fine wines and beers, along with movie rentals. A restaurant is also located within the store and offers a variety of sandwiches, salads, soups and pastries. The store is located at 3024 Mud Bay Road, one and a half miles from the county dock along quiet country roads (southendgen.webs.com).

A dinghy or kayak exploration of nearby Crab Island is always entertaining for the harbor seals who like to sunbathe on the island. Birds and seals alike share the rocky little island and are well worth the trip to watch these curious creatures in their wild habitat. Crab Island, along with nearby Fortress Island, are both National Wildlife Refuges and are closed to public access to protect nesting seabirds and other marine wildlife .

Seabirds on Crab Island with Hunter Bay in the background

Hunter Bay county dock and boat launch

Mud Bay

Mud Bay lies at the southern extreme of Lopez Sound and just around the corner from Hunter Bay. Mud Bay is larger than Hunter Bay with a fairly uniform 1 to 2 fathom depth. Public beach access allows visitors to get off the boat and stretch their legs on the quiet country roads found on the south end of Lopez Island. A mile down the road from Mud Bay is the South End General Store and restaurant, a perfect spot to pick up a treat or enjoy a meal off the boat. With miles of protected shoreline, Mud Bay is also the perfect spot to launch the kayaks and explore the numerous National Wildlife Refuge's rocky islets and islands from the water.

Mud Bay is located at the southern end of Lopez Sound on Lopez Island. Approaches to the bay can be made from Lo-

The anchorage at Mud Bay

pez Sound to the north or Lopez Pass to the east. If approaching via Lopez Pass, the eastern entrance point is marked by a lighted red buoy off the southern most point of Decatur Island. Once through the pass, be aware of a rock danger found west of the pass which is marked by a red day beacon.

Two small islands are found outside the entrance to Mud Bay, Crab Island and Fortress Island. Passage can be taken between the two islands or to the east side of Fortress Island. Keep in mind reefs are found in the small bight east of Fortress Island, so be sure to check your charts. A second reef is located within Mud Bay, southeast of Fortress Island. This small reef is marked with a day beacon.

Anchorage can be taken anywhere within the bay in 1 to 2 fathoms over a mud bottom. The bay offers good southeast and westerly protection. Occasionally, strong winds blowing through the Strait of Juan de Fuca can spill over into Mud Bay. If the weather forecast for the east Strait is for strong winds, there is a chance that some wind could flow over the south end of Lopez Island.

Most of the land surrounding Mud Bay is privately owned, however there is public beach access near the southeast end of the bay. A small beach and stairs leading up from the beach lead to a dirt road. Follow the dirt road a tenth of a mile to Mud Bay Dock Road (gravel road) and another quarter mile to Mud Bay Road. Heading west on Mud Bay

Road for 0.8 miles takes you to the South End General Store and restaurant (southendgen.webs.com). Here you can find most of your grocery needs, including island raised meats, fine wines and beers, along with movie rentals. The restaurant offers homemade salads, soups and sandwiches.

San Juan Islands National Wildlife Refuge

The San Juan Islands National Wildlife Refuge consists of 83 rocks, reefs, grassy islands, and forested islands scattered throughout the San Juan Islands. These islands cover 454 acres and were set aside to protect various marine birds and animals. These refuges are home to colonies of nesting and loafing seabirds including glaucous-winged gulls, cormorants, pigeon guillemots, rhinoceros auklets, black oystercatchers, and a variety of shorebirds. They are also popular sites for bald eagles and harbor seals.

With the exception of Matia Island and Turn Island, all of the national wildlife refuges are closed to the public in order to protect the nesting and resting sites of these birds and animals. Visitors viewing the refuges by boat are asked to stay 200 yards offshore to avoid scaring adult birds off of their nests.

Watmough Bay

Watmough Bay is an anchorage like no other in the San Juan Islands. This off the beaten path locale has not only breathtaking views of the forested fjord-like setting, but also a large sand beach and miles of amazing hiking trails. The beautiful beach and clear water, combined with the grand cliffsides of Chadwick Hill, make this stunning anchorage a high point on most itineraries. With wonderful insight, the majority of the land surrounding this very special area has been preserved and protected for the enjoyment of all who visit the bay. Whether you're looking for a relaxing day at the beach or an invigorated hike up the hill, Watmough Bay is sure to delight and impress!

Watmough Bay is located on the southeastern tip of Lopez Island, near the southern extent of Rosario Strait and nearly due west of Deception Pass. Approaches to the bay can be taken from Rosario Strait to the north, Deception Pass to the east, or the Strait of Juan de Fuca to the south. If approaching from the north via Rosario Strait, be aware of Kellett Ledge, a reef marked by a green buoy, found west

off Cape St. Mary, on the eastern side of Lopez Island. If approaching from the south via the Strait of Juan de Fuca, be sure to consult your charts and navigate with caution around the southern end of Lopez Island due to a number of rocky islets and reefs found in the area. If approaching

Watmough Bay to:		
	Anacortes	12 nm
	Bellingham	23 nm
	Blaine	36 nm
	Blind Bay (Shaw Island)	13 nm
	Deer Harbor (Orcas Island)	20 nm
	Eagle Harbor (Cypress Island)	12 nm
	Fisherman Bay (Lopez Island)	14 nm
	Friday Harbor (San Juan Island)	15 nm
	Roche Harbor (San Juan Island)	24 nm
	Shallow Bay (Sucia Island)	24 nm
	Spencer Spit (Lopez Island)	9 nm
	Victoria (Canada)	27 nm

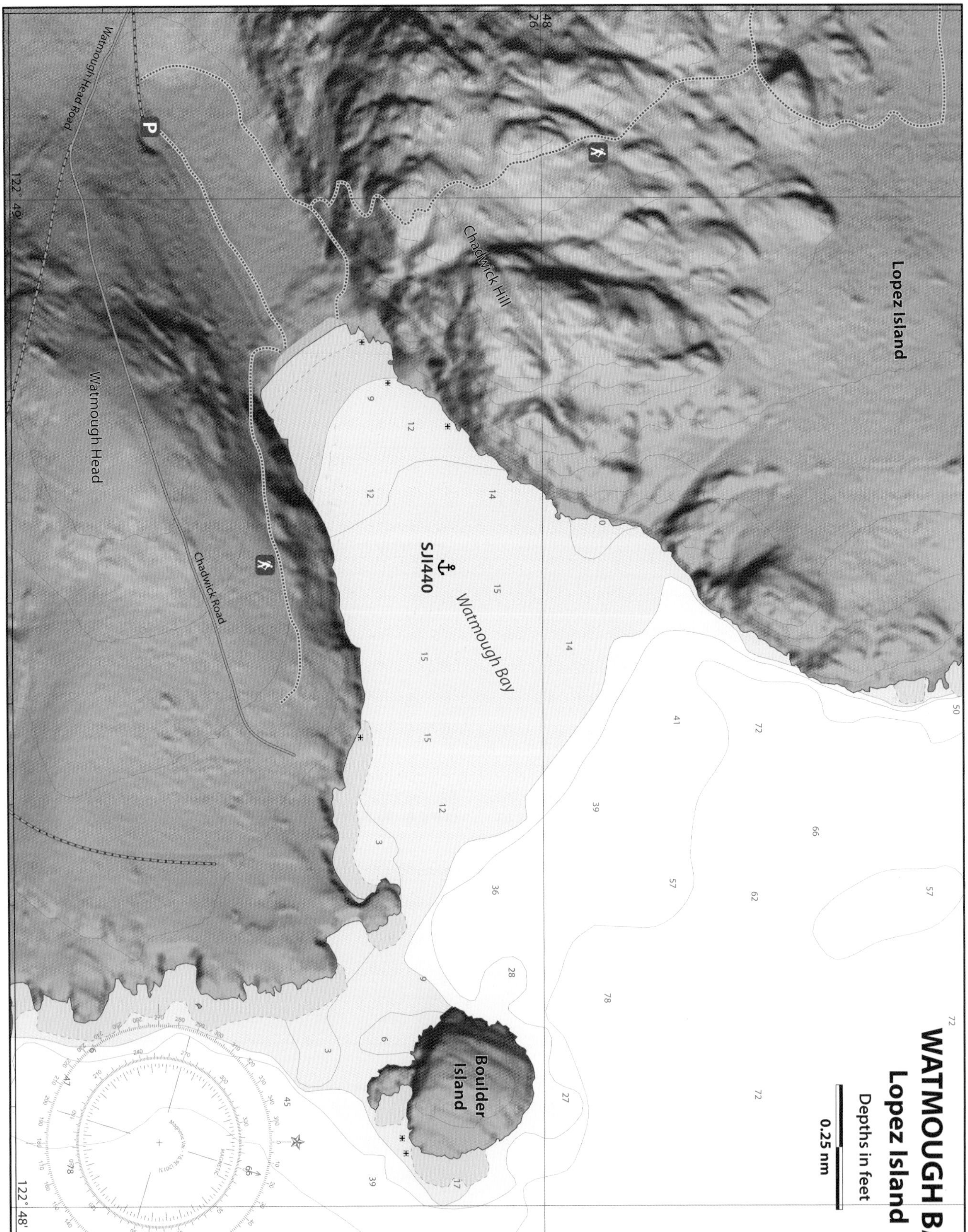

WATMOUGH BAY
Lopez Island
Depths in feet

0.25 nm

Lopez Island

Chadwick Hill

Watmough Bay

SJI440

Boulder Island

Watmough Head

Watmough Head Road

Chadwick Road

P

SJI440 - 48°25.930'N 122°48.630'W

122° 49'

48°
26'

122° 48'

© 2013 Blue Latitude Press - Not for Navigation

from Deception Pass, be aware that strong currents can flow through the pass, up to 8 knots at times, making slack tides a preferable traveling time for some vessels.

The southern shore of Watmough Bay is formed by Watmough Head and nearby Boulder Island. A small passage lies between Watmough Head and the island. Due to shallow depths, this passage should only be used by dinghies and kayaks. Once inside the bay, a fairly uniform shelf extends out from the head of the bay, providing good anchoring depths throughout in 2 to 2½ fathoms over a mostly mud bottom.

View from the top of Chadwick Hill

Watmough Bay provides protection from southerly and westerly weather, but is open to winds from the north or east. During periods of stronger southwesterly or westerly winds (including winds within the Strait of Juan de Fuca), the low stretch of land between Watmough Bay and McArdle Bay does not afford much wind abatement and can occasionally funnel wind through the narrow gap. The anchorage can also experience the occasional wake from commercial traffic traveling through Rosario Strait, however it is infrequent and is over quickly.

Once anchored, Watmough Bay offers a host of activities including lounging on the beach, hiking up Chadwick Hill or exploring the rocky shoreline by kayak or dinghy. The gently sloping sand beach at the head of the bay offers easy beach landings, as well a perfect spot for a toss of the frisbee or a nap in the sunshine. A few trails lead from the beach: a well defined trail heads to a parking lot for visitors arriving by car, a second trail leads around the marsh and splits to head up Chadwick Hill, and a third travels along the southern side of the bay. For those that take the challenge and head up the 450 foot hill, you will be greatly rewarded with sweeping views of the anchorage, the Strait of Juan de Fuca and nearby Whidbey Island - a vista not to miss while here!

The beach at Watmough Bay

Watmough Bay is a special place and will remain preserved and open to all through a number of generous land donations, along with purchases and maintenance by the Bureau of Land Management, San Juan County Land Bank and San Juan Preservation Trust. The beauty and delicate ecology of Watmough Bay will be around for all future generations to enjoy and cherish.

U.S. Department of Agriculture, Farm Service Agency

Aleck Bay

Aleck Bay is the largest of three small coves found at the very southern end of Lopez Island. The bay opens towards the east, offering sweeping views of nearby Whidbey Island and the rugged, snowcapped, Olympic Mountain range. With a handful of National Wildlife Refuge islands surrounding the bay, harbor seal and marine bird sightings are a highlight here.

Aleck Bay is located between Iceberg Point and Watmough Head on the southern end of Lopez Island. Approaches to the bay can be taken from Rosario Strait to the east, Admiralty Inlet to the south and the Strait of Juan de Fuca, Haro Strait or San Juan Channel to the west. Entrance to the bay is protected by a number of off lying rock islets including Colville, Castle, Blind and Swirl Islands, as well as Davidson Rock (marked by a lighted buoy) and Aleck Rocks. These islands are surrounded by rocky reefs and kelp beds, and should be given a wide berth when approaching. Be sure to study your chart and navigate with care when entering the bay.

Anchorage can be taken within Aleck Bay in 4 to 7 fathoms over a mostly mud bottom. The bay offers protection from west and north winds, but is open to weather from the east and southeast. Because the bay lies near the open waters of the Strait of Juan de Fuca, weather here may be different at times than the weather experienced in the more sheltered areas of the San Juan Islands.

While there is no public beach access within Aleck Bay, Blackie Brady County Park, located around the corner in Hughes Bay, is a small niche open to the public. Other activities for the area include kayak or dinghy exploration of the intricate shoreline and nearby rocky islands.

Aleck Bay to:		
	Anacortes	14 nm
	Bellingham	26 nm
	Blaine	39 nm
	Blind Bay *(Shaw Island)*	16 nm
	Clark Island	20 nm
	Eagle Harbor *(Cypress Island)*	15 nm
	Echo Bay *(Sucia Island)*	26 nm
	Friday Harbor *(San Juan Island)*	13 nm
	Reid Harbor *(Stuart Island)*	25 nm
	Roche Harbor *(San Juan Island)*	22 nm
	Spencer Spit *(Lopez Island)*	11 nm
	Victoria *(Canada)*	25 nm

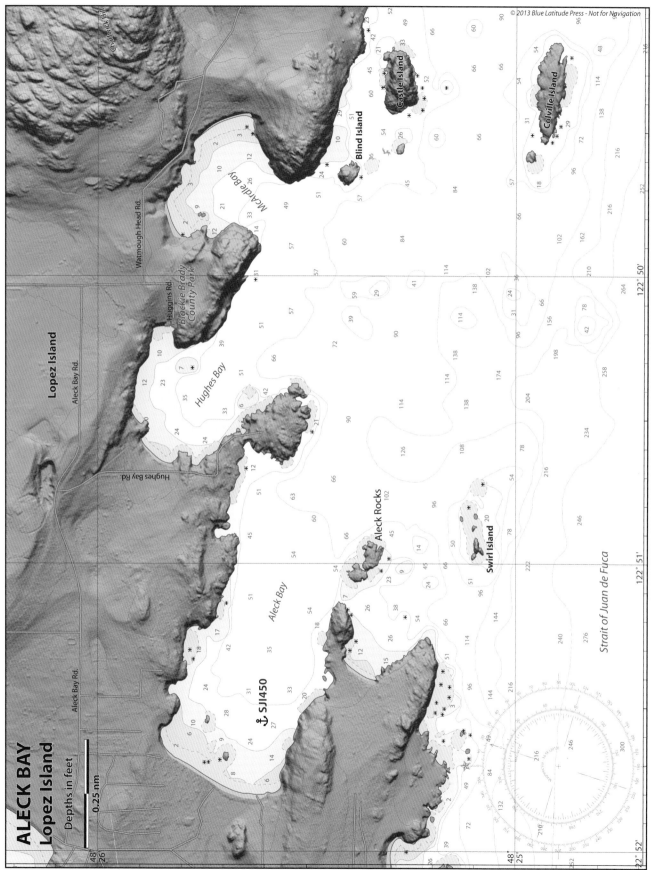

ALECK BAY
Lopez Island

Depths in feet

0.25 nm

SJI450 - 48°25.600'N 122°51.550'W

© 2013 Blue Latitude Press - Not for Navigation

Mackaye Harbor

Mackaye Harbor sits at the southern edge of the San Juan archipelago, allowing for sweeping views of the Strait of Juan de Fuca and the myriad of rocky islets protecting the entrance to the harbor. Found at the southern end of Lopez Island, Mackaye Harbor and nearby Richardson, once dominated the fishing industry with canneries and fishing fleets lining the shores. Today, this peaceful harbor offers boaters a relaxing time on the water with incredible sunset views of the Olympic Mountain range. A small county boat launch is also located in the harbor for trailer boats looking to explore and fish the waters on Lopez's southern shore.

Mackaye Harbor is found at the southern end of Lopez Island, near the confluence of the Strait of Juan de Fuca, Haro Strait and Rosario Strait. Approaches to the harbor can be made via the Strait of Juan de Fuca and Haro Strait to the west, San Juan Channel to the north, Rosario Strait to the east and Admiralty Inlet to the south. Due to commercial traffic and various islands and hazards, it is important to read your charts ahead of time and to have them present when navigating this area.

If approaching from San Juan Channel, be aware that strong currents and tidal rips are found in the constricting area of the channel between the southern end of San Juan and Lopez Islands. If approaching from the west, south or east via one of the straits, be cautious of commercial traffic as a number of shipping lanes are found throughout this area. When approaching the entrance to Mackaye Harbor from the north or west, be aware of the maze of rocky islets, kelp beds and shallow areas found west of the harbor. Depending on the draft of the boat and local knowledge, a few different approaches may be taken into the harbor. The most hazard-free route from San Juan Channel is Middle Channel, which heads west of Whale Rocks, and passes south of Long Island and Hall Island. If approaching via Haro Strait, passage can be taken south of Salmon Bank, a shallow area

Mackaye Harbor to:		
Anacortes	18 nm
Bellingham	30 nm
Blaine	41 nm
Blind Bay (Shaw Island)	13 nm
Clark Island	23 nm
Eagle Harbor (Cypress Island)	18 nm
Fossil Bay (Sucia Island)	25 nm
Friday Harbor (San Juan Island)	10 nm
Hunter Bay (Lopez Island)	12 nm
Roche Harbor (San Juan Island)	20 nm
Spencer Spit (Lopez Island)	15 nm
Victoria (Canada)	23 nm

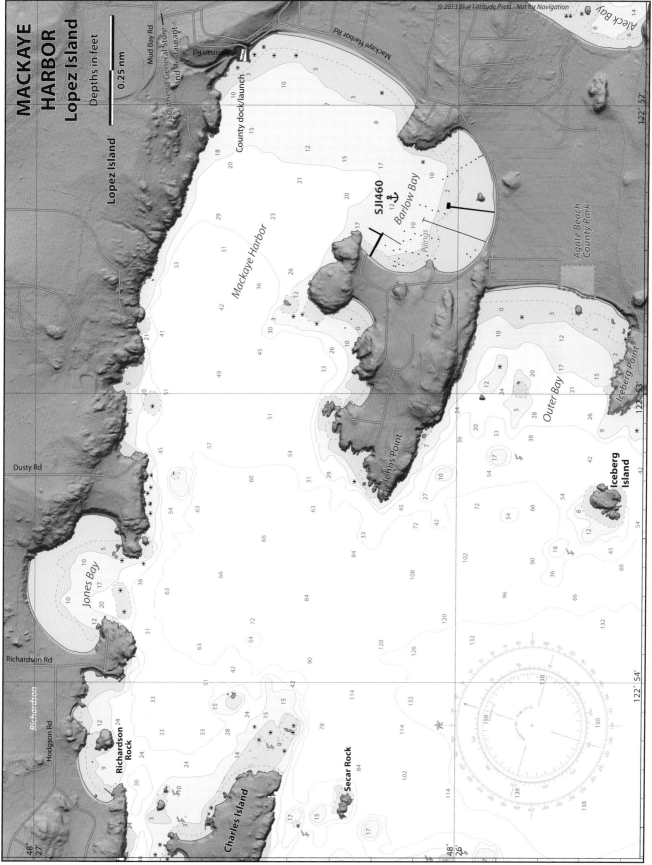

MACKAYE
HARBOR
Lopez Island
Depths in feet

0.25 nm

Mud Bay Rd

Southend General Store
and Restaurant

Lopez Island

© 2013 Blue Latitude Press - Not for Navigation

Aleck Bay

Mackaye Harbor Rd

Norman Rd

County dock/launch

Barlow Bay

SJI460

Pilings

Agate Beach
County Park

Mackaye Harbor

Iceberg Point

Outer Bay

Dusty Rd

John's Point

Iceberg
Island

Jones Bay

Richardson Rd

Richardson

Hodgson Rd

Richardson
Rock

Charles Island

Secar Rock

48° 27'

48° 26'

122° 52'

122° 53'

122° 54'

Sunset off Johns Point with the Olympic Mountains in the background

County dock and boat launch at Mackaye Harbor

found south of Cattle Point. The southern end of Salmon Bank is marked by a lighted gong buoy.

Once inside the harbor, anchorage can be taken in Mackaye Harbor or the inner Barlow Bay in 2 to 4 fathoms over a mostly mud bottom. Keep in mind that a number of pilings and a sunken boat are reported on the NOAA chart for Barlow Bay. A marina, docks and mooring buoys are found within the bay, however these are privately owned and not open to the public. The anchorage offers protection from nearly all directions except from the west near the entrance to the harbor. Because the anchorage is located near the east entrance to the open Strait of Juan de Fuca, weather may be different here at times than the interior of the San Juan Islands. Wrap around swell from the open waters found south of here can also occasionally enter the anchorage, creating a slight roll.

While much of the shore-side land around the harbor is privately owned, beach access can be found at the county boat launch ramp and dock. The South End General Store and restaurant is located a half a mile from the county dock, and can be reached by heading north on Norman Road. Here you can find most of your grocery needs, including island raised meats, fine wines and beers, along with movie rentals. The restaurant offers homemade salads, soups and sandwiches.

A short dinghy ride or kayak excursion around Johns Point leads to Outer Bay and Agate Beach County Park. Agate Beach is a small park with beach access, picnic tables and a pit toilet. The beach is named after the smooth and colorful agate rocks found here. From Agate Beach County Park, you can also access the public lands at Iceberg Point.

Chapter 6
Shaw Island

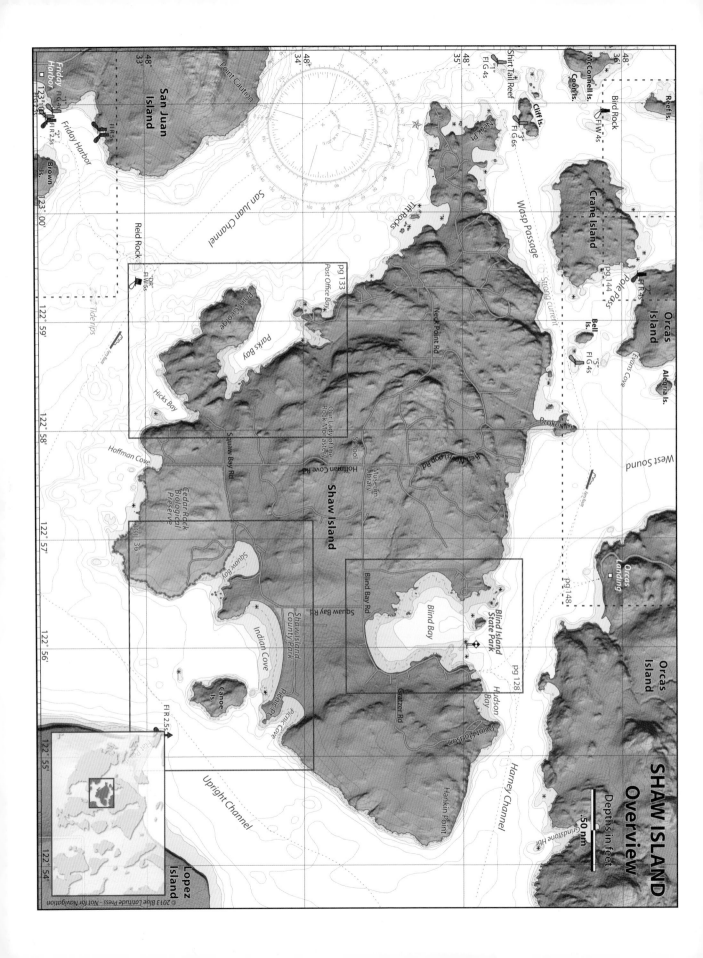

SHAW ISLAND
Overview

Depths in feet

50 nm

Shaw Island

Located in the heart of the San Juan Islands, Shaw Island is 7.7 square miles in size with an approximate year round population of 240 people. Although Shaw Island is serviced by the Washington State Ferries, it has managed to retain its quiet, rural ambiance, taking visitors back to a simpler time. While the island holds only one commercial establishment, the Shaw Island General Store and Silver Bay Cafe, it draws people to the island with its natural beauty, quiet country roads, and well protected anchorages.

Many visit Shaw Island to take advantage of the quiet and relatively flat paved roads to explore the scenic farm lands by bicycle, catching the ferry over for the day, or camping at the county park. Those visiting by boat have the added perk of being able to explore the island by both land and water, while being able to sleep on their boat in a picturesque, quiet anchorages. The island's general store and cafe, offers locals and visitors a historic and waterfront shopping location with everything you might need or want, including homemade meals from their cafe and even overnight accommodations.

History of Shaw Island

Like many of the islands found within the San Juan Archipelago, the original inhabitants of Shaw Island were the Coast Salish people. Evidence of seasonal or possibly year round camps can be seen scattered along Shaw Island's shoreline in the form of midden (or) shell beaches. The Coast Salish people occupied the San Juan area centuries before the first arrival of European explorers and settlers.

European and American settlers began arriving on the island in the late 1800's. Like with many of the islands in the San Juans, early settlers relied on the island's abundant natural resources of rich soils for farming, plentiful salmon runs and thick forests for lumber. In 1887, Shaw Island's first school opened its doors. This small one room log cabin was used for only a few short years before a second school was constructed in 1890. The school, still in use to this day by Shaw Island children, remains the longest continuously operated school in Washington state.

To take advantage of the growing fishing industry, the Shaw Island Canning Company was established in 1912 to process, preserve and can the massive quantities of fish that

In 1976, Shaw Island became home to four nuns of the Franciscan Sisters of the Eucharist. Dedicated to serving the needs of a community, the nuns moved to the island to run the store, ferry terminal, small marina and post office. For nearly 30 years, the nuns were a famous sight for ferry passengers, wearing their brown habits and florescent safety vests, directing ferry traffic and operating the terminal. In 2004, the aging nuns retired their operation at Shaw Island, and moved to Oregon. The store was sold and ferry operations were transferred to the current owners and operators.

Sights to See

While much of the sights to see on quiet Shaw Island lie in the form of its natural beauty and peacefulness, the island does have a few attractions to see while visiting. First on the list is the Shaw Island Library and Historical Society. The historical society's museum, which is housed in a small log cabin at the corner of Blind Bay and Hoffman Cove Roads, was once the original post office of Shaw Island. With rotating exhibits, photographs, and a collection of historical artifacts, the museum is an ideal stop for anyone looking to take in the history of the island. Adjacent to the museum is the island's library designed by Shaw Island artist and architect, Malcolm Cameron. Museum and library hours are limited with a current schedule posted on their website at: **www.shawislanders.org/others/library/library.htm**.

Across from the museum and library is the Little Red Schoolhouse, which is listed on the National Register of Historic Places. Built in 1887, the schoolhouse is the oldest continuously run school within the entire state of Washington, serving kindergarten through eighth grade. The original one room school house has recently become a two room schoolhouse to accommodate more students living on the island.

Shaw Island is also home to Our Lady of the Rock Benedictine Monastery. The all-woman monastery is set amidst 300 acres of forest and farmland, where the nuns raise livestock, produce, flowers and herbs. To help support the monastery, the nuns sell fleeces, rovings, battings, spun wool, hides and knit goods from the sheep raised on the farm. Also available are meats, dairy goods and herbs from the farm. Visitors of all faiths are welcome to take part in the work and prayer of their community and farm by contacting the nuns at **www.ourladyoftherock.com**.

Additional sights to see on the island include the Shaw Island General Store and nearby cannery building, and the Shaw Island County Park (also known as South Beach). Further information is available on the general store within the Blind Bay section (page 129), and on the park within the Indian Cove section (page 135).

were being caught in Puget Sound. Over the years, the cannery processed fish, fruit, and vegetables. When the fishing industry declined, the warehouse was used for boat building, storage of feed and lumber for the general store, and even a small chapel for the nuns. The cannery building can still be seen today on the waterfront between the Shaw Island ferry landing and the Shaw General Store.

In 1899, Eugene and Sadie Fowler opened a small store out of their house near Blind Bay, and in 1924, they built a new general store at today's present location near the ferry terminal. After many decades and generations of Fowler family members operating the general store, it was sold in 1958.

Blind Bay

Blind Bay, located on the north side of Shaw Island, is a popular resting spot for many boaters traveling through the San Juan Islands. This quiet, nearly landlocked bay can accommodate a huge number of anchored boats, though you will rarely see more than a few dozen. With a well stocked general store and cafe just a short dinghy ride away and easy ferry access for visiting friends and family, Blind Bay is a choice and beautiful location to enjoy the San Juan Islands.

Blind Bay is reached via Harney Channel, which separates the north end of Shaw Island from the south shore of Orcas Island. Ferry traffic is frequent in this area due to the landing at the northeast point of Blind Bay, and Orcas Landing one mile to the north-northwest of the bay. Keep in mind that ferries have the law of mass behind them as well as restricted maneuverability, so be sure to give them plenty of space and the right of way when transiting this area.

Entrance to Blind Bay can be taken east of Blind Island, the small state park island located at the north end of the bay. A shoal and rocky area extends west from Shaw Island

into the entrance channel to Blind Bay so caution should be taken on approach. The western edge of this is marked by a tall (unlit) day beacon. The western portion of this reef is visible at low tide, but at high tide the reef is completely submerged. Enter the bay mid channel between Blind Island and the marked reef.

Northwest of Blind Island is a second set of reefs, por-

Blind Bay to:		
	Anacortes	16 nm
	Bellingham	23 nm
	Blaine	31 nm
	Echo Bay (Sucia Island)	16 nm
	Fisherman Bay (Lopez Island)	6 nm
	Friday Harbor (San Juan Island)	7 nm
	Roche Harbor (San Juan Island)	11 nm
	Rosario (Orcas Island)	6 nm
	Sidney (Canada)	20 nm
	Spencer Spit (Lopez Island)	5 nm
	Victoria (Canada)	31 nm

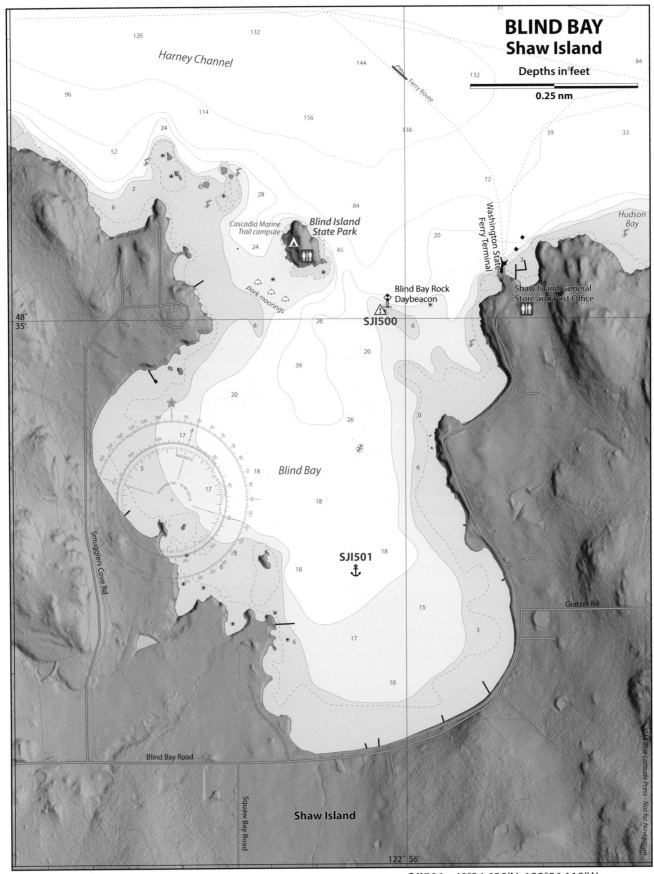

SJI500 - 48°35.015'N 122°56.045'W

SJI501 - 48°34.630'N 122°56.110'W

Day Beacon on Reef

Blind Island

Reefs NW of Blind Island

tions of which are visible at low tide. These unmarked reefs are extensive and are located between Blind Island and the northwestern point of Blind Bay. Because of these unmarked rocks, entrance to Blind Bay is best taken from the eastern side of Blind Island.

Once inside Blind Bay, ample anchorage is available throughout the bay in 3 to 4 fathoms over solid holding mud. Three state park mooring buoys off the southern shore of Blind Island are also available for a nightly fee. A number of private moorings are also located in the southeast portion of the bay.

The bay provides nearly all around protection with the exception of north winds. Orcas Island and to a lesser extent, Blind Island, help to prevent major north wind waves from building in the bay. During southerly blows, Blind Bay provides good protection from wind-driven waves with a solid holding mud bottom.

One of the main shoreside attractions at Blind Bay is the historic Shaw Island General Store. Located directly in front of the store and next to the ferry terminal is the small boat and dinghy marina operated by the store. Daily, weekly, or monthly marina moorage for small boats can also be arranged through the store.

Originally opened in 1898, the Shaw Island General Store has a great selection of grocery items including fresh produce from the local farms found on nearby Waldron Island. Movie rentals, apparel, local island crafts, wine, beer, dairy items, meats and fresh baked goods round out the store's general supplies.

Located in back of the store is the waterfront Silver Bay Cafe. The cafe specializes in fresh baked delicacies, gourmet deli sandwiches, homemade soups, you-bake fresh pizzas, espresso drinks, and delicious ice cream treats. All items can also be taken to go, where you can dine al fresco while enjoying the view of Blind Bay at the small waterfront park across from the store.

For those who have guests visiting and lack the sleeping space on board or for guests who prefer their bed to be on solid ground, the General Store also offers two reasonably priced waterfront accommodation options. For further in-

Shaw Island General Store and dock

Camping on Blind Island

Shaw Island ferry terminal

formation on the Shaw Island General Store and the various services they offer, check their website at: **www.shawgeneralstore.com**, or phone them directly at: (360) 468-2288.

Located next to the store is the Shaw Island Post Office. This is a convenient location for all your mailing needs including general delivery, priority shipping, and sending out post cards to all your loved ones. The office is open Monday through Friday, from 8am to 4pm, although the last pick up is at 3:30pm. Contact the office at: (360) 468-2157.

Located between the post office and the ferry terminal is a large, red waterfront warehouse. This building was originally built for the Shaw Island Canning Company in 1912. The cannery was later used for boat building, as well as a warehouse for feed and lumber sold through the general store.

Additional island activities include an island walking tour to the Shaw Island library, the Historical Society museum, the Little Red Schoolhouse and the sand covered beach at Shaw Island County Park. Detailed information on these sights can be found at the start of the chapter on page 126.

No trip to Blind Bay would be complete without a kayak or dinghy excursion to Blind Island. Blind Island is a state park and open to visitors year round. Part of the Cascadia

Canada Goose

If you are lucky enough to visit the San Juan Islands during the spring and early summer months, you will have a good chance to spot a family of Canada Geese paddling past your boat.

The geese, which are native to North America, generally lay their eggs in the spring months, with the golden colored goslings hatching a month later. Their nests are located in small depressions on the ground and usually close to the shoreline. Both monogamous parents vigorously protect the nest site, with the female primarily incubating the eggs. After nesting, and towards the beginning of summer, the geese undergo an annual molting period where they are flightless for approximately four weeks before they regrow their wing feathers. During this time, geese tend to congregate in open grasslands near water where they are better able to spot approaching prey and can escape to open water.

Blind Bay, including Blind Island, is a popular spotting location, as well as favorite area for nesting geese. Should you hear a hissing sound while walking in the area, be aware that you have most likely stumbled upon a nest, and you are being given a stern warning to steer clear. Canada Geese weigh anywhere between five to eighteen pounds and can have a wing span of four to five feet, so be sure to heed the warning and give the soon-to-be parents their privacy.

Marine Trail system, the island is a popular camping destination for kayakers and boaters exploring the islands. During the spring months, the island is covered with lush wild flowers, and is home to families of Canada geese and their newly hatched golden-colored goslings. Blind Island is also a great vantage point to capture the perfect picture of snow capped Mt. Baker, a Washington State Ferry and the surrounding San Juan Islands. The island has a few fire pits as well for evening campfires under the stars.

The rest of Blind Bay is also great for exploring. The large bay is an ideal spot for kayakers looking for protected paddling waters. Bald eagles, great blue herons and Canada geese frequent these waters. At low tide, harbor seals can be found napping on the reefs northwest of Blind Island. Brightly colored purple, or ochre, sea stars become exposed and millions of mussels can be seen clinging to the well-flushed pilings of the Shaw Island ferry terminal. For kayakers craving a little more adventure or those with a fast dinghy, take the one mile trip across Harney Channel to Orcas Landing on Orcas Island. A dinghy dock is available at Orcas Landing as well. Be aware that Harney Channel can be a busy thoroughfare, especially during the summer months so be prepared for traffic. Current also flows through Harney Channel so consult your current atlas when planning your trip across the channel.

Wikimedia Commons: Dan Huntington

Parks Bay

Parks Bay is a jewel, very near but hidden from summer's hustle and bustle in Friday Harbor. Lying only 2 miles northeast of Friday Harbor, Parks Bay is a quiet piece of solitude on the southern shores of Shaw Island. Since the majority of land surrounding the anchorage has been donated to the University of Washington and protected by a land trust, Parks Bay has the isolated feel of a remote island. For this reason, wildlife here is abundant with small deer found grazing along the water's edge, seals popping their heads up to survey the anchorage, and bald eagles soaring overhead.

Entrance to Parks Bay is taken via San Juan Channel. When approaching from the south, be sure to take note of Reid Rock, located near the middle of San Juan Channel across from Friday Harbor on San Juan Island. Enter Parks Bay mid channel to avoid rocks lying close to shore off the peninsula forming the bay's western shore.

Anchorage can be taken inside the bay in 2 to 9 fathoms over a mostly mud bottom. Much of the bay is deep, though shallower anchoring can be found towards the head of the bay and closer to the shoreline. Anchorage is also available tucked into the small cove at the north end of the bay. The shoreline at the north end of the bay is rocky and the bottom contour is steep so make sure your swinging radius is clear of the rocks.

Charts of the bay also show submerged pilings and logs, as well as moorings. During a survey completed at low tide in 2011, many of the piling locations illustrated on the chart could not be located. While this does not mean that the pil-

Parks Bay to:		
	Anacortes	19 nm
	Bellingham	26 nm
	Blaine	31 nm
	Echo Bay *(Sucia Island)*	16 nm
	Fisherman Bay *(Lopez Island)*	5 nm
	Friday Harbor *(San Juan Island)*	2 nm
	Roche Harbor *(San Juan Island)*	10 nm
	Rosario *(Orcas Island)*	10 nm
	Sidney *(Canada)*	18 nm
	Spencer Spit *(Lopez Island)*	8 nm
	Victoria *(Canada)*	27 nm

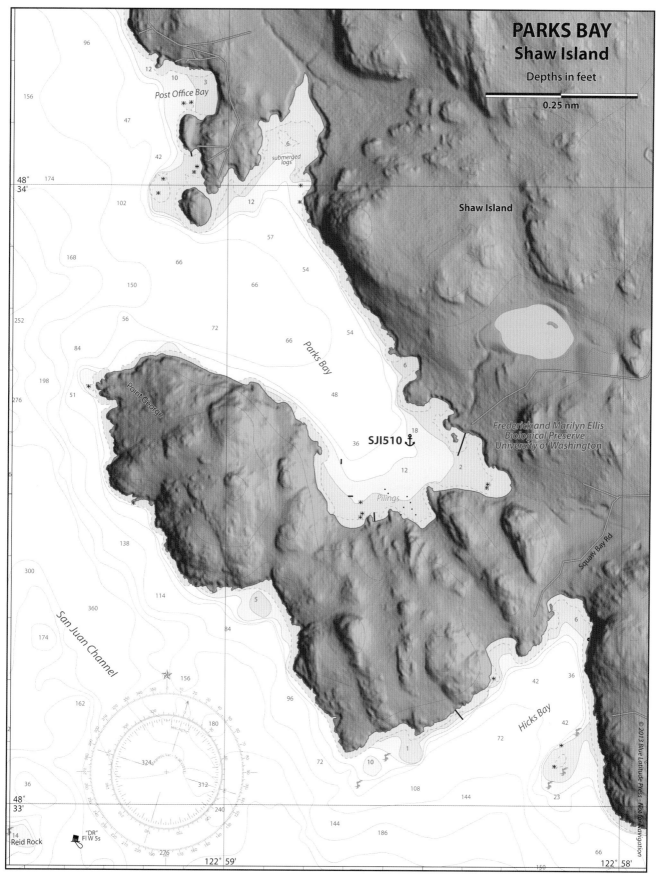

PARKS BAY
Shaw Island

Depths in feet

0.25 nm

Shaw Island

Post Office Bay

submerged logs

Parks Bay

Point George

SJI510 ⚓

Frederick and Marilyn Ellis
Biological Preserve -
University of Washington

Pilings

Squaw Bay Rd

San Juan Channel

Hicks Bay

© 2013 Blue Latitude Press - Not for Navigation

"DR"
Fl W 5s

Reid Rock

48° 34'

48° 33'

122° 59'   122° 58'

SJI510 - 48°33.590'N 122°58.520'W

pilings and logs do not exist, care should be taken when anchoring as the pilings may be deeper underwater. One piling was found during the survey, although it's location was in an area that shows no pilings on the chart. Often, this piling is marked with a float installed by fellow boaters. Keep in mind that it is possible that other pilings may also be located in this area.

Due to the surrounding protected and private land, trips to shore are not allowed. For those boats traveling with pets, this anchorage is best suited as a lunch stop only. Parks Bay is also part of the Shaw Island Marine Preserve, and fishing within the bay is restricted in order to preserve the underwater habitat. To check for current updates on fishing restrictions within the Shaw Island Marine Preserve, check the Department of Fish and Wildlife website at: **www.wdfw.wa.gov/fishing/mpa/shaw_island.html.**

Although a few restrictions limit some activities within the bay, do not let them prevent a stop at this beautiful, serene anchorage. The limitations are there to enhance and protect the natural ecosystem of the San Juan Islands.

One of the best activities in Parks Bay is exploring the shoreline by kayak or dinghy. A quiet paddle around the bay is most often rewarded with sightings of wildlife found throughout the islands. Black-tail deer, harbor seals, bald eagles, cormorants and great blue herons are common sightings in the area. Make sure to have your binoculars ready when visiting Parks Bay!

Shaw Island Biological Preserves

The University of Washington operates five biological preserves on San Juan and Shaw Islands. Through deeded land donations, the University acquired nearly 1,000 acres of land on the south side of Shaw Island. The Frederick and Marilyn Ellis Biological Preserve (donated by Frederick and Marilyn Ellis) includes 496 acres surrounding the Parks Bay area on Shaw Island. The Cedar Rock Biological Preserve, donated by Bob Ellis, is 370 acres of land nearly adjacent to the Fred and Marilyn Ellis Preserve. The Cedar Rock Preserve trails are open to the public during daylight hours only. The entrance and guest book sign in are located along Hoffman Cove Road. Both preserves are administered by the Friday Harbor Laboratories and provide a unique environment for students to study the natural environment.

Indian Cove

With a lengthy stretch of soft, golden colored sand, the shores of Indian Cove, enchant many a boat traveling through Upright Channel. Located on Shaw Island's southeast side, this quiet cove is the perfect stop for those looking to get off the boat and wiggle their toes in the warm sand, or to enjoy a lively game of bocce or frisbee on the beach. Shallow waters are found at the head of the cove, and with the approach of low tide, the beach nearly doubles in size. Indian Cove is also home to Shaw Island County Park, where campers, kayakers and bikers alike are found enjoying the soft, sandy shoreline and beautiful sunrises over Lopez Island.

Entrance to Indian Cove is taken via Upright Channel, which is the narrow waterway separating the southeastern shore of Shaw Island from the northwestern tip of Lopez Island. At its narrowest, off Flat Point on Lopez Island, swirls of current flooding and ebbing can be found. Upright Channel is also used by the Washington State Ferries on passages to and from Friday Harbor and Sidney, so be sure to keep an eye out for ferry traffic.

The eastern portion of the cove is protected by Canoe Island. A small, shallow passage is found between the north end of Canoe Island and the mainland shore of Shaw Island. This shallow passage is marked by a thick bed of kelp, and is bordered to the north by a large reef. For this reason, passage is not recommended for boats.

Indian Cove to:		
	Anacortes	16 nm
	Bellingham	23 nm
	Blaine	33 nm
	Eagle Harbor (Cypress Island)	12 nm
	Echo Bay (Sucia Island)	20 nm
	Fisherman Bay	3 nm
	Friday Harbor (San Juan Island)	4 nm
	Jones Island	8 nm
	Roche Harbor (San Juan Island)	13 nm
	Rosario (Orcas Island)	7 nm
	Sidney (Canada)	21 nm
	Spencer Spit (Lopez Island)	5 nm

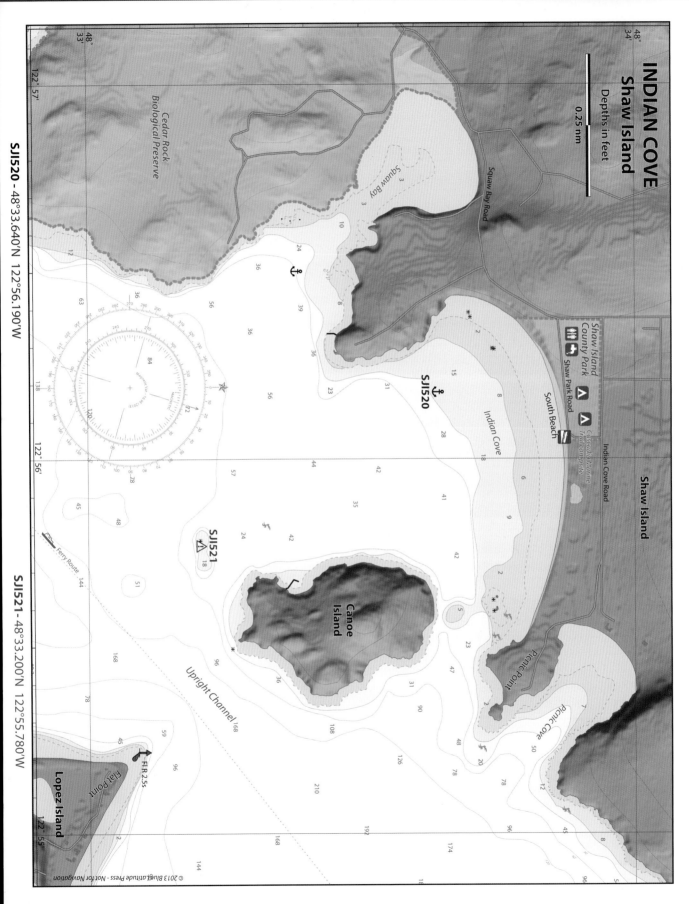

INDIAN COVE
Shaw Island

Depths in feet

0.25 nm

Squaw Bay

Squaw Bay Road

Cedar Rock
Biological Preserve

Shaw Island
County Park

Shaw Park Road

Cascadia Marine
Trail campsite

South Beach

Indian Cove

Indian Cove Road

Shaw Island

Picnic Point

Picnic Cove

SJI520

SJI521

Canoe
Island

Upright Channel

Ferry Route

Flat Point

Fl R 2.5s

Lopez Island

SJI520 - 48°33.640'N 122°56.190'W

SJI521 - 48°33.200'N 122°55.780'W

© 2013 BlueLatitude Press - Not for Navigation

136

Canoe Island

Upright Channel

Lopez Island

Reef SW of Canoe Island

A second reef, marked by a kelp bed, is found off the southwestern shore of Canoe Island. This reef lies approximately 250 yards southwest of the island. While passage can be taken between this reef and Canoe Island, it is recommended to give this unmarked reef ample room and pass well to the west side of the reef when entering Indian Cove.

Once inside Indian Cove, anchorage can be taken throughout the bay in 3 to 7 fathoms over a solid sand and mud bottom. The head of the cove becomes shallow so be sure to check the tide tables to make sure you have plenty of water under the keel. This anchorage provides good protection from west, north and east winds, but is exposed to winds from the south. The cove may also experience a slight roll from the occasional ferry passing by, but the wake is short lived and the ferries end service in the late evening.

Public access to the beach is found on the northwest side of the cove, in front of the county park. The park's boat launch ramp is the dividing line between public and private land. Land west of the ramp is park land and east of the ramp is private land. Dinghy trips to shore are made easy by the soft sand and shallow water.

At the head of the cove is the Shaw Island County Park, which is also part of the Cascadia Marine Trail system. This park is popular with kayakers and campers alike due to its beautiful beach, central location and protected bay. Park amenities include water (shut off during the winter months), restrooms, eleven campsites, a covered shelter, fire pits (firewood is available for sale), a boat launch ramp, and even a solar station for charging small electronic devices like cell phones and iPods. For further information regarding the park including a park map, contact San Juan County Parks by phone: (360) 378-8420, or check their website at: **www.sanjuanco.com**.

Indian Cove is a wonderful location with a wealth of activities for people of all ages. Children love to hit the beach to explore and build forts from drift wood. Those traveling with dogs will enjoy the beach and long stretches of running room to tire out your pup before returning to the boat. Indian Cove is also a great place for kayakers to paddle the shoreline in protected waters. A number of small coves are found in this area, including Picnic Cove, Squaw Bay, Hoffman Cove and Hicks Bay. All are great locations for shoreline explorations by dinghy or kayak.

For hikers, Indian Cove is a good location (depending on the current weather) to leave the boat in order to explore the trails found at the University of Washington's Cedar Rock Biological Preserve.

For those interested in getting off the boat and stretching their legs, a number of nearby walks are within the area. While a number of these walks follow paved roads crossing the island, traffic is minimal, allowing you to enjoy the local scenery without having to dodge cars. One of the most scenic walks on the island is found at the University of Washington's Cedar Rock Biological Preserve (see the sidebar on page 134). The public is welcome to walk the trails on this 370 acre preserve during daylight hours (closed to the public at night). Because this is a preserve with the intent of low impact on the natural environment, dogs and bicycles are not allowed on the trails. To reach the public entrance to Cedar Rock, follow Squaw Bay Road from the county park to the west for approximately 1.25 miles. At Hoffman Cove Road take a left (south) and head down the road towards Hoffman Cove and the gated entrance. A small enclosure is located at the entrance for guests to sign in and/or leave comments regarding the preserve.

Another popular walk heads north from the county park to Blind Bay, on Shaw Island's north side. From the park, head north on Squaw Bay Road for 0.75 miles until you reach Blind Bay Road, where you will take a right (east) towards the bay. From the road, you will have sweeping views of Blind Bay as well as distant Orcas Island. If you are in need of a few extra supplies or a refreshing ice cream treat for your good exercise deed, continue on for 1.25 miles towards the ferry terminal where the Shaw Island General Store is located (see page 129).

Picnic Cove and Squaw Bay

Picnic Cove and Squaw Bay are two small anchorages located just east and west of Indian Cove. These intimate little locales offer a quiet destination with beautiful sunrise views over the nearby islands. Picnic Cove, lying east of Indian Cove, has a steep-to bottom with anchorage for one or two boats in 7 to 9 fathoms. Around the corner to the west of Indian Cove lies Squaw Bay. Squaw Bay also has anchorage for one or two boats in 4 to 6 fathoms. Both of these small anchorages have shallow water at the heads of the bays, preventing anchoring further within. Private mooring buoys are also found within the bays and may prevent anchoring within certain areas. While the surrounding land at Picnic Cove and Squaw Bay is private, public beach access is available at nearby Indian Cove.

Chapter 7
Orcas and Jones Islands

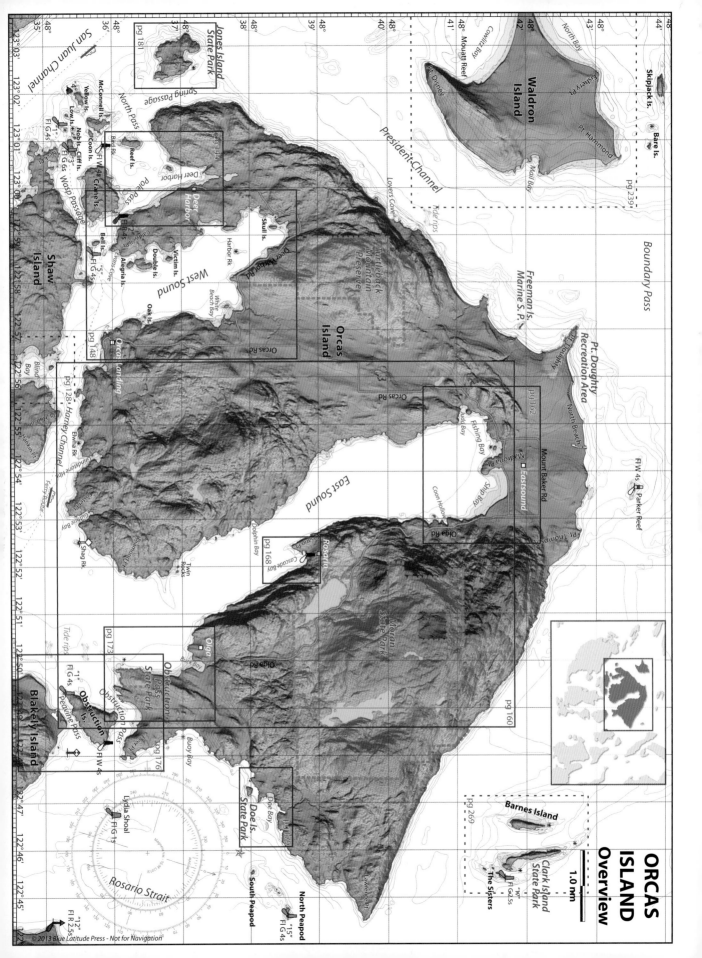

ORCAS ISLAND
Overview

1.0 mm

© 2013 Blue Latitude Press - Not for Navigation

White Beach Bay in West Sound

Orcas Island

With towering mountain views, vibrant pastoral scenes and a seemingly never-ending coastline, Orcas Island is an island like no other. 57 square miles and a 2,409 foot mountain peak make Orcas Island the largest and tallest island in the San Juan archipelago. A scattering of small hamlets dot the shoreline of the island, each with its own unique character and history. Here, wildlife and forest dominate the island, where the occasional traffic jam can be blamed on a wondering, lackadaisical deer. With its unusual horseshoe shape and expansive shoreline, boaters have an abundance of locales to explore.

Orcas Island has a population of just over 5,300 people. Three marinas are found on the island at Deer Harbor, West Sound and Rosario, along with ample anchoring locations. The center of island activity is found at Eastsound, where the small village supports a wonderful waterfront community. Restaurants, hotels, grocery stores, galleries, parks and much more are found within Eastsound, sat-

isfying every need and want. Multiple daily ferry sailings transport visitors and cars to the island along with scheduled seaplane and airline service.

History of Orcas Island

For thousands of years, the coast Salish people were the original inhabitants of Orcas Island, with small family villages and seasonal camps scattered along the shoreline. Numerous midden, or crushed shell beaches can still be seen today from these early settlements. As European explorers began arriving in the 1700's, word of the area's rich natural resources slowly spread. By the 1800's, European hunters, trappers and fishermen began pioneering the area. For the local Salish tribes, many suffered devastation with small pox outbreaks and increased attacks by northern raiding tribes newly equipped with European guns.

Needing a more easily accessible port than the post found at Fort Vancouver on the Columbia River, the Hud-

View from Mt Constitution over Clark Island, Lummi Island and Bellingham

son's Bay Company established Fort Victoria on the southern end of Vancouver Island in 1843. This fort became a vital and strategic base for England as well as one of the main Pacific Northwest trading posts.

Louis Cayou and James Bradshaw, Hudson's Bay employees from Fort Victoria, are credited with being two of the first settlers on Orcas Island in the 1850's. After years of deer hunting expeditions on the island, the two settled in present day Deer Harbor. With the settlement of the land dispute between England and the United States over (see page 186), homesteads began to spring up around the island including those at Eastsound, West Sound, Olga, Doe Bay and Orcas Landing. Access to the water was vital as roads were nearly nonexistent and trails were cumbersome with thick vegetation and steep terrain.

Langdon's Lime Kiln, the first commercial operation on the island, was based out of East Sound, where large rocks of limestone had been found. With bountiful runs of salmon coming through the islands each year, fishing also became a leading industry in the area. Fish traps were erected (they were later banned in 1935) and canneries were built, employing hundreds living in the islands.

Farms were also an important industry on the island. Before irrigation canals were built through Eastern Washington, the islands provided a large amount of fruit, vegetables and wool to the Seattle market. On Orcas Island Italian prunes, apples, pears and strawberries were some of the more successful crops grown.

With regular steamship transport, Orcas Island also became a haven for visitors from the mainland cities looking for a relaxing vacation destination close to home. Orcas' first resort opened in Deer Harbor at Norton's Inn where vacationers rented tents and enjoyed fishing, hiking and beachcombing. Over a hundred years later, the resort remains open today as the Deer Harbor Inn (see page 143). For the adventurous visitor, hiking or wagons could be hired for a trip to the top of Mt. Constitution. In later years, thanks to the philanthropic efforts of Robert Moran, over 5,000 acres, including Mt. Constitution, would be turned into public park land (see pages 170-171 for Robert Moran and Moran State Park).

With increasing development across Orcas, island residents formed the Orcas Power and Light Cooperative (OPALCO) in 1937 under President Franklin D. Roosevelt's Rural Electrification Administration in order to bring power to the island. With 53 miles of overhead power lines and two Worthington General Electric diesel engines, OPALCO established the first power on the island in 1938. By 1951, OPALCO had increased to include coverage of the surrounding islands with more than 200 miles of line on Orcas, San Juan, Lopez and Shaw Islands. In order to obtain cheaper power from the newly constructed Bonneville dam on the Columbia River, OPALCO and the Bonneville Power Administration laid the world's longest submarine power cable, a cable 7.5 miles long, from Anacortes to the San Juan Islands in 1951. Celebrating its 75th anniversary, OPALCO today has over 1,100 miles of power lines serving 20 islands within the San Juan archipelago.

Orcas Island continues on today much like it has over the past decades, warmly welcoming visitors from mainland cities to enjoy the immense beauty of the island.

Deer Harbor

Nestled within the southwestern corner of Orcas Island is the charming little port of Deer Harbor. Protected by the enchanting maze of the nearby Wasp Island group, Deer Harbor offers boaters a large anchorage as well as dock space at the Deer Harbor Marina. With a dramatic cliffside back drop to the west and the Wasp Islands to the south, Deer Harbor offers beautiful vistas in a quiet, secluded setting.

Deer Harbor is located on the southwestern shore of Orcas Island, just west of West Sound and east of Jones Island. Approaches to the harbor can be taken from the main channels of San Juan Channel to the west, President Channel to the north or Harney Channel to the east. With a maze of islands south of the entrance to Deer Harbor, a number of passages lead into the anchorage including Spring Passage, North Pass, Pole Pass and Wasp Passage. Due to the number of islands and reefs in this area, it is important to read your charts carefully and navigate with caution through this area. Tides ebbing and flowing between and around these islands can also produce stronger current in this area, especially through the narrow passages of Pole Pass and Wasp Passage.

If approaching from the west via San Juan Channel, the least obstructed approach to Deer Harbor can be taken through North Pass which lies north of the Wasp Islands and south of Jones Island. North Pass offers deep water passage between Steep Point on the southwestern extreme of Orcas Island and nearby Reef Island. Keep in mind that Reef Island, true to its name, has a number of reefs lying off its western shore, along with reefs and shallow water off the Wasp Islands, so be sure to allow for ample room.

For boats approaching Deer Harbor via Wasp Passage, be sure to have charts and tide tables handy when transiting due to the number of islands and reefs in this area. Approaching from the west, it is best to use the marked route that the Washington State Ferries use through Wasp Passage. For detailed information on Wasp Passage see pages

Michael Bertrand www.michaelbertrandphotography.com

Deer Harbor to:		
Anacortes	20 nm
Bellingham	26 nm
Blaine	28 nm
Blind Bay (Shaw Island)	4 nm
Fisherman Bay (Lopez Island)	9 nm
Fossil Bay (Sucia Island)	12 nm
Friday Harbor (San Juan Island)	5 nm
Jones Island	3 nm
Reid Harbor (Stuart Island)	9 nm
Roche Harbor (San Juan Island)	8 nm
Rosario (Orcas Island)	10 nm
Sidney (Canada)	16 nm

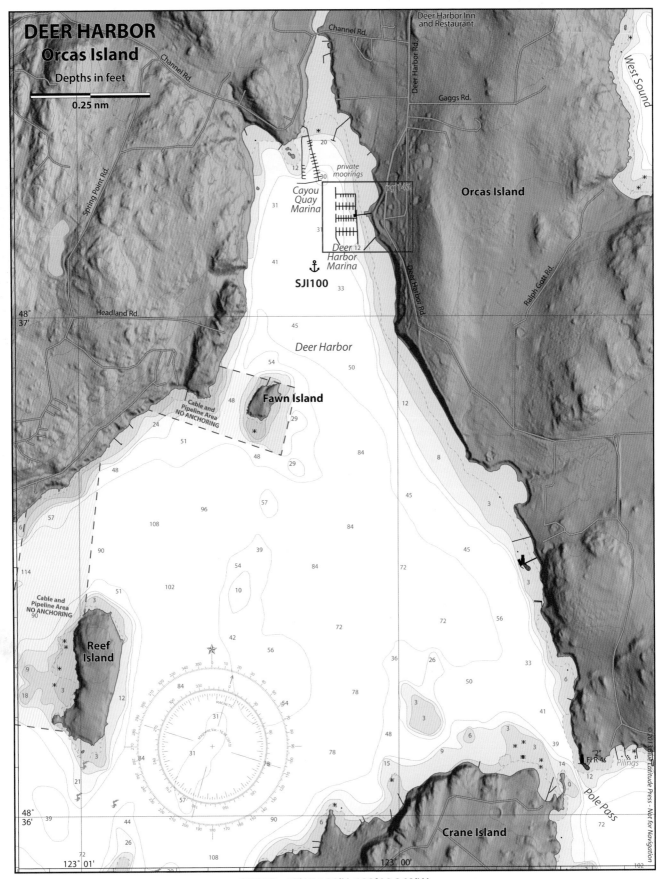

DEER HARBOR
Orcas Island

Depths in feet

0.25 nm

Channel Rd.

Channel Rd.

Deer Harbor Inn and Restaurant

Deer Harbor Rd.

Gaggs Rd.

West Sound

private moorings

pg 146

Orcas Island

Cayou Quay Marina

31

31

Deer Harbor Marina

SJI100

Spring Point Rd.

Ralph Gott Rd.

Deer Harbor Rd.

48° 37'

Headland Rd.

Deer Harbor

Cable and Pipeline Area
NO ANCHORING

Fawn Island

Cable and Pipeline Area
NO ANCHORING

Reef Island

MAGNETIC Var - 16.58 (2013)

Crane Island

Pole Pass

Pilings

Fl R 4s

"2"

48° 36'

123° 01'

123° 00'

SJI600 - 48°37.100'N 123°00.260'W

© 2013 Fine Edge Latitude Press - Not for Navigation

145 and 275. The passage entrance begins between Shirt Tail Reef in the Wasp Islands and Neck Point on Shaw Island's northwestern extreme. Shirt Tail Reef is marked by lighted green beacon #1. Passage heads east between Cliff Island and Neck Point. Lighted green beacon #3 is located on Cliff Island. Once past Cliff Island, boats can turn north and head towards Deer Harbor, passing between the eastern shore of Cliff Island and Crane Island. A large reef, known as Bird Rock, lies between Crane Island and McConnell Island which is marked by a lighted beacon. Pass between Bird Rock and Crane Island, favoring Crane Island.

For boats approaching from the north via President Channel, passage can be taken through Spring Passage. Spring Passage lies between Jones Island and Orcas Island. This passage is large and deep and ties in with North Pass. Be aware of a reef lying off the northeastern shore of Jones Island which is marked by a buoy.

For boats approaching from the east via Harney Channel, Pole Pass or Wasp Passage can be used. See pages 273 and 275 for detailed information on Pole Pass and Wasp Passage. If using Pole Pass, keep in mind that this pass is very narrow and experiences strong current flowing through it so be sure to consult your tidal chart and navigation chart before transiting. Pole Pass lies between Orcas Island and Crane Island. When approaching the pass, a reef is found off the eastern side of Bell Island and is marked by lighted green beacon #5. Passage can be taken either north or south of Bell Island, but keep in mind, shallow water and kelp are found off Caldwell Point on Orcas Island. Pole Pass is marked by lighted red beacon #3 on Orcas Island. The shoreline in this area is rocky and extending reefs and shallow water lie off Crane Island on the north side of the pass.

For boats approaching via Harney Channel using Wasp Passage, the entrance to the pass is marked by lighted green beacon #5. This beacon marks a reef east of Bell Island. Passing south of beacon #5, passage can be taken between Shaw Island and Crane Island. Current can be strong in this area. Once past Crane Island, passage can be taken north towards Deer Harbor between Crane Island and Cliff Island. Be aware of the above mentioned Bird Rock lying between Crane Island and McConnell Island.

Two marinas are located in the harbor, the Deer Harbor Marina and the Cayou Quay Marina. Deer Harbor Marina is the southeastern most marina with transient and permanent moorage options. Cayou Quay Marina is the northern most marina and offers permanent moorage only.

For boats anchoring in Deer Harbor, anchorage can be taken north of Fawn Island near the marinas in 7 to 8 fathoms over a mostly mud bottom. A number of moorings can be found in this area, however they are private and not avail-

Deer Harbor Inn restaurant

The Deer Harbor Waterfront Preserve

able for public use. For trips to shore, public beach access is available at the Deer Harbor Waterfront Preserve located just north of the marina. This two acre preserve was acquired by the San Juan County Land Bank and opened to the public's use. Because this land and the tidal waters are being preserved and protected, it is important not to harm or disturb the surrounding environment. Dogs are allowed on the trails and the meadow as long as they are leashed and that you clean up after your pet.

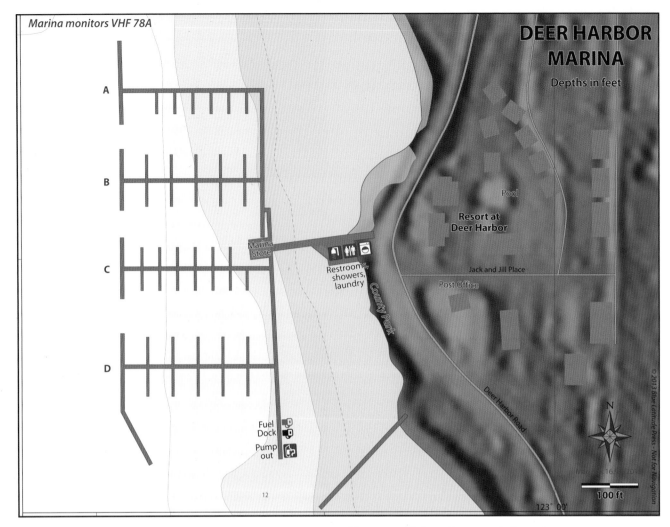

DEER HARBOR MARINA

Depths in feet

A

B

C

D

Marina Store

Restrooms, showers, laundry

Resort at Deer Harbor

Pool

Jack and Jill Place

Post Office

County Park

Deer Harbor Road

Fuel Dock

Pump out

12

© 2013 Blue Latitude Press - Not for Navigation

N

123° 00'

100 ft

Restaurants and Other Services

Deer Harbor Inn Restaurant

The Deer Harbor Inn Restaurant is a wonderful spot to enjoy the view and a delicious meal. Using local ingredients and fresh seafood, the Deer Harbor Inn offers indoor and outdoor seating in a beautiful pastoral setting overlooking the harbor. The restaurant is open nightly for dinners after 5pm. Located a half mile north of the marina on Deer Harbor Road.

Phone: (360) 376-1040

Web: www.deerharborinnrestaurant.com

United States Post Office

Founded in 1893, the Deer Harbor Post Office is a piece of history in this small community. Open Monday through Friday from 8am to 2pm.

Phone: (360) 376-2548   Web: www.usps.com

Deer Harbor Marina

Deer Harbor Marina is located on the southwest end of Orcas Island within Deer Harbor. The marina can accommodate boats up to 120 feet in length with each slip having access to water and power hookups. A fuel dock with easy, open access is operated by the marina. Other services include showers, laundry facilities, a pumpout dock, a small grocery and deli, wireless internet and beach and pool access at the resort. For trips into Eastsound or the ferry terminal, shuttle service is available through San Juan Transit (see page 165).

Deer Harbor Marina
Monitors VHF Channel 78A
5164 Deer Harbor Road
Deer Harbor, WA 98243
(360) 376-3037
mbroman@deerharbormarina.com
www.deerharbormarina.com

View of West Sound and West Sound Marina from the hike at Turtleback Mountain Preserve

West Sound

Located on the western side of Orcas Island, West Sound is a large and protected body of water, filled with numerous nooks and crannies, perfect for the gunkholing boat. Small islands and rocky reefs dot the shoreline, providing interesting locations to spot wildlife from the dinghy or kayak. Tucked into the western edge of the sound is the West Sound Marina. At the head of the bay is the expansive Turtleback Mountain Preserve, which offers sweeping views of the islands throughout its nearly 1,600 acres.

West Sound is found at the southwest end of Orcas Island between Deer Harbor to the west and East Sound to the east. Approaches to the sound can be taken via Harney Channel to the east, which separates Orcas Island and Shaw Island, or from the west via Pole Pass or Wasp Passage. If approaching via Harney Channel, be aware of ferry traffic transiting the channel between the nearby terminals at Orcas Island and Shaw Island.

For boats approaching from the west via Wasp Passage, be sure to have charts and tide tables handy when transiting due to the number of islands, reefs and current in this area. Approaching from the west, it is best to use the marked route that the Washington State Ferries use through Wasp Passage. For detailed information on Wasp Passage see page 275. The passage entrance begins between Shirt Tail Reef in the Wasp Islands and Neck Point on Shaw Island's northwestern extreme. Shirt Tail Reef is marked by lighted green beacon #1. Passage heads east between Cliff Island and Neck Point on Shaw Island. Lighted green beacon #3 is located on Cliff Island. The passage continues east between Cliff Island and Shaw Island, where strong current can be experienced. Lighted green beacon #5 marks a reef lying east of Bell Island. Pass between Shaw Island and the south end of Bell Island, avoiding the reef near beacon #5.

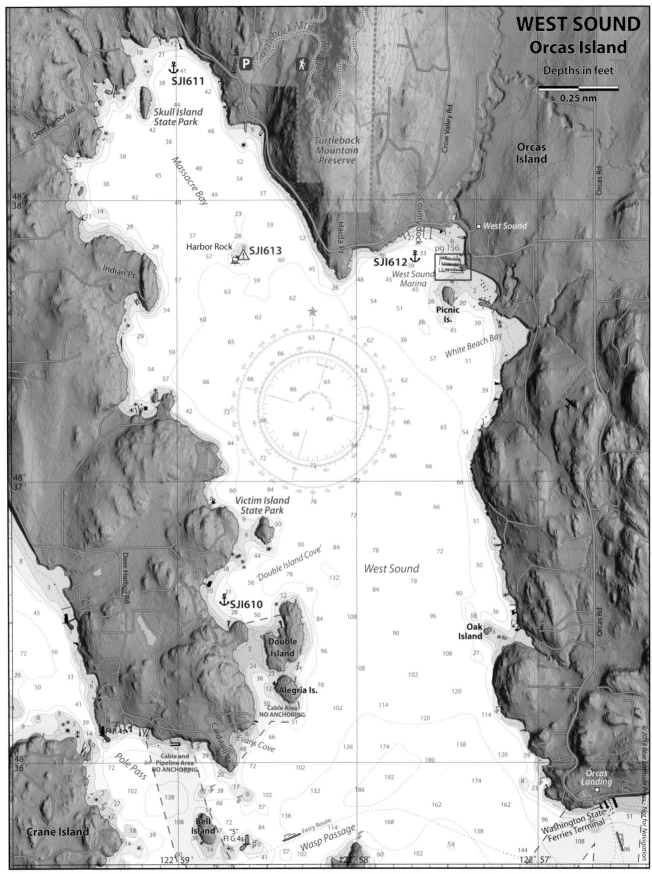

WEST SOUND
Orcas Island
Depths in feet

0.25 nm

Skull Island State Park

SJI611

Turtleback Mountain Preserve

Crow Valley Rd

Orcas Island

Orcas Rd

West Sound

Massacre Bay

Haida Pt

County dock

pg 156

SJI612

West Sound Marina

Harbor Rock

SJI613

Indian Pt

Picnic Is.

White Beach Bay

MAGNETIC

Magnetic Var - 16.98 (2013)

Victim Island State Park

Oak Island

'Double Island Cove'

West Sound

Deer Harbor Rd

SJI610

Double Island

Alegria Is.

Cable Area NO ANCHORING

Evans Cove

Cable and Pipeline Area NO ANCHORING

Crane Island

Pole Pass

Caldwell Pt

Fl R 4s

Bell Island

"5"
Fl G 4s

Ferry Route

Wasp Passage

Orcas Landing

Washington State Ferries Terminal

© 2013 Blue Latitude Press - Not for Navigation

122° 59'

122° 58'

122° 57'

48° 38'

48° 37'

48° 36'

SJI610 - 48°36.580'N 122°58.750'W   **SJI611** - 48°38.480'N 122°59.010'W   **SJI612** - 48°37.800'N 122°57.680'W
                                            SJI613 - 48°37.800'N 122°58.660'W

View of West Sound and Skull Island from the hike at Turtleback Mountain Preserve

If approaching via Pole Pass, keep in mind that this pass is very narrow and experiences strong current, so be sure to consult your tidal chart and navigation chart before transiting (see page 273 for detailed information on Pole Pass). Pole Pass lies between Orcas Island and Crane Island. The shoreline off Crane Island north of the pass is rocky with extending reefs and shallow water. Pole Pass is marked by lighted red beacon #3 on Orcas Island. Once through the pass, passage can be taken either north or south of Bell Island, but keep in mind, shallow water and kelp are found off Caldwell Point on Orcas Island. Reefs are found east of Bell Island, with the eastern most marked by lighted green beacon #5. Due to reefs, there is no passage between Bell Island and beacon #5.

Once within West Sound, there are anchoring options found throughout the sound, as well as moorage options at the West Sound Marina (see page 156) or the San Juan County dock (day use only). Popular anchoring locations can be found within Massacre Bay, Double Island Cove, south of Indian Point and White Beach Bay.

Looking south at Double Island and Victim Island

When traveling in the northern portion of the sound, be sure to locate Harbor Rock which lies roughly near the middle, between Indian Point and Haida Point. This rock is marked by a day buoy.

Double Island Cove

Double Island Cove is a well kept local secret that is off the beaten path, yet lying within the heart of the San Juans. Just moments from the busy waterway of Harney Channel, the secluded anchorage is nestled between the protection of Double and Orcas Islands. Affording nearly all round protection, the cove is a favorite stop to explore two nearby state park islands of Victim Island and Skull Island. Surrounded by the dramatic hills and valleys of Orcas Island, Double Island Cove is a wonderful treat to stumble upon.

Double Island Cove (named by the authors) is located on the western shore of West Sound on Orcas Island and north of Double Island. The approach is via Harney Channel to the east, or Wasp Passage or Pole Pass to the west. If approaching via Wasp Passage (see page 275 for detailed information on the pass), be aware of detached reefs lying off the southeastern side of Bell Island. The eastern most reef is marked by lighted green beacon #5. This passage is also used by the Washington State Ferries so be on the lookout for traffic. If approaching via Pole Pass (see page 273 for detailed information) be sure to note the shallow water and kelp beds found off Caldwell Point on Orcas Island.

To enter Double Island Cove, approach via the east and north side of Double Island and enter mid channel. A small narrow channel lies between the western side of Double Island and Orcas Island, however this channel is not for navigation due to shallow depths and reefs.

Once inside the cove, keep in mind that there are reefs extending off the northwestern tip of Double Island, as well as a large reef extending out from the northern shore of the

Double Island Cove to:		
	Anacortes	18 nm
	Bellingham	25 nm
	Blaine	31 nm
	Eagle Harbor (Cypress Island)	13 nm
	Echo Bay (Sucia Island)	15 nm
	Fisherman Bay (Lopez Island)	8 nm
	Friday Harbor (San Juan Island)	6 nm
	Jones Island	4 nm
	Roche Harbor (San Juan Island)	10 nm
	Rosario (Orcas Island)	8 nm
	Sidney (Canada)	18 nm
	Spencer Spit (Lopez Island)	7 nm

anchorage. A small portion of this reef is visible at low tide. A few mooring buoys are located within the cove, however these are private buoys maintained by local residents.

Anchorage can be taken within the cove in 4 to 9 fathoms over a mostly mud bottom with scattered patches of rock. A small shelf extends out near the western side of the cove providing shallow anchoring depths, with deeper water found near the middle of the cove.

Although most of the surrounding land is privately owned, including Double Island and Alegria Island, Victim Island provides a good stop to get out and stretch your legs. Victim Island is an undeveloped state park island with a few crisscrossing trails providing views of West Sound and Orcas Island. To dinghy ashore, a small sand spit is exposed at low tide off the southwestern shore of the island. Shallower areas along the western shore of the island also provide landing options during higher tides.

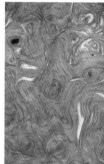
Victim Island State Park

Double Island Cove is also a perfect place to drop the kayak in the water and go for a paddle. With miles of protected water and islands to explore, there's no better way to experience the area than by kayak. 1.75 miles to the north is Skull Island (see page 153), a state park island great for picnicking and tide pooling. Across the sound on the northeastern shore is the public county dock, where boats can tie up for a few hours and enjoy a meal at the West Sound Cafe or walk to the trailhead at Turtleback Mountain for a breathtaking day of hiking (see page 155).

During the summer months, children from the nearby youth camp, Four Winds Westward Ho, can be spotted on the sound in a variety of sailboats, canoes and kayaks, laughing and enjoying island life. The Orcas Island Yacht Club and Sail Orcas also offer youth and adult sailing programs which provide a beautiful backdrop of sailboats in the protected waters of West Sound.

Looking north at West Sound from Victim Island

Massacre Bay

Massacre Bay is located in the far northern reaches of West Sound. Under the protection of nearby Turtle-back Mountain, Massacre Bay offers a beautiful setting with shore access available at Skull Island State Park. This large bay, along with Skull and Victim Islands derive their historic, yet foreboding names from raiding attacks from northern tribes on the Lummi's seasonal camps. Massacre Bay offers a wonderful location to drop the kayak in for a paddle, strap on the hiking boots for a mountain climb or stroll the beach in search of tidepools.

Massacre Bay is located at the northwestern head of West Sound on Orcas Island. Similar to Double Island Cove, approaches can be made via Harney Channel to the east, or Wasp Passage or Pole Pass to the west. If approaching via Wasp Passage or Pole Pass, be sure to consult your navigation charts and tide tables due to numerous reefs in the area and strong currents. For further information, see pages 273 and 275 for Wasp Passage and Pole Pass.

On the approach to Massacre Bay, be sure to locate Harbor Rock within West Sound, lying approximately mid way between Indian Point and Haida Point on Orcas Island. The rock, marked by a day buoy, is found near the entrance to Massacre Bay.

Massacre Bay to:		
Anacortes	20 nm
Bellingham	26 nm
Blaine	32 nm
Deer Harbor *(Orcas Island)*	4 nm
Double Island Cove *(Orcas Island)*	2 nm
Fisherman Bay *(Lopez Island)*	10 nm
Echo Bay *(Sucia Island)*	17 nm
Friday Harbor *(San Juan Island)*	8 nm
Jones Island	6 nm
Roche Harbor *(San Juan Island)*	13 nm
Rosario *(Orcas Island)*	10 nm
White Beach Bay *(Orcas Island)*	1 nm

Anchorage can be taken within the bay in 6 to 8 fathoms over a mostly mud bottom. The shoreline in this area is rocky with a few reefs extending into the bay, including detached reefs lying north of Skull Island. Massacre Bay offers good north, west and east wind protection, but is open to southerly weather. South wind protection can be found at nearby Double Island Cove or Blind Bay on Shaw Island.

For shore side excursions, dinghies or kayaks can be landed at Skull Island, Victim Island or the county dock at White Beach Bay. Nearby Skull Island offers a wonderful island setting to take in the natural beauty of the plant life, marine life and the history of the area. Landing on the white midden, or crushed shell beach, visitors are instantly brought back in time to when the Lummi's used the island and surrounding lands for their seasonal camps. Arriving at low tide exposes the island's rocky shore, creating perfect tidepools for catching a glimpse of tidal marine life. Trails traverse the rocky and sparse island offering great views of the surrounding waters.

For those looking for a little adventure, a dinghy or kayak trip to the county dock at White Beach Bay is a perfect landing spot to tackle the hiking trails on Turtleback Mountain Preserve (see page 155). After an exhilarating hike, treat yourself to a delicious dinner at the West Sound Cafe found near the head of the county dock (see page 155).

Down near the southwestern edge of West Sound is Victim Island. This small island is an undeveloped State Park island with public access. While much of the island's shore is rocky, a couple of small beaches can be found on the western side at low tide to land a dinghy or kayak. Rough trails meander across the island providing nice views of West Sound and Orcas Island.

Dungeness Crab

Dungeness crab is widely known through the San Juan Islands for is sweet and tender meat in both the legs and the body. Named after the Washington port town along the Strait of Juan de Fuca, Dungeness crab is caught both commercially and recreationally in gated pots that lie on the ocean floor. Dungeness have a purplish colored exoskeleton on top and a cream colored belly. Two very strong pincers are used for defense, tearing and grasping so watch your fingers when handling! At approximately 4 to 5 years of age, the male crabs are of legal size to be caught, while the females are returned to the ocean to continue laying eggs. Adult females carry eggs under an appendage on their bellies, where large females can hold over 2.5 million eggs. One of the favored habitats for crab, especially juveniles, is shallow eelgrass beds.

Red Rock (l) and Dungeness (r) Crabs

White Beach Bay

White Beach Bay, found on the eastern shore of West Sound on Orcas Island, is home to the West Sound Marina. A small community is centered around the bay including a county dock, restaurant, lodging, marine chandlery and marina. For boaters, White Beach Bay is also the closest access to the hiking trails found within the nearly 1,600 acre Turtleback Mountain Preserve.

White Beach Bay is located within a small bight on the eastern side of West Sound on Orcas Island. Similar to the approaches to Massacre Bay and Double Island Cove, approaches can be made via Harney Channel to the east, or Wasp Passage or Pole Pass to the west. If approaching via Wasp Passage or Pole Pass, be sure to consult your navigation charts and tide tables due to numerous reefs and strong currents in the area. For further information, see pages 273 and 275 for Wasp Passage and Pole Pass descriptions.

Picnic Island is a small island found near the middle of White Beach Bay that is surrounded by shallow water. A narrow sandy spit extends northeast from the island, connecting it to a small islet. When approaching the bay, it is best to transit around the west and north side of Picnic Island to avoid shallow water found between Picnic Island and Orcas Island.

White Beach Bay to:		
	Anacortes	19 nm
	Bellingham	25 nm
	Blaine	31 nm
	Blind Bay (Shaw Island)	3 nm
	Deer Harbor (Orcas Island)	3 nm
	Double Island Cove (Orcas Island)	1 nm
	Fisherman Bay (Lopez Island)	9 nm
	Fossil Bay (Sucia Island)	15 nm
	Friday Harbor (San Juan Island)	7 nm
	Jones Island	5 nm
	Roche Harbor (San Juan Island)	12 nm
	Rosario (Orcas Island)	9 nm

Anchorage can be taken in the northern portion of the bay in 5 to 7 fathoms, offering both north and east wind protection. A few mooring buoys are found scattered throughout the bay, although these are private and not available for public use. A roughly, 75-foot county dock is also located in this northern portion of the bay. The dock, with tie-ups on either side, is available for public day use (no overnight stays). The West Sound Marina is located north of Picnic Island and offers a fuel dock and transient moorage (see page 156 for detailed marina information).

For trips to shore the county dock provides easy and convenient dinghy and kayak access. Just up from the head of the dock is the West Sound Cafe which offers nightly dinners (closed Tuesdays) overlooking West Sound. The cafe specializes in local, fresh ingredients including seafood. Dinner reservations are recommended: (360) 376-4440 or visit their website at **www.westsoundcafe.com**.

For those looking for an adventure and amazing views of the surrounding islands, hiking trails are found at nearby Turtleback Mountain Preserve. Thanks to the dedicated efforts of the San Juan Preservation Trust, the San Juan County Land Bank, and the Trust for Public Land, nearly 1,600 acres was purchased in 2006 for $18.5 million to protect and preserve the land for public use. Seven miles of trails climb and traverse the mountain, affording views of the San Juan Islands, Gulf Islands, Olympic Mountains and Cascade Mountains from atop the 1,519 foot peak.

The south trailhead for Turtleback Mountain is located approximately 1.35 miles from the head of the county dock. To reach the trailhead, follow Deer Harbor Road to the west and around Haida Point. Stay on Deer Harbor Road until you reach an open field and Wild Rose Lane. Take a right onto Wild Rose Lane, following the field until you reach the parking lot for the trailhead. From here, the trail begins heading up the mountain to a series of peaks and overlooks, connecting with numerous trails. Be sure to bring a lunch, water and a camera along to enjoy this pristine and undeveloped preserve. For further information on the Turtleback Mountain Preserve, including trail maps and donation information, visit the San Juan Preservation Trust website at: **www.sjpt.org** or the San Juan County Land Bank website at: **www.sjclandbank.org**.

West Sound county dock

West Sound county dock

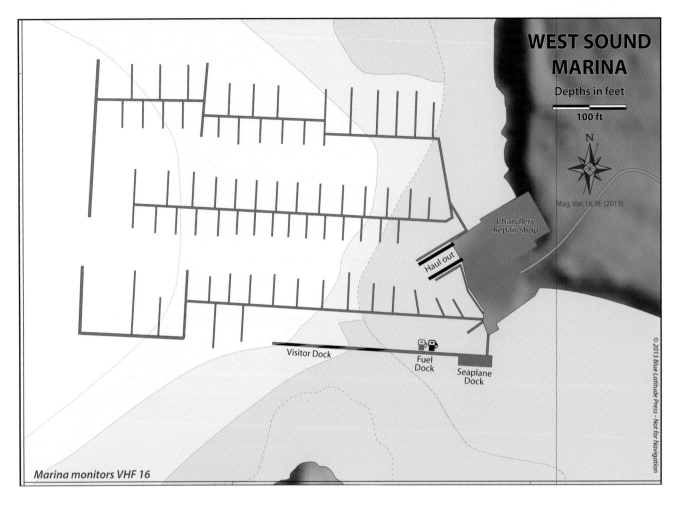

WEST SOUND MARINA

Depths in feet

100 ft

N

Mag. Var. 16.9E (2013)

Chandlery Repair Shop

Haul out

Visitor Dock

Fuel Dock

Seaplane Dock

Marina monitors VHF 16

© 2013 Blue Latitude Press - Not for Navigation

West Sound Marina

Located on the northeast shore of West Sound, West Sound Marina is the largest marina on Orcas Island. The marina has over 180 slips and can accommodate boats up to 80 feet in length. The majority of the slips are for permanent moorage, although a 250 foot side-tie dock is available for visitor moorage. Each slip has access to power (30 amps) and water hook ups. Services include a gas and diesel fuel dock, pumpout station and showers.

The marina also operates a travel lift, repair and maintenance yard, storage facility and marine chandlery. The 30-ton travel lift is able to accommodate boats up to an 18 foot beam, with a covered warehouse able to house a boat up to 60 feet in length. Indoor and outdoor dry storage for trailer boats is also available. The marina store stocks a wide variety of marine chandlery items including engine parts, propane, charts, ice and snacks. A seaplane dock is located next to the fuel dock with Kenmore Air providing scheduled flights.

West Sound Marina
Monitors VHF channel 16
525 Deer Harbor Road
Orcas, WA 98280
(360) 376-2314
betsy@westsoundmarina.com
www.westsoundmarina.net

Orcas Landing

Orcas Landing is an iconic waterfront scene with staggered white washed buildings topped with red roofs, all centered around the island hub of transportation, the Washington State Ferry. During the summer months, the landing is filled with residents and tourists alike, visiting the shops or waiting in line for the next island ferry. The casual and friendly atmosphere is evident everywhere, welcoming visitors to the relaxed pace of "island time." Orcas Landing also provides a good stop to pick up visitors arriving on the ferry or gather a few extra essentials and treats from the grocery.

Orcas Landing is located near the eastern entrance point to West Sound along Harney Channel on Orcas Island. Approaches to Orcas Landing can be taken from Harney Channel to the east and Wasp Passage or Pole Pass to the west. If approaching via Wasp Passage or Pole Pass, be sure to consult your navigation charts and tide tables due to numerous reefs in the area and strong currents. For further information see pages 273 and 275 for Wasp Passage and Pole Pass descriptions.

For brief stops to pick up visitors or supplies, the Orcas Landing public dock is the most convenient option. The county dock offers over 400 feet of moorage without charge for up to four hours during the day for visiting boats, dinghies and kayaks. The public dock is located just west of the ferry terminal, within the heart of the village. When

Orcas Landing to:		
Anacortes	16 nm
Bellingham	23 nm
Blaine	30 nm
Deer Harbor (Orcas Island)	3 nm
Fisherman Bay (Lopez Island)	7 nm
Eagle Harbor (Cypress Island)	12 nm
Echo Bay (Sucia Island)	16 nm
Friday Harbor (San Juan Island)	6 nm
Roche Harbor (San Juan Island)	11 nm
Sidney (Canada)	19 nm
Spencer Spit (Lopez Island)	5 nm
Watmough Bay (Lopez Island)	14 nm

Orcas Village Store

across the channel at Blind Bay on Shaw Island or within West Sound. A number of mooring buoys are also found in the area, although these are private and not available for public use. Two small private marinas are located near the landing, however they are permanent moorage marinas and do not offer transient moorage for visiting boats.

On shore, a number of picturesque shops, restaurants and a hotel can be found. From boutique tourist shops to a deli serving luscious pates, Orcas Landing is a unique stop with a little something for everyone.

Provisioning and Other Services

Orcas Hotel

Originally opened in 1904, the Orcas Hotel features lodging, a cafe and bakery, and a fine dining restaurant. There's no better location to enjoy a hot espresso drink and pastry, or a gourmet dinner overlooking the water. Located on the hill, next to the ferry terminal.

Phone: (360) 376-4300   Web: www.orcashotel.com

Orcas Mopeds

For traveling around the island, Orcas Mopeds has a variety of transportation options from hourly to weekly rentals. Orcas Mopeds offers bicycle, moped, three-wheeled scootcars, and car rentals. Located up the hill from the ferry terminal.

Phone: (360) 376-5266   Web: www.orcasmopeds.com

Orcas Village Store

Located at the top of the ferry landing ramp, the Orcas Village Store is a well supplied grocery including a gourmet deli, bakery, made to order take & bake pizzas, meats, fresh produce, wine and beer.

Phone: (360) 376-8860   Web: www.orcasvillagestore.com

tying up, be sure to put out plenty of fenders as the dock is exposed south winds and wake from the ferries and boats traveling through Harney Channel.

Anchorage is available east of the ferry terminal in deeper water of approximately 8 to 9 fathoms. Due to the large amount of traffic transiting Harney Channel, anchorage here can be a bit rolly. Better protection can be found

Fishing Bay and Indian Island in East Sound

East Sound

East Sound is the long, narrow body of water that nearly divides the horseshoe-shaped island of Orcas in two. This lengthy sound is a popular destination for visitors to the island. The main village is located at the head of the bay, with Rosario Resort (see page 167) and Moran State Park (see page 171), found on the eastern shores. With the towering 2,409 foot Mt. Constitution flanking the eastern edge of the sound, East Sound is an unmistakable location within the islands.

The entrance to East Sound is centrally located in the heart of the San Juans, with the islands of Shaw, Lopez and Blakely nearby. If approaching the entrance to East Sound from the east via Obstruction Pass or Peavine Pass (see pages 273 for further information on these passes), be sure to note the detached rocks found off the western point of Obstruction Pass State Park. If approaching the sound from the west via Harney Channel, be on the lookout for Shag Rock, lying off the western entrance point to East Sound, between Foster Point and Diamond Point on Orcas Island. Shag Rock is also marked by a day beacon. Once inside the sound, a clear channel and deep water can be found throughout the middle of the sound. The shoreline around the sound remains relatively steep-to with the exception of the head of the sound and the bay near Olga.

Occasional winds found within East Sound, known as gap winds, are also a notable phenomenon. These winds are low-elevation winds found within gaps or valleys in a mountainous area. With the low valley of Eastsound village at the head, Mt. Constitution to the east and Mt. Woolard to the west, the constricting mountainous sides of the sound funnel and accelerate north wind breezes down the length of the sound. If a northerly wind is blowing, one can predict that strong, accelerated north winds will be blowing through East Sound. For sailboats approaching from the usually windless passes of Obstruction or Peavine, they can occasionally be caught off guard by stronger winds flowing down the Sound. When approaching the East Sound area, look for signs of stronger winds like whitecaps and heavily heeled sailboats and adjust accordingly.

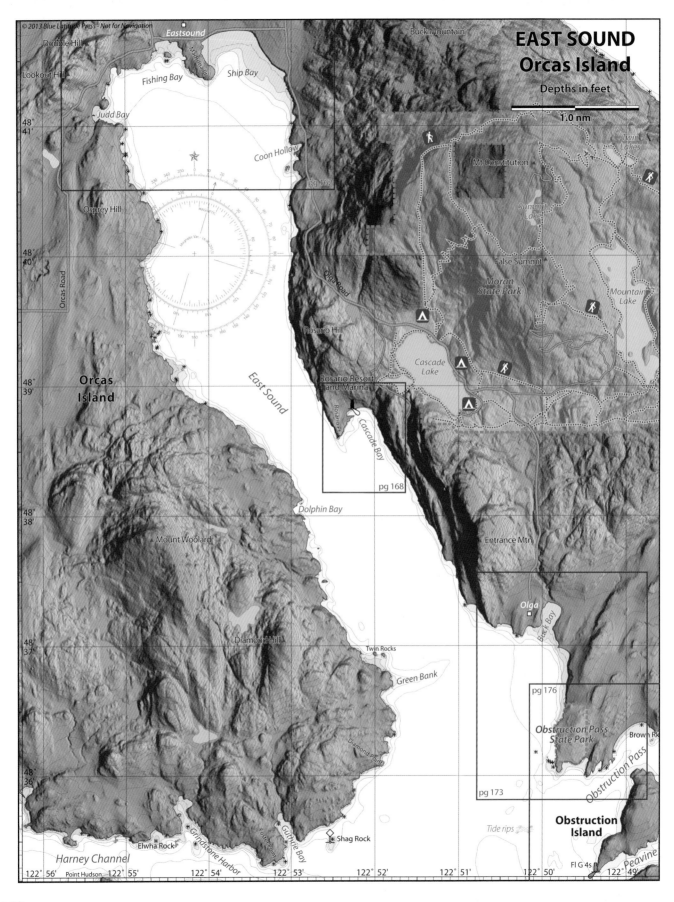

© 2013 Blue Latitude Press - Not for Navigation

EAST SOUND
Orcas Island

Depths in feet

1.0 nm

Double Hill

Eastsound

Buck Mountain

Lookout Hill

Fishing Bay

Ship Bay

Twin Lakes

Judd Bay

Coon Hollow

Mt Constitution

pg 162

Osprey Hill

Summit Lake

48° 41'

48° 40'

False Summit

Orcas Road

Moran State Park

Mountain Lake

Olga Road

Rosario Hill

Cascade Lake

Orcas Island

East Sound

Rosario Resort and Marina

Rosario Pt

Cascade Bay

48° 39'

pg 168

Dolphin Bay

48° 38'

Mount Woolard

Entrance Mtn

Olga

Buck Bay

Diamond Hill

48° 37'

Twin Rocks

pg 176

Green Bank

Obstruction Pass State Park

Brown Rk

Diamond Pt

Obstruction Pass

48° 36'

pg 173

Tide rips

Obstruction Island

Harney Channel

Elwha Rock

Grindstone Harbor

Foster Point

Guthrie Bay

Shag Rock

Fl G 4s

Peavine

Point Hudson

122° 56'   122° 55'   122° 54'   122° 53'   122° 52'   122° 51'   122° 50'   122° 49'

Eastsound

The village of Eastsound, found at the head of its name-sake, is an alluring coastal community set amidst the hills and valleys on Orcas Island. With street names like Enchanted Forest Road and Lover's Lane, it is easy to get the sense of the serenity and beauty found here. Eastsound is the largest village on the island and boasts a "downtown" with easy walking distances. Excellent shopping and a wide variety of delectable restaurants, with many serving up island grown or raised produce, meats and seafood, are some of the many highlights found at Eastsound.

The village of Eastsound is located at the northern extreme of East Sound on Orcas Island. Approaches to the sound can be made via Obstruction Pass or Peavine Pass (see pages 273 for detailed information on these passes) to the east, Harney Channel to the west, or Lopez Sound or Upright Channel to the south. If approaching from the east, be aware of detached rocks found off the western point of Obstruction Pass State Park. If approaching from Harney Channel, be on the lookout for Shag Rock (marked with a day beacon) which lies offshore between Diamond Point and Foster Point on Orcas Island. If approaching from the south via Lopez Sound, Blakely Island Shoal lies roughly

midway between the northern tip of Lopez Island and the western shore of Blakely Island. The shoal is marked by a lighted buoy off the southwestern extent of the shoal.

Once inside East Sound, a clear channel with relatively deep water can be found through the middle of the sound. The shoreline around the sound remains relatively steep-to with the exception of the head of the sound and the bay at Olga. Anchorage can be taken near the village of Eastsound within Fishing Bay, west of Madrona Point and south of In-

Eastsound to:		
	Anacortes	19 nm
	Bellingham	25 nm
	Blaine	34 nm
	Blind Bay (Shaw Island)	10 nm
	Deer Harbor (Orcas Island)	13 nm
	Fisherman Bay (Lopez Island)	21 nm
	Friday Harbor (San Juan Island)	13 nm
	Roche Harbor (San Juan Island)	20 nm
	Rosario (Orcas Island)	4 nm
	Shallow Bay (Sucia Island)	22 nm
	Spencer Spit (Lopez Island)	10 nm
	Victoria (Canada)	36 nm

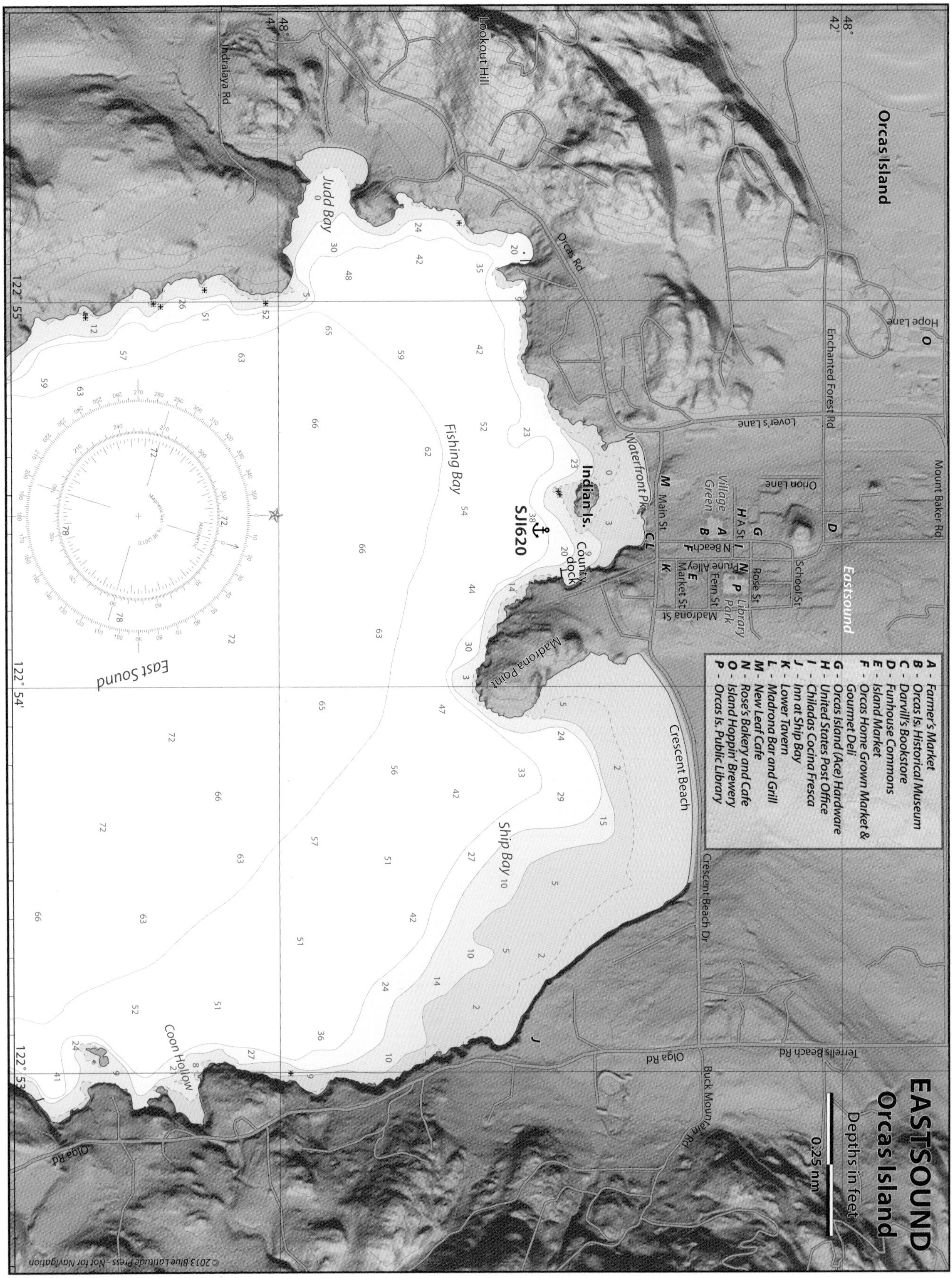

Orcas Island

Lookout Hill

Indralaya Rd

Judd Bay

Orcas Rd

Hope Lane

O

Enchanted Forest Rd

Lover's Lane

Mount Baker Rd

Fishing Bay

Indian Is.

SJI620

Waterfront Pk

County dock

Orion Lane

Village Green

Eastsound

School St

M Main St
H A St
G
D
A Beach
B N Beach
F
C L
N Rose St
P Library
Park
E
K
Prune Alley
Fern St
Market St
Madrona St

East Sound

A - Farmer's Market
B - Orcas Is. Historical Museum
C - Darvill's Bookstore
D - Funhouse Commons
E - Island Market
F - Orcas Home Grown Market & Gourmet Deli
G - Orcas Island (Ace) Hardware
H - United States Post Office
J - Chilidas Cocina Fresca
K - Inn at Ship Bay
L - Lower Tavern
M - Madrona Bar and Grill
N - New Leaf Cafe
O - Rose's Bakery and Cafe
P - Island Hoppin' Brewery
Orcas Is. Public Library

Madrona Point

Crescent Beach

Ship Bay

Crescent Beach Dr

Coon Hollow

Olga Rd

Terrells Beach Rd

Buck Mountain Rd

SJI620 - 48°41.460'N 122°54.410'W

EASTSOUND
Orcas Island

Depths in feet

0.25 nm

© 2013 Blue Latitude Press - Not for Navigation

162

dian Island. Anchorage in Fishing Bay ranges from 6 to 9 fathoms over mixed mud and rock. A seasonal county dock is available for day use and lies off the western shore of Madrona Point, making for easy and convenient dinghy trips to shore.

The anchorage at Eastsound offers north, west and east protection, but is open to southerly winds. Northerly gap winds (see page 159 can be experienced within Eastsound as well as stronger southerly winds constricted and funneled up the sound. South wind protection can be found at nearby Judd Bay or Blakely Island Marina, off the northern end of Blakely Island.

Orcas Island Historical Museum

Sights to See

The waterfront village of Eastsound is a beautiful and picturesque place to take a stroll, grab a bite to eat and do a little shopping. Being the largest village on Orcas, Eastsound has a lot to offer visitors, all within easy walking distance.

One of the highlights to town is the Orcas Island Historical Museum found on North Beach Road next to the Village Green park. The museum is comprised of six original homestead cabins built during the 1870s and 1890s that were moved from various sites around the island to the museum's present site. Each cabin houses historical exhibits from artifacts to photographs, depicting island history from the first inhabitants to present day. The museum is open from 11am to 4pm Tuesdays through Sundays. For more information, visit their website at: **www.orcasmuseum.org**.

If you happen to visit the island on a Saturday during the summer months, be sure to visit the Orcas Island Farmers' Market located next door to the museum at the Village Green. Farmers and artisans from around the island can be found here selling produce, seafood, meats, bakery items, flowers, art, jewelry, and clothing. Be sure to bring your appetite as a number of food and beverage vendors can also be found at the weekly event. For a list of vendors visit the market's website at: **www.orcasislandfarmersmarket.org**.

Eastsound storefronts

View of Fishing Bay from town

For kids, there is no better place for entertainment and education than the Funhouse Commons located on the corner of Enchanted Forest Road and Pea Patch Lane. The Funhouse has dozens of hands-on kid-friendly science exhibits, audio and video production studios complete with musical instruments, computer labs, an arts and crafts yurt and much more. The Funhouse is open to all with nominal daily or annual admission packages. To check hours and current classes and programs, visit the Funhouse website at: **www.funhousecommons.org**.

For some beachside strolling, Waterfront Park is a perfect place to soak up a bit of sunshine and wade through the cooling and shallow waters found at the head of East Sound. Located near the west entrance to the village, the open grassy park offers picnic tables and a drift wood covered beach to explore. At low tide, it is possible to wade across the shallow bay along a sandy bar to nearby Indian Island.

Orcas Island Farmer's Market

Provisioning and Other Services
Darvill's Bookstore
Located along the waterfront on Main Street, Darvill's carries a wide selection of books for all interests including fiction, local guides, nautical and children's books.
Phone: (360) 376-2135   Web: www.darvillsbookstore.com

Island Hardware & Supply
Island Hardware is a full service hardware and home supply store. Located two miles southwest of Eastsound at 21 West Beach Road.
Phone: (360) 376-4200   Web: www.islandhardware.com

Island Market
Island Market is the largest grocery store on Orcas Island, stocking everything including fresh produce, meats, dairy items and even a deli with salads and sandwiches. Located on the corner of Prune Alley and Market Street.
Phone: (360) 376-6000

Orcas Home Grown Market & Gourmet Deli
Specializing in natural and organic groceries and produce, fresh local seafood, vitamins, and bulk foods. Complete

Rose's Cafe & Bakery

with a gourmet deli, fresh juice and espresso bar. Located at 138 North Beach Road.
Phone: (360) 376-2009   Web: orcashomegrownmarket.com

Orcas Island Farmers' Market
Every Saturday from May through September (10am to 3pm) join farmers, chefs and artists at the Village Green for locally grown produce, fresh baked goods, flowers, arts and crafts and much more.
Web: www.orcasislandfarmersmarket.org

Orcas Island Hardware
An Ace Hardware store featuring hardware, building, home and gardening supplies is located at 421 North Beach Road.
Phone: (360) 376-3833   Web: www.acehardware.com

Rose's Bakery & Cafe
Rose's Bakery offers freshly baked artisan breads and pastries, along with a large selection of fine wines, cheeses, meats and chocolates. Sandwiches made with the bakery's fresh bread, as well as homemade soups and salads are available at the cafe. Located next to Library Park on Prune Alley.
Phone: (360) 376-5805

United States Postal Service
The Eastsound post office is open Monday through Friday from 7:30am to 3pm. The office is located at 221 A Street.
Phone: (360) 376-4121   Web: www.usps.com

Transportation
Kenmore Air
Kenmore Air provides daily, year-round flights between Seattle and seven locations in the San Juan Islands, including Friday Harbor, on both seaplanes and wheeled aircraft.
Phone: (425) 486-1257   Web: www.kenmoreair.com

Northwest Sky Ferry
Northwest Sky Ferry has scheduled and chartered flights available to and from Bellingham and the San Juan Islands.
Phone: (360) 676-9999   Web: www.skyferrynw.com

NW Seaplanes
NW Seaplanes offers charter and sight seeing flights for western Washington and Canada's British Columbia coast.
Phone: (425) 277-1590   Web: www.nwseaplanes.com

Orcas Island Shuttle
Car rentals including delivery anywhere on the island. Reservations recommended with sedans, convertibles and mini vans available.
Phone: (360) 376-RIDE   Web: www.orcasislandshuttle.com

San Juan Airlines
Offering scheduled, charter, and scenic flights from Anacortes, Bellingham, and Seattle to the San Juan Islands and British Columbia.
Phone: 800-874-4434   Web: www.sanjuanairlines.com

San Juan Transit
San Juan Transit offers daily, scheduled transportation around the island, including Eastsound, West Sound, Turtleback Trail, Moran State Park, Rosario Resort, the Golf Course and the ferry landing. Schedules vary by season.
Phone: (360) 378-8887   Web: www.sanjuantransit.com

Outdoor seating at the New Leaf Cafe

Restaurants

Chiladas Cocina Fresca

With a wonderful outdoor courtyard, Chiladas serves delicious Mexican style meals along with quenching, margaritas. Daily happy hour specials from 4 to 6pm. Located on the corner of A Street and North Beach Road.

Phone: (360) 376-ORCA   Web: www.chiladas.com

Inn at Ship Bay

Inn at Ship Bay is an elegant fine dining experience overlooking the waters of East Sound. The Inn offers seasonal menus that feature fresh, delicious, locally farmed products. The Inn is open for dinner with indoor and outdoor seating. Located at 326 Olga Road, one mile east of Eastsound.

Phone: (360) 376-5886   Web: www.innatshipbay.com

Island Hoppin' Brewery

Locally brewing tasty brews such as Parker's Reef Pilsner, Old Salts Brown Ale and K-Pod Kolsch this is a great place for the thirsty island hopper to quench their thirst or pick up a growler to go. Located at 33 Hope Lane.

Phone: (360) 376-6079   Web: www.islandhoppinbrewery.com

Lower Tavern

If you're looking for a cold beer, a mouth-watering burger and friendly local island camaraderie, look no further than the Lower Tavern. With three big screens, it's also a great spot to catch those not-to-be-missed televised games. Located at 46 Prune Alley.

Phone: (360) 376-4848   Web: www.lowertavern.com

Madrona Bar and Grill

The Madrona Bar and Grill boasts one of the finest views of East Sound in town. Situated waterfront, the restaurant serves grilled meats and seafood, burgers, sandwiches and salads for lunch and dinner. Located at 310 Main Street.

Phone: 360-376-7171   Web: www.madronabarandgrill.com

New Leaf Cafe

The New Leaf Cafe offers a fine dining experience across from the water with both indoor and outdoor seating. Local and organic produce, free range meats and fresh northwest seafoods are used to prepare beautiful and delicious meals. Open for breakfast and dinner at 171 Main Street.

Phone: (360) 376-2200   Web: www.newleafcafeorcas.com

Rose's Bakery and Cafe

Rose's Cafe serves fresh and flavorful meals using mostly island grown and raised produce and meats. With an excellent wine list, in-house made artisan breads and pastries, Rose's is a place not to miss! Located at 382 Prune Alley.

Phone: (360) 376-5805

Cascade Bay (Rosario)

The enchanting Rosario Resort & Spa, located within Cascade Bay, is a marvelous look back at Northwest history. Set amidst a beautiful island landscape with sweeping ocean views, Rosario Resort retains its old world charm over one hundred years later. While the large bay affords room for anchoring, the resort offers protected slips within its 36-slip marina as well as mooring buoys within the bay. With lodging, restaurants and daily ferry service to the island or scheduled seaplane flights from Seattle, Rosario makes for a convenient and unique experience for friends and family to visit.

Cascade Bay is located on the eastern shore of East Sound on Orcas Island, roughly 2.25 miles northwest of Olga. Approaches to East Sound can be made via Lopez Sound or Upright Passage to the south, Obstruction or Peavine Passes to the east or Harney Channel to the west. If approaching from Obstruction or Peavine Passes (see pages 273 for detailed information), be aware of detached rocks found off the western point of Obstruction Pass State Park. If approaching from Harney Channel, be on the lookout for Shag Rock (marked with a day beacon) which lies offshore between Diamond Point and Foster Point on Orcas Island. If approaching from the south via Lopez Sound, Blakely Island Shoal lies roughly midway between the northern tip of Lopez Island and the western shore of Blakely Island. The

shoal is marked by a lighted buoy off the southwestern extent of the shoal. If approaching from the north from the village of Eastsound, be aware of shallow water found off Rosario Point, the western entrance point into the bay.

Cascade Bay is a large and fairly deep bay. A number of mooring buoys are found within the bay, a mixture of private moorings and moorings available for nightly rental through Rosario Marina (see the marina contact information on page 170). Anchorage can be taken within the bay in 9 to 11 fathoms over a mixture of mud and rock.

Cascade Bay to:		
Anacortes		16 nm
Bellingham		21 nm
Blaine		31 nm
Blind Bay *(Shaw Island)*		6 nm
Eagle Harbor *(Cypress Island)*		10 nm
Fossil Bay *(Sucia Island)*		17 nm
Fisherman Bay *(Lopez Island)*		9 nm
Friday Harbor *(San Juan Island)*		10 nm
Jones Island		11 nm
Roche Harbor *(San Juan Island)*		17 nm
Spencer Spit *(Lopez Island)*		7 nm
Sidney *(Canada)*		25 nm

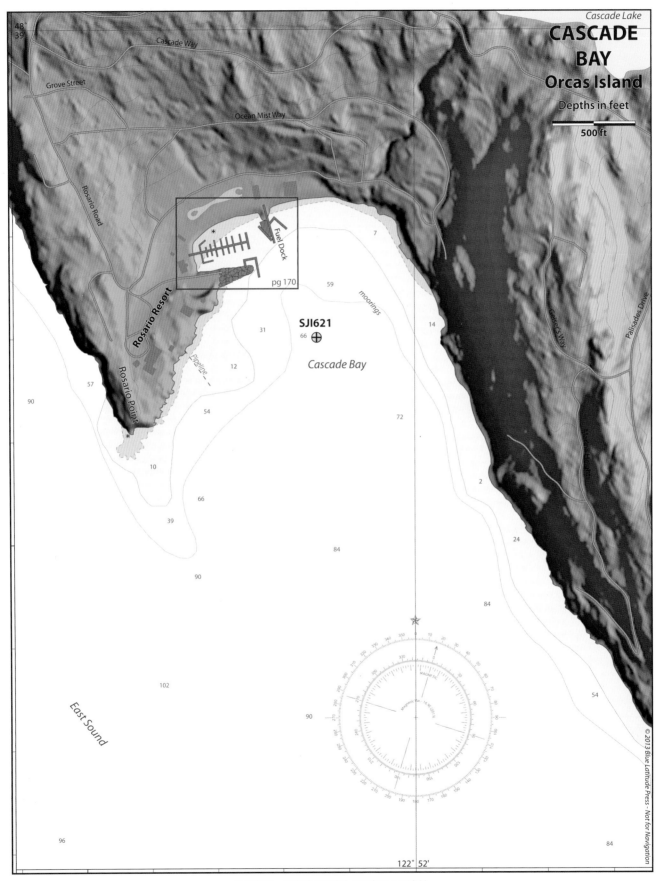

Cascade Lake

CASCADE BAY
Orcas Island

Depths in feet

500 ft

Cascade Way

Grove Street

Ocean Mist Way

Rosario Road

Rosario Resort

Fuel Dock

pg 170

7

59

moorings

14

SJI621
66 ⊕

31

Cascade Bay

12

Pipeline

57

54

72

Rosario Point

90

10

66

39

84

90

2

24

102

90

84

54

East Sound

96

84

122° 52'

© 2013 Blue Latitude Press - Not for Navigation

SJI621 - 48°38.700'N 122°52.150'W

Cascade Bay provides protection from north and east winds and some west winds depending on the moorage location, but is open to the south. As mentioned in the East Sound description on page 159, East Sound can experience gap winds through the narrow waterway. The mountains found on either side of the sound can funnel north winds down the sound, and occasionally enhance south winds.

The whole family can enjoy activities at the resort, from swimming pools to kayak tours, there's something for everyone at Rosario. Walking trails stretch around the grounds and a historical museum is located within the mansion detailing the construction of the estate and the history of Robert Moran. Restaurants at the resort also offer a night away from the galley with superb waterfront views.

Rosario Resort was originally developed and built by Seattle ship builder and mayor of Seattle, Robert Moran, as his retirement residence. Moran purchased over 7,000 acres on Orcas Island and completed the construction on his Arts and Crafts style mansion in 1909. The estate would become the largest in the islands, employing approximately 50 people during its construction.

Robert Moran was also a nature enthusiast, spending his days on the island enjoying the outdoor world and hiking across his thousands of acres of property. Inspired by preservationist John Muir and the conservation policies of President Theodore Roosevelt, Moran donated more than 2,700 acres to the state of Washington to be used for park lands. This park was dedicated to Moran and given the name Moran State Park (see page 171). Most of the trails, roads, bridges, and buildings in the park were built by the Civilian Conservation Corps (CCC) during the 1930s.

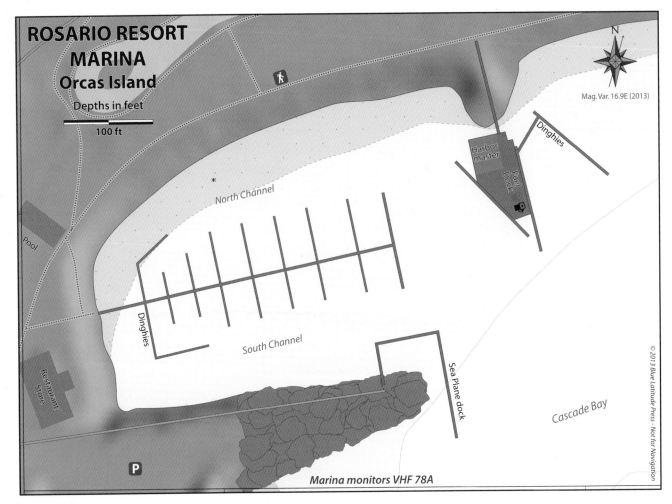

ROSARIO RESORT MARINA
Orcas Island
Depths in feet

100 ft

North Channel

South Channel

Dinghies

Dinghies

Harbor master

Fuel Dock

Pool

Restaurant/ Store

Sea Plane dock

Cascade Bay

Mag. Var. 16.9E (2013)

Marina monitors VHF 78A

© 2013 Blue Latitude Press - Not for Navigation

Rosario Marina

Rosario Marina is located within the Rosario Resort & Spa in Cascade Bay. The 36-slip marina can accommodate boats up to 105 feet in length, and up to 140 feet pending the harbormaster's approval, all with water and power hookups (30 and limited 50 amp power). Eight resort moorings are also available for nightly rental. Marina services include a fuel dock with diesel and gasoline, cafe, small grocery, showers, swimming pool, and fitness center.

Rosario Resort & Spa Marina
Monitors VHF Channel 78A
1400 Rosario Road
Eastsound, WA 98245
(360) 376-2152
harbormaster@rosarioresort.com
www.rosarioresort.com

Moran State Park

Moran State Park is an extraordinary 5,252 acre park that includes nearly 40 miles of trails, campgrounds, five lakes, several waterfalls and an old growth forest. The park is situated around the 2,409 foot high Mount Constitution, which is the highest peak in the San Juans, and offers sweeping views from every direction. The park's namesake, Robert Moran, originally donated 2,700 acres of land next to his mansion at Rosario to be set aside as park land in 1921. In the 1930's the Civilian Conservation Corps (CCC) was brought to the park where they built a watchtower, bridges, rock walls and various other structures that are still in use today.

One of the highlights to visiting Moran State Park is a trip to the top of Mount Constitution. Various hiking trails lead to the top, along with a winding paved road for vehicles. At the top, visitors are treated to amazing views of the islands and the Cascade and Olympic Mountain ranges. Visitors also have access to the watch tower, where interpretive signs and history of the park are on display. Other activities at the park include 38 miles of hiking trails crisscrossing the 5,252 acres. And for mountain bikers, the park's trails are open from September 15th through May 15th, and closed to bikers during the summer season. For further park information visit the state park website at: www.parks.wa.gov or by phone at (360) 902-8844.

Olga

The small village of Olga dates back to the late 1800's where its prosperity centered around the commercial dock extending out into East Sound. Today, a newer version of this dock still brings commerce into this quiet seaside village. Tourists drop in to visit the cafe, art galleries and post office Olga is known for. With the convenience of the county dock, Olga is a delightful stop to take in the history of Orcas Island and its once grand fields of strawberries, or to enjoy the art of local residents over a fresh gooey cinnamon roll at the cafe.

Olga is located on the southeastern edge of East Sound on Orcas Island at Buck Bay. Approaches to Olga can be made via East Sound from either the north or south. If approaching from the south, be sure to note the detached rocks extending out from the far southern point of the bay, near Obstruction Pass State Park.

The water extending out from Buck Bay is a popular summer mooring location and crabbing ground for island residents due to its large, relatively flat shelf. At times, this area can be littered with various buoys marking moorings or crab pots so keep a lookout when approaching or leaving Olga.

The county dock, which stretches out from the west entrance point of Buck Bay, is available for visiting boats. The 95 foot long dock has tie ups on either side and can be used for day or overnight moorage for a nightly fee. The moorings within Buck Bay are privately owned and therefore not for use by visiting boats. If anchoring, be sure to avoid the cable crossing area identified on the NOAA navigation charts. The dock and surrounding water at Olga provide

Olga to:		
	Anacortes	14 nm
	Bellingham	19 nm
	Blaine	29 nm
	Blind Bay (Shaw Island)	5 nm
	Echo Bay (Sucia Island)	16 nm
	Fisherman Bay (Lopez Island)	8 nm
	Friday Harbor (San Juan Island)	9 nm
	Hunter Bay (Lopez Island)	9 nm
	Jones Island	10 nm
	Roche Harbor (San Juan Island)	16 nm
	Spencer Spit (Lopez Island)	5 nm
	Victoria (Canada)	32 nm

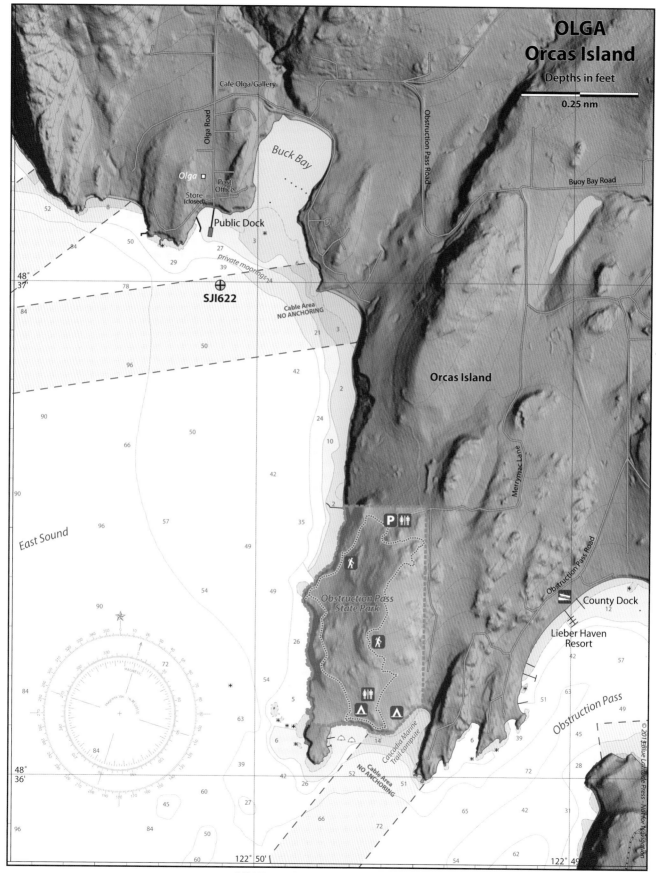

OLGA
Orcas Island

Depths in feet

0.25 nm

Cafe Olga/Gallery

Buck Bay

Olga Road

Obstruction Pass Road

Buoy Bay Road

Olga

Post Office

Store (closed)

Public Dock

private moorings

48° 37'

SJI622

Cable Area
NO ANCHORING

Orcas Island

Merrymac Lane

East Sound

Obstruction Pass Road

P

County Dock

Lieber Haven Resort

Obstruction Pass State Park

Cascadia Marine Trail campsite

Cable Area
NO ANCHORING

48° 36'

Obstruction Pass

122° 50'

122° 49'

© 2013 Blue Latitude Press - Nor'or Navigation

SJI622 - 48°36.990'N 122°50.130'W

north and east wind protection, but is open to winds from the south and west. Keep in mind that East Sound is also affected by gap winds (see page 159) which can enhance and funnel winds through the sound.

The town of Olga was founded in 1860 and named by John Ohlert after his mother. Ohlert operated the town's store and post office, with a dance hall located upstairs. By the early 1900's, Olga became the port town for processing and distribution of the island's renowned strawberries. Today, Olga retains its peaceful charm with the post office still in operation and the old barreling plant renovated into a beautiful art studio and cafe. The old Olga Store is currently closed down, but hopefully this charming shop will be back in operation once again someday soon.

While visiting Olga, be sure to stop by the Artworks building where the past and present of this wonderful village are on display. While there, enjoy local residents' works of art in the studio, and with the delicious smells of Cafe Olga wafting in, there's no better place to enjoy a coffee, pastry or meal.

Orcas Island Berry Growers Assoc.

The Orcas Island Berry Growers Association was formed in 1935 by independent strawberry farmers on Orcas Island. With hundreds of acres of berries being grown around Orcas island, farmers needed an efficient way to process their prized crop to sell the berries and plants at various markets. Under a collective group, the farmers were able to negotiate an agreement with the National Fruit Canning Company out of Olympia to provide the materials and equipment for a berry processing plant. In conjunction with the first underwater cable reaching Orcas Island in 1938 and bringing electricity with it, the Olga Barreling Plant was officially opened.

Farmers trucked their strawberries to the plant where the berries were weighed, washed and sorted. The strawberries were then graded for either immediate consumption or packed with sugar into fifty gallon barrels where they were taken each evening by ferry to the mainland for cold storage. Berries alone were not the only product handled at the plant. Year old strawberry plants were also dug up from the fields and taken to the barreling plant where they were cleaned, trimmed and bundled for sale.

According to the *Friday Harbor Journal*, at the end of the 1941 season, Orcas farmers produced 241 tons of strawberries. This banner year was to be the start of decline in the berry industry. By the end of that year, the U.S. entered World War II and islanders began leaving the farms to help join the fight.

Today the history of the berry industry is kept alive by local residents who formed the Olga Strawberry Council. This group joined together to help purchase and preserve the Artworks building which is the renovated sight of the Olga Barreling Plant. The Artworks building now houses a few historical artifacts from the berry days, along with an artists' co-op gallery, the James Hardman Gallery and Cafe Olga.

Obstruction Pass State Park

The intimate anchorage at Obstruction Pass State Park is a hidden gem for those in the know. While the small cove is easy to miss on your transit through Obstruction Pass, it would be a shame to pass by this perfect little anchorage without stopping to explore the sights. Due to its prime location and inclusion in the Cascadia Marine Trail system, the state park is popular with seakayakers as a camping destination or as a resting spot while waiting for tidal changes within Obstruction Pass. Fronted by a beautiful sand and pebble crescent-shaped beach, along with hiking trails looping through the forest, the state park is a wonderful location to take in the sights of the San Juan Islands.

Obstruction Pass State Park is located on the western edge of Obstruction Pass, near the entrance to East Sound on Orcas Island. Approaches to the cove can be made from the east via Obstruction or Peavine Passes, from the north via Eastsound, the south via Lopez Sound, or the west via Upright or Harney Channels. If approaching from the north or northwest, be aware that detached rocks lie off the western point to the cove, and to give this area a wide berth when rounding into the anchorage. If approaching via Ob-

struction Pass or Peavine Pass, note that swift currents can flow through these passes (see page 273 for further information on these areas).

The state park offers two mooring buoys for use within the cove. Due to the small size of the cove and the proximity to underwater cable crossing in the area, the park mooring buoys are a great option when visiting Obstruction Pass State Park. The anchorage offers protection from north and

Obstruction Pass to:		
Anacortes	12 nm
Bellingham	18 nm
Blaine	28 nm
Blind Bay (Shaw Island)	5 nm
Eagle Harbor (Cypress Island)	7 nm
Fisherman Bay (Lopez Island)	7 nm
Fossil Bay (Sucia Island)	14 nm
Friday Harbor (San Juan Island)	9 nm
Roche Harbor (San Juan Island)	15 nm
Rosario (Orcas Island)	3 nm
Sidney (Canada)	24 nm
Spencer Spit (Lopez Island)	4 nm

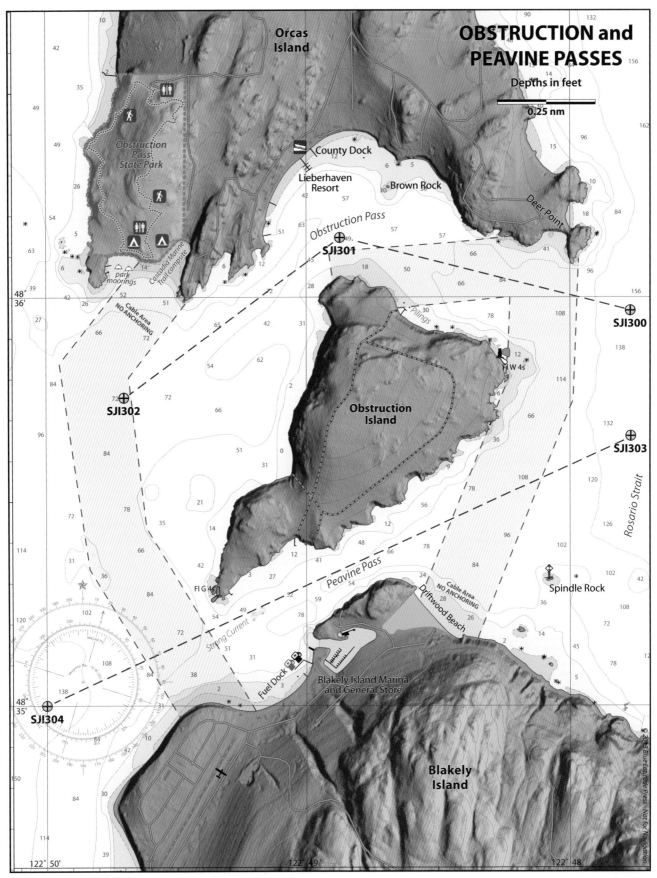

OBSTRUCTION and PEAVINE PASSES

Depths in feet

0.25 nm

Orcas Island

Obstruction Pass State Park

park moorings

Cascadia Marine Trail campsite

Cable Area NO ANCHORING

County Dock

Lieberhaven Resort

Brown Rock

Deer Point

Obstruction Pass

SJI301

SJI300

Pilings

Fl W 4s

Obstruction Island

SJI302

SJI303

Rosario Strait

Spindle Rock

Peavine Pass

Cable Area NO ANCHORING

Fl G 4s

Strong Current

Driftwood Beach

Fuel Dock

Blakely Island Marina and General Store

MAGNETIC

SJI304

Blakely Island

48° 36'

48° 35'

122° 50'

122° 49'

122° 48'

SJI300 - 48°35.970'N 122°47.770'W   **SJI301** - 48°36.130'N 122°48.870'W   **SJI302** - 48°35.750'N 122°49.700'W

SJI303 - 48°35.660'N 122°47.760'W   **SJI304** - 48°35.000'N 122°50.000'W

east winds, but is open to south and west winds. During the typically calm summer months, Obstruction Pass makes for a perfect evening anchorage.

On shore, the park offers campsites, fire rings, pit toilets and hiking trails. Stairs heading up from the beach lead visitors to a park information kiosk with a payment drop box for use of the moorings and campsites. While the campground is accessible by car, visitors must hike a half mile in from the parking lot.

A few trails loop around the park, taking visitors past informational signs on the local flora and geology of the area. These well defined trails traverse through the surrounding forest and nearby shorelines. A couple of picnic sites on the western edge of the park are prime locations for a relaxing view of the sun setting over the islands.

Lieber Haven

The quaint coastal village of Lieber Haven is located along the shores of Obstruction Pass on Orcas Island. One of the main attractions here is the Lieber Haven county dock and boat launch ramp which is open to the public. A small private marina and mooring buoys are also located nearby. Keep in mind that Obstruction Pass has stronger currents flowing through it reaching estimated velocities near 2 to 3 knots.

Doe Bay and the Doe Bay Resort and Retreat

Doe Bay and Doe Island

Historic Doe Bay was once a lively port town with a village dock that was responsible for shuttling people and goods to and from Orcas Island. Today, Doe Bay continues to see people visiting its shores, although most arrive by car now, to enjoy the rustic and laid back charm of Doe Bay Resort and Retreat. With a near cult following, the Doe Bay Resort offers a relaxing and peaceful experience with campsites, cabins and yurts available, along with soaking tubs and a dry sauna. Nearby Doe Island State Park is a perfect destination to explore by foot and by kayak or dinghy. Although the park dock was removed due to damage by a storm, the island still affords the picture perfect setting for a lunch picnic site.

Doe Bay and Doe Island are located on the eastern side of Orcas Island, roughly 2.5 miles southwest of Lawrence Point. Approaches to the bay and island can be made via Rosario Strait. If approaching from the south, be on the lookout for Lydia Shoal which is marked by a lighted gong style buoy. If approaching from the north or crossing Rosario Strait from the east, be cautious of Peapod Rocks which lie approximately 1 mile east of Doe Bay. Only the northern most rock is marked by a lighted beacon. Rosario Strait is also a main channel for commercial ships and experiences current so be sure to keep an eye out for traffic and watch your compass for drift.

Just outside of Doe Bay lies a small patch of shallow water, approximately 2 fathoms deep. Deeper draft vessels may choose to navigate around this area. Anchorage can be taken within the bay in 3 to 6 fathoms. A few private moorings are also located within the bay, however they are not

Doe Bay to:		
	Anacortes	13 nm
	Bellingham	15 nm
	Blaine	25 nm
	Blind Bay (Shaw Island)	9 nm
	Eagle Harbor (Cypress Island)	5 nm
	Fisherman Bay (Lopez Island)	11 nm
	Fossil Bay (Sucia Island)	11 nm
	Friday Harbor (San Juan Island)	13 nm
	Roche Harbor (San Juan Island)	20 nm
	Rosario (Orcas Island)	7 nm

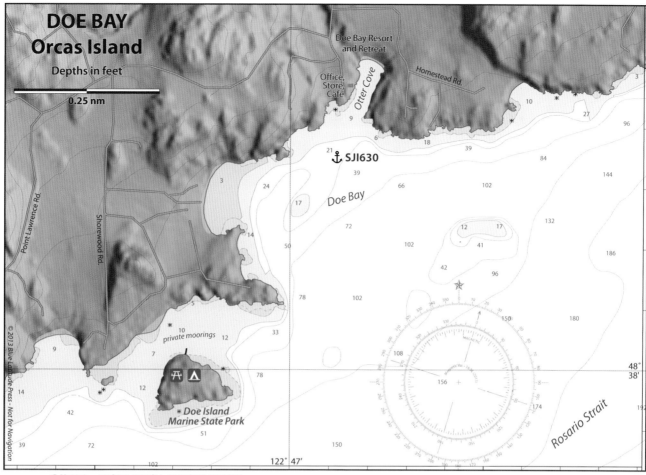

DOE BAY
Orcas Island

Depths in feet

0.25 nm

Doe Bay Resort and Retreat

Office, Store, Cafe

Otter Cove

⚓ SJI630

Homestead Rd.

Doe Bay

Point Lawrence Rd.

Shorewood Rd.

© 2013 Blue Latitude Press - Not for Navigation

private moorings

Doe Island Marine State Park

Rosario Strait

122° 47'

48° 38'

122° 46'

SJI630 - 48°38.350'N 122°46.880'W

available to the public. Anchorage may be possible on the northeastern side of Doe Island, although this area contains private moorings and has a steep-to bottom gradient that drops off into deep water. Doe Bay and Doe Island are both open to weather from the south with a large amount of fetch via Rosario Strait. These anchorages are best suited during periods of calm weather or as day stops.

For trips to shore, Doe Island is open to the public with small pebble and rock beaches located on the east and south sides of the island for dinghy or kayak landings. Much of the shoreline of Doe Island is rocky. For guests of Doe Bay Resort and Retreat, dinghies and kayaks can be landed on the beach in front of the resort. The resort offers lodging along with yoga and spa opportunities, including clothing-optional soaking tubs and a sauna. The Doe Bay Cafe is also located at the resort and is open for breakfast, lunch and dinner. The cafe features a seasonal menu, using fresh produce from its own garden as well as produce, eggs, meat and seafood from local farms and fisheries around the islands. For further information regarding the Doe Bay Resort and Retreat visit their website at: **www.doebay.com** or call (360) 376-2291. For the Doe Bay Cafe call (360) 376-8059.

Doe Island State Park

Remnants of the Doe Island dock

Jones Island

This magical little state park island is a favorite stop for everyone, from boaters to campers, offering scenic beauty and wildlife encounters in the heart of the San Juan Islands. With a public dock, mooring buoys and room for anchoring, Jones Island is a popular stop for boaters, lying only three miles from Deer Harbor and six miles from Friday Harbor for day trips or overnight stays. One of the island's highlights is the herd of blacktail deer that live on Jones. Over the years, while sharing the island with boaters and campers, the deer have become quite acclimated to the presence of people, affording many close encounters with these petite, graceful creatures. The island also offers walking trails traversing the island and a beautiful shoreline to explore by kayak.

Jones Island is located off the western tip of Orcas Island, near the intersection of San Juan, Spieden and President Channels. Approaches to the island can be made from a variety of directions, using various channels. Approaches from the north can be made via President Channel, from the east via North Pass or Wasp Passage, from the south via San Juan Channel, or from the west via Spieden Channel or New Channel. Lying near the vicinity of a number of channels, current and occasional tide rips can be found in the area, especially near Spieden Channel.

Jones Island to:		
	Anacortes	21 nm
	Bellingham	27 nm
	Blaine	26 nm
	Blind Bay (Shaw Island)	6 nm
	Deer Harbor (Orcas Island)	3 nm
	Eagle Harbor (Cypress Island)	16 nm
	Echo Bay (Sucia Island)	12 nm
	Fisherman Bay (Lopez Island)	9 nm
	Friday Harbor (San Juan Island)	6 nm
	Reid Harbor (Stuart Island)	7 nm
	Roche Harbor (San Juan Island)	6 nm

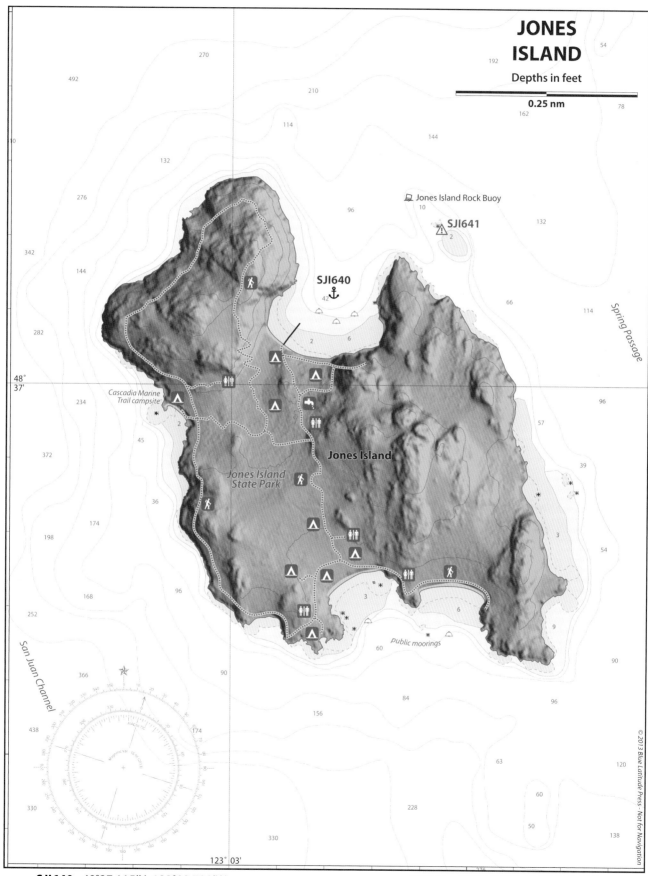

JONES ISLAND

Depths in feet

0.25 nm

Jones Island Rock Buoy

SJI641

SJI640

Spring Passage

Cascadia Marine
Trail campsite

Jones Island

Jones Island
State Park

public moorings

San Juan Channel

SJI640 - 48°37.115'N 123°02.790'W

SJI641 - 48°37.220'N 123°02.580'W

© 2013 Blue Latitude Press - Not for Navigation

When approaching the entrance to the north cove, be sure to locate the detached rocks found off the eastern entrance point. These rocks are marked by an unlit buoy, and passage should not be taken between the rocks and Jones Island.

For boats choosing to anchor in the north cove, a stern line to shore may be required due to the depth of the anchorage and limited swinging room. The park dock and mooring buoys are also available to visiting boats for a nightly fee with a payment drop box located near the top of the ramp. During the winter months, the dock is removed, but the mooring buoys remain in place. The north cove provides protection from southerly, west and east winds, but is open to the north.

A couple of park mooring buoys are also available at the south end of the island. While this anchorage is open to the area's predominate southerly winds, it is a fair anchorage in calm or north winds. Be aware that this area is rocky with an unmarked detached rock lying off the small point dividing the two coves of the anchorage. This area is steep-to and deep with a rocky shoreline making anchoring a less than desirable option.

Much of Jones Island is steep-to with the exception of the eastern and northeastern shore where shallow water and detached rocks can be found. Mooring options are found on the north and south side of the island, with the north cove providing dock space, mooring buoys and room for anchoring.

For trips to shore, the dock in the north cove provides a convenient landing location. On the south side, dinghies can be landed on the pebble and sand beaches. The 188-acre park provides 24 campsites, which also includes two sites dedicated to the Cascadia Marine Trail system. Composting and pit toilets are available, along with fresh water during the summer months. Trails link the north and south coves, along with a waterfront looping trail that traverses the western side of the island.

Jones Island is well noted for its herd of blacktail deer and are the stars for many photographs taken at the island.

Blacktail Deer

Blacktail deer are a common site within the San Juan Islands. These petite deer are native to the area and can often be spotted grazing on the lush undergrowth found on the islands. Adult blacktail deer bucks weigh on average between 100 to 200 pounds, and adult does weigh between 90 to 130 pounds. The rut, or breeding season, for blacktail deer is generally during the months of November and December. Each year, bucks shed their antlers after the rut season, usually in January or February. The dropped antlers are a favorite of mice, rats, squirrels, and hares, helping to providing them with calcium and other essential minerals. Does will give birth during the spring months, with younger does generally giving birth to one fawn, while more mature does often give birth to twins. Does, needing additional nutrients while nursing, will often leave new born fawns in grassy, hidden locations while they venture out to graze. Should you come across a lone, healthy looking sleeping fawn, do not fear that it is orphaned, its mother is most likely out feeding and keeping a careful eye on you from a distance.

It is not uncommon to find deer on the trails or grazing on the grassy meadows near the center of the island. Over the years the deer have become accustomed to the presence of humans on their island, but keep in mind that they are still wild creatures that desire a respectful distance. Raccoons are also found on the island and can at times be quite forthcoming when searching out the delicious smells of camp food. Be sure to securely pack your food away to avoid a pesky late night visitor!

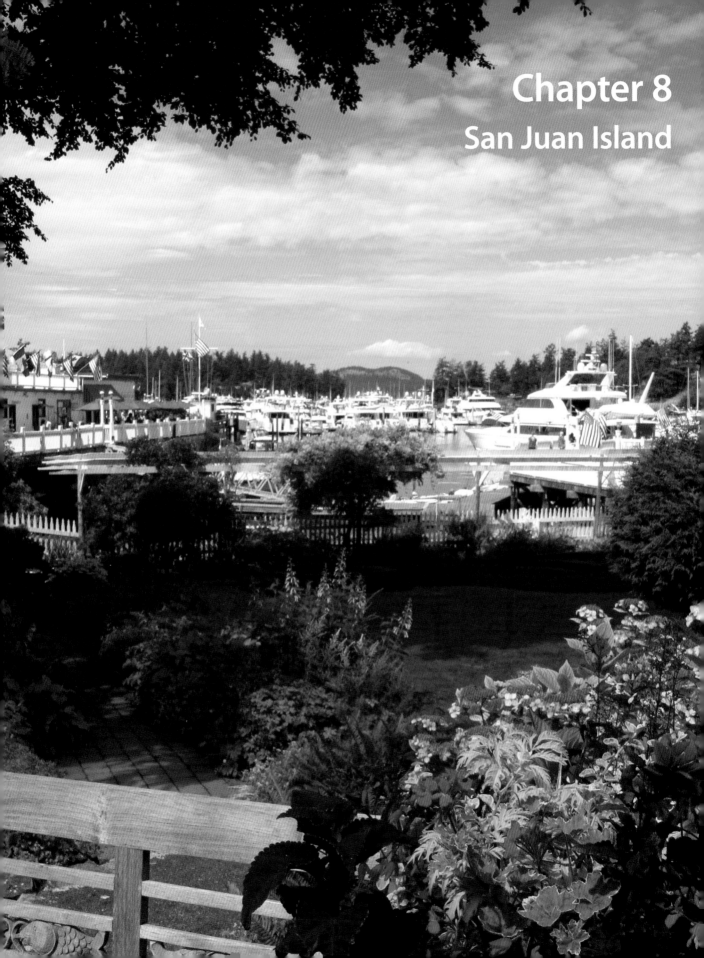

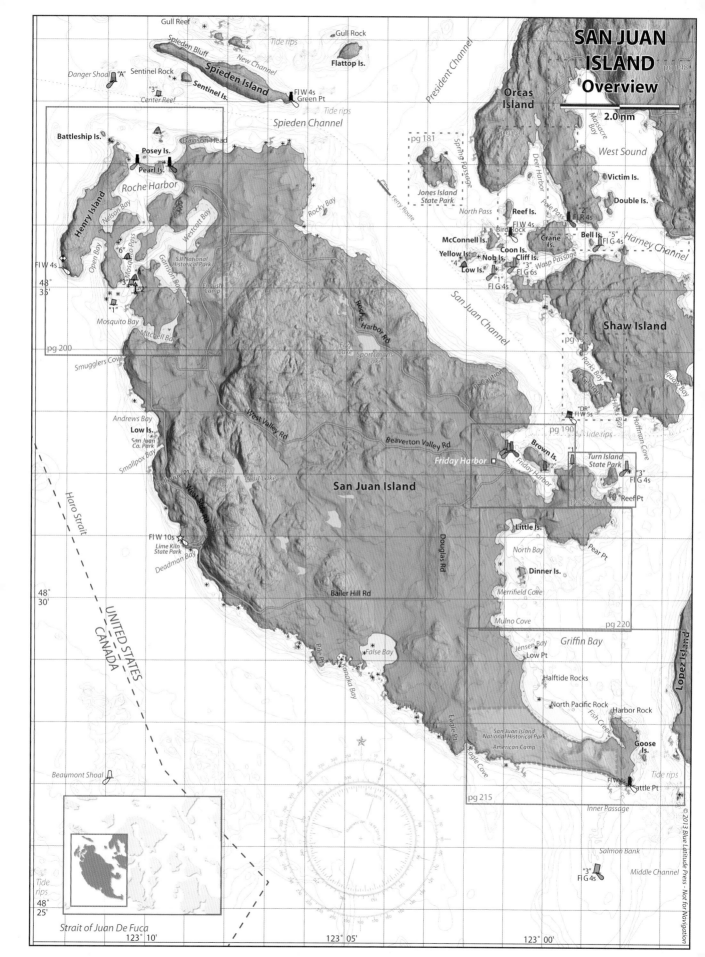

Gull Reef

Spieden Bluff

Gull Rock

Flattop Is.

Tide rips

New Channel

Danger Shoal   "A"   Sentinel Rock

Spieden Island

Sentinel Is.

"3"   Center Reef

Fl W 4s
Green Pt

Spieden Channel

Tide rips

Orcas Island

President Channel

Massacre Bay

pg 148

pg 181

pg 144

West Sound

Battleship Is.

Davison Head

Spring Passage

Deer Harbor

Victim Is.

Double Is.

Posey Is.

Pearl Is.

Roche Harbor

Ferry Route

North Pass

Pole Pass

Reef Is.

"2"
Fl R 4s

Henry Island

Nelson Bay

Rocky Bay

Westcott Bay

SJI National Historical Park

Fl W 4s
Bird Rock

Crane Is.

Bell Is.   "5"
Fl G 4s

Harney Channel

Open Bay

Garrison Bay

"6"

"4"

McConnell Is.

Yellow Is.
"4"

Coon Is.   Cliff Is.

Low Is.   "3"
Fl G 6s

Wasp Passage

Fl W 4s

48°
35'

"3"   "2"

English Camp

"1"

Nob Is.

"1"
Fl G 4s

San Juan Channel

Shaw Island

pg 200

Mosquito Bay

Mitchell Bay

Smugglers Cove

Roche Harbor Rd

Ego Lake

Sportsmans Lake

Caution

Parks Bay

Indian Cove

pg 133

Squaw Bay

Andrews Bay

Low Is.
San Juan Co. Park

West Valley Rd

Beaverton Valley Rd

"DR"
Fl W 4s

pg 190

Tide rips

Hicks Bay

Hoffman Cove

Smallpox Bay

Bellevue Pt

Trout Lake

San Juan Island

Friday Harbor

Brown Is.   "1"

"2"

Turn Island
State Park

"3"
Fl G 4s

Reef Pt

pg 223

Fl W 10s
*Lime Kiln
State Park*

West Side Rd

Douglas Rd

Bailer Hill Rd

Little Is.

North Bay

Dinner Is.

Merrifield Cove

Pear Pt

Haro Strait

48°
30'

UNITED STATES
CANADA

Deadman Bay

Mulno Cove

pg 220

Griffin Bay

Jensen Bay
Low Pt

Lopez Island

Pile Pt

Kanaka Bay

False Bay

Eagle Pt

*San Juan Island
National Historical Park*

American Camp

Halftide Rocks

North Pacific Rock

Harbor Rock

Goose Is.

Tide rips

Fish Creek

Eagle Cove

Fl W 4
Cattle Pt

pg 215

Inner Passage

© 2013 Blue Latitude Press - Not for Navigation

Beaumont Shoal

Tide rips

Salmon Bank

48°
25'

Strait of Juan De Fuca

Middle Channel

"3"
Fl G 4s

123° 10'   123° 05'   123° 00'

Michael Bertrand www.michaelbertrandphotography.com

San Juan Island

San Juan Island is a magical place, able to satisfy all types of boating desires, from picture perfect harbor towns and marinas to quiet secluded anchorages. For many visitors, San Juan Island is their first experience into the laid back, friendly attitude of island life. Schedules and stresses from everyday life seem to melt away as you sit back and enjoy the maritime show of ferries, seaplanes and pleasure boats coming and going from the island's ports of call at Friday Harbor and Roche Harbor. San Juan Island's population is approximately 7,600 residents making it the largest within San Juan County. The island hosts two National Historic Parks at American Camp and English Camp, a whale watching State Park at Lime Kiln, and county parks scattered throughout the island.

History of San Juan Island

San Juan Island was first inhabited by the Coast Salish people, thousands of years before the first European explorers. With the area's protected waters and abundant natural resources, camps were established throughout the islands. These were supported by fishing, hunting, and gathering. Many of these old campsites can still be seen today in the form of white midden beaches.

By the late 1700's, European explorers began entering the waters of the Pacific Northwest. Gonzalo Lopez de Haro of Spain is believed to be the first of these explorers to spot the San Juan Islands. A few years later, Francisco Eliza made an attempt to explore the area, but rather than recognizing the San Juans as an archipelago, he mapped the area as one large land mass. It was not until 1792 when English lieutenant William Broughton, under the direction of Captain George Vancouver, explored the area and discovered the many islands comprising the San Juan archipelago.

With bountiful salmon runs, rich soils for farming and old growth timber, the islands held great wealth and opportunity. By the turn of the century, both England and the United States were staking claim to the rich lands of the Pacific Northwest. In 1818, a treaty was signed between the two countries, allowing for joint occupation and settlement of the Oregon Territory. As both countries began to expand settlements and business opportunities in the territory, land disputes and tensions grew. In 1846, the Oregon Treaty was signed to help clarify boundaries and ease tensions between the two countries.

"From the point of the forty-ninth parallel of north latitude, where the boundary laid down in existing treaties and conventions between the United States and Great Britain terminates, the line of boundary between the territories of the United States and those of her Britannic Majesty shall be continued westward along the said forty-ninth parallel of north latitude to the middle of the channel which separates the continent from Vancouver's Island, and thence southerly through the middle of the said channel, and of Fuca's Straits, to the Pacific Ocean: Provided, however, That the navigation of the whole of the said channel and straits, south of the forty-ninth parallel of north latitude, remain free and open to both parties."

- Article 1 of The Oregon Treaty, 1846

Lime Kiln Lighthouse

Unfortunately, those present at the negotiations and signing of the treaty were unfamiliar with the actual charting of the Salish Sea. Not one, but two major channels separate mainland Washington and Vancouver Island: Haro Strait to the west and Rosario Strait to the east. Lying between these two major bodies of water are the San Juan Islands, with England interpreting "the channel" to be Rosario Strait, and the U.S. believing it to be Haro Strait.

The English-owned, Hudson's Bay Company had already staked a claim on San Juan Island. Believing greater occupation of the area would enhance England's right to ownership of the islands, the Hudson's Bay Company opened a salmon curing station near what is today known as Roche Harbor, and the Belle Vue sheep farm near what became known as American Camp.

Friday Harbor

American Camp

As the two countries continued to dispute the location of the boundary and therefore ownership of the San Juan Islands, tensions between the English and American settlers living within the islands began to escalate. Tensions came to a head on the fateful day of June 15, 1859, when American, Lyman Cutlar, shot and killed a Hudson's Bay Company pig found rooting in his garden. After refusing to pay for the pig he shot, British authorities were called in, and threatened to arrest and evict Cutlar, as well as his countrymen from San Juan Island.

Tensions quickly rose when the U.S. dispatched a military unit to protect American settlers living on San Juan as well as to maintain an official presence on the island. In response, England dispatched warships in hopes of peacefully forcing the Americans to leave. Until a settlement could be reached between England and the United States over the location of "the channel," England and the U.S. agreed to a joint occupation of the island in 1859 with respective camps occupying either end of San Juan Island. For twelve years, San Juan Island remained peaceful, jointly occupied by the

Farm lands with Olympic Mountain backdrop

two nations. During these years, the British and American camps developed a somewhat social relationship, celebrating respective national holidays and holding various athletic competitions to pass the time.

Friday Harbor waterfront

Finally in 1871, with the signing of the Treaty of Washington, the land dispute issue was sent to Kaiser Wilhelm I of Germany for settlement. An arbitration commission was formed and tackled the issue for nearly a year. On October 21, 1872, the commission determined "the channel" to be Haro Strait, and therefore ownership of the San Juan Islands belonged to the United States. A month later, England's Royal Marines left their post of twelve years and returned to Vancouver Island, ending one of history's most peaceful wars, known as the Pig War.

With the ownership of the islands settled, pioneers began to stake claims, enjoying the area's rich natural resources. San Juan Island provided large salmon runs for salt curing or canning, lush evergreen forests for lumber, rich soil beds for grazing livestock and growing crops, as well as deposits of lime for mining. Small towns began springing up, including Friday Harbor, which was incorporated in 1909, and today remains the only incorporated town in San Juan county. In 1951, Washington state purchased the majority of the holdings from the Puget Sound Navigation Company, and began operating the scheduled ferry routes that we know today. With direct ferry service to the islands, tourists from the mainland cities were able to easily visit. Slowly, the traditional, resource based work on the islands began to shift toward a more tourist based economy.

Michael Bertrand www.michaelbertrandphotography.com

Friday Harbor

Friday Harbor is one of the top destinations within the San Juan Islands. With a year-round population of approximately 2,300 people, Friday Harbor is a thriving, yet quaint island town. A 500-slip marina and a large sheltered harbor make it a popular stop for visiting boaters looking to stock up on provisions, sample one of the many excellent restaurants, or to see the sights in this historic town.

Friday Harbor is located on the eastern shore of San Juan Island, and is accessed by San Juan Channel. Brown Island lies in front of the town, and affords additional protection within the harbor. The main, deep water entrance to Friday Harbor is taken between San Juan Island and the northwest side of Brown Island. This is the entrance used by the Washington State Ferries and most other traffic including seaplanes. At times it can a busy port, therefore requiring good attention at the helm. Ferries approaching or leaving the port (Friday Harbor can dock two ferries at a time) have the right of way so be sure to leave a clear path for their maneuvering, if not, the ferry captain will let you know by five very loud horn blasts!

Additionally, entrance to Friday Harbor can also be taken off the southeast side of Brown Island. A reef extending off the southeast corner of Brown Island is marked by red beacon "2," and should be given a wide berth. Farther from town, this entrance sees less traffic and leads through a number of moorings and anchored boats.

Friday Harbor has a large public marina operated by the Port of Friday Harbor as well as ample room for anchor-

Friday Harbor to:		
Anacortes		19 nm
Bellingham		26 nm
Blaine		31 nm
Blind Bay (Shaw Island)		7 nm
Echo Bay (Sucia Island)		17 nm
Fisherman Bay (Lopez Island)		5 nm
Roche Harbor (San Juan Island)		11 nm
Rosario (Orcas Island)		10 nm
Sidney (Canada)		19 nm
Spencer Spit (Lopez Island)		8 nm
Victoria (Canada)		27 nm

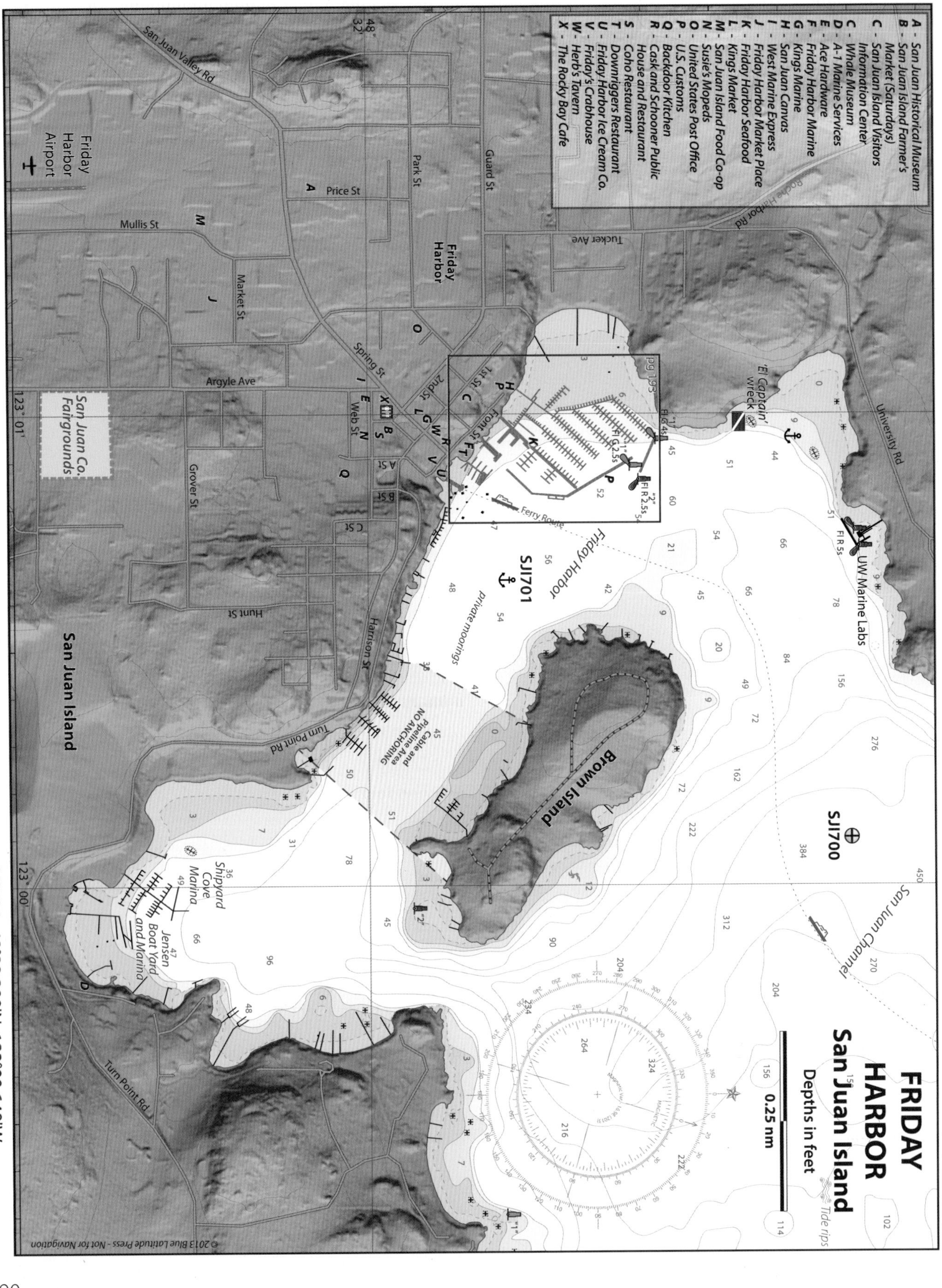

FRIDAY HARBOR
San Juan Island
Depths in feet
0.25 nm
Tide rips
A - San Juan Historical Museum
B - San Juan Island Farmer's Market (Saturdays)
C - San Juan Island Visitors Information Center
D - Whale Museum
E - A-1 Marine Services
F - Ace Hardware
G - Friday Harbor Marine
H - Kings Marine
I - San Juan Canvas
J - West Marine Express
K - Friday Harbor Market Place
L - Friday Harbor Seafood
M - Kings Market
N - San Juan Island Food Co-op
O - Susie's Mopeds
P - United States Post Office
Q - U.S. Customs
R - Backdoor Kitchen
S - Cask and Schooner Public House and Restaurant
T - Coho Restaurant
U - Downriggers Restaurant
V - Friday Harbor Ice Cream Co.
W - Friday's Crabhouse
X - Herb's Tavern
Z - The Rocky Bay Cafe
Friday Harbor
Brown Island
San Juan Island
San Juan Channel
SJI700
SJI701
UW Marine Labs
'El Capitan' wreck
pg 193
private moorings
Cable and Pipeline Area NO ANCHORING
Shipyard Cove Marina
Jensen Boat Yard and Marina
Friday Harbor Airport
San Juan Co. Fairgrounds
Ferry Route
San Juan Valley Rd
Roche Harbor Rd
Tucker Ave
Guard St
Park St
Price St
Mullis St
Market St
Spring St
Argyle Ave
1st St
2nd St
Front St
Web St
A St
B St
C St
Grover St
Hunt St
Harrison St
Turn Point Rd
University Rd
© 2013 Blue Latitude Press - Not for Navigation

SJI700 - 48°32.700'N 123°00.100'W

SJI701 - 48°32.200'N 123°00.640'W

ing. If you plan to anchor within the harbor, keep in mind that much of the anchorage area is relatively deep (40 to 60+ feet), with some current running through the harbor. Anchorage is not permitted within the path of the ferries or the cable and pipeline crossing area.

The most popular anchorage areas are located north of the marina and also east of the ferry terminal. Due to underwater cables stretching from San Juan Island to Brown Island, a small corridor between the two islands is designated as a no anchoring zone. Be sure to check your chart and find the signs on shore marking the cable crossing area if anchoring near the area east of the ferry terminal.

While much of the anchorage at Friday Harbor is deep, the holding is good with a mostly solid mud bottom. However, due to current running through the harbor, especially east of the ferry terminal, be sure your anchor is well set before heading into town.

To dinghy ashore, the Port of Friday Harbor Marina offers a dinghy dock for visiting boaters near the main pier (check with the marina office for fees). Showers, laundry, provisions, restaurants, shopping and even a movie theater are all available in town within easy walking distance.

Michael Bertrand www.michaelbertrandphotography.com

Port of Friday Harbor Marina

The Port of Friday Harbor Marina is a modern 500-slip marina that can accommodate boats up to 150 feet in length. Each slip has access to water and power hookups. Services at the marina include a fuel dock, US Customs dock, seaplane dock, showers, restrooms, laundry, pump out facilities, trash and recycling.

During the busy summer months, the marina operates various check-in stations to help coordinate slip assignments, directions, and handling of docklines (look for staff on the docks). The main pier check-in station, located just below the port office, also serves as a concierge service, assisting with check-ins, city maps, directions, phone numbers and transportation.

When approaching the marina and your slip, be aware that some current flows through the harbor, and can occasionally make docking at the marina tricky during big tides.

Port of Friday Harbor Marina
Monitors VHF channel 66A
204 Front Street North
Friday Harbor, WA 98250
Phone: (360) 378-2688
Fax: (360) 378-6114
tamih@portfridayharbor.org
www.portfridayharbor.org

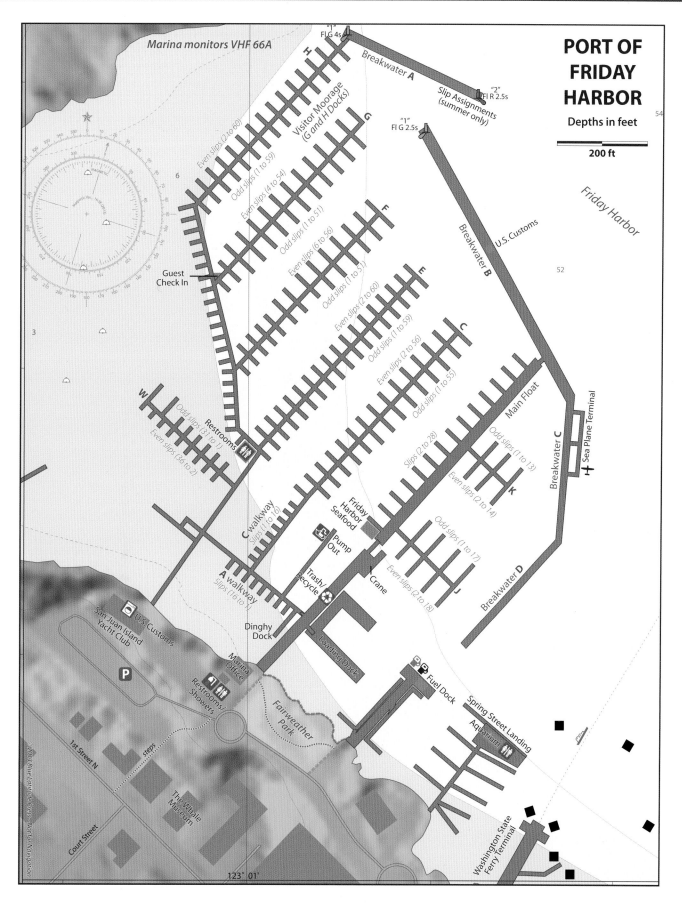

Marina monitors VHF 66A

**PORT OF
FRIDAY
HARBOR**

Depths in feet

200 ft

"1"
Fl G 4s

Breakwater **A**

Slip Assignments
(summer only)

"2"
Fl R 2.5s

"1"
Fl G 2.5s

H

Visitor Moorage
(G and H Docks)

G

Even slips (2 to 60)

Odd slips (1 to 59)

Even slips (4 to 54)

Odd slips (1 to 51)

Even slips (6 to 56)

F

Odd slips (1 to 51)

Even slips (2 to 60)

E

Odd slips (1 to 51)

Even slips (1 to 59)

C

Odd slips (2 to 56)

Even slips (2 to 59)

Odd slips (1 to 55)

Guest
Check In

Breakwater **B**

U.S. Customs

Friday Harbor

54

52

6

3

W

Odd slips (31 to 1)

Even slips (36 to 2)

Restrooms

C walkway
Slips (1 to 16)

Slips (2 to 28)

Main Float

Breakwater **C**

Sea Plane Terminal

Odd slips (1 to 13)

Even slips (2 to 14)

K

Odd slips (1 to 17)

A walkway
Slips (16 to 1)

Friday
Harbor
Seafood

Pump
Out

Trash/
Recycle

Crane

Even slips (2 to 18)

J

Breakwater **D**

Dinghy
Dock

San Juan Island
Yacht Club

U.S Customs

Marina
Office

Restrooms/
Showers

P

Fairweather
Park

Loading Dock

Fuel Dock

Spring Street Landing

Aquarium

1st Street N

steps

The Whale
Museum

Court Street

Washington State
Ferry Terminal

123° 01'

© 2013 Blue Latitude Press-Not for Navigation

History of Friday Harbor

The original inhabitants of the San Juan Islands were the Coast Salish people who used many locations throughout the islands as seasonal camps for harvesting fish and shellfish, as well as many other natural resources found throughout the area. The abundance of these same resources were also the attraction for early European settlers to the islands. As more people started claiming lands in the west, land ownership issues between countries began to arise. The most historic dispute began in the 1800's between the United States and England (see pages 186-188 for a full description).

In order to solidify their ownership of San Juan Island, England backed a claim established by the Hudson's Bay Company who ran a sheep ranch and salmon curing station on San Juan Island. In 1853, the Hudson's Bay Company transported 1,300 sheep to their Belle Vue ranch located on the southern end of the island. It is believed that one of the ranch hands, by the nickname of "Friday," settled in to the area of what is now the town of Friday Harbor. Over time this area began to be referred to as "Friday's Harbor," and the name continues on today.

San Juan Historical Museum

San Juan Historical Museum

San Juan Vineyards

San Juan Vineyards

With its sheltered deep water port, Friday Harbor soon flourished as more settlers moved to the island, and general stores, hotels, and saloons were established. By the early 1900's, Friday Harbor was a full fledged town with a bank, U.S. Customs office, school, theatre, churches, a cannery, and a dairy. The majority of settlers on the island were ranchers, farmers, fishermen, miners, and lumbermen.

Over the next couple of decades, Friday Harbor continued to grow and prosper because of its natural resources. However, by the time of the Great Depression, the economic downturn as well as increased competition from industry, Friday Harbor's prosperity began to falter. It was not until the 1960's that Friday Harbor started to rebound as tourism and real estate surpassed the island's original industries. Today, Friday Harbor is a thriving tourist town and the hub of the islands, drawing thousands of visitors each year.

Sights to See

The first thing on the list for many visitors to Friday Harbor is a stop at the renowned Whale Museum. Located up the stairs from the marina, the museum provides a fascinating look at the natural history of marine mammals, focusing on the stars of the Salish Sea, the orcas of J, K and L pods (see page 15). Within the Gallery of Whales, you will find a wonderful collection of exhibits, artwork, models, and artifacts, including real whale skeletons and a family tree of the resident orcas. After your visit through the museum, you can browse through the museum's store for gifts from books and posters, to t-shirts, stuffed animals, jewelry, and even a whale adoption program. For more information, see page 195.

To complete your sealife tour in Friday Harbor, stop in at the Spring Street Landing Aquarium, at the end of the pier next to the ferry landing. Inside is a 400 gallon aquarium fed with water directly from the harbor. Within the tank you will be captivated by the colorful array of local creatures including surf perch, gunnel fish, cling fish, sea cucumbers, scallops, tube worms, nudibranchs, and much more.

For a glimpse into the past history of San Juan Island, take a trip to the San Juan Historical Museum. The museum is located at the old James King farm, with a number of exhibits housed in the original farm buildings. The museum is located near the corner of Price and Spring Street, approximately one mile southwest from the ferry terminal.

After stepping back in time at the museum, continue your history lesson of Friday Harbor by taking a self-guided historical walking tour of the town. The tour takes you past many of the historical buildings that still stand today. Download the 44-page booklet (pdf)at: www.historicfridayharbor.org/wp/wp-content/uploads/2011/07/walking_tour.pdf

The Whale Museum

The Whale Museum in Friday Harbor is a must stop while visiting San Juan Island. The museum teaches visitors about the natural history of marine mammals, focusing particularly on the Southern Resident orcas found in the waters around the San Juan Islands.

The museum began in the late sixties for the purpose of studying whales. Called the Moclips Cetalogical Society, the organization was based in Moclips, Washington. In 1976, the Society moved to Friday Harbor and began working with the National Marine Fisheries Service to research the Southern Resident Community of orca whales.

The museum includes a wonderful collection of exhibits, artwork, models, and artifacts, including whale skeletons and a family tree of the resident orcas. The museum has a large, well stocked gift store, as well as an orca adoption program which helps to fund additional research of the orcas and other marine mammals in the area. For further information about The Whale Museum and their programs, visit their website at: www.whalemuseum.org.

San Juan Island Farmer's Market

San Juan Island Farmer's Market

If you're looking for a taste of the island's bounty, consider visiting the San Juan Island Farmer's Market. Outside in the Brickworks Plaza, farmers and craftsmen from around the islands set up colorful tables and umbrellas with their local produce and art. Come hungry as a number of food vendors, including bakeries are too tempting to miss. The market is open each Saturday in the spring and summer months from 10am to 1pm.

Wine lovers should consider a trip out to the beautiful vineyards and tasting room at San Juan Vineyards. This locally owned winery began in 1996 and has been producing and bottling their wines ever since. San Juan Vineyards is located on Roche Harbor Road, three miles northwest of Friday Harbor, and is easily spotted by the renovated chapel and schoolhouse buildings.

Marine Chandleries and Services
Ace Hardware
Ace Hardware carries a wide range of hardware, plumbing, electrical, and painting supplies including housewares, outdoor and sporting gear. Located at 340 Argyle Avenue.
Phone: (360) 378-4622   Web: www.acefh.com

Albert Jensen & Sons Boatyard and Marina

In operation since 1910, Jensen & Sons offers permanent marina slips, including covered slips. The boatyard operates a 35 ton travel lift and offers repairs and dry storage. An on site store also carries supplies, oil and more.
Phone: (360) 378-4343   Web: www.jensenshipyard.com

Friday Harbor Marine

Friday Harbor Marine specializes in boat rentals, brokerage, and marine repair services. Located on the waterfront, below Downrigger's Restaurant.
Phone: (360) 378-6202   Web: www.sjimarine.com

Kings Marine

Kings Marine carries a large selection of marine supplies, including electronics, fishing gear, charts and guides for fishing and boating in the San Juans. Located upstairs above the Kings Market grocery store on Spring Street.
Phone: (360) 378-4593   Web: www.kings-market.com

San Juan Canvas

San Juan Canvas specializes in custom sails and canvas work as well as repairs and marine cabinetry. Located under the San Juan Yacht Club at Friday Harbor Marina.
Phone: (360) 378-4119   Web: www.sanjuancanvas.com

US Customs

The US Customs dock at Friday Harbor is open seven days a week, 8am-8pm during the summer months and 8am-5pm during the rest of the year. The customs office is located next to the marina office at 271 Front Street.
Phone: (360) 378-2080 or 1-800-562-5943 after hours
Web: www.cbp.gov

Vessel Assist Friday Harbor

Vessel Assist response boats are located at Friday Harbor and Roche Harbor on San Juan Island. Each boat is rigged for marine towing, and salvage work, as well as carrying extra fuel, engine fluids, pumps, dive gear and battery charging packs. Recreational boaters can call Vessel Assist Friday Harbor 24-hours a day at (360) 378-1111, through the Boat US toll-free Dispatch Service at 800-391-4869, or by hailing on VHF radio channel 16.

West Marine Express

The well renowned marine chandlery has a small express store in Friday Harbor for your boating needs. Located up the hill at the corner of Spring Street and Argyle Avenue.
Phone: (360) 378-1086   Web: www.westmarine.com

Provisioning and Other Services

Friday Harbor Market Place

The Market Place is a popular grocery store for local islanders due to its location away from the busy tourist center in Friday Harbor and its competitive prices. Located towards the airport at 515 Market Street.
Phone: (360) 378-3238

Friday Harbor Seafood

Friday Harbor Seafood specializes in live dungeness crab, prawns, mussels, oysters, scallops and clams, as well as freshly caught (and smoked too) salmon, halibut, cod. Take out items include party platters, chowders, cocktails and more. The quaintly decorated floating market is located on the main dock at the Friday Harbor Marina.
Phone: (360) 378-5779 Web: www.interisland.net/fishcreek/

Griffin Bay Bookstore

Griffin Bay carries a nice selection of books and is centrally located at 155 Spring Street
Phone: (360) 378-5511   Web: www.griffinbaybook.com

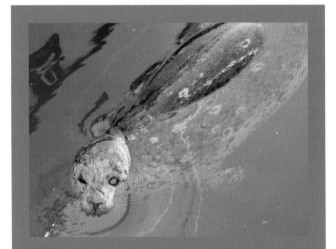

Popeye the Harbor Seal

Popeye the harbor seal is the Port of Friday Harbor's most well known celebrity. After approximately 15 years of patrolling the fairways around Friday Harbor's marina, Popeye's not-so-slender physique is telling of her easy living days. With one cloudy eye and her unusual boldness around people, Popeye is well recognizable around the port. The seal's nose for opportunity frequently leads her to the waters around the Friday Harbor Seafood float in hopes that a small morsel might come her way. In 2005, a sculpture was unveiled at Fairweather Waterfront park honoring this beloved seal. "Popeye," by Matthew Gray Palmer, is a life-size granite sculpture depicting the seal, complete with a mother-of-pearl eye. Popeye is a cherished icon of Friday Harbor and hopefully she will continue to entertain visitors to the marina for years to come.

Harbor Bookstore

Harbor Bookstore is conveniently located next to the ferry landing, and offers a wide selection of books including a local islands section. Located at 22 Cannery Landing.
Phone: (360) 378-7222   Web: www.harborbookstore.com

Kings Market

Kings Market has a great selection of foods, fresh produce, seafood, meats, gourmet deli specialties, wines, and more. Kings Market is conveniently located on Spring Street, one block up from the water.
Phone: (360) 378-4505   Web: www.kings-market.com

San Juan Island Farmer's Market

The San Juan Islands Farmer's Market includes farmers and their produce as well as artisans from throughout the San Juan Islands. The market is open each Saturday from 10am to 1pm at the Brickworks Plaza on Nichols Street.
Web: www.sjifarmersmarket.com

San Juan Island Food Co-op

The Co-op is a cooperatively owned and operated grocery store that sells local and organic products. Located on Mullis street, near the Friday Harbor Airport.
Phone: (360) 370-5170   Web: www.sanjuancoop.org

United States Postal Service

The Friday Harbor post office is open Monday through Friday from 7am to 3pm. The office is located at 220 Blair Avenue, on the corner of Blair and Reed.
Phone: (360) 378-4511   Web: www.usps.com

Transportation

Friday Harbor Taxi

Friday Harbor Taxi serves San Juan Island and also provides packages for guided driving tours of the island.
Phone: (360) 298-4434   Web: www.fridayharbortaxi.com

Island Air

Island Air operates charter, scenic and ambulance flights from Friday Harbor.
Phone: (360) 378-2376   Web: www.sanjuan-islandair.com

Kenmore Air

Kenmore Air provides daily, year-round flights between Seattle and seven locations in the San Juan Islands, including Friday Harbor, on both seaplanes and wheeled aircraft.
Phone: (425) 486-1257   Web: www.kenmoreair.com

Northwest Sky Ferry

Northwest Sky Ferry has scheduled and chartered flights available to and from Bellingham and the San Juan Islands.
Phone: (360) 676-9999   Web: www.skyferrynw.com

NW Seaplanes

NW Seaplanes offers charter and sight seeing flights for western Washington and Canada's British Columbia coast.
Phone: (425) 277-1590   Web: www.nwseaplanes.com

San Juan Airlines

Offering scheduled, charter, and scenic flights from Anacortes, Bellingham, and Seattle to the San Juan Islands and British Columbia.
Phone: 800-874-4434   Web: www.sanjuanairlines.com

San Juan Taxi and Tours
Taxi and island tour service for San Juan Island.
Phone: (360) 378-TAXI   Web: www.sjtaxi.com

San Juan Transit
San Juan Transit offers daily, scheduled transportation around the island, including Friday Harbor, Roche Harbor, Pelindaba Lavender Farm, Krystal Acres Alpaca Ranch, San Juan Vineyard, Lime Kiln Point State Park, English Camp and Lakedale Campground Resort. Schedules vary by season.
Phone: (360) 378-8887   Web: www.sanjuantransit.com

Susie's Mopeds
Susie's Mopeds offers a variety of rental vehicles for those looking to explore the sights of inland San Juan Island. Rentals are available by the hour or by the day. The rental office is located at 125 Nichols, just up from the ferry terminal.
Phone: (360) 378-5244   Web: www.susiesmopeds.com

Victoria Clipper
The Clipper offers daily high-speed passenger-only ferry service between Seattle and Victoria, Canada year-round, and seasonal service between Seattle and Friday Harbor.
Phone: (206) 448-5000   Web: www.clippervacations.com

Washington State Ferries
Washington State Ferries operates numerous passenger and vehicle ferries everyday traveling between Anacortes, the San Juan Islands and Sidney, British Columbia. The port of call for San Juan Island is Friday Harbor. For current schedules and fares, visit their website or call the ferry hotline.
Phone: (206) 464-6400   Web: www.wsdot.wa.gov/ferries/

Restaurants
Backdoor Kitchen
The Backdoor Kitchen is a fine dining experience with international cuisine mixed with a northwest flare. Indoor and outdoor seating set with beautiful ambiance. Open for din-
ner Wednesday through Saturday seasonally (call to check hours in the off season). Located at 400b "A" Street.
Phone: (360) 378-9540   Web: www.backdoorkitchen.com

Cask and Schooner Public House and Restaurant
This newly renovated restaurant has old world nautical charm along with a great location. Meat pies and a cold beer can't be beat. Located on the corner of Front Street and Spring Street.
Phone: (360) 378-2922   Web: www.caskandschooner.com

Coho Restaurant
Coho Restaurant offers seasonally fresh and delicious meals combined with an amazing list of wines. An intimate and fine dining experience including locally farmed and harvested ingredients. Located at 120 Nichols Street.
Phone: (360) 378-6330   Web: www.cohorestaurant.com

Downriggers
With a prime waterfront location and open for breakfast, lunch and dinner, Downriggers is a favorite dining option for those visiting Friday Harbor. Specializing in Pacific Northwest fare and happy hour specials.
Phone: (360) 378-2700 Web: www.downriggerssanjuan.com

Friday Harbor Ice Cream Co.
When walking the waterfront or just getting off the ferry, it is impossible to pass by this ice cream shop. With more than 50 flavors to choose from, one visit is just not enough. Located north of the ferry landing.
Phone: (360) 298-0716

Friday's Crabhouse
Friday's Crabhouse, with it's fantastic view of the harbor and outdoor seating, is a popular stop for ferry goers. Serving fresh seafood as well as grilled burgers. Located directly across from the ferry terminal.
Phone: (360) 378-8801   Web: www.fridayscrabhouse.com

Herb's Tavern
Herb's Tavern is Friday Harbor's local neighborhood bar, with friendly service, excellent burgers, and a long list of cold draft beer to choose from. Pool tables, dart boards, big screen TV's and live music round out this local tavern's entertainment. Located on the corner of 1st and Spring Streets.
Phone: (360) 378-7076

The Rocky Bay Cafe
Rocky Bay Cafe is Friday Harbor's breakfast hotspot. Serving all your breakfast favorites (and lunch too) including an espresso bar. Located at 225 Spring Street.
Phone: (360) 378-5051

Michael Bertrand www.michaelbertrandphotography.com

Roche Harbor

Roche Harbor is a wonderful feast for the senses. This quaint resort village has evolved from an 1800's era lime mining company town. The large, nearly landlocked bay includes plenty of room for anchoring as well as a 377 slip marina. With a fuel and US Customs dock, marine chandlery, grocery, post office, internet, laundry, showers, and restaurants, Roche Harbor is a one-stop-shop for boaters traveling throughout the islands. Boats, dinghies and seaplanes are constantly on the move during the day, adding to the hustle and bustle of the harbor. As sunset approaches, a quiet serenity takes over the harbor for a peaceful evening under the stars. With festive and historic grace, Roche Harbor quickly becomes a top favorite of all who visit.

Roche Harbor is located on the northwestern side of San Juan Island (as well as the southern border of the Canadian Gulf Islands). For this reason, Roche Harbor tends to be a popular entry point for boats clearing customs.

Entrance to the harbor can be taken via Spieden Channel to the north, or Mosquito Pass to the south. The most common and hazard-free approach is taken off Spieden Channel between Pearl Island and Henry Island. This is a clear and deep water entrance, able to accommodate large yachts and deep draft vessels.

When transiting Spieden Channel, keep in mind that strong currents can flow through this area, so you may want

Roche Harbor to:		
	Anacortes	28 nm
	Bellingham	34 nm
	Blaine	31 nm
	Blind Bay *(Shaw Island)*	11 nm
	Echo Bay *(Sucia Island)*	16 nm
	Fisherman Bay *(Lopez Island)*	14 nm
	Friday Harbor *(San Juan Island)*	11 nm
	Jones Island	6 nm
	Rosario *(Orcas Island)*	17 nm
	Sidney *(Canada)*	10 nm
	Spencer Spit *(Lopez Island)*	16 nm
	Victoria *(Canada)*	21 nm

199

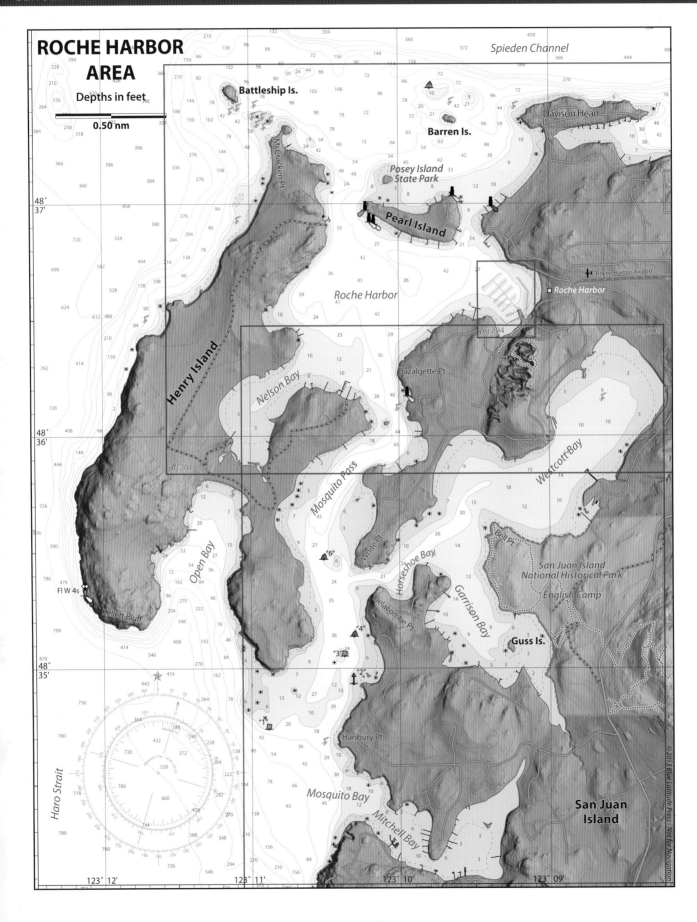

ROCHE HARBOR
AREA

Depths in feet

0.50 nm

Spieden Channel

Battleship Is.

Barren Is.

Davison Head

Posey Island
State Park

Pearl Island

Roche Harbor Airport

Roche Harbor

pg 204

pg 209

Roche Harbor

Henry Island

Bazalgette Pt.

Nelson Bay

Westcott Bay

pg 201

Mosquito Pass

San Juan Island
National Historical Park

Open Bay

White Pt.

Horseshoe Bay

English Camp

Bell Pt.

Kellett Bluff

FI W 4s

Delacombe Pt.

Garrison Bay

Guss Is.

"4"

"3"

"2"

"1"

Hanbury Pt.

Mosquito Bay

**San Juan
Island**

Haro Strait

Mitchell Bay

123° 12'

123° 11'

123° 10'

123° 09'

48°
37'

48°
36'

48°
35'

© 2013 Blue Latitude Press - Not for Navigation

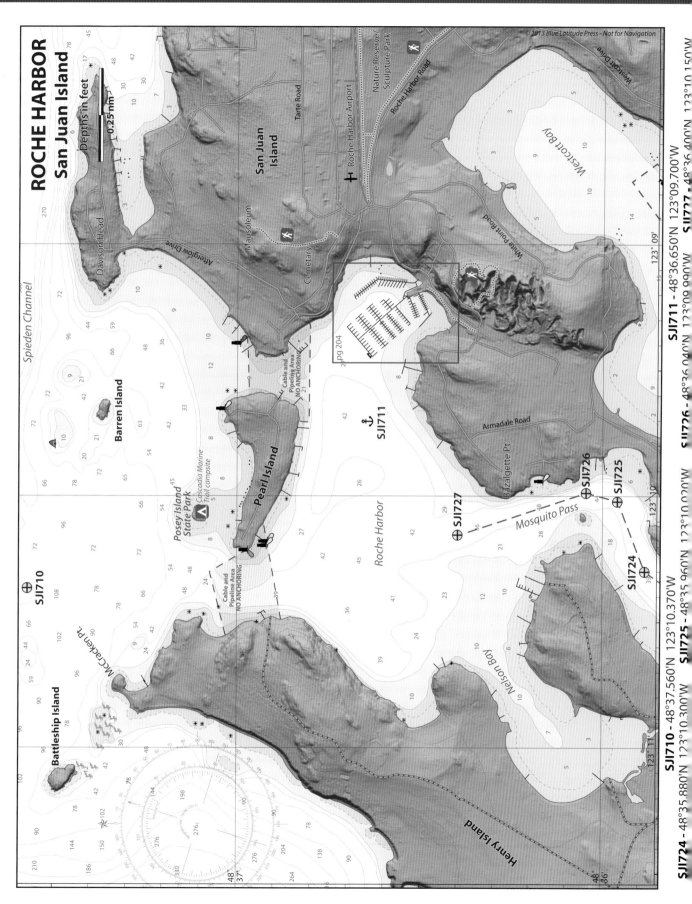

ROCHE HARBOR
San Juan Island

Depths in feet

0.25 nm

Spieden Channel

Davison Head

Afterglow Drive

San Juan Island

Mausoleum

Cemetery

Tarte Road

Nature Reserve/
Sculpture Park

Roche Harbor Airport

Roche Harbor Road

White Point Road

Westcott Bay

Westcott Drive

Barren Island

Cable and
Pipeline Area
NO ANCHORING

pg 204

Armadale Road

Bazalgette Pt.

Mosquito Pass

Cascadia Marine
Trail campsite

Posey Island
State Park

Pearl Island

Cable and
Pipeline Area
NO ANCHORING

SJI711

Roche Harbor

SJI727

SJI726

SJI725

SJI724

Nelson Bay

McCracken Pt.

SJI710

Battleship Island

Henry Island

© 2013 Blue Latitude Press - Not for Navigation

SJI711 - 48°36.650'N 123°09.700'W

SJI726 - 48°36.040'N 123°09.000'W

SJI727 - 48°36.400'N 123°09.150'W

SJI710 - 48°37.560'N 123°10.370'W

SJI725 - 48°35.960'N 123°10.300'W

SJI724 - 48°35.880'N 123°10.300'W

123° 09'

123° 10'

123° 11'

48° 37'

48° 36'

201

to time your approach accordingly if possible. A few hazards are also located near this area, fortunately they are marked by lighted buoys. Center Reef is located approximately 0.75 miles south of Spieden Island's western tip, with Danger Shoal being located 1 mile to the southwest. Both are covered in kelp. If approaching Roche Harbor from Stuart Island, be sure to take note of these hazards. Shallow water is also found 0.6 miles northeast of the main entrance to Roche Harbor, directly north of Barren Island. The northwestern extent of this shallow water is marked by a buoy. If approaching from the east via Spieden Channel, be sure to not cut the corner here.

Entrance to Roche Harbor can also be taken between Pearl Island and San Juan Island for those with local knowledge and shallow draft boats. This passage is shallow and has a few unmarked reefs, including one that is mostly covered at

Unmarked reef northeast of Pearl Island

high water off the northeastern shore of Pearl Island. If using this approach, be sure to check the tide first and to keep a careful watch for reefs.

Entrance to Roche Harbor can also be taken from the south from Haro Strait via Mosquito Pass. This winding channel is narrow and has sections of shallow water, but is well marked with channel buoys. Be aware that current runs through this channel, with stronger currents found along the dogleg turn. When approaching Mosquito Pass from Haro Strait, be sure to note the large reef extending off the southeastern tip of Henry Island, marked by buoy #1. Do not cut the corner around Henry Island, and be sure to give the reef a wide berth.

Mosquito Pass and Roche Harbor are *No Wake Zones*. During the summer months, these areas receive a tremendous amount of traffic from kayakers and small dinghies to large yachts and seaplanes. For the safety of others on the water, as well as preventing shoreline and dock destruction, be sure to look behind your boat and reduce your speed accordingly to ensure you are not creating a wake.

Once inside Roche Harbor, protected anchorage can be taken anywhere within the bay in 5 to 7 fathoms over a good holding mud bottom. Some current can flow through this anchorage. Depending on a boat's hull and ground tackle (chain or nylon rode), boats may sit or turn differently at anchor, so be sure to give ample room to your neighbors. A number of mooring buoys are also located within the harbor, however these moorings are private and are not for public use.

Michael Bertrand www.michaelbertrandphotography.com

Roche Harbor Marina

The Roche Harbor Marina can accommodate boats up to 150 feet in length with 377 slips available. Each slip has water and power hookups (30 to 100 amp available). Services include a fuel dock, US Customs, seaplane dock, restrooms, showers, laundry, wireless internet, mobile pump out services by the M/V *Pheacal Phreak*, trash and recycling. The marina

also offers guests access to the resort's amenities like the pool, tennis and bocce courts, walking trails and the gardens.

Upon arrival, staff members will greet you at your slip and assist with your docklines. During the summer months, the marina is very active with visiting and resident boats, along with hosting a number of boating events including more than 30 different rendezvous and the popular Fourth of July celebration. The marina also performs a colors ceremony each evening twenty minutes prior to sunset, from May through September, complete with music and lowering of the flags.

Roche Harbor Marina
Monitors VHF channel 78a
248 Reuben Memorial Drive
Roche Harbor, WA 98250
Phone: (360) 378-2155 ext. 450, or 1-800-586-3590
marina@rocheharbor.com
www.rocheharbor.com

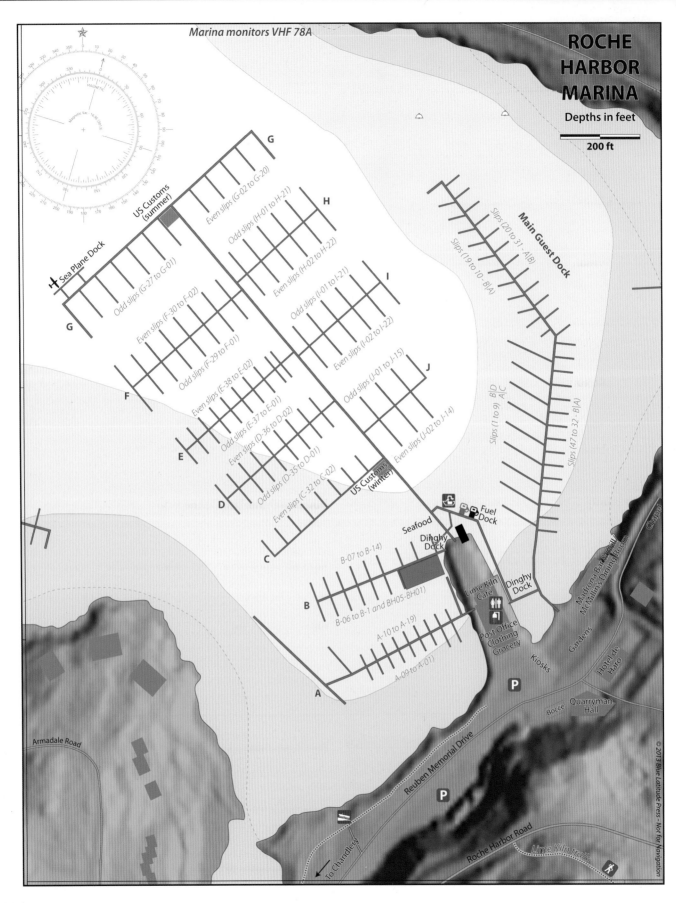

Marina monitors VHF 78A

ROCHE HARBOR MARINA

Depths in feet

200 ft

MAGNETIC

Magnetic Var. 16 56' 2003

Sea Plane Dock

US Customs (summer)

G

Even slips (G-02 to G-20)

Odd slips (G-27 to G-01)

H

Odd slips (H-01 to H-21)

Even slips (H-02 to H-22)

I

Odd slips (I-01 to I-21)

Even slips (I-02 to I-22)

Odd slips (I-01 to J-15)

Even slips (F-30 to F-02)

Odd slips (F-29 to F-01)

Even slips (E-38 to E-02)

Odd slips (E-37 to E-01)

Even slips (D-36 to D-02)

Odd slips (D-35 to D-01)

J

Even slips (J-02 to J-14)

Main Guest Dock

Slips (20 to 31 - A|B)

Slips (19 to 10 - B|A)

Slips (1 to 9) B|D A|C

Slips (47 to 32 - B|A)

G

F

E

D

C

B

A

Even slips (C-32 to C-02)

US Customs (winter)

Seafood

Dinghy Dock

Fuel Dock

Dinghy Dock

B-07 to B-14

B-06 to B-1 and BH05-BH01

A-10 to A-19

A-09 to A-01

Lime Kiln Cafe

Post Office Clothing Grocery

Madrona Bar & Grill McMillin's Dining Room

Gardens

Hotel de Haro

Chapel

Kiosks

P

Bocce

Quarryman Hall

Armadale Road

Reuben Memorial Drive

P

To Chandlery

Roche Harbor Road

Lime Kiln Trail

Roche Harbor Resort formal gardens

History of Roche Harbor

Roche Harbor was originally named after the British Royal Marine, Lieutenant Richard Roche. During the Pig War (1860-1872), when British and American military troops jointly occupied San Juan Island over land dispute issues, the British built a fort at nearby Garrison Bay. Previously, this area had been inhabited for thousands of years by Coast Salish people who fished, hunted and gathered the rich natural resources of San Juan Island and surrounding waters.

During the British military occupation, limestone was found in large quantities around the area of Roche Harbor. Troops were soon thereafter commissioned to mine the lime deposits. In 1872, at the end of the Pig War, British troops returned to Vancouver Island and an American settler named Joe Ruff put a homestead claim on the land around Roche Harbor.

John S. McMillin, who moved with his family from Indiana to Washington in 1884, was an attorney and partner in the Tacoma Lime Company. After learning of the large deposits of limestone found on San Juan Island, McMillin and his partners purchased the Roche Harbor quarry from the Scurr brothers in 1886. McMillin developed the quarry into a large scale operation, complete with a company town to serve the workers and their families.

During its peak, the Roche Harbor Lime and Cement Company was the largest lime mining operation on the

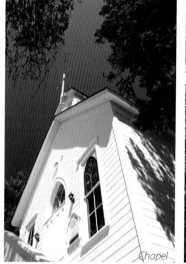
Chapel

McMillin Mausoleum

Artist kiosks

Reserve Sculpture Park

Nightly colors ceremony

west coast, employing roughly 800 workers. The town included the lime mining and kiln operations, the Hotel de Haro, wood barrel fabrication, numerous piers and docks, transport ships, a church and school, a company store, and houses along the hillside for employees and their families.

By the 1930's, lime production was beginning to slow due to decreased demand in building materials caused by the Great Depression and subsequent economic downturn. In 1956, the McMillin family sold the Roche Harbor property to Seattle businessman, Reuben J. Tarte, who began a new era for the company town.

The Tarte family reclaimed many of the old buildings, and transformed the old company town into a new maritime-based resort, complete with a modern marina. For over three decades, the Tarte family improved and operated Roche Harbor Resort. In 1988, the resort was sold to Rich Komen and Saltchuk Resources. Today, Roche Harbor is once again in a new phase of development, combining a premier northwest boating resort with a luxurious year-round permanent community with plans to develop a residential neighborhood and new commercial buildings.

Sights to See

The resort at Roche Harbor has a long list of activities for everyone to enjoy. From walking trails to shopping, history lessons to sculpture gardens, Roche Harbor is sure to keep you busy throughout your stay.

The sight that most everyone encounters when first arriving at the resort are the formal gardens found in front of the Hotel de Haro. During the summer months these gardens are a vibrant mixture of electric greens and brilliant fuchsias. Cobblestone walking paths wind through the well designed gardens and under a rose-filled trellis, with benches available for taking in the beauty of the surroundings.

For those looking for a little lively competition, check out the newly constructed bocce courts or nearby disc golf course. The popular Italian ball sport of bocce has become quite a hit at the resort, with two courts available for use next to the Quarryman Hall suites (game rules posted nearby). For a unique combination of frisbee and golf, bring your discs and hit the course located at 401 Rouleau Rd. (in the Roche Harbor Trails area). And if you are looking for a little more exercise in your sport, head to one of the resort's tennis courts, located next to the swimming pool on the north side of property.

For those looking to do some shopping while visiting Roche Harbor, a number of options are found around the central courtyard of the resort. Clothing stores, gift and household boutique stores and a grocery store can be found here. Also located in this area are artist kiosks, where you can find handmade crafts, as well as a few treats like candy, ice cream and espresso drinks.

Just north of the formal gardens and hotel is the historic, Our Lady of Good Voyage Chapel. This chapel was originally built for the McMillin family as a Methodist Church in the late 1800's. During this time it was also used as a schoolhouse for the children living in the company town. When Roche Harbor was sold to the Tarte family, the chapel was refurbished and dedicated as a Catholic Church.

Roche Harbor is also a wonderful place to take a stroll and enjoy the many walking trails and interpretive signs found throughout the property. One of the most popular trails takes you north of the resort to the cemetery and Mc-Millin Mausoleum. Scattered throughout the forest, you will find headstones for many of the people who lived and worked at the Roche Harbor Lime and Cement Company town. Continuing further down the trail you will come upon the stately and very unique McMillin family mausoleum. This limestone structure features symbolic icons that represent McMillin's family, the Masonic Order and the stages of physical and spiritual life.

Additional trails are found throughout the property as well as the nearby surrounding land (see **sanjuanislandtrails. org/trailsw/** for trail maps). Many of the walking paths on the resort property also display interpretive signs with photos and history of the former mining town. A noteworthy stop for art lovers is the Reserve Sculpture Park found near the entrance to the resort and next to the airfield. The sculpture park houses a rotating exhibit of over 100 sculptures in an open 19-acre setting from artists found locally and around the world.

Theater lovers will also enjoy the *Shakespeare Under the Stars* series in July and August at the resort. Presented by Island Stage Left, this free production provides professional theatre in a stunning outdoor amphitheater located just south of the main resort complex (donations are also welcome). Check the Island Stage Left website at **www.islandstageleft. org** for a current schedule of performances and show times.

Marine Chandleries, Provisioning and Services
Roche Harbor Marine, Inc.
Roche Harbor Marine handles service and repairs of marine engines and electronics. The shop also includes a parts department, well stocked marine chandlery and trailer boat storage. Located near the maintenance building at the southwest corner of the resort.
Phone: (360) 378-6510   Web: www.rocheharbormarine.com

The Company Store
The Company Store is the local one-stop shopping for Roche Harbor. The well stocked grocery has a wide selection of fresh produce, dairy, meats and staples, along with a large selection of wine and beer. The store also sells fishing licenses, fishing gear and a few marine chandlery items.

North Sound Seafood
For the freshest locally caught seafood including live dungeness crab and spot prawns, North Sound Seafood is your source. North Sound is located at the bottom of the main

ramp with daily summer hours from 11am to 7pm.
Phone: (360) 378-3904 Web: www.northsoundseafood.com

Susie's Mopeds
Susie's Mopeds offers a variety of rental vehicles for those looking to explore the sights of inland San Juan Island. Rentals are available by the hour or by the day. The rental office is located at resort entrance, across from the airport.
Phone: (360) 378-5244   Web: www.susiesmopeds.com

United States Postal Service
Located next to The Company Store and the public restrooms is a small office of the USPS. This office can handle all your shipping needs as well as delivery options including post office boxes and general delivery. Office hours are Monday through Friday from 10:30am to 1:30pm.
Phone: (360) 370-7709   Web: www.usps.com

US Customs
The US Customs dock at Roche Harbor is open year round with seasonal hours. Customs is located next to the marina office on G dock during the summer months.
Phone: (360) 378-2080

Village Artist Kiosks
Local artists including photographers, painters, jewelry makers, knitters, and more gather each day in front of The Company Store to display their colorful arts and crafts. A popular espresso/ice cream kiosk as well as a candy kiosk are also located within the mix.

Restaurants
Lime Kiln Cafe
The Lime Kiln Cafe, located at the top of the ramp from the marina is a popular breakfast and lunch hotspot. Freshly made doughnuts, hearty egg dishes, gourmet sandwiches and fish and chips highlight the menu. Outdoor seating is also available. Summer cafe hours are 7am to 4pm daily.

McMillin's Dining Room
McMillin's is a San Juan County Certified Local restaurant specializing in fresh, local ingredients. Gourmet Pacific Northwest cuisine is paired with an impressive wine list to create a memorable waterfront dining experience. Summer restaurant hours are 5pm to 10pm daily.

Madrona Bar and Grill
The Madrona Bar and Grill is a popular casual dining location with an outdoor deck perfect for catching sunsets over the harbor. Fresh salads and seafood, grilled sandwiches, and kiln-fired pizzas are menu favorites. Summer restaurant hours are 11am to 10pm daily.

Overlooking Garrison Bay from Young Hill

Garrison Bay

Garrison Bay is the place we all dream about when looking for the perfect intimate anchorage with nearly 360° protection. Not only does this charming bay have full protection from the elements, it is also adjacent to a national historic park. The park is the historical location of English Camp, when England occupied San Juan Island through the mid 1800's during the infamous Pig War. With beautiful hikes throughout the surrounding park, tours of the historical museum, and a perfectly protected anchorage, Garrison Bay is a must stop on every boater's list.

Garrison Bay is found on the northwest corner of San Juan Island, only 3 miles south of Roche Harbor. To reach the bay, passage must be taken using Mosquito Pass. This winding channel is narrow and has sections of shallow water, but is well marked with channel buoys. Be aware that current runs through this channel, with stronger currents found along the dogleg turn. When approaching Mosquito Pass from Haro Strait, be sure to note the large reef extending off the southeastern tip of Henry Island, marked by buoy #1, and to give the reef a wide berth.

The entrance to Garrison Bay and Westcott Bay is found nearly midway through Mosquito Pass. This entrance is marked by White Point to the north and Delacombe Point to the south. A finger of shallow water extends northwest off Delacombe Point so be sure to not cut the corner when approaching the entrance. Although the entrance is somewhat narrow, mid channel has a depth of 3 to 4 fathoms. From

Garrison Bay to:		
	Anacortes	30 nm
	Bellingham	37 nm
	Blaine	33 nm
	Blind Bay (Shaw Island)	13 nm
	Echo Bay (Sucia Island)	18 nm
	Fisherman Bay (Lopez Island)	16 nm
	Friday Harbor (San Juan Island)	12 nm
	Reid Harbor (Stuart Island)	6 nm
	Rosario (Orcas Island)	19 nm
	Sidney (Canada)	12 nm
	Spencer Spit (Lopez Island)	18 nm
	Victoria (Canada)	20 nm

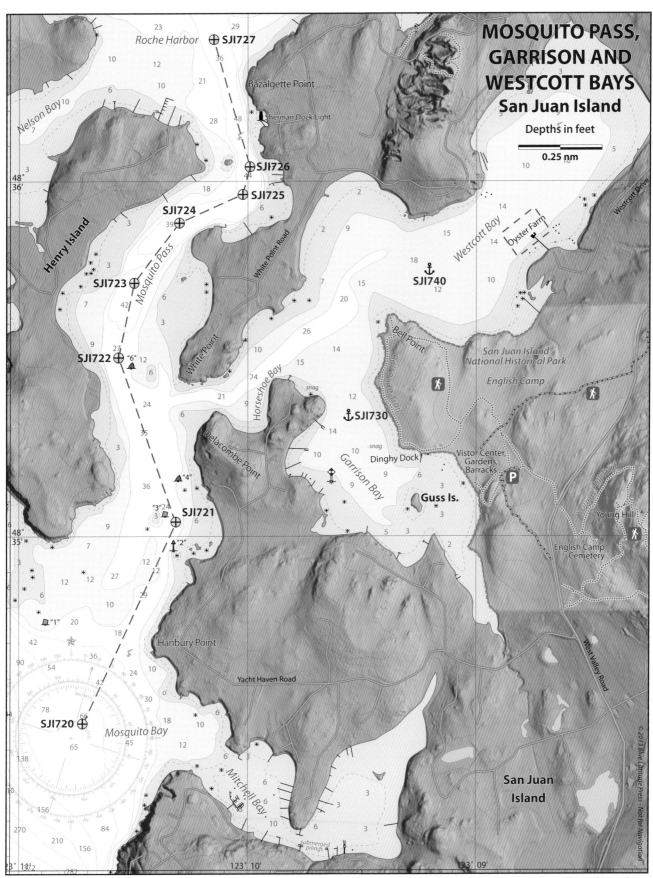

MOSQUITO PASS, GARRISON AND WESTCOTT BAYS
San Juan Island
Depths in feet

0.25 nm

SJI720 - 48°34.470'N 123°10.730'W   SJI721 - 48°35.040'N 123°10.320'W   SJI722 - 48°35.500'N 123°10.570'W   SJI723 - 48°35.710'N 123°10.500'W
SJI724 - 48°35.880'N 123°10.300'W   SJI725 - 48°35.960'N 123°10.020'W   SJI726 - 48°36.040'N 123°09.990'W   SJI727 - 48°36.400'N 123°10.150'W
SJI730 - 48°35.330'N 123°09.560'W   SJI740 - 48°35.730'N 123°09.200'W

this entrance, the bay then splits in two, with Garrison Bay to the south and Westcott Bay to the north.

When anchoring in or near Garrison Bay, keep in mind that much of the bay is shoal, especially towards the head of the bay and sections of the shoreline. Be sure to check with the tide tables before dropping your anchor to make sure you have enough depth at low water. For the deepest water, most boats choose to anchor close to the entrance to Garrison Bay, either inside or outside the bay. The bottom is solid holding mud, although during the summer months, kelp growth on the bottom can increase here. Depending on your anchor, it may take longer to properly set through the kelp.

Once settled in, a trip to shore to explore the museum and the labyrinth of trails around the park is a must. To dinghy ashore, the National Historic Park has provided easy access with a dock for dinghies twenty feet and under. At the top of the landing is a sign detailing a map of the park walking trails, and information regarding the museum and renovated structures found at English Camp.

History of English Camp

The original inhabitants of English Camp were the Coast Salish people. Due to its all-round protection, English Camp is believed to have been a winter village site where canoes could easily be launched to fish within the protec-

tion of the bay. Evidence of these villages can still be seen today in the form of midden beaches. Over the course of approximately two thousand years, clam shells were discarded on the shoreline and eventually broken down to form thick, brilliant, white beaches. These same village sites attracted many of the early explorers and settlers, including the English military who formed a camp at Garrison Bay.

In 1860, commander of the *H.M.S. Satellite*, Captain James Prevost selected the site on Garrison Bay to house the military camp for English soldiers during the joint occupation of San Juan Island by the U.S. and English (see page 186 for details leading up to the joint occupation). Under the recommendation of Lieutenant Richard Roche, Garrison Bay was chosen for its sheltered harbor, open grass area for field maneuvers, fresh water supply, and trail that led to the Hudson's Bay Company sheep farm at Belle Vue.

A commissary or storage building was first erected, followed shortly by barracks, cook houses and other military storage buildings. During the first years of the camp, life was not easy as the men worked hard clearing the land and building structures.

In 1867, a new camp commander arrived, Captain William Delacombe. The captain is believed to be responsible for building the formal garden that stands today, along with new officer's quarters located on the hill overlooking the garden. Looking back over historical photos, it is believed the formal garden may have actually been a strawberry garden. Today's formal garden was recreated during the 1970's.

Life in the camp improved each year as men moved out of tents and into the more sheltered buildings. Gardens were grown to provide a fresh food source as well. By 1872, the land dispute between the U.S. and England had been resolved, and the English soldiers moved back to Victoria, British Columbia.

In 1876, William and Mary Crook homesteaded the majority of the English Camp site. They lived in and used a number of the military buildings, and planted fruit trees, some of which can still be seen today. The property remained with the Crook family until the 1960's, when the remaining Crook family members sold the property to the National Park Service.

Sights to See

When anchoring in Garrison Bay, the obvious sight to see is English Camp. A park dinghy dock is available for use by visiting boaters and kayakers. At the end of the dock is a park sign with maps and information regarding the park. From here, the trail heads to the north for a nice, mostly flat, mile-long loop to Bell Point, or to the south towards the main buildings, museum and gift shop at English Camp. A self-guided walking tour is available through the park service and is a great way to see the sights and learn the history of the camp. A paper version of the tour is usually available at the head of the dock or museum, or a handy full-color pdf version is available for download at: **www.nps.gov/sajh/historyculture/upload/English_Camp_History_Walk_online.pdf**

After checking out the sites of English Camp, take a hike up to Young Hill (650 feet), where you will be rewarded with sweeping views of Garrison Bay, as well as the San Juan and Gulf Islands. Along the way, the trail also passes by the old cemetery for English Camp.

For those looking to get off the boat and get a little extra exercise, there is a maze of trails adjacent to English Camp and Roche Harbor. To download trail maps to your smart phone or to print off copies, the San Juan Island Trails Committee has a wonderful website with pdf versions of maps available for the entire island at: **www.sanjuanislandtrails.org/trailsw/**

Westcott Bay

Westcott Bay is located within the landlocked protection of San Juan Island's northwestern shore. This shallow, yet spacious bay has lots of room for anchoring, and is located next to Garrison Bay and the national historic park of English Camp. During the peak summer months when Garrison Bay fills with boats, Westcott Bay offers a nice alternative for anchoring while still having close access to the park land and trail system.

Westcott Bay is found just northeast of Garrison Bay and south of Roche Harbor on San Juan Island. Approaches to the bay can be taken via Haro Strait or Spieden Channel to Mosquito Pass. The narrow entrance to both Westcott and Garrison Bays is located on Mosquito Pass, the winding waterway between Henry Island and San Juan Island. When approaching Mosquito Pass, be sure to consult your charts and current atlas, and to follow the navigational buoys marking the channel through the pass. For a full description of the pass and entrance to the bays, the Garrison Bay section on page 208.

At the entrance, the waterway widens and splits in two, with Westcott Bay to the north and Garrison Bay to the south. A marginally deeper section of water (3 to 4 fathoms) is found mid channel up to Bell Point, which marks the southern entrance point to Westcott Bay. Anchorage can be taken north and east of Bell Point in 2 to 3 fathoms over a mud bottom. Be aware of shallow water and pilings found along the shoreline, and to check your tide tables before anchoring. Private moorings and a shellfish "farm" from Westcott Bay Sea Farms are also located within the bay.

Shore access is available at English Camp in Garrison Bay, where a small park dinghy dock is available for visitors. At the park, self-guided walking tours are available of the preserved historical grounds, as well as access to miles of Roche Harbor, Highlands, English Camp and Mitchell Hill Trails. Trail maps can be viewed and downloaded at: **www.sanjua-nislandtrails.org/trailsw/**. These trails are not to be missed and offer amazing sights and nature viewing opportunities including wetlands, a fresh water lake and mountain views.

Westcott Bay to:		
Anacortes		30 nm
Bellingham		37 nm
Blaine		33 nm
Blind Bay *(Shaw Island)*		13 nm
Echo Bay *(Sucia Island)*		18 nm
Fisherman Bay *(Lopez Island)*		16 nm
Friday Harbor *(San Juan Island)*		12 nm
Rosario *(Orcas Island)*		19 nm
Sidney *(Canada)*		12 nm
Spencer Spit *(Lopez Island)*		18 nm
Victoria *(Canada)*		20 nm

Snug Harbor Resort

Mitchell Bay

Lined with waterfront homes and a small marina, the shallow waters of Mitchell Bay offer boaters a protected haven on the northwest shore of San Juan Island. A narrow entrance guarded by reefs, opens to a small, pleasant bay that is home to the Snug Harbor Resort and Marina. The calm and shallow waters of the harbor provide a perfect setting for a leisurely paddle along the shoreline, while keeping an eye out for marine wildlife.

Mitchell Bay is located just south of the western entrance to Mosquito Pass on San Juan Island. Approaches to the bay can be taken from Haro Strait or Mosquito Pass. Before entering the bay, keep in mind that the majority of Mitchell Bay has a depth of one fathom or less, and is therefore inaccessible to deep draft boats.

The entrance to Mitchell Bay is located within Mosquito Bay, south of Hanbury Point. Due to rocks within the narrow entrance, be sure to consult your charts prior to entering. At the entrance, a rock 3 feet high lies in the center of the narrow waterway. Boats must pass to the north of this charted rock as shoal water and rocks lie to the south and west. Once inside, shallow anchorage can found over a mud bottom in 1 fathom. Private buoys are located throughout, however these are not available to the public.

Snug Harbor Resort

Snug Harbor Resort and Marina offers 50 slips, each with electricity and water. Services at the marina include a boat launch ramp, restrooms, showers, a small grocery and gift shop, along with cabin rentals and a campground.

Snug Harbor Resort
1997 Mitchell Bay Road
Friday Harbor, WA 98250
Phone: (360) 378-4762
sneakaway@snugresort.com
www.snugresort.com

Mosquito Bay

Charted rock lying mid-channel

Michael Bertrand www.michaelbertrandphotography.com

Griffin Bay

While often overlooked for the popular anchorages of Friday Harbor, Roche Harbor and Fisherman Bay, Griffin Bay is a hidden gem on San Juan Island. The bay hits the trifecta for many with its remote and isolated feel, public beaches and hiking trails, and it's amazing scenic beauty. Miles of sandy public beaches and walking trails frame this expansive south wind protected anchorage. Although you will generally not find more than a handful of boats peacefully swinging at anchor here, there are enough beaches and public lands for hundreds of boats to enjoy. And to top the list of accolades for this great bay, is the National Historical Park of American Camp, where U.S. soldiers once stood vigil during the "Pig War" with England in the 1800's.

Griffin Bay is located on the southeastern side of San Juan Island within the protection of Cattle Point. Approaches to the bay can be made via San Juan Channel, which separates San Juan and Lopez Islands. When approaching from the south near Cattle Point, be aware that tip rips and stronger current flows through the narrow passage between the point and Lopez Island. Current flowing between Goose Island and Deadman Island averages around 2.6 knots and

can reach up to 5 knots or more. Be sure to check your tide and current tables when transiting through this area.

This southern entrance to San Juan Channel is also flanked by shallow areas and reefs. Salmon Bank is located south of Cattle Point with depths ranging from 1 to 3 fathoms. Boats approaching San Juan Channel from the west should pass south of the lighted gong buoy marking the southern reaches of the bank. Once in the channel, pass

Griffin Bay to:		
Anacortes	22 nm
Bellingham	28 nm
Blaine	36 nm
Blind Bay *(Shaw Island)*	10 nm
Echo Bay *(Sucia Island)*	25 nm
Fisherman Bay *(Lopez Island)*	5 nm
Friday Harbor *(San Juan Island)*	6 nm
Jones Island	14 nm
Pelican Beach *(Cypress Island)*	16 nm
Roche Harbor *(San Juan Island)*	16 nm
Victoria *(Canada)*	22 nm
Watmough Bay *(Lopez Island)*	10 nm

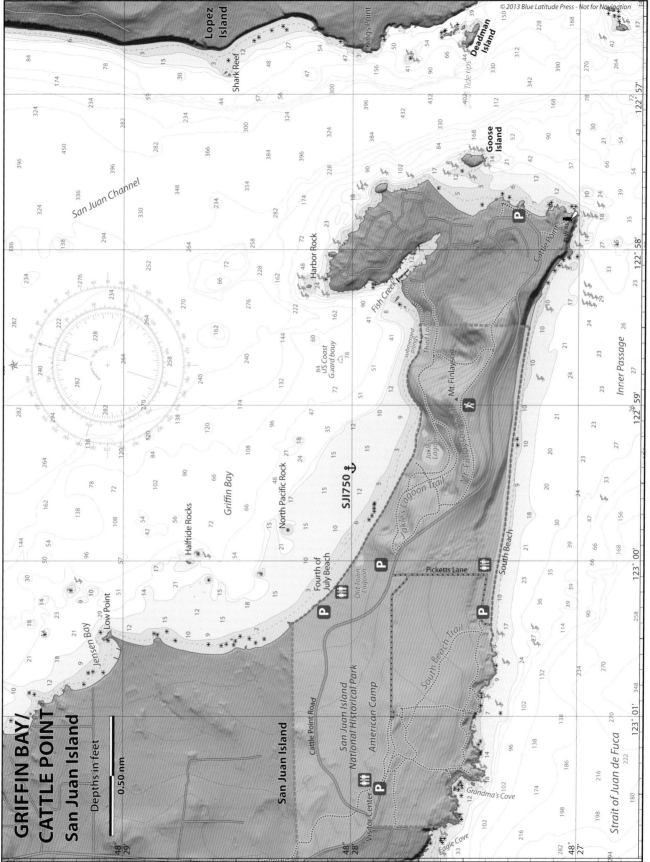

© 2013 Blue Latitude Press - Not for Navigation

**GRIFFIN BAY/
CATTLE POINT**
San Juan Island

Depths in feet

0.50 nm

Lopez Island

Shark Reef

Kings Point

Deadman Island

Goose Island

San Juan Channel

Harbor Rock

Cattle Point

Fish Creek

submerged pilings

Third Lagoon

Mt. Finlayson

US Coast Guard bouy

Inner Passage

Jakles Lagoon

Mt. Finlayson Trail

Jakles Lagoon Trail

SJI750

North Pacific Rock

Griffin Bay

Halftide Rocks

Fourth of July Beach

Old Town Lagoon

Picketts Lane

South Beach

Jensen Bay

Low Point

San Juan Island

Cattle Point Road

San Juan Island National Historical Park

American Camp

South Beach Trail

Visitor Center

Grandma's Cove

Eagle Cove

Strait of Juan de Fuca

48° 29'

48° 28'

48° 27'

123° 01'

123° 00'

122° 59'

122° 58'

122° 57'

SJI750 - 48°28.000'N 122°59.400'W

215

between Deadman Island and Goose Island. Do not pass between San Juan Island and Goose Island.

When rounding into Griffin Bay from the south, be sure to give the peninsula of land north of Fish Creek ample room as Harbor Rock lies just to the north.

History of American Camp

Camp San Juan Island, or American Camp as most know it as today, was originally established in 1860 by the United States Army during the land dispute with England over the San Juan Islands region (see page 186 for information on the Pig War). It was near this location, on the south side of the island, where Englishman, Charles J. Griffin of the Hudson's Bay Company, established his Belle Vue Sheep Farm, and where American farmer, Lyman Cutlar, established a potato farm. Tensions began to rise when Griffin's pig was shot by Cutlar. This escalation, ultimately resulted in a joint military occupation of San Juan Island.

Brigadier General William S. Harney was first to land on the scene at San Juan Island. Fearing that England was trying to gain control over the island, he sent orders to Captain George E. Pickett, stationed at Fort Bellingham, to occupy the island and protect U.S. interests. On July 26, 1859, Pickett landed near Old Town Lagoon on Griffin Bay and set up camp. In response, the English sent three gun ships, the *HMS Tribune*, the *HMS Plumper* and the *HMS Satellite* to Griffin Bay to monitor Pickett's new camp. Wary of the ships, Pickett moved his camp over the hill above South Beach.

On August 10th, Lieutenant Colonel Silas Casey, along with 180 U.S. Army soldiers, arrived at South Beach to back up Pickett's stand on the island. As the new commander, Casey sought out a more protected location for the growing camp, settling on the present day site. Buildings, tents and materials, many of which came from Fort Bellingham, where shipped to the island. On the high ground east of the camp, an earthen redoubt was dug, which can still be seen today. Eight 32-pound guns, removed from the *USS Massachusetts*, were planned for the redoubt. Only one gun was ever put in place though, and fired only once in honor of visiting Lieutenant Colonel Winfield Scott.

With neither countries willing to back down, English and U.S. governments agreed to equal military occupation of the island until the dispute over the islands could be settled. For the next twelve years the U.S. would occupy Camp San Juan Island at Cattle Point, with the English on the other side of the island at Garrison Bay (see English Camp on page 210). While it was a peaceful occupation, hardships abounded for the U.S. soldiers as they endured frigid winter winds and rain at the exposed camp. Once the U.S. entered into the Civil War, funding for the forgotten camp was severely limited. Shelters for the soldiers were lacking and in disrepair, food was minimal, and boredom was rampant.

The dispute over the San Juan Islands was resolved by late 1872, and English soldiers left their post at Garrison Bay shortly thereafter. The last of the American soldiers departed American Camp in July 1874. The U.S. government auctioned off the majority of the camp buildings and opened the land to homestead claims.

In 1966, the San Juan Island National Historical Park was created to preserve the unique and fascinating history of two countries' dispute over these amazing islands. Today, the park is the largest tract of public land on San Juan Island, with more than six miles of public shoreline.

Sights to See

With miles of public beach access and trails looping through this unique park land, it is easy to guess that one of the most popular activities at Griffin Bay are nature walks. From Griffin Bay, dinghies can be landed on soft sand beaches at Third Lagoon, Jakle's Lagoon, or Old Town Lagoon. Each of these spots offer access to the park's walking trails, taking visitors on tours through American Camp, the driftwood studded South Beach, the overlook of Mt. Finlayson, or to the lighthouse at Cattle Point. Each offers amazing views across the narrow peninsula. To the south, the expansive Strait of Juan de Fuca backed by the snow

Cattle Point Lighthouse

Cattle Point Park

View of Griffin Bay and Mt Baker from American Camp

capped Olympic mountain range, to the east is Lopez Island with a beautiful view of Mt. Baker, and to the north lies the entire San Juan Islands archipelago. For a view of the park's trail systems, see the chart on page 215, or visit: **www.sanjua-nislandtrails.org/trailsw/american-camp/** for a downloadable version of the park map. Maps are also available at the park.

One of the great highlights at Griffin Bay is the preserved historical site of American Camp. A visitor's information center lies at the park's western end where park rangers, self guided interpretive walking maps (also available for download at: **www.nps.gov/sajh/planyourvisit/brochures.htm**), bathrooms, and a small museum can be found. During the summer months, ranger guided walking tours through the camp are also available.

At the far eastern side of the park lies the Cattle Point Lighthouse and the Cattle Point Interpretive Center. Along with spectacular ocean front scenic vistas, the interpretive center also has two beautiful sand covered beaches for picnicking and soaking up the sunshine. The converted center was once part of the Navy's Radio Compass Station that began operating in the 1920's. Radio operators at the station aided mariners traveling through the Strait of Juan de Fuca by sending morse code messages to the ships with their true bearing. Using three stations, Cattle Point, New Dungeness Spit, and Smith Island, ships were able to pin point their location in foggy conditions.

Red Fox

The red fox is a non-native, yet common site on San Juan Island, particularly on the prairie lands at American Camp. Although known as "red," this fox can be brown, black or orange, but all have the characteristic white-tipped bushy tail. The red foxes have superior hearing, allowing them to locate mice, voles, rabbits and other prairie dwelling animals. Spring and summer is the time to spot mothers with their playful kits in tow.

North Bay

North Bay is a pleasant anchorage found just two miles south of downtown Friday Harbor. The anchorage boasts sweeping views of Griffin Bay and the distant Olympic mountain range, as well as nearby Lopez Island and the snow-capped Mount Baker. On shore Jackson Beach, owned by the Port of Friday Harbor, offers visitors a chance to wiggle their toes in the sand while beachcombing the driftwood strewn beach. Jackson Beach is also popular for its protected two lane paved boat ramp with dock for trailer boats, kayaks and canoes. For aircraft enthusiasts, North Bay is also located near the Friday Harbor Airport, were small passenger and cargo planes frequent the airstrip.

North Bay is located on the eastern side of San Juan Island and north of Griffin Bay. Approaches to the bay can be made via San Juan Channel. If approaching from the northeast, be aware of detached reefs found northeast of Pear Point including Turn Rock, Reef Point and Danger Rock. If approaching from the south via Griffin Bay, be aware of rocks lying offshore and shallow areas around Low Point including North Pacific Rock, Halftide Rocks and unnamed rocks east-northeast of Low Point.

The entrance to North Bay contains a few unmarked rock dangers, and therefore requires careful navigation and attention to your charts. Dinner Island, which lies in the southern portion of North Bay, has extending reefs off the south side of the island. Passage is not recommended between Dinner Island and San Juan Island. Lying approximately 0.25 nm southeast of Dinner Island is a covered rock which is unmarked. 0.65 nm east of Dinner Island is

North Bay to:		
	Anacortes	20 nm
	Bellingham	27 nm
	Blaine	35 nm
	Blind Bay (Shaw Island)	9 nm
	Eagle Harbor (Cypress Island)	16 nm
	Fisherman Bay (Lopez Island)	5 nm
	Friday Harbor (San Juan Island)	5 nm
	Jones Island	9 nm
	Mackaye Harbor (Lopez Island)	8 nm
	Roche Harbor (San Juan Island)	14 nm
	Rosario (Orcas Island)	11 nm
	Shallow Bay (Sucia Island)	20 nm

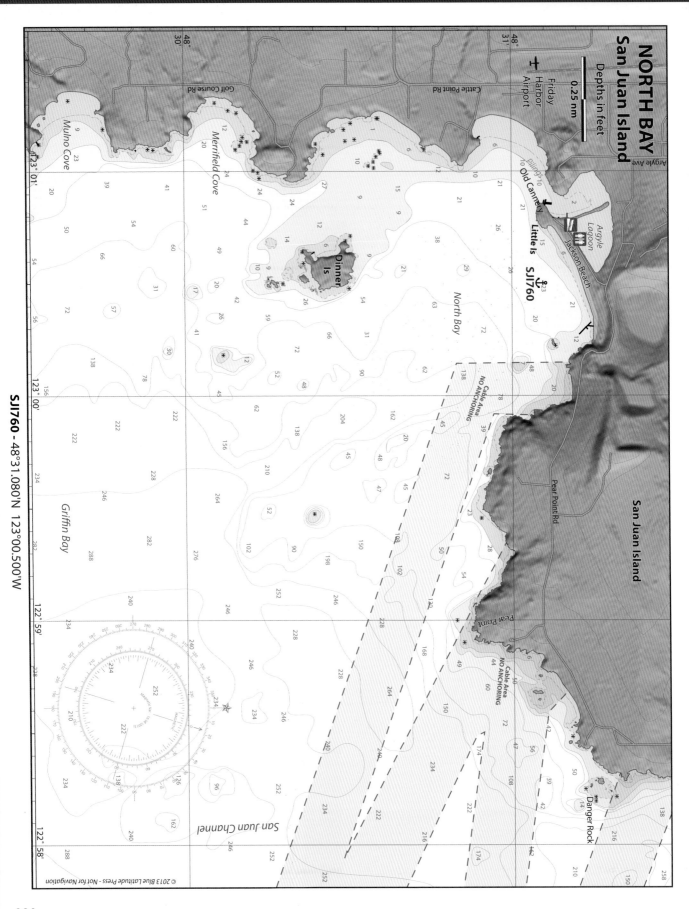

NORTH BAY
San Juan Island

Depths in feet

0.25 nm

Friday Harbor Airport

SJI760 - 48°31.080'N 123°00.500'W

San Juan Island

North Bay

Dinner Is

Little Is SJI760

Old Cannery

Argyle Lagoon

Jackson Beach

Pear Point

Pear Point Rd

Danger Rock

Cable Area NO ANCHORING

Cable Area NO ANCHORING

Mulno Cove

Merrifield Cove

Golf Course Rd

Cattle Point Rd

Argyle Ave

Griffin Bay

San Juan Channel

© 2013 Blue Latitude Press - Not for Navigation

Jackson Beach

a second covered, unmarked rock. Navigate with caution in this area. Once inside the bay, an uncovered rock can be found lying 0.1 miles south from the eastern edge of Jackson Beach. A one fathom shallow area can be found southeast of this rock.

Anchorage can be taken within the bay in 3 to 5 fathoms over a rock and mud bottom. North Bay offers protection from west, north and northeast winds, but is open to the predominate wind and waves from the south. With the stacks of driftwood found on Jackson Beach, it is a telling story of the exposure North Bay has to winter time southerly winds with its close proximity to the Strait of Juan de Fuca. North Bay is therefore best suited in settled and calm conditions, or as a lunch stop to picnic on the beautiful Jackson Beach.

For trips to shore, dinghies and kayaks can be landed on the gently sloping and sandy shores of Jackson Beach. The Port of Friday Harbor also maintains a paved, two-lane boat launch ramp with dock, located on the protected west side of the beach. Dinghies can be landed at the dock, allowing room for trucks to back their trailers down the ramp. The port does not charge a launching fee for boats, and allows vehicles with trailers up to 72 hours of parking.

Amenities at Jackson Beach include restrooms, volleyball courts, picnic sites, barbecue grills, firepits and nearly a half mile of sand beach. The park also includes the adjacent Argyle Lagoon Biological Preserve, owned by the University of Washington. For trips to town, Friday Harbor is located roughly two miles north of Jackson Beach. For provisioning, the well stocked, Friday Harbor Market Place (see page 196), is located one mile northeast following Pear Point Road to Argyle Avenue.

View from North Bay

Old cannery at Jackson Beach

Dinner Island

Looking at the western shore of Turn Island at sunset

Turn Island

Located less than two miles from Friday Harbor, Turn Island State Park and San Juan National Wildlife Refuge is a popular kayak and boat destination. This beautiful 35-acre park offers campsites, mooring buoys and hiking trails. With its close proximity to town, Turn Island is also a favorite picnic site for day-long kayak excursions from Friday Harbor.

Turn Island is located directly off the eastern shore of San Juan Island near Turn Rock. Approaches to the island can be made via Upright Channel to the northeast, or San Juan Channel from the south or northwest. Keep in mind that both channels experience current and can have tidal rips in certain areas. If approaching via San Juan Channel from the northwest, be on the lookout for the lighted buoy marking Reid Rock, which lies near the center of the channel of the entrance to Friday Harbor. If approaching from the south, be aware that the shoreline around Pear Point on San Juan Island is rocky with detached reefs, including the aptly named Danger Rock and Reef Point.

Located approximately 0.2 miles east of Turn Island is Turn Rock. This rock ledge is exposed at low tide, and is also marked by a lighted beacon and surrounded by kelp. Current can be strong in this area so be sure to give Turn Rock a wide berth when passing.

A narrow waterway separates Turn Island and San Juan Island. This passage is flanked by numerous rocks and ex-tending reefs with sections of shallow water. This passage is best suited for shoal-draft dinghies and kayaks.

Three park mooring buoys and room for anchoring can be found on the northwestern shore of Turn Island. Current flows through this area so be sure to set your anchor well, or have a back up line if attached to the moorings (always prudent).

Shore access to the island can be made on one of the fine pebble and sand beaches found along the west and southwest sides of the island. A nearly mile long trail loops around the island with the trailhead beginning near the campground on the southwest shore. The rocky and scenic shoreline in this area also provides a great kayak destination, although currents can be swift so be sure to check your current tables before heading out.

Turn Island to:		
	Anacortes	18 nm
	Bellingham	25 nm
	Blaine	32 nm
	Blind Bay (Shaw Island)	6 nm
	Eagle Harbor (Cypress Island)	14 nm
	Fisherman Bay (Lopez Island)	3 nm
	Fossil Bay (Sucia Island)	16 nm
	Friday Harbor (San Juan Island)	2 nm
	Roche Harbor (San Juan Island)	11 nm
	Rosario (Orcas Island)	9 nm

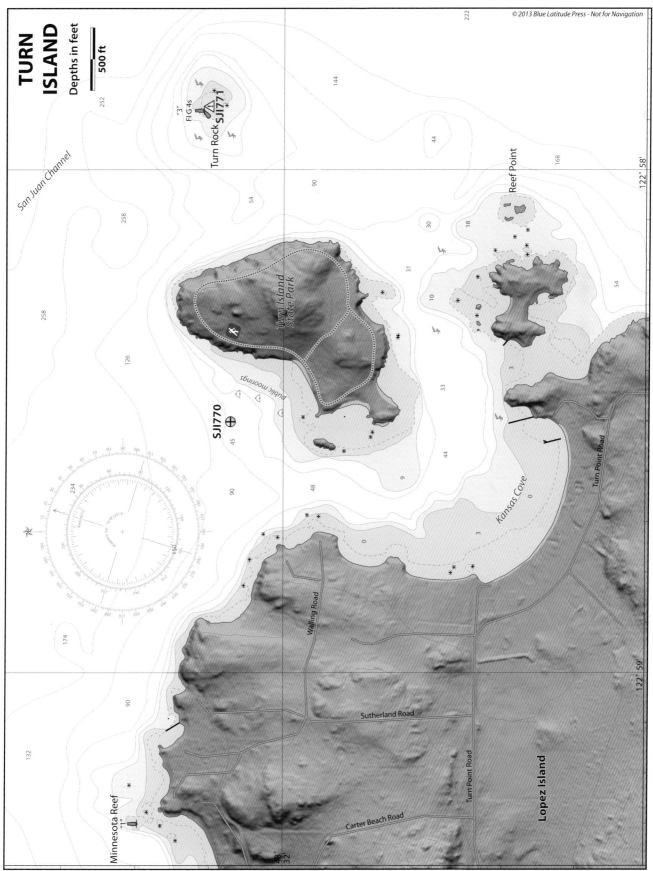

TURN ISLAND

Depths in feet

500 ft

© 2013 Blue Latitude Press - Not for Navigation

San Juan Channel

252

258

258

258

126

174

132

90

90

45

48

90

MAGNETIC

234

90

150

SJI770

Public moorings

Turn Island
State Park

Minnesota Reef
"1"

Walling Road

Sutherland Road

Carter Beach Road

Turn Point Road

Lopez Island

Kansas Cove

Turn Point Road

Reef Point

Turn Rock
SJI771
"3" Fl G 4s

222

144

44

168

90

54

30

18

10

31

33

44

9

3

0

0

3

54

3

SJI771 - 48°32.100'N 122°57.870'W

SJI770 - 48°32.070'N 122°58.500'W

122° 58'

122° 59'

48°
32'

Chapter 9
Stuart Island Area

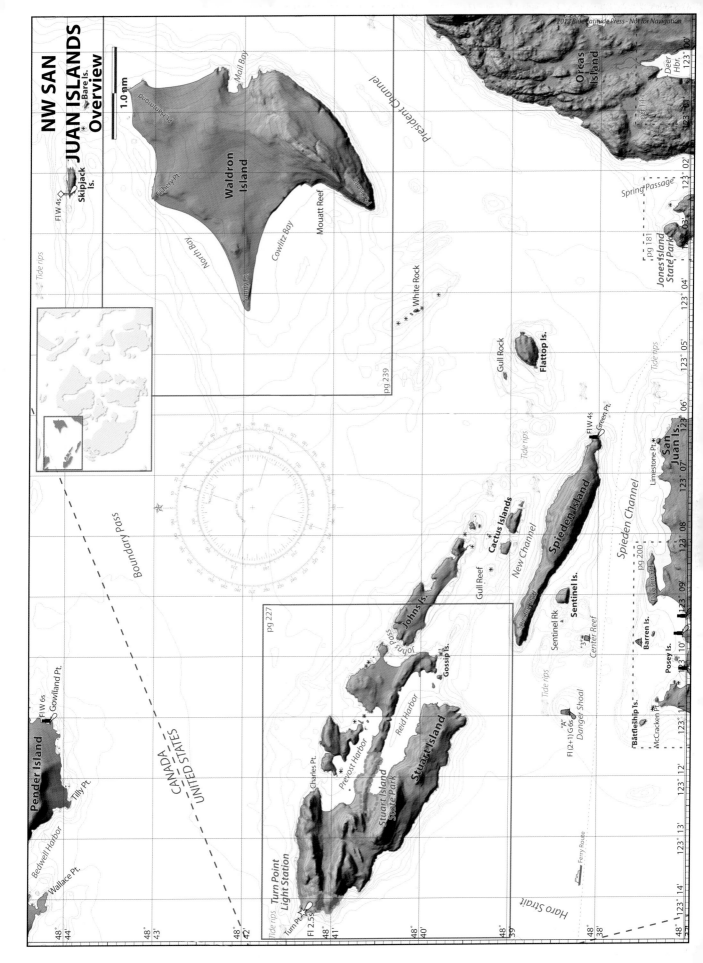

NW SAN
JUAN ISLANDS
Bare Is.
Skipjack Is.
Overview

1.0 nm

2013 Blue Latitude Press - Not for Navigation

FlW 4s
Skipjack Is.

Tide rips

Mail Bay

Pt. Hammond

Waldron Island

Fishery Pt.

North Bay

Sandy Pt.

Cowlitz Bay

Mouatt Reef

President Channel

Orcas Island

Deer Hbr.

pg 144

123° 01'

123° 00'

Spring Passage

pg 181

Jones Island State Park

123° 02'

123° 03'

123° 04'

White Rock

pg 239

Gull Rock

Flattop Is.

123° 05'

123° 06'

Tide rips

FlW 4s

Green Pt.

Limestone Pt.

San Juan Is.

123° 07'

Boundary Pass

Cactus Islands

New Channel

Spieden Island

Spieden Channel

Gull Reef

Sentinel Is.

Sentinel Rk

Center Reef

"3"

pg 200

Davison Hd.

123° 08'

123° 09'

CANADA
UNITED STATES

pg 227

Johns Is.

Johns Pass

Gossip Is.

Danger Shoal

Fl (2+1) G 6s
"A"

Battleship Is.

Barren Is.

Posey Is.

McCracken Pt.

123° 10'

123° 11'

Pender Island

FlW 6s
Gowlland Pt.

Tilly Pt.

Bedwell Harbor

Wallace Pt.

Charles Pt.

Prevost Harbor

Reid Harbor

Stuart Island

Stuart Island State Park

123° 12'

123° 13'

Turn Point
Light Station

Turn Pt.
Fl 2.5s

Tide rips

Haro Strait

Ferry Route

123° 14'

48° 44'

48° 43'

48° 42'

48° 41'

48° 40'

48° 39'

48° 38'

Michael Bertrand www.michaelbertrandphotography.com

Stuart Island

Picturesque Stuart Island is a haven for boaters who are looking to escape the noise and stress of city life. All of that quickly melts away when relaxing on the placid, peaceful waters of Reid and Prevost Harbors. With spotty reception, there is no guilt in turning your cell phone off to enjoy a simple, distraction-free way of life during your stay!

Hosting a number of popular activities, including a tour of the historic U.S. Lighthouse Station at Turn Point, Stuart Island welcomes visitors to explore the beauty of the island and to enjoy its quiet, well protected harbors. The island is also home to Stuart Island State Park, an 85 acre marine park, which is part of Puget Sound's Cascadia Marine Trail system. State park facilities include docks, mooring buoys, campsites and hiking trails at both Prevost and Reid Harbors (a pumpout station is located at Reid Harbor only).

Although it is seemingly one of the more remote islands, the boating mecca of Roche Harbor lies only 4 miles south of Reid Harbor, and Canada's popular boating destination and customs dock at Bedwell Harbor lies only four miles north of Prevost Harbor.

History of Stuart Island

The history of Stuart Island begins with the original inhabitants of the island, the Coast Salish people, who established seasonal camps hundreds to thousands of years ago in order to take advantage of the area's bountiful natural resources. Evidence of these camp sites can be seen today in the form of white midden beaches which are scattered around the island. These beaches were created from centuries of discarded shells, bleached by the sun, from the island's plentiful stocks of oysters, clams, and scallops.

In 1841, the Wilkes Expedition was exploring the islands and gave Stuart Island its current namesake in honor of Frederick D. Stuart, the captain's clerk on the expedition. By the mid to late 1800's, European and U.S. pioneers began moving to the area and homesteaded much of the

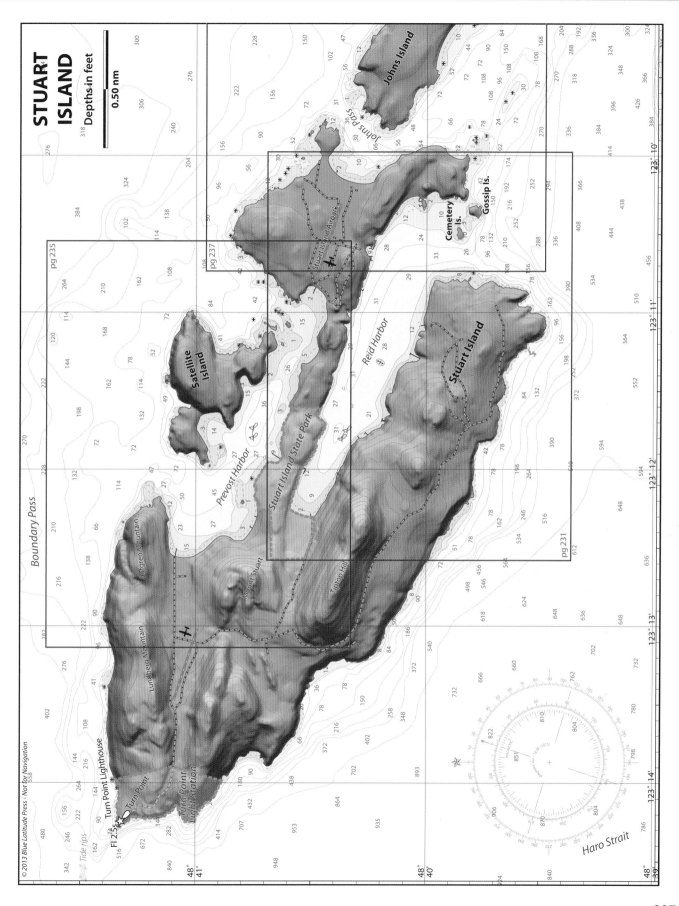

STUART ISLAND

Depths in feet

0.50 nm

Johns Island

Johns Pass

Cemetery Is.

Gossip Is.

Stuart Island Airpark

pg 235

pg 237

Satellite Island

Reid Harbor

Stuart Island

Prevost Harbor

Stuart Island State Park

pg 231

Boundary Pass

Lofgren Mountain

Lundberg Mountain

Mount Stuart

Tiptop Hill

Turn Point Lighthouse

Turn Point

Turn Point Light Station

Haro Strait

Tide rips

Fl 2.5s

© 2013 Blue Latitude Press - Not for Navigation

227

View of Prevost Harbor

Turn Point Lighthouse

island. Farming, fishing, and some mining were the main occupations on the island.

In 1893, recognizing the importance of the major shipping channels of Haro Strait and Boundary Pass, the U.S. government commissioned the building of the Turn Point light and fog station on Stuart Island. The first fixed white lens lantern was visible up to seven miles away, and during periods of fog, a Daboll trumpet signal was used to alert passing ships.

With the opening of the lighthouse station on the island, many of the keepers and their assistants brought their families to live with them on the island. Coupled with a newly growing local community, a need for a school on Stuart Island arose. In 1897, the first public classes on the island began in the barn of the new lighthouse station, and by 1904, a proper, one-room school house was built on donated land. Over the years the school remained mostly open (closing during World War II and during various years when there were no children present), serving the needs of children living on the island and surrounding nearby islands. In 1967, the elementary school was granted "remote and necessary" status and became an official school of the San Juan Island School District.

In 1974, the U.S. Coast Guard fully automated the station at Turn Point. Today, Turn Point is managed by two entities, with the Coast Guard maintaining the navigation light and equipment, and the Bureau of Land Management maintaining the surrounding grounds. In 2005, working jointly, the Coast Guard and Bureau, along with the help of the Turn Point Lighthouse Preservation Society, began a renovation project to preserve the historical buildings of the Turn Point Light Station.

Sights to See

One of everyone's favorite past times on Stuart Island is meandering along the miles of trails and county dirt roads, taking the island in one step at a time. Whether anchored in Prevost or Reid Harbor, state park trails join the two areas and wind through the lush forest with occasional sweeping views of the harbors. These well marked trails will also deposit hikers on the main county dirt road which takes visitors past the Stuart Island school and its museum, the Prevost Harbor county dock, and the Turn Point lighthouse.

While exploring the island, it is well worth a stop at the Stuart Island School to visit the museum which displays the history of this one of a kind school. The small museum is adjacent to the school and the school's library. Inside the one room museum are numerous photos depicting the unique hundred plus years of the school's operation. Next door is the school and island's public library. The library was originally built in 1904 and was used as the schoolhouse until 1980, when the new school was built. Today, the one room library houses shelves of books as well as colorful island postcards for sale created by the students themselves. The school's fund raising efforts include bake sales and postcard sales to the island's numerous visitors. These funds are used by the local PTSA to purchase books, fund field trips and pay for visiting artists to supplement the educational program for the students on the island.

Along the road to the school and lighthouse, visitors will come across an eclectic roadside display of tourist merchandise for sale. The Treasure Chests of Stuart Island (displays found near the school and road to the Prevost Harbor county dock) are operated by the Benson family, island residents

Museum and library

Stuart Island School

Louise Bryant

Louise Bryant was an American journalist, feminist and writer born in December 1885. Bryant is best known for the radical activist movements she participated in during the early 1900's, as well as her marriage to bohemian journalist, John Reed.

Bryant attended school at the University of Oregon, and upon graduation in 1909, she attempted to break into the male dominated world of journalism. Unable to land a job with one of Portland's newspapers, Bryant accepted a teaching position in the San Juans on Stuart Island. Here, Bryant lived with the Borcher family, who were the light keepers at Turn Point. Shortly after taking her teaching position, Bryant returned to Portland for what most assumed to be a visit, however she never returned to Stuart Island again.

Bryant had been offered a writing position in Portland and later married. It was during this time that Bryant became a very active member in the woman's suffrage movement and became familiar with John Reed's reporting on labor disputes, revolutions and war. The two met while Reed was in Oregon and fell in love at first sight. Bryant who was already separated from her husband, moved to New York to be with Reed and later marry. In 1917, the two traveled to Europe and Russia where they reported first hand on the Bolshevik Revolution. In 1920, Reed passed away from typhus while in Russia, and was buried at the Kremlin Wall Necropolis.

Bryant returned to the U.S. where she became a leading reporter for the Hearst newspapers. In 1923, she married Ambassador William C. Bullitt and had a child. In January of 1936, Louise Bryant died while in Paris, where she is buried.

In 1981, Hollywood depicted the radical lives of John Reed and Louise Bryant in the movie, "Reds," starring Warren Beatty, Diane Keaton and Jack Nickolson (winning three Academy Awards).

whose wares, especially t-shirts, have achieved cult status. These stands operate on an honor system, with each item packaged with a special IOU envelope for payment once you return home, or via online with a credit card (www.boundarypasstradersnw.com).

One of the great highlights while visiting Stuart Island is a visit to the historic Turn Point Light Station and museum. While the navigation light was fully automated in 1974, the buildings from the original 1893 station have been restored for the public to visit. A museum is housed in the station's original barn, where visitors can read about the history of the light station and the light keepers, as well as viewing historical artifacts and photographs.

Turn Point is also a great vantage point to watch for the stars of the San Juan Islands, the orca whales. From Turn Point, visitors can view Haro Strait and Boundary Pass, two areas where whales can frequently be spotted. Whale watchers can take advantage of the light station's grassy lawns and picnic tables to enjoy a sack lunch and the beautiful vista of Canada's Vancouver Island and nearby Gulf Islands.

Stuart Island also offers kayakers a wonderful opportunity of exploration. The well protected harbors of Reid and Prevost offer paddlers the chance to explore the shoreline, reaching every nook and rocky cranny the island has to offer. With the advantage of being able to navigate in areas of very shallow depths, kayaks allow visitors close access to the shoreline and reef areas, where views of the underwater world can be seen.

Michael Bertrand www.michaelbertrandphotography.cor

Reid Harbor

Reid Harbor is a haven for boats with over a mile of protected mooring options found on the western edge of the border between the San Juan and Gulf Islands. With the start of the summer season, boaters flock to this nearly landlocked anchorage to enjoy the island's laid back atmosphere and sublime natural surroundings. The Stuart Island State Park is located between the two harbors of Reid and Prevost, offering boaters dock space, mooring buoys, campsites and miles of hiking trails. A county road links Reid Harbor to the western side of the island, where visitors can explore the scenic, forested interior, as well as venture to the historic Turn Point light station and museum. Reid Harbor is a popular destination, and for good reason. Whether your passion is hiking, kayaking, wildlife viewing, or just enjoying a peaceful anchorage, Reid Harbor is sure to impress and quick to be a favorite.

Stuart Island lies on the western edge of the San Juan Island group, with the entrance to Reid Harbor located on the island's southeastern shore, only 4 miles north of Roche Harbor. Reid Harbor is reached from the southwest via Haro Strait, or from the southeast via Spieden Channel south of Spieden Island or New Channel north of Spieden Island. Reid Harbor can also be approached from the north

Reid Harbor to:		
Anacortes		29 nm
Bellingham		33 nm
Blaine		31 nm
Blind Bay (Shaw Island)		12 nm
Eagle Harbor (Cypress Island)		23 nm
Echo Bay (Sucia Island)		16 nm
Fisherman Bay (Lopez Island)		15 nm
Friday Harbor (San Juan Island)		12 nm
Jones Island		7 nm
Roche Harbor (San Juan Island)		4 nm
Rosario (Orcas Island)		18 nm
Sidney (Canada)		10 nm
Spencer Spit (Lopez Island)		17 nm

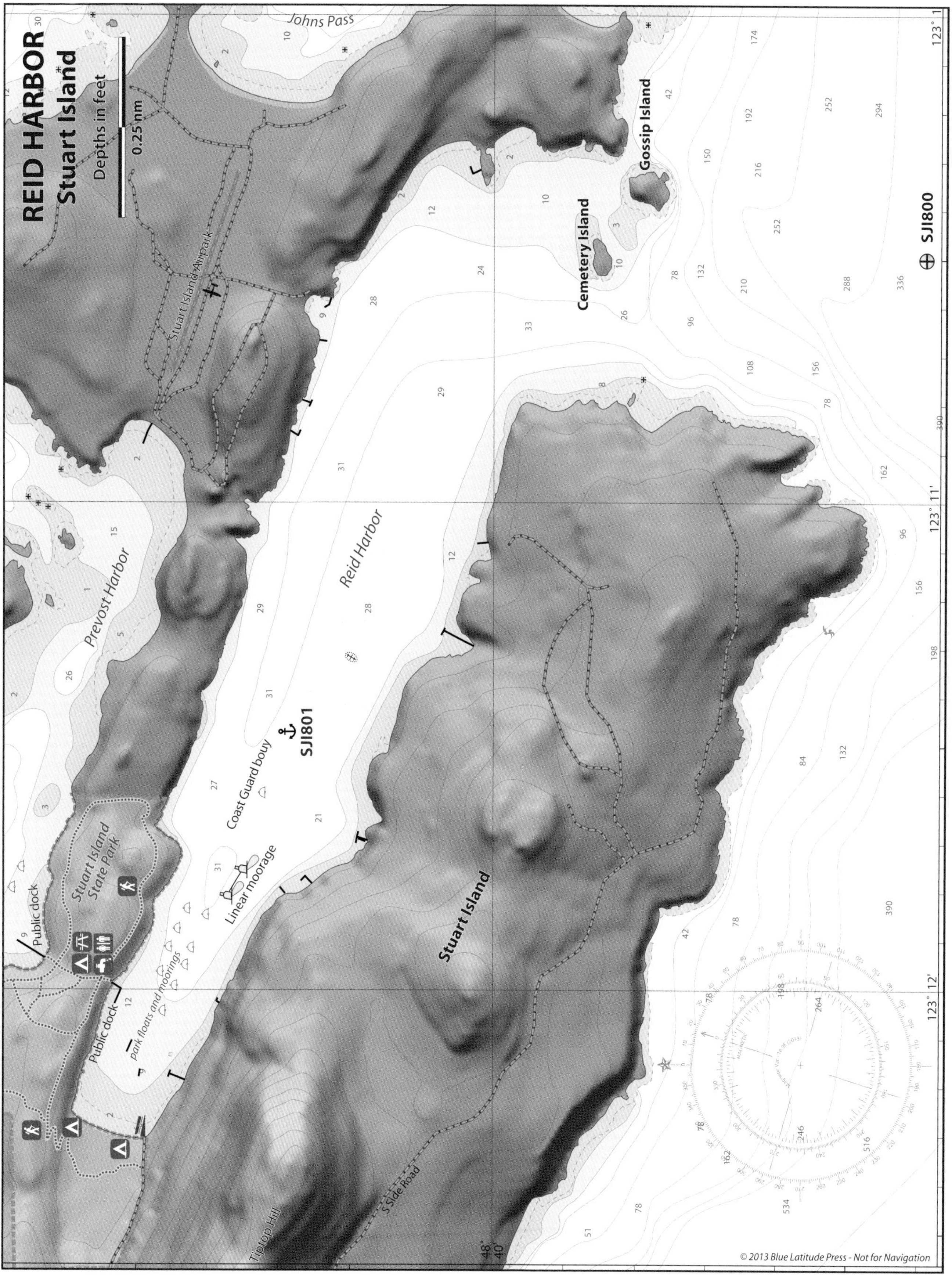

REID HARBOR
Stuart Island

Depths in feet

0.25 nm

Johns Pass

Gossip Island

Cemetery Island

Stuart Island Airpark

Prevost Harbor

Reid Harbor

Coast Guard bouy

SJI801

Linear moorage

Stuart Island State Park

Public dock

park floats and moorings

Public dock

Stuart Island

S. Side Road

Tiptop Hill

SJI801 - 48°40.270'N 123°11.480'W

⊕ SJI800

123° 11'

123° 12'

123° 1

48° 40'

SJI800 - 48°39.370'N 123°10.560'W

© 2013 Blue Latitude Press - Not for Navigation

231

Stuart Island

Gossip Island

Cemetery Island

Spieden Island

Stuart Island

Reid Harbor entrance

via the narrow channel of Johns Pass which separates the eastern side of Stuart Island from nearby Johns Island. Be aware that currents in this area can be strong so be sure to check your heading and compensate for drift.

When approaching Reid Harbor via Haro Strait or Spieden Channel, and especially when crossing from Roche Harbor, be sure to check your charts and locate the hazards of Danger Shoal, Center Reef and Sentinel Rock. Both Danger Shoal and Center Reef are marked by lighted buoys and are generally surrounded by kelp. When transiting off the southern shore of Spieden Island and near Sentinel Island, be aware that a large detached reef, including Sentinel Rock, extends off the western shore of Sentinel Island, and is not marked by a buoy. If crossing from Roche Harbor to Reid Harbor, clear passage can be taken mid-way between Danger Shoal and Center Reef.

The approach to Reid Harbor can also be taken along the north shore of Spieden Island via New Channel. This channel passes between the islands of Spieden and Cactus. Be sure to check your charts when transiting in this area as a number of rocks and detached reefs can be found off Cactus Islands and Johns Island.

If approaching from the north, the narrow channel of Johns Pass can be taken between the islands of Stuart and Johns (see page 237 for the chart and full description). At the

southern end of this pass, extending off the east-southeastern shore of Stuart Island, is a long reef covered by kelp. A small pass through the middle of this reef is occasionally used by boats with local knowledge of the area, but is unmarked. Be sure to give this reef, as well as Gull Reef lying further southeast, ample room when transiting. Because this pass has a number of nearby reefs and areas of shallow water, it is important to consult your charts before approaching this area.

The entrance to Reid Harbor is guarded by two islands, Gossip Island to the southeast and Cemetery Island to the northwest. Passage into Reid Harbor should be taken west of these islands. Reefs and shallow water are found between the islands and along their eastern shores. Enter the harbor mid channel between the Stuart Island and the west side of Cemetery Island.

Once inside the entrance to Reid Harbor, the bottom contour rises rapidly, allowing boats to anchor nearly anywhere within its 1.25 mile stretch. Anchorage can be taken in 4 to 5 fathoms within the harbor over a solid holding mud bottom. Near the head of the harbor, the state park offers mooring buoys, dock space and linear mooring options for a nightly fee. Reid Harbor also offers a pump out station located near the main dock, operated by the park department.

Reid Harbor offers nearly all round protection from weather with the exception of strong southeasterlies. Dur-

ing periods of strong southeasterly winds, better protection can be found at nearby Roche Harbor or Garrison Bay on San Juan Island.

Up the ramp from the dock, near the head of the bay, is the state park campground, trail heads, information kiosks and payment drop boxes. The campground offers 18 campsites with access to composting toilets, fire pits and water. Four of the campsites are designated Cascadia Marine Trail sites for human or wind-powered watercraft, and are located near the beach at the head of the bay.

It is a short walk, only 500 feet, across the narrow stretch of land separating Prevost and Reid Harbors. A scenic loop trail is found near the top of this isthmus, taking hikers on a tour of the state park grounds towards the eastern side of the island. A second trail leads west, through a beautiful madrona filled forest, towards the beach at the head of the harbor. From the beach, hikers can find the county dirt road, located on the far southern end, which will take visitors on an exploration of the island, including the school museum, cemetery and Turn Point lighthouse.

The expansive harbor is also a great place to explore by dinghy or kayak. A handful of midden beaches can be spotted on the shore as well as on Cemetery and Gossips Islands. These bright white beaches mark the historical camps of the Coast Salish people who were the first inhabitants of the islands. During the summer salmon runs, the southwestern side of the island comes alive with fishermen vying for a chance to catch one of these grand fish as they make their way towards the mainland rivers.

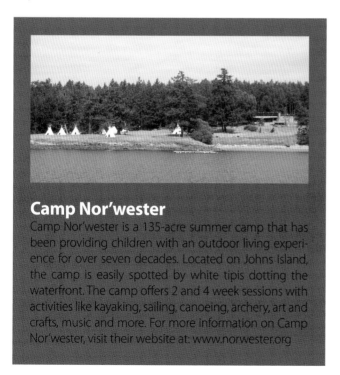

Camp Nor'wester

Camp Nor'wester is a 135-acre summer camp that has been providing children with an outdoor living experience for over seven decades. Located on Johns Island, the camp is easily spotted by white tipis dotting the waterfront. The camp offers 2 and 4 week sessions with activities like kayaking, sailing, canoeing, archery, art and crafts, music and more. For more information on Camp Nor'wester, visit their website at: www.norwester.org

Prevost Harbor

The protected waters and peaceful atmosphere of Prevost Harbor draw boaters from around the San Juan and Gulf Islands to its forest-lined shores. With its state park facilities geared towards the boating crowd, Prevost Harbor is a hot spot of boating traffic during the summer season. Stuart Island hosts a number of on shore activities ranging from scenic hiking trails to informative historical sites, allowing visitors the chance to explore island life at its best. Dock space, mooring buoys and ample anchoring room allow boaters to sit back, relax and take in the beauty of this pleasant, one of a kind, rural island.

Prevost Harbor is located on the north side of Stuart Island. Entrance to the harbor is taken via Boundary Pass, which is a main shipping channel and the northwestern boundary water separating the Canadian Gulf Islands and the U.S. San Juan Islands.

For boats approaching from the south, passage can be taken either around Turn Point on the west side of Stuart Island, or through Johns Pass on the east side of Stuart Island. If approaching via the west side of Stuart Island, keep in mind that Haro Strait and Boundary Pass are commercial shipping channels, and some of the larger tankers and container ships have limited maneuverability in the narrow

dog-leg turn around Turn Point, at the western tip of Stuart Island. This area also experiences current and occasional tide rips, particularly off Turn Point. For larger yachts approaching from the south, this is the preferred passage to Prevost Harbor rather than navigating the narrow channel of Johns Pass.

Prevost Harbor is protected to the north by Satellite Island, creating two passages into the anchorage. The primary entrance used by nearly all boats is located between the

Prevost Harbor to:		
Anacortes		31 nm
Bedwell Harbor (Canada)		4 nm
Bellingham		32 nm
Blaine		27 nm
Blind Bay (Shaw Island)		13 nm
Fisherman Bay (Lopez Island)		17 nm
Friday Harbor (San Juan Island)		13 nm
Jones Island		8 nm
Olga (Orcas Island)		18 nm
Pelican Beach (Cypress Island)		22 nm
Roche Harbor (San Juan Island)		7 nm
Shallow Bay (Sucia Island)		13 nm
Spencer Spit (Lopez Island)		18 nm

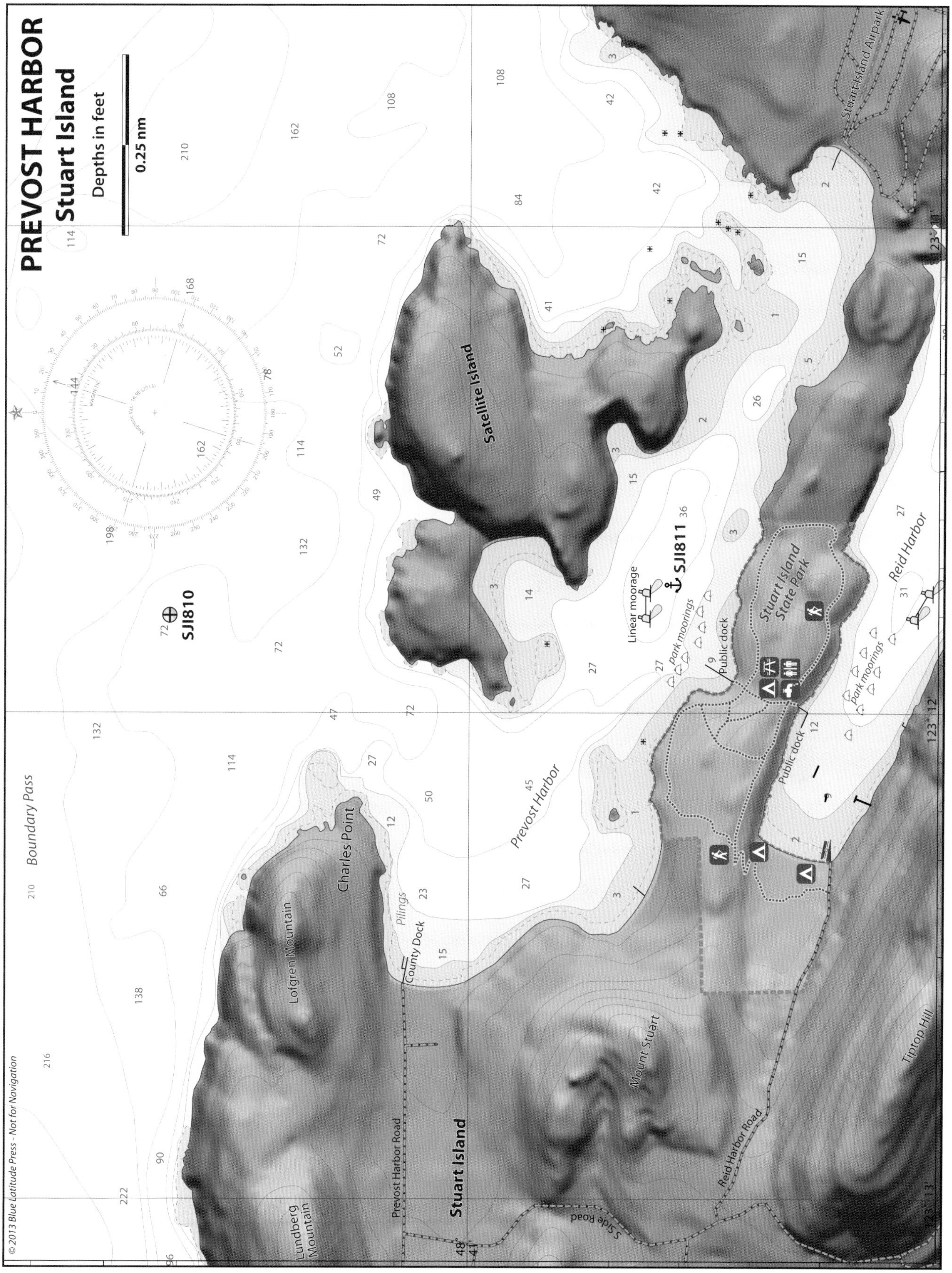

PREVOST HARBOR
Stuart Island

Depths in feet

0.25 nm

Boundary Pass

Lofgren Mountain

Charles Point

Lundberg Mountain

Prevost Harbor Road

Stuart Island

Mount Stuart

Reid Harbor Road

S Side Road

Tiptop Hill

County Dock

Pilings

Prevost Harbor

Satellite Island

Linear moorage

SJI811

park moorings

Public dock

Stuart Island State Park

Reid Harbor

park moorings

Public dock

Stuart Island Airpark

SJI810

SJI810 - 48°41.400'N 123°11.800'W

SJI811 - 48°40.700'N 123°11.730'W

235

western shore of Satellite Island and Charles Point on Stuart Island. This western entrance is relatively free from obstructions with the exception of a small reef located near shore off Charles Point. The eastern entrance to Prevost Harbor, located off the eastern shore of Satellite Island, is reef strewn and shallow. This entrance should therefore be avoided due to these unmarked dangers.

Once inside the harbor, the main anchorage and mooring area is located off the state park dock near the middle of Prevost Harbor. When navigating towards the state park facilities, be sure to locate two reefs, one near the western edge of the state park facilities, and the other near the entrance to the small cove on the southwestern side of Satellite Island. At low tide, both of these reefs are visible.

Anchorage can be taken inside the harbor in 4 to 6 fathoms over a mostly mud bottom, and nearly all round protection. Be aware that during certain times of the year, including the summer season, heavy growth on the bottom can clog anchors. Be sure your anchor is well set before heading to shore. The state park also offers a number of mooring buoys, dock space and a linear moorage option for a nightly fee. At the northern head of the harbor, near the open pasture land, a county dock is also available for short term tie ups (no overnights).

For trips to shore, dinghy space is available at the back of the state park dock (for those looking to shorten their walk to the Turn Point light station, dinghies can also be tied to the county dock at the north end of the harbor). Once on shore, the state park offers campsites, water, composting toilets and numerous hiking trails. At the head of the ramp is a park information kiosk, including island maps, along with a payment drop box for those using park facilities.

A short walk up the hill takes visitors to an overlook of nearby Reid Harbor. From here, a scenic loop trail heads east, exploring beautiful evergreen forests, including vibrant madrona trees. Be sure to keep your eyes open while on the trail for the island's resident population of black tail deer.

A second trail at the top of the hill separating Prevost and Reid Harbors, takes visitors on a walk to the small sand and gravel beach found at the head of Reid Harbor. At the opposite end of this beach is a county boat launch as well as the start of the county dirt road which will take visitors past the school house and out to the Turn Point light station.

For those boaters continuing on into Canada and the Gulf Islands, Prevost Harbor is an excellent jumping off point due to its close proximity. Boaters and charters, who are on a tighter time schedule and would like to experience Canada, can make the short four mile trip over to Bedwell Harbor on South Pender Island. Bedwell Harbor has a customs dock for clearing into the country as well as a marina, fuel dock, and

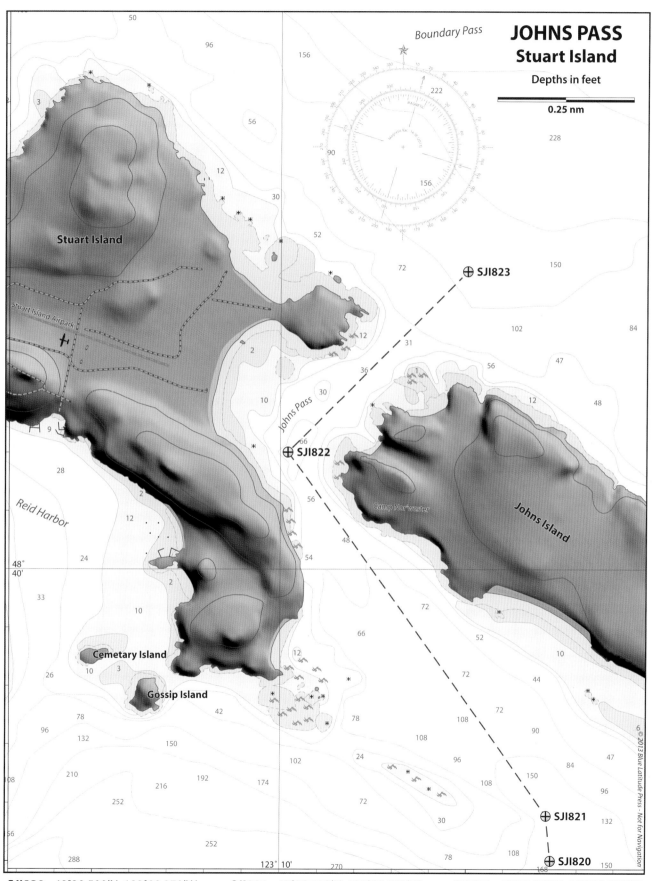

JOHNS PASS
Stuart Island

Depths in feet

0.25 nm

Boundary Pass

Stuart Island

Stuart Island Airpark

Johns Pass

SJI823

SJI822

SJI821

SJI820

Reid Harbor

Camp Nor'wester

Johns Island

Cemetary Island

Gossip Island

48°
40'

123° 10'

© 2013 Blue Latitude Press - Not for Navigation

SJI820 - 48°39.500'N 123°09.270'W   **SJI821** - 48°39.580'N 123°09.280'W   **SJI822** - 48°40.200'N 123°09.980'W
SJI823 - 48°40.510'N 123°09.500'W

Michael Bertrand www.michaelbertrandphotography.com

small grocery. Bedwell Harbor is also home to the beautiful and luxurious, Poet's Cove Resort and Spa (www.poetscove. com). Even if just for a quick night's stay, Bedwell Harbor is an easy and fun way to experience a bit of Canada's Gulf Islands. For those returning to the U.S., a customs dock is conveniently located at Roche Harbor and Friday Harbor).

Johns Pass

Johns Pass is the narrow waterway located between Johns Island (Johns Island is private and home to Camp Nor'wester) and Stuart Island. While this pass is a convenient shortcut through the islands, it contains a few unmarked reef hazards. Boaters should consult their charts before approaching this area, as well as practice careful and attentive navigation once in the area. This pass can also experience current on the flood and ebb tides.

The southern entrance to Johns Pass is guarded by a long reef extending off the southeastern tip of Stuart Island. This reef extends out nearly 0.6 miles with a small break located approximately mid way. This break in the reef is occasionally used by boats with local knowledge, but keep in mind that none of these reefs or the break are marked by navigational aids and could be a danger to those new to the area. Much of this extending reef is covered by kelp beds which can help to distinguish the reef's location.

Boaters approaching from the east through New Channel should also keep a look out for two detached reefs lying off the northwestern side of Cactus Islands. The northwestern most reef is named Gull Reef and is unmarked. When approaching Johns Pass from this direction, be sure to give Gull Reef and the above mentioned reef extending off Stuart Island plenty of room.

When transiting through Johns Pass, stay mid channel to avoid reefs found near the shoreline. Within the pass, a small cove is located off Stuart Island with a number of moored boats. This cove is shallow and also contains a reef in the northern portion. When exiting Johns Pass (or approaching Johns Pass from the north), be cautious of the reefs found off the northern tip of Johns Island, and do not cut the corner.

Spieden Island

Spieden Island, located two miles north of Roche Harbor along Spieden Channel, is a privately owned island with a unique history. Heavily forested on its northern side with barren grassland on its southern side, Spieden Island, once known as "Safari Island," was developed into a big game hunting destination. The island was stocked with grazing animals and game birds found around the world including African Barbary sheep, Corsican mouflons, Spanish goats, Indian spotted deer, Japanese sika deer, European fallow deer, ringneck pheasants, guinea fowl, wild turkeys and more. Although the resort shut down not long after it opened and the island has since been sold, deer and sheep can still be spotted grazing throughout the 3-mile long island.

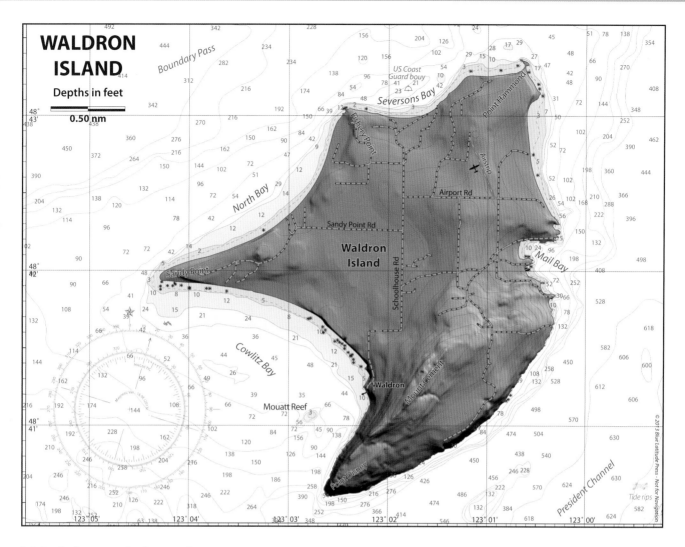

Waldron Island

Waldron Island is truly a unique locale within the San Juan Islands. Lying along the boundary waters between the United States and Canada, Waldron is an off-the-beaten path destination for most boaters. With no ferry service and no power to the island, Waldron has retained much of its simple and quiet ways - much to the liking of island residents. Approximately 100 people reside on the island, with a handful of farms supplying residents and markets on surrounding islands with fresh, local produce.

Waldron Island is located between Boundary Pass and President Channel, roughly 1.25 miles northwest of Orcas Island. The island may be approached from any direction, keeping in mind that Skipjack and Bare Islands, along with nearby detached reefs lie 0.5 miles off the northern end of Waldron. The unmarked Mouatt Reef, located in Cowlitz Bay, should also be taken to caution.

Depending on wind and wave conditions, boats can be found anchored or moored at Mail Bay, North Bay, Cowlitz Bay, as well as off the beach between Point Hammond and Mail Bay. A county dock is found in Cowlitz Bay and is available for public use for loading and unloading as well as for small boat tie ups. If anchoring in Mail Bay, be cautious of the numerous old pilings, rocky shore, and steep-to bottom contour. Mooring buoys can be found scattered around the island, however these moorings are private and not available to the public.

The majority of these bays are large and relatively open, thus best suited for periods of settled weather and calm conditions. Due to Waldron's location between two main passes, strong current can also be experienced within the anchorages.

Visitors are welcome to use the county dock and sight see the beautiful farms and forest land along the public road, or visit the very unique Waldron Post Office. The majority of Waldron however, is privately owned and visitors to the island should respect the privacy and property of residents who cherish the peace and quiet of this unique island.

Chapter 10
Sucia Island Area

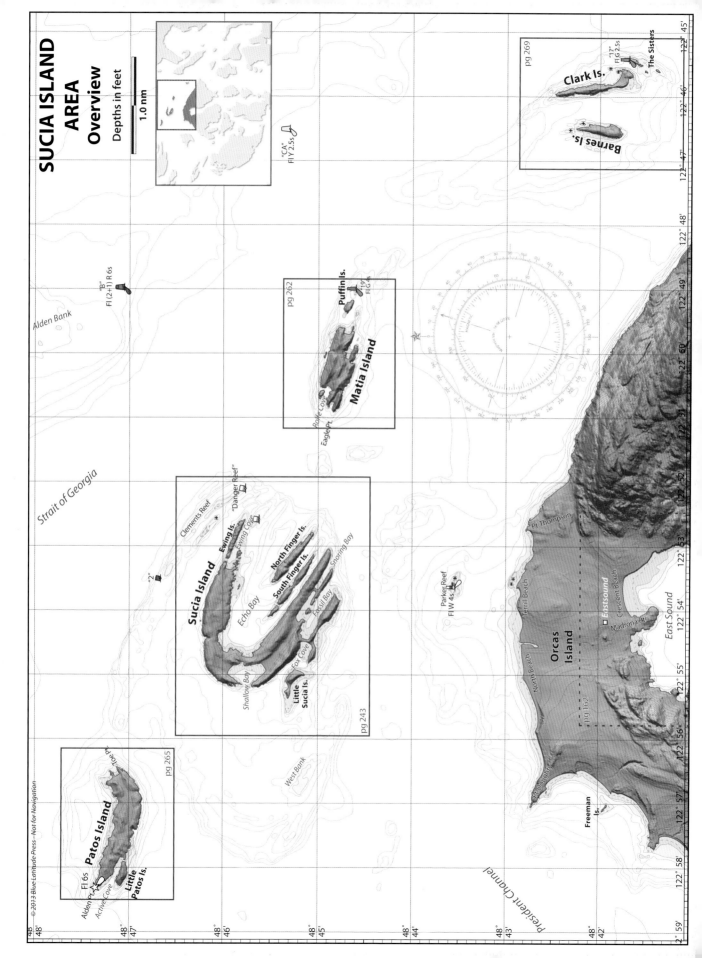

SUCIA ISLAND AREA Overview

Depths in feet

1.0 nm

© 2013 Blue Latitude Press – Not for Navigation

"CA"
Fl Y 2.5s

pg 269

Clark Is.
"17"
Fl G 2.5s
The Sisters

Barnes Is.

Fl (2+1) R 6s
"B"

Alden Bank

Strait of Georgia

pg 262

Puffin Is.
"19"
Fl G 4s

Matia Island

Rolfe Cove

Eagle Pt.

MAG VAR

Clements Reef

"Danger Reef"

Ewing Is.
Ewing Cove

"2"

Sucia Island

North Finger Is.

South Finger Is.

Snoring Bay

Echo Bay

Fossil Bay

Fox Cove

Shallow Bay

Little Sucia Is.

pg 243

West Bank

Parker Reef
Fl W 4s

Pt Thompson

Terrill Beach

Eastsound

Crescent Beach

Madrona Pt.

Orcas Island

East Sound

North Beach

pg 162

Pt Doughty

Freeman Is.

Patos Island

Little Patos Is.

Alden Pt.
Fl 6s
Active Cove

pg 265

President Channel

48°
48'

48°
47'

48°
46'

48°
45'

48°
44'

48°
43'

48°
42'

2° 59'

122° 58'

122° 57'

122° 56'

122° 55'

122° 54'

122° 53'

122° 52'

122° 51'

122° 50'

122° 49'

122° 48'

122° 47'

122° 46'

122° 45'

Michael Bertrand www.michaelbertrandphotography.com

Sucia Island

Sucia Island is the ultimate highlight of any cruise through the San Juan Islands. The shining star of the marine state park system, Sucia's unique geography and surrounding finger islands offer boaters an endless array of anchorage possibilities, including docks and mooring buoys. Thick, vibrant evergreen forests blanket the island, while delicate, lace-like sandstone formations line the rocky shoreline. Miles of scenic trails intersect the island, allowing visitors an endless array of maritime vistas.

History of Sucia Island

With its unique horseshoe shape and surrounding finger islands, Sucia Island has fascinated geological researchers for years. The deep coves used today for protected and scenic anchorages have been formed by the continual erosion of the soft layers of sedimentary deposits found on the island. Evidence of the erosion can be seen in the island's soft shoreside sandstone where thousands of years of wave action has eaten through the rock to create honeycomb-like rock formations and caves.

The first human inhabitants of Sucia Island were the Coast Salish people who used the island as a seasonal camp to hunt, fish and gather local plants. Archaeological evidence found on the island dates these camps back to more than 2,500 years ago. This evidence also indicates that deer once lived on the island, though today, the only mammals found are mink, river otters, mice, harbor seals and sea lions.

The first European contact in the area came with the Eliza Expedition in 1791. These Spanish explorers named many of the northern islands, including Sucia (pronounced soo-see-ah in Spanish). This translates to "dirty," referring to the many rocky reefs found within the bays and surround the island.

Sucia Island was first homesteaded by the Wiggins family in the mid 1800's. In 1902, a sandstone quarry company set up operations in what is now known as Fossil Bay. Much

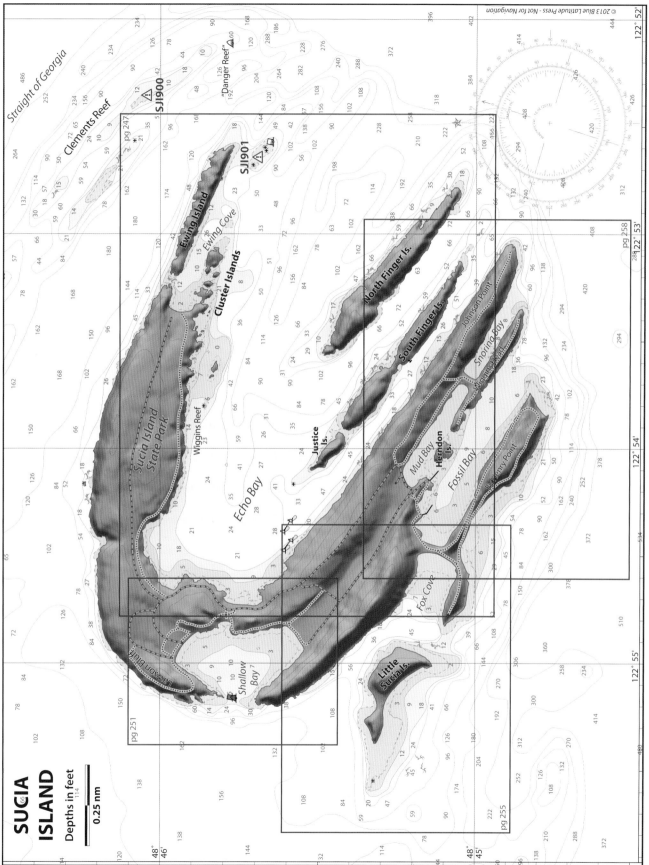

SUCIA ISLAND

Depths in feet

0.25 nm

© 2013 Blue Latitude Press - Not for Navigation

SJI901 - 48°45.690'N 122°52.630'W

SJI900 - 48°46.040'N 122°52.360'W

Little Sucia Island

Sandstone formations

of this sandstone was shipped to Seattle and southern Puget Sound communities to provide paving for streets, but the company was short lived and closed down operations. In 1918, William Harnden and his family moved to the island and also settled in Fossil Bay. Harnden owned and operated the 47 foot passenger boat, *Tulip King*, which was used to ferry passengers, mail and supplies to the San Juan Islands. The Harnden family lived on the island until 1942, when they moved to nearby Orcas Island.

Over the decades, Sucia Island has been reputed to be one of the many islands used for smuggling. Tales of opium, sheep's wool, alcohol, and even Chinese laborers intertwine into the history of the island. While the items being smuggled have changed over the years, the US Customs and Border Patrol continue plying the same waters in search of illegal activity.

Recognizing the importance of keeping a portion of Sucia Island open to the public, the Washington State Parks and Recreation Commission acquired approximately one-third of the island in 1952. With the remainder of the land available for private purchase, developers looked to the island as a possible location to build vacation cabins. Everett (Ev) Henry along with local recreational boaters and the Puget Sound Interclub Association (known now as the Recreational Boating Association of Washington), intervened and managed to raise $25,000 to purchase the majority of the remaining land. In 1960, Interclub donated this land to Washington State Parks where it continues to be used as a marine park, open to all visitors to share its wonders.

Sights to See

Every adventure to Sucia Island begins with an exploration of the island on one of the many well maintained trails. In total, Sucia Island has roughly ten miles of trails to keep visitors busy (see page 243 for a map of the trails). Each trail weaves across the island, taking visitors past wind-sculpted madrona trees and crescent shaped sand beaches. The distant barks of sea lion bulls and the sharp cries of bald eagles drift in through the thick forest of evergreens.

For kayakers, Sucia Island has a seemingly never ending expanse of protected shoreline. There is no better way to explore the numerous nooks and crannies, rocky reefs and tree studded shorelines than by a quiet morning paddle around the island. Be sure to pack a lunch and take advantage of some of the more remote sandy beaches.

Sucia is also a great location to spot harbor seals, Steller and California sea lions sun bathing on a few of the more isolated rocky cliffs and reefs. Both seals and sea lions tend to stick to their familiar haulout sites, which are generally near choice feeding grounds. Low tide, when more of the rocky reef is exposed and more seals can haulout, is a good

Sea lions and harbor seals on Clements Reef

time to view these protected marine mammals. Seals are curious creatures, popping their heads out of the water to survey and investigate the above water scene, but are quick to disappear when approached too close. Sea lions on the other hand, especially the enormous bulls, are territorial, and it is important to give these massive creatures plenty of space and to respect their privacy. Adult male sea lions dwarf the smaller harbor seals on the rocky reefs, with mature males weighing over two thousand pounds. In the water, harbor seals and sea lions can most easily be differentiated by their ears. Sea lions have small ear flaps located on the sides of their head, while seals have ear holes but lack an external ear flap.

Sucia Island is also a hotspot for diving. In Ewing Cove, an underwater marine park has been established for divers, including a sunken boat that has created an artificial reef. Another popular site is a wall dive off Lawson Bluff. Keep in mind that strong currents can flow through this area, making it prudent to dive with someone who has local knowledge. Check with your local dive shop for further information on these sites. A number of dive companies operate out of the islands as well as Seattle, Bellingham, and Anacortes.

Although Sucia is primarily visited by those who own or charter their own boats, the island is accessible to campers and kayakers via water taxi. A number of water taxi companies operate from nearby Orcas, San Juan and Lopez Islands, as well as the mainland cities of Anacortes, Bellingham and Blaine. With dock space and carts available in Fossil Bay for easy loading and unloading of gear, water taxis provide easy and accessible transportation to everyone wishing to visit this amazing island.

Echo Bay

Echo Bay is by far the most popular and the largest bay at Sucia Island. With sweeping views of nearby Mt. Baker and the Cascade mountain range, Echo Bay affords visitors a breathtaking backdrop of classic Pacific Northwest terrain. The bay offers an expanse of anchoring possibilities as well as a number of park mooring buoys and two linear mooring sites. At the head of the bay, a system of trails takes visitors on a scenic tour around the island, meandering through lush evergreens and thick fern undergrowth. For the early birds, there is no better place to watch the sunrise over the mountains with a steaming cup of coffee and the perfect waterfront seat.

Echo Bay is located on the eastern side of horseshoe-shaped Sucia Island. True to its name (the Spanish translation is "dirty" or "foul"), Sucia Island is surrounded by numerous rocky reefs, both above and below the water. Pay close attention to the charts of the area and navigate with care when approaching the island as well as once inside the bay.

Echo Bay to:		
Anacortes		21 nm
Bellingham		19 nm
Blaine		17 nm
Blind Bay *(Shaw Island)*		16 nm
Deer Harbor *(Orcas Island)*		13 nm
Eagle Harbor *(Cypress Island)*		14 nm
Fisherman Bay *(Lopez Island)*		22 nm
Friday Harbor *(San Juan Island)*		17 nm
Jones Island		12 nm
Patos Island		6 nm
Prevost Harbor *(Stuart Island)*		15 nm
Roche Harbor *(San Juan Island)*		16 nm
Sidney *(Canada)*		24 nm

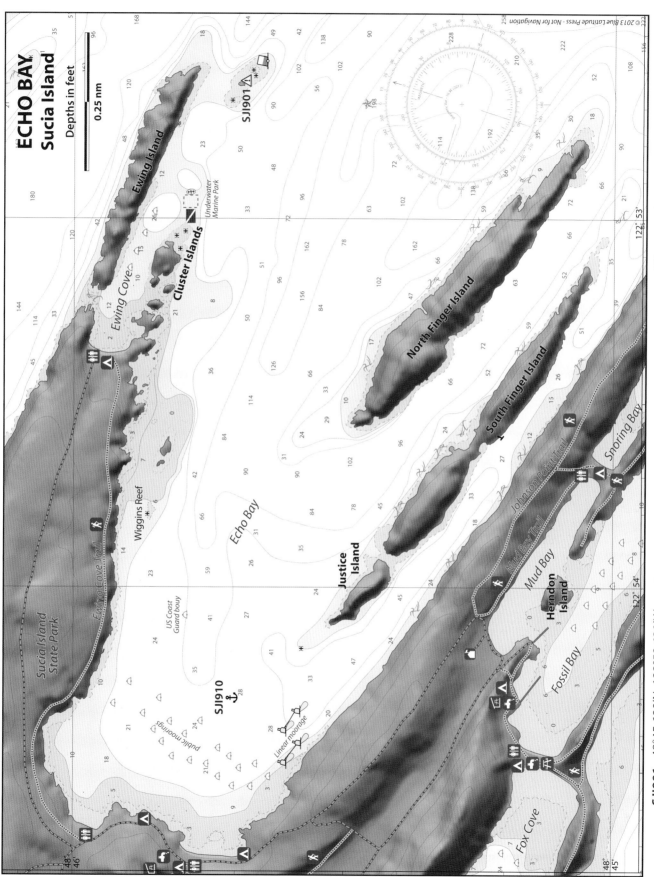

ECHO BAY
Sucia Island

Depths in feet

0.25 nm

Ewing Island

Ewing Cove

Cluster Islands

Underwater Marine Park

SJI901

Sucia Island State Park

Ewing Cove Trail

Wiggins Reef

Echo Bay

US Coast Guard bouy

SJI910

public moorings

Linear moorage

North Finger Island

South Finger Island

Justice Island

Johnson Point Trail

Mud Bay Trail

Snoring Bay

Mud Bay

Herndon Island

Fossil Bay

Fox Cove

© 2013 Blue Latitude Press - Not for Navigation

SJI910 - 48°45.700'N 122°54.300'W

SJI901 - 48°45.690'N 122°52.630'W

247

For those approaching from the north or east, be aware of the expansive Clements Reef guarding the northeastern shore of Sucia Island. With only a small section of this reef exposed, it is important to look for the buoys marking the far northwestern and southeastern tips of the reef. This long, narrow reef is also marked by kelp beds, and can many times be located by the sounds of barking and gurgling sea lions perched on its exposed sections. Passage can be taken between Clements Reef and the north side of Sucia Island, although take note of the reefs found off the eastern tip of Ewing Island.

For boats approaching from the south, Parker Reef (marked by a lighted beacon) is located approximately 0.6 miles north of Terrill Beach on the northern shore of Orcas Island.

When approaching the main entrance to Echo Bay, between Ewing Island and the North Finger Island, be aware that a detached reef is located off the southeastern side of Ewing Island. The eastern extent of this reef is marked by a day beacon. Make sure to give this reef ample room when passing.

Entrance to the bay can also be taken between the Finger Islands. A deep water channel can be found between the North and South Finger Islands. Passage between Sucia Island and the South Finger Island is narrow and shallower, and therefore best suited for small draft boats. Both passages have rocky shorelines so it is best to stay mid channel when transiting.

Keep in mind when approaching Echo Bay, and while once inside the bay, that both the North and South Finger Islands have extending underwater reefs found off both the northwestern and southeastern tips of each island. Be sure to give a wide berth to the ends of these islands, especially the South Finger Island, as its reefs are more extensive and closer to the main anchorage area of Echo Bay.

Once inside Echo Bay, anchorage can be taken in 4 to 5 fathoms over a mostly mud bottom. A number of park mooring buoys are scattered throughout the bay, as well as two unique linear mooring systems. These linear mooring options are a nice alternative for group gatherings as Echo Bay does not have docks for group raft-ups. All park moorings are available for a nightly fee or for those with an annual state park moorage permit (see page 12).

Echo Bay provides good protection from northerly and westerly winds and waves, but is open to east and southeast weather. Protected anchorage from east and southeast winds is available on the west side of Sucia Island at Shallow Bay.

Linear mooring in Echo Bay

To dinghy ashore, a few sand covered beaches are located at the head of the bay. From here, the park service dirt access road runs near the shoreline and provides a scenic walking tour, as well as access to the many side trails crossing the island. A number of individual and group campsites are located in this area, including covered shelters for the occasional periods of rain. Composting toilets, water, park information kiosks, firewood for sale and payment drop boxes are also located in this area.

During the peak summer months, especially on sunny weekends, it is not uncommon to find fifty or more boats anchored within Echo Bay. This alone is true testament to the amazing beauty and multitude of activities for people of all ages, and why the island is most certainly a top destination for boaters. During the quieter winter months, visitors are rewarded for their cooler weather cruising with a peaceful anchorage and dramatic, snow-covered views of Mt. Baker and surrounding mountain ranges.

Ewing Cove

Ewing Cove is located on the northeastern corner of Sucia Island, near the entrance to Echo Bay. This narrow little anchorage can accommodate only a few boats. Studded by surrounding reefs and rocky islands, this anchorage is one of Sucia Island's more intimate and remote locations. With its close proximity to Clements Reef, boaters are occasionally serenaded by vocal sea lions found sunbathing on the reef.

Ewing Cove is formed by Ewing Island to the north and Sucia Island to the west. Surrounding the cove are a number of reefs and rocky islets so pay close attention when navigating in this area. Clements Reef, found north of Ew-

ing Island, is extensive, but well marked with lighted buoys. See page 248 for a description of Clements Reef.

A second reef to be aware of when approaching the entrance to Ewing Cove is located south from the southern tip of Ewing Island. A very small portion of this reef is visible at high tide, and the reef's eastern extreme is marked by a day beacon. Also be aware that the underwater marine park is located in this area. Be on the lookout for dive flags and avoid divers when they are in the area.

Four state park mooring buoys are available for use within the cove. Dinghy and kayak trips to shore are easily made at the head of the cove on the soft sand beach. Hours can be spent in this secluded, rocky little cove inspecting the lace-like rock formations, scouting for seals and sea lions, and tide pooling among the various shoreside rocks at low water. A trail head is also located at the head of the cove and follows the shoreline around the north side of Echo Bay.

Beach at Ewing Cove

Shallow Bay

Shallow Bay is the quintessential boater's dream for a perfect island anchorage. This well enclosed bay offers beautiful beaches backed by lush forests and intricate sandstone formations. Located on the west side of Sucia Island, Shallow Bay offers visitors unforgettable sunset views over the Canadian Gulf Islands. With miles of trails traversing the island, hikers are afforded waterfront views of nearly every shore of this uniquely formed island. Whether frolicking on the beaches, enjoying a moonlit campfire or paddling the diverse shoreline, Shallow Bay will be sure to please.

Shallow Bay is found on the west side of Sucia Island off the fringes of Boundary Pass and the Strait of Georgia. Approaches to the bay can be made from most directions, but keep in mind reefs and commercial traffic lanes are found

Shallow Bay to:		
Anacortes		22 nm
Bellingham		21 nm
Blaine		16 nm
Blind Bay (Shaw Island)		15 nm
Eagle Harbor (Cypress Island)		15 nm
Fisherman Bay (Lopez Island)		19 nm
Friday Harbor (San Juan Island)		16 nm
Jones Island		11 nm
Patos Island		3 nm
Prevost Harbor (Stuart Island)		13 nm
Roche Harbor (San Juan Island)		15 nm
Rosario (Orcas Island)		19 nm
Sidney (Canada)		21 nm

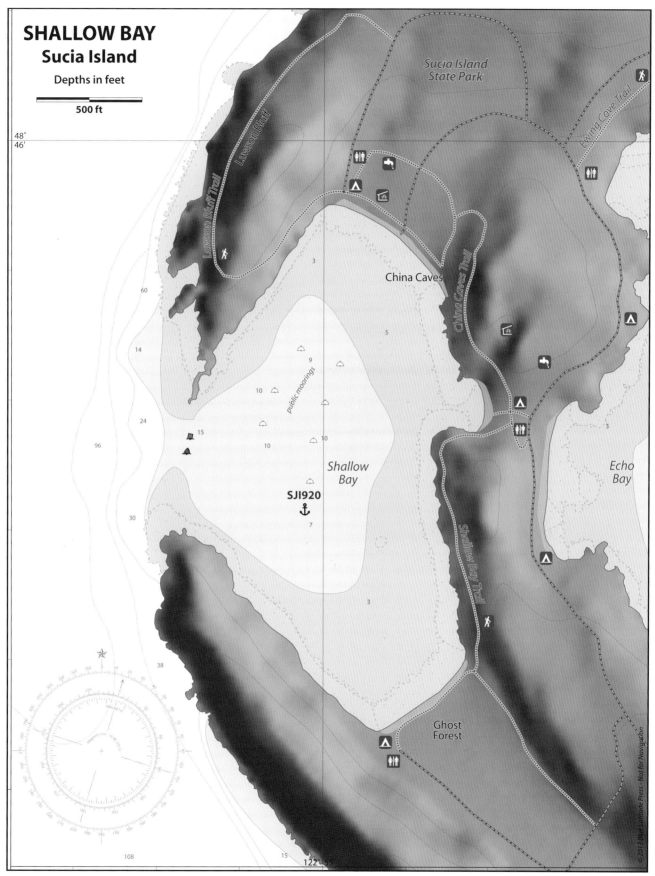

SHALLOW BAY
Sucia Island

Depths in feet

500 ft

Sucia Island
State Park

Ewing Cove Trail

Lawson Bluff

Lawson Bluff Trail

48°
46'

China Caves

China Caves Trail

60

14

3

24

5

96

15

9

public moorings

10

10

30

10

10

Shallow
Bay

SJI920
⚓

7

Echo
Bay

3

Shallow Bay Trail

38

3

Ghost
Forest

108

15

122°55'

©2013 Blue Latitude Press - Not for Navigation

SJI920 - 48°45.710'N 122°55.020'W

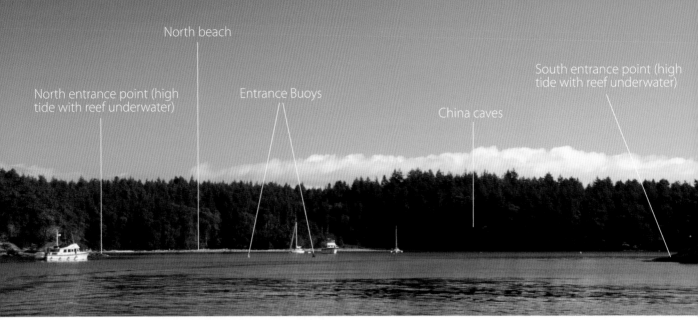

North beach

North entrance point (high tide with reef underwater)

Entrance Buoys

China caves

South entrance point (high tide with reef underwater)

nearby so have your charts at hand. Both Boundary Pass and the Strait of Georgia, which links to Rosario Strait, are commercial traffic areas where large tankers and tugs in tow can frequently be found.

Surrounding Sucia Island are a few reefs and shallow areas to take note of including Parker Reef, Clements Reef, Alden Bank and West Bank. For boats approaching from the north or east, Clements Reef, which lies off the northeastern shore of Sucia Island, stretches roughly 1 mile in length from the northwest to the southeast. The northwest and southeast ends of the reef are marked by day buoys. Lying 3 miles north of Matia Island is Alden Bank. The shallowest depths for this bank are found in the southeast end (approximately 2 to 4 fathoms) and can often be spotted by crab pot buoys floating on the surface. For boats approaching from the west or southwest, the aptly named West Bank lies west of Little Sucia Island. The shallowest depths on West Bank range from 1 to 4 fathoms with current found between the bank and Sucia Island.

Once at the entrance to Shallow Bay, red and green buoys mark the narrow channel into the bay. Inside, park mooring buoys and ample room for anchoring can be found. Anchorage can be taken in 1 to 2 fathoms over a mud bottom. As the name suggests, portions of the bay can become shallow depending on the level of the tide, so be sure your swinging radius keeps you out of the shallows. Shallow Bay provides protection from north, south and east winds, but is open to the west. Lying at the southern end of the Strait of Georgia, weather here can be different than the weather found in the more protected inner San Juan Islands.

For trips to shore, three main beaches can be found at the north, south and east areas of the bay. A mixture of sand

and pebble provides the perfect platform for landing a dinghy, or for a refreshing dip into the ocean. On shore, numerous campsites are scattered throughout the island including covered shelters, firepits, composting toilets and fresh water.

Sucia Island also has one of the finest trail systems around. Miles of trails loop and intersect the island, traveling through lush forests, gaining vantage from overlooking bluffs, and ending at sublime beaches. From any one of the three beaches at Shallow Bay, trails head off across the island reaching the picturesque destinations of Ewing Cove, Snoring Bay, Fox Cove and many more.

One of the attractions at Shallow Bay is China Caves. Located between the north and east beaches, the caves have been carved out of the sandstone cliffside by thousands of years of ocean waves. Surrounded by folk lore, the caves are said to have been the perfect hiding location for smuggled Chinese laborers as well as Canadian liquor smuggled in during prohibition times.

Shallow Bay is also a great, protected location to launch the kayak or paddle board to explore the unique shoreline. Beautiful and elaborate sandstone formations can be found within and outside the bay. These rock formations are a true highlight when visiting Sucia Island and there's no better way to view them than by a peaceful sunset paddle.

Shallow Bay is also known to be home to families of river otters. These playful, curious creatures are entertaining to watch and are amazing fishermen. To spot the otters, keep a watch along the shoreline where you are likely to spot a mother and her pups coming and going from her den. River otters make a variety of squeals and chirps to communicate, as well as warning hisses if they feel threatened.

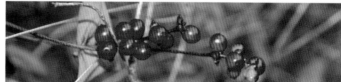

Sandstone

Over millions of years, the rocks of Sucia Island were laid down in sedimentary layers from rivers, seas and glaciers. Year after year, sand, mud, gravel, boulders and even marine invertebrates contributed to the sandstone layers. With the convergence of tectonic plates, the land around Sucia Island began to bend and lift, resulting in the island's unique horseshoe shape. During the Ice Age, glaciers and ice thousands of feet thick blanketed the area, carving the land and depositing debris. As the climate began to warm and melt the ice, islands emerged within the sea. The soft sedimentary layers of sandstone were slowly eroded away by the ocean, creating the finger islands, reefs and coves found on and around Sucia. The water's erosion continues on cutting ledges, digging caves and weaving a honeycomb lace-like formations in the golden colored stone.

Fox Cove

Fox Cove is a charming location, surrounded by the stunning beauty that makes Sucia Island a one of a kind destination. At the head of the cove lies a beautiful beach with golden sand, and flanked by striking rock formations to the north and the picturesque, Little Sucia Island to the west. With room for only a handful boats, Fox Cove is an intimate anchorage with a perfect setting for watching the slow, vibrant sunsets the San Juans' are known for.

Fox Cove is located on the southwestern shore of Sucia Island. As stated in previous sections, Sucia Island has a number of rocky reefs and shallow areas both attached and off lying. When approaching, be sure to read the charts and navigate with caution. Hazards to be aware of when approaching the island include the long, narrow Clements Reef found just northeast of the island (see page 248), the shallow waters of West Bank found off Sucia's western shore (see page 252), and Parker Reef found between Orcas Island and Sucia Island.

Guarding the entrance to Fox Cove is Little Sucia Island. This island is surrounded by extensive reefs and kelp beds so be sure to give this island a wide berth when passing, especially off the island's western tip.

To enter the cove, passage can be taken off the north side or off the southeast side of Little Sucia Island. Current runs through this area, and tends to accelerate through the narrowing channel between the southeast side of Little Sucia Island and the main island of Sucia. If taking the entrance off the southeastern end of Little Sucia, be aware that this entrance is shallow and somewhat narrow due to extending reefs from Little Sucia and Sucia Islands. If rounding Little Sucia Island to the west in order to enter Fox Cove from the

Fox Cove to:		
	Anacortes	22 nm
	Bellingham	20 nm
	Blaine	17 nm
	Blind Bay *(Shaw Island)*	20 nm
	Clark Island	7 nm
	Eagle Harbor *(Cypress Island)*	14 nm
	Friday Harbor *(San Juan Island)*	15 nm
	Jones Island	10 nm
	Prevost Harbor *(Stuart Island)*	12 nm
	Roche Harbor *(San Juan Island)*	14 nm
	Sidney *(Canada)*	21 nm
	Spencer Spit *(Lopez Island)*	18 nm

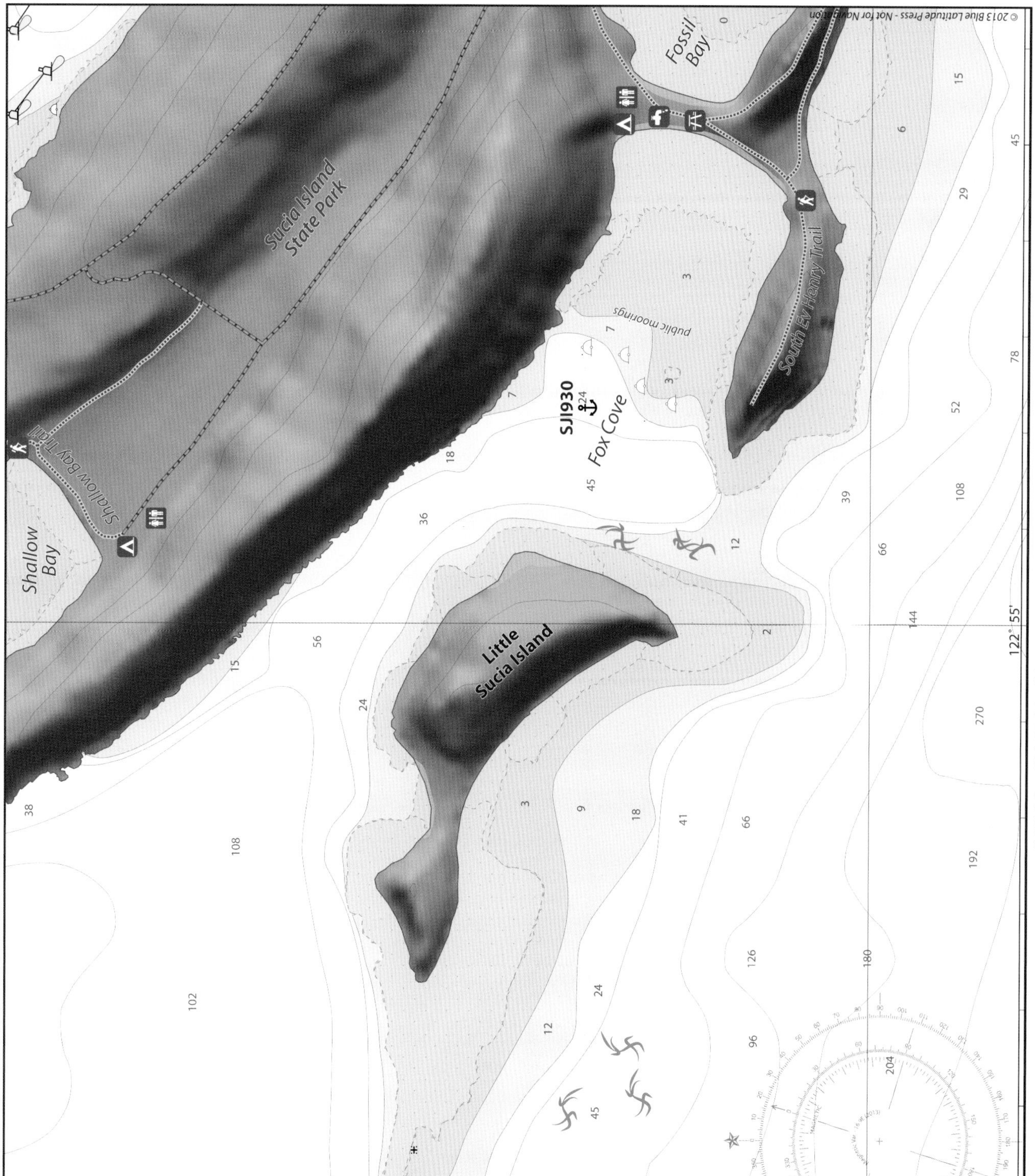

FOX COVE
Sucia Island

Depths in feet

500 ft

Shallow Bay

Shallow Bay Trail

Sucia Island State Park

Fossil Bay

South EV Henry Trail

public moorings

SJI930
Fox Cove

Little Sucia Island

© 2013 Blue Latitude Press – Not for Navigation

0

15

6

45

29

78

52

108

66

39

3

3

3

7

1

24

45

12

2

144

270

18

9

3

24

41

66

12

24

45

192

126

96

180

204

174

222

90

59

59

47

20

84

102

108

38

15

56

36

18

7

5

SJI930 - 48°45.200'N 122°54.770'W

122° 55'

48° 45'

255

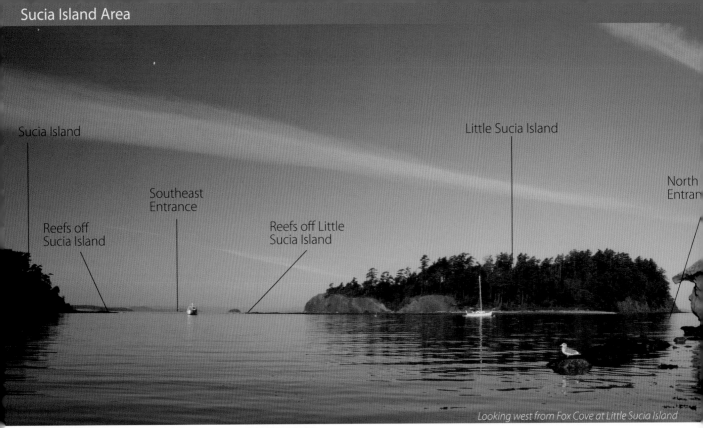

Sucia Island

Little Sucia Island

North Entran[ce]

Southeast Entrance

Reefs off Sucia Island

Reefs off Little Sucia Island

Looking west from Fox Cove at Little Sucia Island

Sucia Island

Little Sucia Island

Southeast Entrance

Orcas Island

Fox Cove

Looking southeast into Fox Cove

north, be sure to clear well past the reef lying off the island's western shore. The western extent of this reef is not marked.

Once inside Fox Cove, a few state park mooring buoys are available. Unfortunately, much of Fox Cove is very shallow, causing most boats to anchor or moor near the entrance areas to the cove where the water is deeper. This area can experience current flowing between Little Sucia and Sucia Islands so be sure to have a secondary line attached to the mooring buoy in case the first chafes through (always a good idea).

Fox Cove is exposed to northwest and southwest winds. Because most boats have to moor further back in the cove in deeper water, swell from strong southerly winds tends to wrap into the cove between Little Sucia and Sucia Islands, causing some boats to roll about. Better anchorage for strong southerly winds can be found around the corner at Shallow Bay.

At the head of the bay is a narrow isthmus that separates Fox Cove and Fossil Bay. This isthmus has a soft sand beach, making for easy dinghy trips to shore. A number of camping sites are found here as well as trail heads for exploring Sucia Island. Park information kiosks and payment drop boxes are found towards the Fossil Bay side of the island.

Little Sucia Island is also part of the Sucia Island State Park, however, due to nesting birds, the park is closed to the public from January 1 through August 31.

Camping on the beach at Fox Cove

Fossil Bay

Surrounded by pristine park land, choice camping locations and two large docks, Fossil Bay is a festive and ideal hub for the outdoor enthusiast. Boaters, kayakers and campers alike convene at this pleasant bay, sharing picnic tables, hiking trails and even impromptu musical jam sessions around the campfire. For boaters, Fossil Bay is a favorite and popular destination with options for dock space, mooring buoys and anchoring. Fossil Bay's charm and easy access to outdoor activities will quickly win your heart, and have you planning your next trip out to Sucia Island.

Fossil Bay is located on the southern end of Sucia Island. Depending on your direction of approach, be aware of the reefs and shallow areas surrounding the island, including Clements Reef (see page 248) and West Bank (see page 252). On approach to the bay, be sure to give a wide berth to Ev Henry Point to avoid an extending reef. Enter Fossil Bay mid channel, slightly favoring Wiggins Head to avoid this reef area.

At the entrance to the bay, the bottom contour shallows rapidly providing good anchoring depths throughout the bay. At first glance, Mud Bay appears to be an attractive and nearly landlocked anchoring option, however, the entire bay is shoal and not suitable for anchoring. Anchorage can be taken in Fossil Bay in 1 to 2 fathoms over a solid mud bottom. Two linear rows of park mooring buoys are also found run-

Fossil Bay to:		
	Anacortes	21 nm
	Bellingham	19 nm
	Blaine	18 nm
	Blind Bay (Shaw Island)	15 nm
	Clark Island	7 nm
	Deer Harbor (Orcas Island)	12 nm
	Eagle Harbor (Cypress Island)	13 nm
	Fisherman Bay (Lopez Island)	19 nm
	Friday Harbor (San Juan Island)	16 nm
	Jones Island	10 nm
	Prevost Harbor (Stuart Island)	14 nm
	Roche Harbor (San Juan Island)	15 nm
	Sidney (Canada)	22 nm

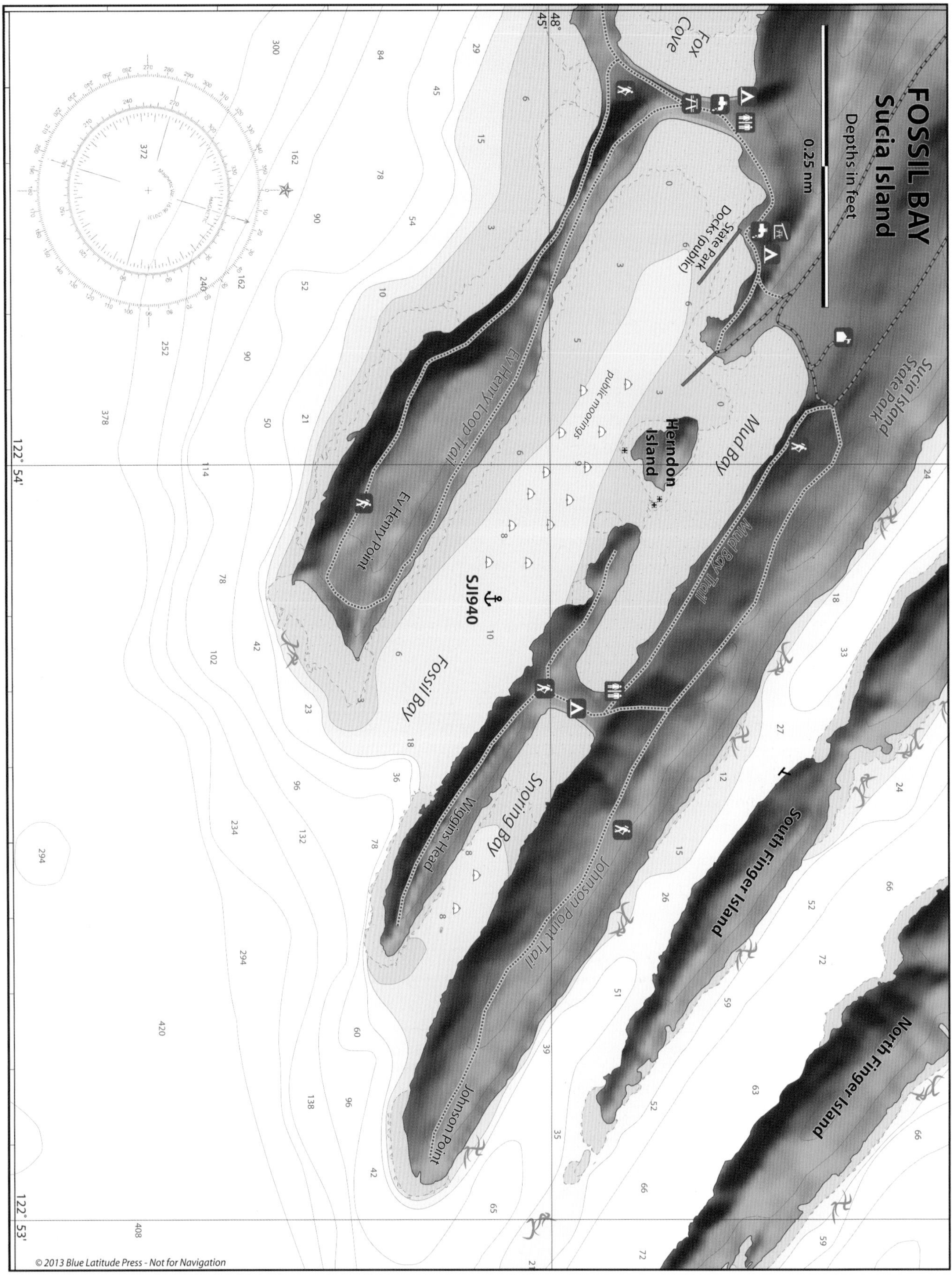

FOSSIL BAY
Sucia Island

Depths in feet

0.25 nm

Fox Cove

State Park Docks (public)

Sucia Island State Park

Ev Henry Loop Trail

Ev Henry Point

Herndon Island

Mud Bay

Mud Bay Trail

public moorings

SJI940

SJI940

Fossil Bay

Snoring Bay

Wiggins Head

South Finger Island

North Finger Island

Johnson Point Trail

Johnson Point

372

162

162

300

84

29

45

15

6

78

54

90

52

10

3

3

0

6

9

3

5

3

6

0

6

9

8

8

8

8

10

6

3

18

50

21

90

114

378

252

240

21

78

42

102

23

96

132

234

294

294

420

138

60

96

35

39

42

65

408

294

18

33

27

12

15

26

51

24

52

72

66

59

63

66

59

72

24

45

48° 45'

48°

122° 54'

122° 53'

ning through the bay for additional moorage options. The state park has installed two 180-foot long docks, which are found near the head of the bay, and are available on a first come basis. For those with deeper draft vessels, be sure to check the tides and the depth at the dock as these areas can become shallow.

Fossil Bay provides good protection from nearly all weather with the exception of southeast winds, to which the bay is exposed. During periods of southeast weather, better protection can be found on the island's western shore at Shallow Bay.

For easy and convenient trips to shore, designated dinghy space is available on both park docks. For those who prefer beach landings, a large, soft sand beach is located at the head of the bay. Campsites surround the shoreline, from grass-covered beach front sites, to scenic rocky vistas overlooking the anchorage. Covered shelters, water, composting toilets, firewood for purchase, park information kiosks and payment drop boxes are also located on shore.

Fossil Bay holds a feast of activities for all, keeping you busy from day to night. Nearly everyone's favorite pastime is to lace up the hiking shoes and head towards one of the many trail heads located at Fossil Bay. A number of different trails meander across the island, taking hikers on a scenic tour to island highlights like Ev Henry Point, Wiggins Head, Johnson Point, Shallow Bay, Echo Bay and Ewing Cove. Whether out for a quick stroll or an all day affair, you are sure to take in the grandeur of Sucia Island.

For those traveling with kayaks, there is no better place to paddle than the protected bays and coves of Sucia Island. Depending on the time of year, the waters around Sucia can be quite clear, allowing shoreside paddlers a "virtual" snorkeling experience without having to brave the chilly Pacific waters. Paddlers also have the silent advantage when searching for some of the area's marine mammals and birds.

One of the highlights at Fossil Bay is the large expanse of green grass found on the narrow isthmus separating Fox Cove and Fossil Bay. This grassy area, along with the lengthy stretch of sand beach found on either side of the isthmus is a perfect location for a game of frisbee, bocce, volleyball or even a mid-afternoon siesta under the sun. There's little doubt that Fossil Bay will capture the hearts of everyone lucky enough to visit this picturesque cove.

Snoring Bay

Snoring Bay is the sleepy little sister to the ever popular favorites of Echo Bay and Fossil Bay. The narrow cove with surrounding high hill sides lends to a feeling of having your own personal fjord to enjoy for the night. With limited space for moored or anchored boats, the bay retains its peaceful charm while still being in the heart of island activities like hiking trails and strolls on the beach.

Snoring Bay is a small cove located on the southeastern shore of Sucia Island, between Echo Bay and Fossil Bay. Entrance to Snoring Bay is found between Wiggins Head and Johnson Point. The shoreline around these two points is marked by reefs so give them plenty of room when rounding into the bay. Once inside, the bay is relatively shallow with depths around 1 to 1½ fathoms and shoal areas located at the head. Two park mooring buoys are available for public use for a nightly fee. Room for anchoring is limited due to the moorings, shallow water and small confines of the bay. Anchoring is best suited for small, shallow draft boats. Snoring Bay provides protection from most directions with the exception of southeast winds to which the bay is open.

The sand and pebble beach at the head of the bay offers a good landing spot for dinghies and kayaks. Campsites, along with composting toilets are located in the area with fresh water available at Fossil Bay. Trails found near the beach connect Snoring Bay with the miles of paths found traversing the entire island, including trails following the hills out to Wiggins Head and Johnson Point.

Snoring Bay to:		
Anacortes		21 nm
Bellingham		19 nm
Blaine		18 nm
Blind Bay (Shaw Island)		15 nm
Eagle Harbor (Cypress Island)		13 nm
Fisherman Bay (Lopez Island)		19 nm
Friday Harbor (San Juan Island)		16 nm
Jones Island		10 nm
Matia Island		2 nm
Roche Harbor (San Juan Island)		15 nm
Rosario (Orcas Island)		17 nm
Sidney (Canada)		22 nm

Matia Island

Matia Island is a small, yet beautiful island paradise situated along the northern boundary waters, one and a half miles east of Sucia Island. The 145-acre island is part of the San Juan National Wildlife Refuge, with five acres at Rolfe Cove dedicated as state park land. Along with a public dock, the park offers mooring buoys and campsites for visitors to the island. A looping trail around the island takes hikers past old growth trees and dense forest land. With Matia's popularity and limited boat accessibility, it is a true treat to experience the wilderness of this alluring island.

Matia Island is located at the southern end of the Strait of Georgia and lies approximately 2.5 miles north of Orcas Island. Approaches to the island can be made from most directions including Rosario Strait, Boundary Pass, President Channel and the Strait of Georgia. If approaching from the north, be aware of the extensive Clements Reef lying northeast of Sucia Island (see page 248). If approaching from the southwest via President Channel, be on the lookout for the lighted beacon marking Parker Reef which lies roughly 0.7

miles north of the northern shore of Orcas Island. Shallow water and kelp lie west and south of this reef. Keep in mind that Matia Island also lies near the commercial shipping lanes of Rosario Strait, the Strait of Georgia and Boundary Pass. Tanker ships and tug boats in tow are frequently seen transiting these waters. These ships can travel quickly

Matia Island to:		
	Anacortes	19 nm
	Bellingham	17 nm
	Blaine	17 nm
	Blind Bay (Shaw Island)	17 nm
	Eagle Harbor (Cypress Island)	12 nm
	Friday Harbor (San Juan Island)	17 nm
	Jones Island	12 nm
	Patos Island	6 nm
	Roche Harbor (San Juan Island)	16 nm
	Rosario (Orcas Island)	16 nm
	Sidney (Canada)	23 nm
	Spencer Spit (Lopez Island)	16 nm

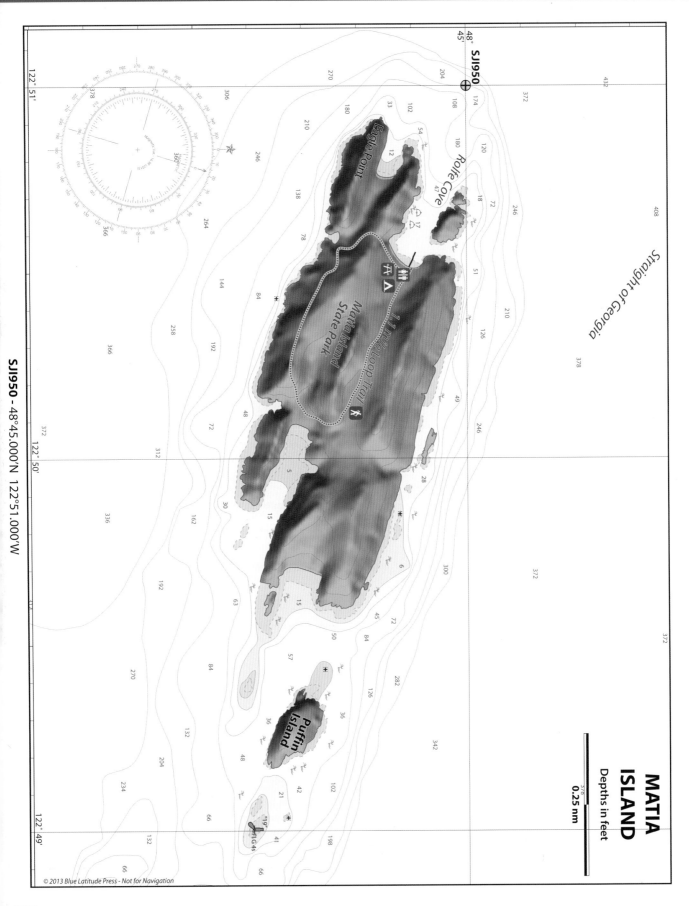

SJI950

SJI950 - 48°45.000'N 122°51.000'W

MATIA
ISLAND

Depths in feet

0.25 nm

Eagle Point

Rolfe Cove

Matia Island State Park

1.1 mile Loop Trail

Straight of Georgia

Puffin Island

G 4s

Rolfe Cove provides south and east wind protection, but is open to weather from the north or west. Lying at the southern fringes of the expansive Strait of Georgia, west and northwest winds blowing down the strait will affect the anchorage at Rolfe Cove. Due to the large distance of fetch (the distance that wind has traveled over open water), west and northwest winds in the Strait of Georgia can create larger waves and a rough anchorage at Rolfe Cove. Better west and northwest wind and wave protection can be found at nearby Sucia Island at Fossil and Echo Bays.

For those using the park mooring buoys, trips to shore are easily made by tying the dinghy up to the dock. At the head of the ramp is a park information kiosk detailing information about the island. A payment drop box is located nearby for those using the dock, moorings or campground. Six campsites and a composting toilet are available for use at Rolfe Cove, with potable water available at nearby Sucia Island. Campfires or beach fires are not permitted on the island.

A scenic one mile loop trail beginning at the campground takes hikers through the forest lands of Matia Island. Old growth cedar trees and various birds taking shelter in the foliage are a couple of the highlights while walking the trail. Aside from the 5 acres at Rolfe Cove and the hiking trail, the remainder of Matia Island is closed to the public to protect and preserve the wilderness and wildlife refuge.

With crystal clear waters and nutrient rich currents feeding the marine life, Rolfe Cove and the nearby cove to the south are also great places for a dinghy or kayak exploration. Starfish, crabs, fish and other marine life can be spotted through the clear water, giving a glimpse into the thriving underwater world of the islands.

The Hermit of Matia Island

Born in Wisconsin, Elvin Smith, was a Civil War veteran who headed west to find opportunity in the newly developing west. In 1892, Smith moved to Matia Island in hopes of staking a homesteading claim on the yet to be released island. Unfortunately, the government never did release the island, but Smith, who fell in love with the quiet beauty of the island, continued on with his squatter's lifestyle. For the next thirty years Smith made Matia Island his home, rowing and later motoring the three mile stretch of water to Orcas Island for supplies, mail and socializing. In 1921, Smith and a friend were returning home from a trip to Orcas. Encountering rough weather, neither Smith, his friend or the boat were ever seen again, but his legend of the Hermit of Matia Island continues to live on.

and have limited maneuverability so be sure to navigate with care and give them sufficient room.

Rolfe Cove is located on the island's northwestern shore. When entering the cove, use the main west entrance. Do not attempt to enter from the north between Matia Island and the small island forming the northern shore of the cove due to shallow water and rocks. Two state park mooring buoys along with a 64-foot dock (side ties on both sides) are available for public use. For smaller boats, anchoring is possible using both a bow and stern anchor, or stern line ashore. However, the cove is narrow, rocky and has current flowing through it, making the dock or moorings a more convenient and attractive option. The dock is removed each October in preparation for winter weather and is replaced at the end of March.

Michael Bertrand www.michaelbertrandphotography.com

Patos Island

Lying at the far northern reaches of the San Juan Islands, Patos Island has served as a beacon to mariners for 120 years. In 1893, the Patos Island Light Station was put into service to aid ships transiting the waters of Boundary Pass and the Strait of Georgia. Now fully automated, the renovated lighthouse remains a historical icon of a time when ships were the life source for the coastal communities of Washington and British Columbia. Today, the 207-acre island has been designated as state park land complete with mooring buoys and a campground for visiting boaters. With it's solitary location and breathtaking vistas, Patos Island is a magical destination that will easily win your heart over.

Patos Island is located 1.4 miles northwest of Sucia Island, at the intersection of Boundary Pass and the Strait of Georgia. Approaches to the island can be taken from most directions including Rosario Strait, Boundary Pass, President Channel and the Strait of Georgia. If approaching from the south, be aware of the shallow waters and kelp beds found at West Bank, lying west of Sucia Island. If approaching from

the east and north of Sucia Island, be sure to avoid the extensive Clements Reef which lies northeast of Sucia (see page 248). Due to Patos Island's close proximity to the major shipping lanes of the Strait of Georgia and Boundary Pass, be sure to keep an eye out for commercial traffic frequenting

Patos Island to:		
	Anacortes	24 nm
	Bellingham	23 nm
	Blaine	16 nm
	Blind Bay (Shaw Island)	16 nm
	Eagle Harbor (Cypress Island)	17 nm
	Friday Harbor (San Juan Island)	16 nm
	Jones Island	11 nm
	Prevost Harbor (Stuart Island)	12 nm
	Roche Harbor (San Juan Island)	15 nm
	Rolfe Cove (Matia Island)	6 nm
	Rosario (Orcas Island)	21 nm
	Spencer Spit (Lopez Island)	20 nm
	Sidney (Canada)	19 nm

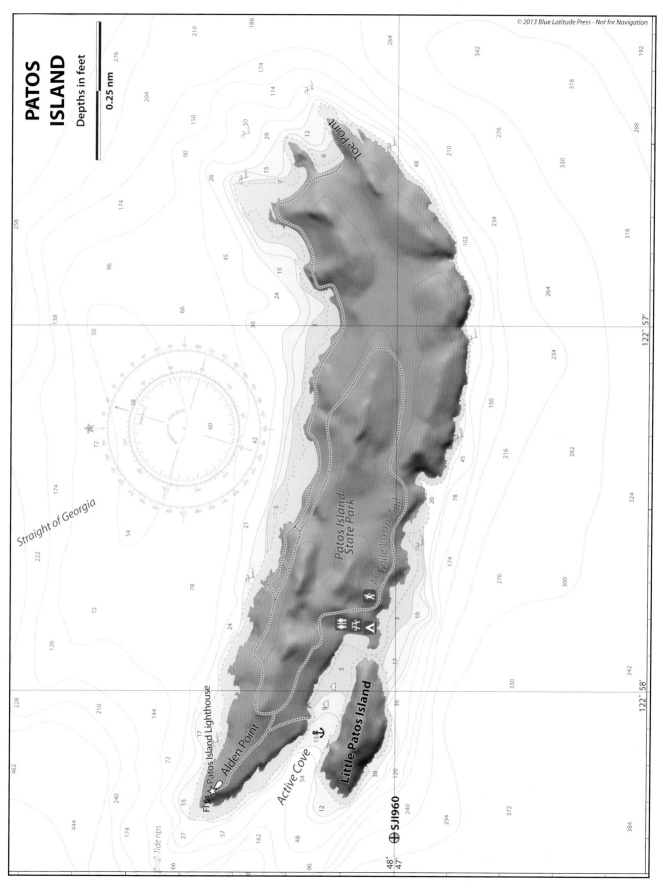

© 2013 Blue Latitude Press - Not for Navigation

PATOS ISLAND
Depths in feet

0.25 nm

Straight of Georgia

Tide rips

Toe Point

Patos Island State Park

1.5 mile Loop Trail

Fl 6s Patos Island Lighthouse

Alden Point

Active Cove

Little Patos Island

⊕ SJI960

SJI960 - 48°47.000'N 122°58.400'W

the area. Tanker ships and tug boats in tow can travel quickly and have limited maneuverability so be sure to navigate with care and give them ample room. With Patos Island lying near the merging of two major deep water channels, current will also be experienced in the area. Steep underwater gradients around the island, especially on the island's northern and western sides, also lends to tide rips in the area.

Moorage can be taken on the island's western side within Active Cove. The cove is formed by Little Patos Island to the south and Alden Point, marked by the lighthouse, to the north. The state park offers two mooring buoys for visiting boats for a nightly fee. While anchoring may be possible for small vessels within the cove, the narrow confines, along with a rocky bottom and current flowing through the anchorage make the moorings a very attractive option. If using a mooring, a second back up line is advisable due to current flowing through the anchorage.

While Active Cove offers protection from northeast, east and south winds, its location at the south end of the Strait of Georgia leaves it open to winds out of the west and northwest. Due to the large distance of fetch (the distance that wind has traveled over open water), west and northwest winds in the Strait of Georgia can create larger waves and a rough anchorage at Active Cove. Better west and northwest

wind and wave protection can be found at nearby Sucia Island at Fossil and Echo Bays.

For trips to shore, a nice sand and pebble beach is found at the head of the cove for landing dinghies and kayaks. The state park offers seven campsites and toilet facilities at Active Cove. A park bulletin board is located near the beach with park information, and a payment drop box nearby.

One of the many highlights at Patos Island is the walking trail to Alden Point and the lighthouse. The original light station was built in 1893, with a light and trumpet fog signal. In 1908, a 38 foot tower was added, housing a new fog signal and a fourth order Fresnel lens. By 1974, the light became automated, flashing white with 2 red sectors as it remains today. With the exception of the lighthouse, which was renovated in 2007, the outbuildings and houses at the light station have been removed.

Thanks to the writings of Helene Glidden, life on Patos Island in the early 1900's has been captured forever in her book, titled *The Light on the Island*. Glidden's father, Edward Durgan took the position of lightkeeper in 1905, and moved his family including his wife and thirteen children to the remote island. For the next eight years the family lived, worked and played on Patos, forming life-long memories.

While Glidden's book is fictional, it is based on her upbringing at the island and is a must read if visiting Patos.

Another popular activity is taking the 1.5 mile trail which loops around the island. This scenic trail takes visitors through the island's towering forests of cedar and madrona. From this trail, be sure to keep an eye out and listen for the sharp of cries of bald eagles who are frequent visitors to the island. The eagles are also known to nest on the island, with their large twig and branch nests tucked high into the foliage of the trees.

At low tide, a shoreside walk is a wonderful way to check out the intricate honeycomb detail of the surrounding sandstone rock formations. Similar to Sucia Island, the softer portions of sandstone on Patos Island has eroded over thousands of years by water and wave action. The result that we see today are delicate lace-like formations and large overhangs in the rocky shoresides of Active Cove.

Keep in mind when touring the island that Patos is designated a federal Wilderness Area. Visitors are free to enjoy the trails, light station and camping area at Active Cove. The remainder of the island as well as Little Patos Island are closed to public access in order to preserve and protect the wilderness and wildlife.

Moorings off the west side of Clark Island

Clark Island

Clark Island is the remote Pacific Northwest island paradise we all dream about. Boasting soft white sand and agate-laden beaches, framed by clear blue water, electric green forests, and sweeping views of the 10,700 foot snow-capped Mt. Baker, island paradises don't get much better than this! With state park status, Clark Island has been preserved for all generations to enjoy the beauty of this amazing island. The island is also a popular camping destination for kayakers paddling the northern stretches of the San Juan Islands.

Clark, and its sister island, Barnes, are located between Orcas and Lummi Islands in the far southern reaches of the Strait of Georgia. Approaches to Clark Island can be made via Rosario Strait from the south or the Strait of Georgia from the north. Both straits are main shipping channels and the nearby Cherry Point refinery brings traffic into the area so be sure to keep an eye out for large commercial ships. With current running through both the Strait of Georgia and Rosario Strait on the flood and ebb tides, boaters may need to accommodate for drift as well when traveling in this area.

When approaching Clark Island from the south, be aware of the off lying islands of Little Sister and The Sisters Islands. These islands are rocky and have extending reefs, particularly off the north end of The Sisters. When transiting this area, be sure to give a wide berth to these off lying islands to avoid the extending and detached reefs.

Careful navigation should also be taken around the south end of Clark Island. Extending reefs and shallow water can be found in this area, so have your charts at the ready. A

Clark Island to:		
Anacortes		15 nm
Bellingham		16 nm
Blaine		20 nm
Blind Bay *(Shaw Island)*		13 nm
Eagle Harbor *(Cypress Island)*		8 nm
Friday Harbor *(San Juan Island)*		17 nm
Jones Island		18 nm
Prevost Harbor *(Stuart Island)*		20 nm
Roche Harbor *(San Juan Island)*		20 nm
Rolfe Cove *(Matia Island)*		5 nm
Rosario *(Orcas Island)*		12 nm
Spencer Spit *(Lopez Island)*		11 nm
Sidney *(Canada)*		27 nm

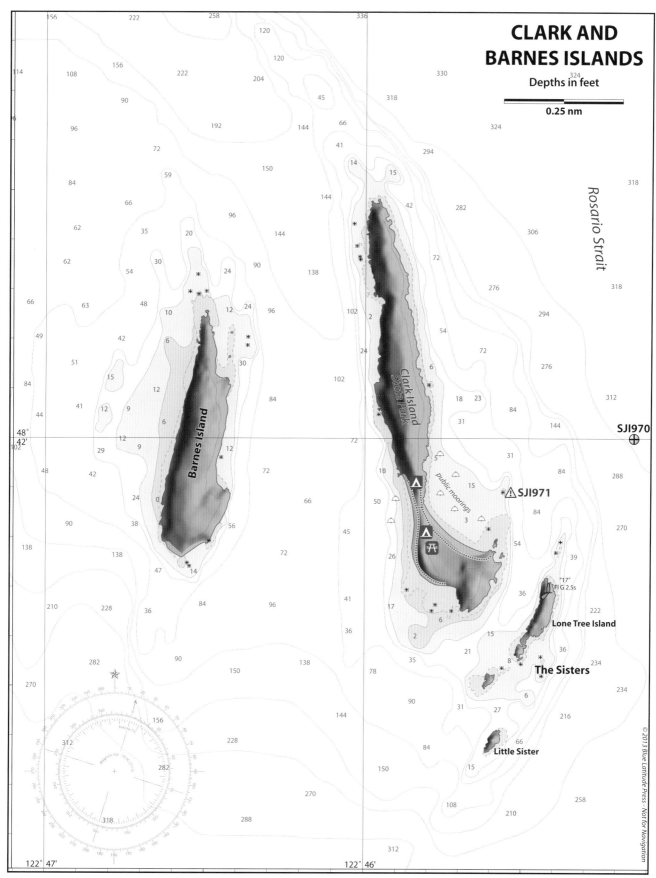

CLARK AND
BARNES ISLANDS

Depths in feet

0.25 nm

Rosario Strait

Barnes Island

Clark Island State Park

public moorings

SJI970

SJI971

"17"
Fl G 2.5s

Lone Tree Island

The Sisters

Little Sister

© 2013 Blue Latitude Press - Not for Navigation

SJI970 - 48°42.000'N 122°45.150'W   **SJI971** - 48°41.890'N 122°45.555'W

269

dangerous reef (SJI971) that catches boaters off guard every year is located on the southeast side of Clark Island. This unmarked reef lies west of the main mooring area on the east side of Clark Island. At low tide this reef is exposed, but is underwater at high tide. When approaching this east anchorage from the south, be sure to round into the anchorage by passing to the north of this reef - do not try to cut between the southeast tip of Clark Island and the unmarked reef.

For those approaching from the north, be aware that reefs also extend off the northern tip of nearby Barnes Island. When approaching the anchorage on the west side of Clark Island from the north, be sure to give the north end of Barnes Island ample room to avoid these extending and detached reefs. It should also be noted that the west side of Barnes Island is shallow and care should be taken when traveling in this area.

Due to the steep underwater gradient surrounding Clark Island, as well as the currents running through the area (especially between Clark and Barnes Islands), anchoring here can be difficult. Luckily, the state park offers eight mooring buoys for use, two on the west side and six on the east side. Because of the area's possible currents or waves, it is best to use a secondary backup line when using the park's mooring buoys.

Clark Island affords marginal protection from wind and waves, and is best suited during periods of calm weather. Because the island lies at the southern end of the Strait of Georgia and the northern end of Rosario Strait, the island is exposed to wind and waves coming from the north or south. East or west wind protection can be found on either side of the island. Because the island is near the shipping lanes through the straits, the occasional boat wake can felt within the anchorages, but they are short lived and usually infrequent.

For trips to shore, dinghies can easily be landed on either side of the island on the soft sand or pebble beach. Once on shore, a number of trails, including beachside walks, lead around the long, narrow island. For campers, fifteen campsites are found on the east and south side of the island with sweeping views of the islands and mountains. Composting pit toilets are located within the campground as well.

Beach and campground off the southeast shore of Clark Island

Pacific Madrona Trees

Clinging to rocky cliffsides and twisting from the power of the winter winds, the Pacific Madrona is a frequent site along the shorelines of the San Juan Islands. The deep reddish-brown smooth bark is one of the tree's most distinguishing traits, making it easily spotted in the forest. Spreading its roots wide, the tree provides excellent erosion control and is thus able to thrive in many extraordinary locations. This broad leaved evergreen can grow to 75 feet high and live over 200 years. The red bark continuously peels off the tree in paper thin curls revealing a pale green trunk. Madronas thrive in drier locations with western exposures, producing fragrant white flowers in the spring months that are large attractants to hummingbirds and bees. By summer, the flowers mature into red berries, and along with the protection of the foliage, provide a welcome habitat and food source to birds, deer and other forest animals.

Pacific Madrona forest

ADDITIONAL PASSES, CHANNELS, ISLANDS AND ROCKS

Depending on your destination and approach, there are a few passes, channels and islands within the San Juans that you may encounter in your travels. The following is a descriptive list of these areas. Keep in mind this guide is meant as an anchorage guide and planning aid only. Navigation through the San Juan Islands and these areas is the responsibility of the captain of the vessel who should always be equipped with the appropriate charts, tide and current tables, and boating knowledge.

Crane Island

Crane Island lies at the east entrance to Wasp Passage, between Orcas Island and Shaw Island. The north shore of the island has covered and exposed rocks within 250 yards of the shore. A shoal covered by a three feet is 350 yards north of the center of the north side of the island. A rock that uncovers at five feet is 200 yards off the east point, with foul ground between it and the shore.

Eliza Island

Eliza Island is located one mile northeast of Carter Point on Lummi Island within Bellingham Bay. Eliza is a private island with full time caretakers and numerous homes and cabins along its shore. While Eliza Island is closed to the general public, good anchorage can be found off the island's southern and northwestern shores. Much of the island is surrounded by reefs and shoal areas so check your charts before approaching. A rock covered by one fathom is approximately 500 yards north of the western tip of the island. Eliza Rock, marked by a lighted beacon lies off the island's south-southeastern point.

Guemes Channel

Guemes Channel lies between the south end of Guemes Island and the north end of Fidalgo Island, leading from Rosario Strait to Padilla Bay. The three mile long channel has depths of 8 to 18 fathoms with lighted buoys marking the channel at the west end. Current runs through the channel and can exceed 5 knots during extreme tides. Ship Harbor is found south of the western entrance point to the channel, near Shannon Point. The Anacortes Washington State ferry terminal is located here with frequent traffic by the ferries. Southeast of Kelly Point, off from Fidalgo Island lies City of Seattle Rock. This rock is covered by 1½ fathoms, and is located is 200 yards offshore. The Skagit County Guemes Island ferry also operates within Guemes Channel, transiting between the island and Anacortes, roughly every half hour.

Guemes Island

Guemes Island lies 0.6 miles north of the city of Anacortes. This relatively large island has a population of year round residents and is served by a car and passenger ferry from Anacortes. Clark Point lies at the northern end of the island with a reef extending 300 yards north from the point. Red buoy #6 is found off this point. Bellingham Channel is found on the western side of Guemes and Padilla Bay is found off the eastern side. Guemes Channel lies off the southern shore of the island and separates Guemes from Fidalgo Island. Huckleberry, Saddlebag and Dot Islands are found off Guemes' southeastern shore near the aptly named Southeast Point.

Looking east through Peavine Pass.

Peapod Rocks

Peapod Rocks lie roughly one mile south of Lawrence Point on the east side of Orcas Island. This group of rocky islets is approximately one mile in length and marked by a lighted beacon on the northeast most rock. The Peapod Rocks lie a half mile off the Orcas Island shore.

Peavine Pass

Peavine Pass (see the chart on page 275) lies on the south side of Obstruction Island, and south of Obstruction Pass. The straight passage separates the north end of Blakely Island from Obstruction Island. The pass is approximately 200 yards wide at its narrowest point, and has a mid channel least depth is of six fathoms. A lighted beacon on Obstruction Island marks the western entrance point to Peavine Pass. Spindle Rock, which lies approximately 0.2 miles offshore from Blakely Island at the eastern entrance to Peavine Pass is marked by a day beacon. The currents through both Obstruction and nearby Peavine Passes can have estimated velocities of 5.5 to 6.5 knots during times of extreme tides. Heavy tide rips can also occur east of Obstruction Island.

Pole Pass

Pole Pass is a very narrow waterway that leads from Deer Harbor to West Sound. The pass separates Crane Island from Orcas Island and is approximately 75 yards wide at its narrowest point. A 7-knot speed limit is enforced through Pole Pass. Strong current is found within the pass, along with numerous rocks surrounding the nearby shorelines of Crane, Bell and Orcas Island. This pass should not be attempted without local knowledge and proper charts. A lighted beacon marks the northeast side of the pass on Orcas Island.

Obstruction Pass

Obstruction Pass (see the chart on page 275) is a narrow waterway that separates Obstruction Island from Orcas Island. The well-traveled pass leads west from Rosario Strait to the inner passages and sounds of the San Juan Islands. The small community of Lieber Haven is also located within the pass on Orcas Island. A lighted beacon on the northeast side of Obstruction Island marks the east entrance. On approach from the east, be sure to locate Lydia Shoal buoy which lies roughly one mile east of the pass entrance. The currents through both Obstruction and nearby Peavine Passes can have estimated velocities of 5.5 to 6.5 knots during times of extreme tides. Heavy tide rips can also occur east of Obstruction Island.

Sinclair Island

Sinclair Island lies 0.7 miles north of Cypress Island and 2.5 miles west-southwest of Carter Point on Lummi Island. Sinclair Island is a private island with a number of homes and cabins found throughout the island. While the southern shore of the island is steep-to and deep, the remainder of the shoreline is shallow with extending reefs. Boulder Reef extends 0.8 miles off the northwestern shore, with portions of the outermost reef uncovered at half tide. The northern extent of this reef is marked by lighted red bell buoy #2. For boats transiting north of Sinclair Island, it is important to stay north of buoy #2 and nearby buoy #4 to avoid the dangers of Boulder Reef and the shallow waters off Sinclair Island. Current is present in this area and during ebb tides, current can push boats traveling north of Sinclair Island south towards the buoys and reef. Be sure to watch your compass and compensate for drift.

Looking southeast through Pole Pass.

Looking northwest through Pole Pass.

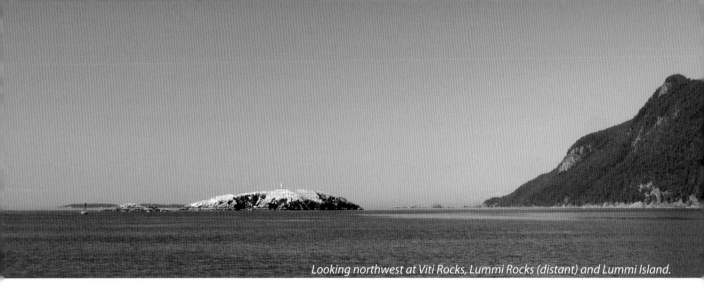
Looking northwest at Viti Rocks, Lummi Rocks (distant) and Lummi Island.

Spieden Channel

Spieden Channel lies between the southern shore of Spieden Island and the northern end of San Juan Island. The channel connects Haro Strait to President Channel and San Juan Channel. The deep channel experiences strong current throughout. On the flood current, heavy tide rips can be experienced at the east entrance as east flowing current through Spieden Channel meets northwest moving current up San Juan Channel. On the ebb current, be aware that current heading south through President Channel will set boats towards Limestone Point on San Juan Island (see the current diagrams on pages 9-10).

Thatcher Pass

Thatcher Pass lies between Blakely Island to the north and Decatur Island to the south. Thatcher Pass is approximately 0.5 miles wide at its narrowest, and is deep and free of danger with the exception of Lawson Rock. For this reason, it is the primary pass used by the Washington State ferries when transiting to and from the San Juan Islands and Sidney from Anacortes. Lawson Rock is found 0.4 miles north of Fauntleroy Point on Decatur Island and near mid channel at the east entrance to Thatcher Pass. The rock is marked by a lighted buoy, as is the southern tip of Blakely Island. During south winds and an ebb current, heavy tide rips can be encountered off the eastern entrance to Thatcher Pass.

Viti Rocks

Viti Rocks lie 0.7 miles southwest of Carter Point on Lummi Island. The northern most rock is 35 feet high, 200 yards long, and is marked by a lighted beacon. A lighted bell buoy marks the shoal extending south-southeast from the southern most rock.

Wasp Islands

The Wasp Islands are a group of small islands found between Shaw Island and the west end of Orcas Island. The Wasp Islands include Yellow, Cliff, Low, Nob, McConnell and Reef Islands. Several narrow channels lead between the islands, most of which are encumbered by rocks and reefs. The most common routes near these islands is taken via Wasp Passage (see page 276) and North Pass.

Yellow Island is the western most of the Wasp Islands. The island is small, grassy and nearly bare of trees, with a shoal that extends 300 yards west of the island and ends in a rock that uncovers at three feet and is marked by kelp. The island was purchased by the Nature Conservancy in 1979 and opened to the public. The grasslands on Yellow Island are unique and thrive in the absence of grazing deer. More than 50 species of wildflowers grow on Yellow Island during the spring and summer months including the brittle prickly pear cactus. Dinghies and kayaks can be landed only at the southeast beach, below the wooden Dodd cabin. The east spit is open to landings only in the spring and fall. No camping or overnight mooring is allowed at the island.

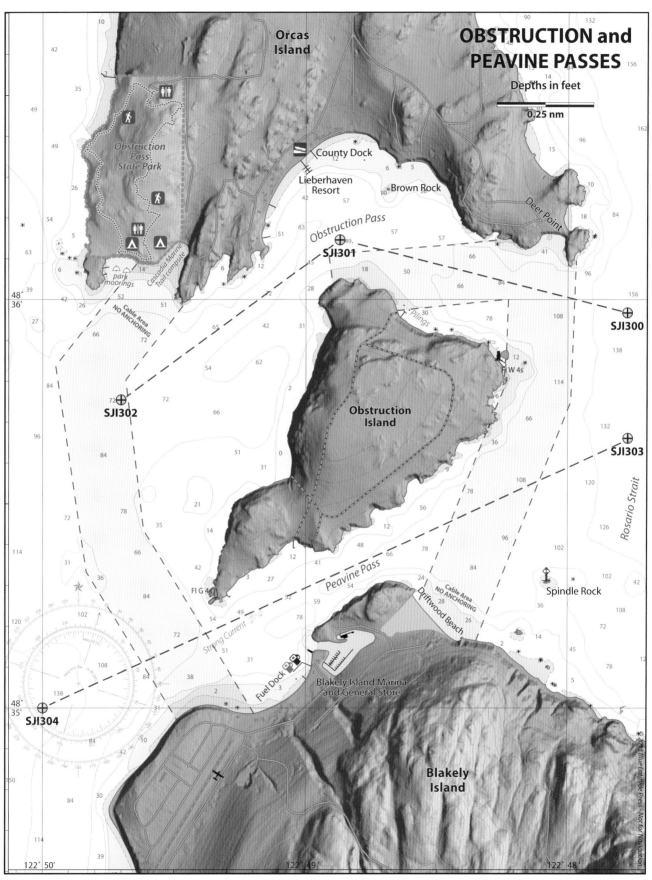

OBSTRUCTION and PEAVINE PASSES

Depths in feet

0.25 nm

Orcas Island

Obstruction Pass State Park

County Dock

Lieberhaven Resort

Brown Rock

Deer Point

Obstruction Pass

⊕ SJI301

Cascadia Marine Trail campsite

park moorings

Cable Area NO ANCHORING

48° 36'

⊕ SJI300

⊕ SJI302

W 4s

Obstruction Island

⊕ SJI303

Rosario Strait

Pilings

Spindle Rock

Fl G 4s

Peavine Pass

Cable Area NO ANCHORING

Driftwood Beach

Strong Current

Fuel Dock

Blakely Island Marina and General Store

48° 35'

⊕ SJI304

Blakely Island

MAGNETIC

122° 50'

122° 49'

122° 48'

© 2015 Blue Latitude Press - Not for Navigation

SJI300 - 48°35.970'N 122°47.770'W   **SJI301** - 48°36.130'N 122°48.870'W   **SJI302** - 48°35.750'N 122°49.700'W

SJI303 - 48°35.660'N 122°47.760'W   **SJI304** - 48°35.000'N 122°50.000'W

Steep Point

Orcas Island

West Sound

Deer Harbor

Reef Island

Cliff Island

Crane Island

McConnell Island

Shaw Island

Shirt Tail Reef

Neck Point

Michael Bertrand www.michaelbertrandphotography.com

Looking west at the Wasp Passage eastern entrance

Wasp Passage

Wasp Passage is a narrow pass that lies off the northwestern shore of Shaw Island and south of the Wasp Islands. The pass leads from San Juan Channel to West Sound and Harney Channel. This pass is used by the Washington State Ferries and experiences strong current throughout. The western entrance is marked by lighted green beacon #1, which also marks Shirt Tail Reef. From the west, enter between green beacon #1 and Neck Point on Shaw Island. Keep in mind that Neck Point is surrounded by detached rocks and shallow water. The channel then leads between Cliff Island and Neck Point. Lighted green beacon #3 marks the southern shore of Cliff Island. The pass continues east between the southern shore of Crane Island and the north shore of Shaw Island. The eastern end of the pass lies between the southern shore of Bell Island and the northern shore of Shaw Island. This eastern entrance point is marked by lighted green beacon #5. Beacon #5 marks the eastern extent of the detached reefs lying off the east side of Bell Island.

WAYPOINTS

Name	Description	Waypoint	
Chapter 1: Bellingham Bay			
SJI100	Squalicum Marina Approach	48°44.900'N	122°31.000'W
SJI101	Fairhaven Anchorage	48°43.490'N	122°30.550'W
SJI110	Chuckanut Rock	48°41.100'N	122°30.170'W
SJI111	North Chuckanut Bay Anchorage	48°41.750'N	122°30.300'W
SJI112	Pleasant Bay Anchorage	48°39.970'N	122°30.030'W
SJI120	Danger Rock North of Inati Bay	48°40.490'N	122°37.240'W
SJI121	Inati Bay Anchorage	48°40.320'N	122°37.340'W
SJI130	Vendovi Island Approach	48°37.000'N	122°36.820'W
Chapter 2: Anacortes			
SJI160	Cap Sante Marina Approach	48°30.700'N	122°36.175'W
SJI165	Skyline Marina Approach	48°29.340'N	122°40.625'W
Chapter 3: Cypress Island			
SJI200	Pelican Beach Approach	48°36.170'N	122°42.000'W
SJI210	Eagle Harbor Approach	48°35.240'N	122°41.400'W
SJI220	Cypress Head Approach	48°34.300'N	122°40.000'W
Chapter 4: Blakely, James and Decatur Islands			
SJI300	Obstruction Pass Approach East	48°35.970'N	122°47.770'W
SJI301	Obstruction Pass Approach Middle	48°36.130'N	122°48.870'W
SJI302	Obstruction Pass Approach West	48°35.750'N	122°49.700'W
SJI303	Peavine Pass Approach East	48°35.660'N	122°47.760'W
SJI304	Peavine Pass Approach West	48°35.000'N	122°50.000'W
SJI310	James Island Approach East	48°31.000'N	122°46.000'W
SJI311	Decatur Head Anchorage	48°30.750'N	122°47.400'W
SJI320	Reads Bay Anchorage	48°29.710'N	122°49.590'W

Name	Description	Waypoint	
Chapter 5: Lopez Island			
SJI400	Fisherman Bay Approach #1	48°31.700'N	122°55.300'W
SJI401	Fisherman Bay Approach #2	48°31.520'N	122°55.100'W
SJI402	Fisherman Bay Approach #3	48°31.370'N	122°55.020'W
SJI403	Fisherman Bay Approach #4	48°31.330'N	122°55.010'W
SJI404	Fisherman Bay Approach #5	48°31.170'N	122°55.150'W
SJI405	Fisherman Bay Approach #6	48°31.125'N	122°55.130'W
SJI406	Fisherman Bay Approach #7	48°30.980'N	122°54.910'W
SJI407	Fisherman Bay Approach #8	48°30.920'N	122°54.900'W
SJI408	Fisherman Bay Anchorage	48°30.720'N	122°55.070'W
SJI410	Shoal Bay Anchorage	48°33.410'N	122°52.600'W
SJI411	Swifts Bay Anchorage	48°32.620'N	122°52.060'W
SJI412	Rocks West of Leo Reef	48°33.130'N	122°51.380'W
SJI420	Spencer Spit Anchorage North	48°32.340'N	122°51.230'W
SJI421	Spencer Spit Anchorage South	48°31.980'N	122°51.280'W
SJI430	Lopez Pass Approach East	48°28.800'N	122°49.000'W
SJI431	Lopez Pass Approach Middle	48°28.690'N	122°49.520'W
SJI432	Lopez Pass Approach West	48°28.200'N	122°50.240'W
SJI433	Hunter Bay Anchorage	48°27.560'N	122°51.450'W
SJI434	Mud Bay Anchorage	48°27.210'N	122°50.710'W
SJI440	Watmough Bay Anchorage	48°25.930'N	122°48.630'W
SJI450	Aleck Bay Anchorage	48°25.600'N	122°51.550'W
SJI460	Mackaye Harbor Anchorage	48°26.160'N	122°52.320'W
Chapter 6: Shaw Island			
SJI500	Marked Reef East of Blind Island	48°35.015'N	122°56.045'W
SJI501	Blind Bay Anchorage	48°34.630'N	122°56.110'W
SJI510	Parks Bay Anchorage	48°33.590'N	122°58.520'W
SJI520	Indian Cove Anchorage	48°33.640'N	122°56.190'W
SJI521	Reef Southeast of Canoe Island	48°33.200'N	122°55.780'W

Name	Description	Waypoint	
Chapter 7: Orcas and Jones Islands			
SJI600	Deer Harbor Anchorage	48°37.100'N	123°00.260'W
SJI610	Double Island Cove Anchorage	48°36.580'N	122°58.750'W
SJI611	Massacre Bay Anchorage	48°38.480'N	122°59.010'W
SJI612	White Beach Bay Anchorage	48°37.800'N	122°57.680'W
SJI613	Harbor Rock	48°37.800'N	122°58.660'W
SJI620	Fishing Bay Anchorage	48°41.460'N	122°54.410'W
SJI621	Rosario Resort and Marina Approach	48°38.700'N	122°52.150'W
SJI622	Olga Approach	48°36.990'N	122°50.130'W
SJI630	Doe Bay Anchorage	48°38.350'N	122°46.880'W
SJI640	Jones Island Anchorage North	48°37.115'N	123°02.790'W
SJI641	Jones Island Rock	48°37.220'N	123°02.580'W
Chapter 8: San Juan Island			
SJI700	Friday Harbor Approach	48°32.700'N	123°00.100'W
SJI701	Friday Harbor Anchorage	48°32.200'N	123°00.640'W
SJI710	Roche Harbor Approach North	48°37.560'N	123°10.370'W
SJI711	Roche Harbor Anchorage	48°36.650'N	123°09.700'W
SJI720	Mosquito Pass #1	48°34.470'N	123°10.730'W
SJI721	Mosquito Pass #2	48°35.040'N	123°10.320'W
SJI722	Mosquito Pass #3	48°35.500'N	123°10.570'W
SJI723	Mosquito Pass #4	48°35.710'N	123°10.500'W
SJI724	Mosquito Pass #5	48°35.880'N	123°10.300'W
SJI725	Mosquito Pass #6	48°35.960'N	123°10.020'W
SJI726	Mosquito Pass #7	48°36.040'N	123°09.990'W
SJI727	Mosquito Pass #8	48°36.400'N	123°10.150'W
SJI730	Garrison Bay Anchorage	48°35.330'N	123°09.560'W
SJI740	Westcott Bay Anchorage	48°35.730'N	123°09.200'W
SJI750	Griffin Bay Anchorage	48°28.000'N	122°59.400'W
SJI760	North Bay Anchorage	48°31.080'N	123°00.500'W
SJI770	Turn Island Anchorage	48°32.070'N	122°58.500'W
SJI771	Turn Rock	48°32.100'N	122°57.870'W

Name	Description	Waypoint	
Chapter 9: Stuart island			
SJI800	Reid Harbor Approach	48°39.370'N	123°10.560'W
SJI801	Reid Harbor Anchorage	48°40.270'N	123°11.480'W
SJI810	Prevost Harbor Approach	48°41.400'N	123°11.800'W
SJI811	Prevost Harbor Anchorage	48°40.700'N	123°11.730'W
SJI820	Johns Pass #1	48°39.500'N	123°09.270'W
SJI821	Johns Pass #2	48°39.580'N	123°09.280'W
SJI822	Johns Pass #3	48°40.200'N	123°09.980'W
SJI823	Johns Pass #4	48°40.510'N	123°09.500'W
Chapter 10: Sucia Island Area			
SJI900	Clements Reef	48°46.040'N	122°52.360'W
SJI901	Reef Southeast of Ewing Island	48°45.690'N	122°52.630'W
SJI910	Echo Bay Anchorage	48°45.700'N	122°54.300'W
SJI920	Shallow Bay Anchorage	48°45.710'N	122°55.020'W
SJI930	Fox Cove Anchorage	48°45.200'N	122°54.770'W
SJI940	Fossil Bay Anchorage	48°44.940'N	122°53.820'W
SJI950	Rolfe Cove Approach	48°45.000'N	122°51.000'W
SJI960	Active Cove Approach	48°47.000'N	122°58.400'W
SJI970	Clark Island	48°42.000'N	122°45.150'W
SJI971	Clark Island Reef	48°41.890'N	122°45.555'W

SUGGESTED READING

Free Local Publications

The following are a list of local area publications that provide the latest news stories, featured articles, classified ads, calendars of events and more. And best of all, these publications are available for free. Pick up copies at your local chandlery or visit their online sites.

Three Sheets
N O R T H W E S T

Three Sheets Northwest is an online publication bringing daily news stories, resources and social media to boaters in the Northwest. Sign up for the Three Sheets weekly newsletter to keep current on all the local happenings.
www.threesheetsnw.com

48° North

48° North is a monthly magazine available in both printed form and on-line. The magazine, which is written for sailors by sailors, is dedicated to the sailing scene in Washington, Oregon, British Columbia and Alaska. Magazines are available at most marine chandleries and marinas.
www.48north.com

Northwest Yachting Magazine

Northwest Yachting is one of the largest boating publications devoted to boating news and stories of the Pacific Northwest. Monthly editions of Northwest Yachting are available in print at most marine chandleries as well as on-line.
www.nwyachting.com

Books

Atkinson, Scott; Sharpe, Fred; and Macaree, David. Wild Plants of the San Juan Islands. Washington, The Mountaineers, 1993.

Biery, Galen and Koert, Dorothy. Looking Back: The Collectors' Edition. Memories of Whatcom County/Bellingham. Washington, Grandpa's Attic, 2003.

Domico, Terry. A Guide to Marine Mammals of Greater Puget Sound. Washington, Turtleback Books Publishing, 2007.

Ferguson, Susan and the Lopez Island Historical Society and Museum. Images of America: Lopez Island. California, Arcadia Publishing, 2010.

Ford, John K. B. and Ellis, Graeme M. Transients: Mammal-Hunting Killer Whales of British Columbia, Washington, and Southeastern Alaska. University of British Columbia Press, 1999.

Ford, John K. B.; Ellis, Graeme M; and Balcomb, Kenneth C. Killer Whales: The Natural History and Genealogy of Orcinus Orca in British Columbia and Washington State. University of British Columbia Press, 1999.

Glidden, Helene. The Light on the Island. Washington, San Juan Publishing, 2001.

Lewis, Mark G. and Sharpe, Fred A. Birding in the San Juan Islands. Washington, The Mountaineers, 1987.

Orcas Island Historical Society and Museum. Images of America: Orcas Island. California, Arcadia Publishing, 2006.

Osborne, Richard; Calambokidis, John ; and Dorsey Eleanor M. A Guide to Marine Mammals of Greater Puget Sound. Washington, Island Pub., 1988.

Pickens, Steven J., Images of America: Ferries of Puget Sound. California, Arcadia Publishing, 2006.

Renner, Jeff. Northwest Marine Weather: From the Columbia River to Cape Scott. Washington, The Mountaineers Books, 1994.

Richardson, David. Magic Islands: A Treasure-Trove of San Juan Islands Lore. Washington, Orcas Publishing Co, 2000.

U.S. Coast Pilot 7: Pacific Coast. 2013. 45th Edition. "Strait of Juan De Fuca and Georgia." Chapter 12.

Vouri, Mike, Julia Vouri, and the San Juan Historical Society. Images of America: San Juan Island. California, Arcadia Publishing, 2010.

White, Charlie. Living Off the Sea. Canada, Heritage House Publishing Co, 2010.

White, Christopher L. The Rise and Fall of Civilization on Cypress Island: An Historical Report. Department of Natural Resources, Division of Land and Water Conservation, 1991.

Websites

www.atmos.washington.edu/data/marine_report.html The University of Washington repeats the Washington Coastal Waters forecast by the National Weather Service in text format.

www.cbp.gov/xp/cgov/travel/pleasure_boats/ U.S. Customs and Border Patrol lists up to date information on entering U.S. ports for pleasure boaters.

www.cityofanacortes.org/Parks/WaPark/wa_park_maps.htm The City of Anacortes Washington park map.

www.cob.org/services/recreation/parks-trails/trail-guide.aspx The City of Bellingham city parks trail maps.

www.co.san-juan.wa.us/parks/ San Juan County lists all of the public county parks and camping information for San Juan, Orcas, Lopez and Shaw Islands.

fishhunt.dfw.wa.gov/ Washington State Department of Fish and Wildlife offers information on fishing openings, licenses, vendors and online license purchases.

www.lopezisland.com The Lopez Island Chamber of Commerce offers local business and visitor information.

lopezmuseum.org The Lopez Island Historical Society and Museum has preserved the history of Lopez Island.

www.nauticalcharts.noaa.gov/staff/chartspubs.html The National Oceanic and Atmospheric Administration (NOAA) provides nautical charts and publications online.

www.nps.gov/sajh/index.htm The National Park Service offers information on the historical parks of San Juan Island including history and nature.

www.orcasmuseum.org The Orcas Island Historical Society and Museum has preserved the history of Orcas Island.

www.orcasislandchamber.com The Orcas Island Chamber of Commerce represents local businesses and provides lodging, dining, and travel information for Orcas Islands.

www.parks.wa.gov Washington State Parks provides information and online camping reservations for all the state parks in the San Juan Islands.

www.sanjuanisland.org The San Juan Island Chamber of Commerce provides useful island information for visitors.

www.sanjuanislander.com Daily online news site covering San Juan Islands and Friday Harbor, Washington.

sanjuanislandtrails.org/trailsw/ The San Juan Island Trails Committee publishes a number of maps for public trails around San Juan Island.

sjmuseum.org The San Juan Historical Society and Museum has preserved the history of Friday Harbor and San Juan Island.

www.visitsanjuans.com The San Juan Islands Washington Visitors Bureau provides information for travelers to the San Juan Islands, including accommodations, events and seasonal attractions, shopping and ferries.

www.whaleresearch.com The Center for Whale Research provides a wealth of information on whales within the San Juans including the orcas.

INDEX

*B*lue Latitude Press was established by cruisers for cruisers. From round-the-world voyagers to armchair dreamers, we strive to bring superior quality, and one-of-a-kind books to our readers.

Also by Blue Latitude Press:

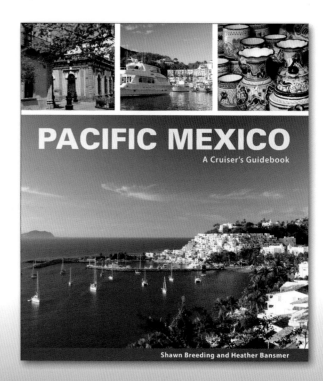